MARCOS AND MARTIAL LAW
IN THE PHILIPPINES

Marcos and Martial Law in the Philippines

EDITED BY
David A. Rosenberg

Cornell University Press

ITHACA AND LONDON

First published 1979 by Cornell University Press.
Published in the United Kingdom by
Cornell University Press Ltd.,
2–4 Brook Street, London W1Y 1AA.

International Standard Book Number 0-8014-1195-5
Library of Congress Catalog Card Number 78-15145
Printed in the United States of America by
York Composition Co., Inc.
Librarians: Library of Congress cataloging information appears on the last page of the book.

Contents

Preface   9

Introduction: Creating a "New Society"   13
   DAVID A. ROSENBERG

1. Ideology and Practice in the "New Society"   32
   JOSE VELOSO ABUEVA

2. Constitutionality and Judicial Politics   85
   ROLANDO V. DEL CARMEN

3. Land Reform: Emancipation or Counterinsurgency?   113
   BENEDICT J. KERKVLIET

4. Liberty versus Loyalty: The Transformation of Philippine
   News Media under Martial Law   145
   DAVID A. ROSENBERG

5. The Political Economy of Refeudalization   180
   ROBERT B. STAUFFER

Appendixes   219

   1. Statement of President Ferdinand E. Marcos on the Decla-
     ration of Martial Law   219
   2. Proclamation No. 1081, Proclaiming a State of Martial Law
     in the Philippines   225
   3. General Order No. 1, That President Ferdinand E. Marcos
     Will Govern the Nation and Direct the Operation of the
     Entire Government   241
   4. General Order No. 3, On the Continuous Operation of All
     Government Instrumentalities under Their Present Officers
     and Employees; On Limitations on the Jurisdiction of the
     Judiciary   242
   5. General Order No. 8, On the Creation of Military Tribunals   244

6. General Order No. 12, On the Jurisdictions of Civil Courts and Military Tribunals 244

7. Proclamation No. 1102, Announcing the Ratification by the Filipino People of the Constitution Proposed by the 1971 Constitutional Convention 248

8. Proclamation No. 1103, Declaring that the Interim National Assembly Provided for in Article XVII (Transitory Provisions) of the New Constitution Be Not Convened 250

9. Transitory Powers and Prerogatives of the President as Provided in Article XVII, Sec. 3, of the New Constitution 251

10. Proclamation No. 1104, Declaring the Continuation of Martial Law 252

11. Report of the National Committee for the Restoration of Civil Liberties in the Philippines 253

12. A Statement of the Civil Liberties Union of the Philippines on the State of the Nation after Three Years of Martial Law 286

13. Philippine Church-State Relations since Martial Law 298

14. Chronology of Church-State Conflicts in the Philippines, from September 21, 1972, to February 4, 1975 303

Index 311

A popular government, without popular information or the means of acquiring it, is but the prologue to a farce or a tragedy; or perhaps both. Knowledge will forever govern ignorance. And a people who mean to be their own governors must arm themselves with the power knowledge gives.

—James Madison, letter to W. T. Barry, August 4, 1822

Preface

This book examines the decline of constitutional democracy and the rise of authoritarian government in the Philippines under the martial law administration of President Ferdinand E. Marcos. We, its contributing authors, have attempted several tasks: to explain how and why martial law was imposed; to present a documentary record of this political transformation; to provide a preliminary assessment of the early years of the New Society program of Mr. Marcos; to examine the wider historical and theoretical significance of this transition to authoritarian government; and to inquire further into the problem of establishing a legitimate political order in a developing country.

We, two Filipinos and three Americans, attempt to achieve these objectives by presenting detailed case studies on several major aspects of this political transformation, concentrating on the period from 1970 to 1975. The record has been updated where appropriate to include information available on significant events occurring through May 1978. Our perspectives and evaluations vary, but all are substantiated by extensive research and thoughtful analysis. Earlier versions of these essays were circulated individually in manuscript form or as short articles in professional journals. They have since been revised and extended to ensure overall coherence and comprehensiveness and to make them accessible to readers with a general interest in world affairs and developing countries as well as to those with a particular interest in Philippine politics. We believe that these essays, taken together, provide the first major attempt at a thorough, scholarly analysis of the decline of constitutional democracy and the rise of authoritarian government in the Philippines.

While our objective has been to provide as complete an analysis as possible, this book is not an exhaustive or definitive treatment of the subject. As is noted in the introduction, there are some important issues that remain clouded by conjecture and contention. Yet it is our hope that this book, by stimulating others to think about the Marcos years, will speed the process of filling in the remaining gaps in our knowledge of this period, rather than merely make it evident that gaps exist. In the meantime, we contribute this book and its knowledge, mindful of James Madison's insight that "a people who mean to be their own governors must arm themselves with the power knowledge gives."

This book had its origin in a panel, "Martial Law in the Philippines," held at the 1974 meetings of the Association for Asian Studies. We acknowledge a debt of gratitude to the organizer and moderator of that session, Professor Michael Onorato. We are grateful to Middlebury College for its research support at several critical stages of this project. We also thank the following for permission to publish materials which appeared under different titles in earlier versions in their journals: *Asian Survey* for Rolando del Carmen, "The Supreme Court and Judicial Politics under Martial Law in the Philippines" Vol. 13, No. 11 (November 1973), and *Pacific Affairs* for Benedict J. Kerkvliet, "Land Reform in the Philippines since the Marcos Coup" (Fall 1974), and for David A. Rosenberg, "Civil Liberties and Martial Law in the Philippines" (Winter 1974–75).

Middlebury, Vermont   DAVID A. ROSENBERG

MARCOS AND MARTIAL LAW
IN THE PHILIPPINES

Introduction:
Creating a "New Society"

David A. Rosenberg
MIDDLEBURY COLLEGE

On September 21, 1972, the Philippines ended its long experiment
with Western-style democracy. President Ferdinand E. Marcos proclaimed martial law throughout the country and began a drastic
transformation of Philippine political institutions. He rapidly began
to dismantle the superstructure of constitutional government that
had been transplanted to the Philippines under American colonial
rule. Congress was dissolved, civil liberties were sharply curtailed,
and the constitution of 1935 was replaced. A "New Society" was
proposed by President Marcos, to be implemented by a new style
of government, "constitutional authoritarianism."

The declaration of martial law was not widely noted outside the
Philippines. Other events in Asia during 1972 competed for international attention: the intensification of the Vietnam War, President Richard Nixon's highly publicized visit to Peking, and yet
another declaration of martial law, by President Park Chung Hee
in South Korea. However, the political upheavals in the Philippines
raise several questions that deserve much closer scrutiny than they
have so far been accorded.

To begin with, the political transformation of the Philippines
provides an opportunity to reexamine many long-standing beliefs
about the nature of Philippine politics. The Philippines was once
popularly regarded as the "showcase of democracy in the Orient." Its
political process was also described by scholars as "an amiable, profitable, and socially undisruptive competition for office among the gen-
try," chiefly characterized by "smooth, interpersonal bargaining."
Freedoms of speech, press, and association were aggressively asserted. The country was governed by alternating political parties determined through periodic general elections. The Philippines was

not without its problems of graft and corruption or social and economic injustices; nevertheless, it had a relatively well-justified claim to representative government and a democratic political ethos. Indeed, shortly before the declaration of martial law, a study by the Rand Corporation reported that the Philippine political system appeared to be stable and responsive; that the economy was performing well; that crime and violence were concentrated in only a few areas; and that dissident groups were not a serious threat to the country. Why, then, was martial law deemed necessary? What justification was there for the elimination of democratic political institutions nurtured over three generations of Philippine history? Did democracy "fail" in the Philippines? Or were the popular beliefs and scholarly observations simply inaccurate?

Martial law also provides a suitable vehicle for reassessing Philippine politics in the context of Southeast Asian culture. The Philippines has long been regarded as an exceptional case in Southeast Asia. It was not noticeably affected by Hindu or Confucian ideas. It never had a monarchy or any extensive, centralized city-states. It was colonized not once, but twice—by Spain and the United States—over three and a half centuries. The Spanish colonial legacy made the Philippines the only Christian country in Asia. The American colonial legacy left English as the first national language. Political independence was accepted, without violence, by an established indigenous elite that had emerged under a paternalistic American colonial rule. These accommodations to colonial rule have made the Philippines perhaps the most Westernized among Asian nations. Indeed, some scholarly texts on Southeast Asia even excluded the Philippines from consideration, despite its obvious geographic and ethnolinguistic affinities, because of these exceptional circumstances.

On the other hand, the Philippines shares several very basic characteristics with the rest of Southeast Asia. The basic unit of society is the kinship group. The overwhelming majority of the population lives in relatively isolated rural areas. Like many Asian nations, it remained a diverse collection of ethnolinguistic regions until colonial rule imposed uniform authority within territorial boundaries. As elsewhere in Southeast Asia, there was frequent resistance to colonial rule in the Philippines; indeed, Filipino nationalists were the first in Asia to declare their independence from Western colonial rule. Since the Jones Act of 1916 which promised "eventual independence," the dynamics of the Filipino nationalist movement have worked at a more moderate pace than elsewhere in the region, largely owing to the influence of a benevolent American colonial policy. The turn to authoritarian government, however, suggests that the Philippines' particular colonial experience has not enabled it to avoid common Southeast Asian problems. Increasingly, the Philippines resembles its Southeast Asian neighbors in their attempts to find a legitimate and effective political order. It is no longer the exceptional case in Southeast Asia.

The turn to authoritarian government in the Philippines also raises questions that have special significance for the United States. U.S. colonial rule and commonwealth tutelage in the Philippines represent the most determined and most extensive attempt to export American ideals and institutions to another country. This was true from the very beginning of American civil government of the newly annexed territory. The instructions of President William McKinley to the Second Philippine Commission, headed by William Howard Taft, made this clear:

The people of the islands should be made plainly to understand, that there are certain great principles of government which have been made the basis of our maintenance of individual freedom, and of which they have, unfortunately, been denied the experience possessed by us; that there are also certain practical rules of government which we have found to be essential to the preservation of these great principles of liberty and law, and that these principles and these rules of government must be established and maintained in their islands for the sake of their liberty and happiness, however much they may conflict with the customs of law and procedure with which they are familiar.[1]

McKinley's instructions became guiding principles for American colonial rule. The political vocabulary, electoral practices, system of party government, jurisprudence, doctrines of constitutionalism, and theories of administrative management all reflected an American origin, according to one prominent Filipino historian, O. D. Corpuz. The same was largely true of the Philippine market economy. But more than these, observes Corpuz, the United States exported its language, its ideas of education, its manufactures, and other less

1. From Appendix III of Dean Worcester, *The Philippines, Past and Present* (New York: Macmillan, 1930).

tangible but equally significant aspects of its way of life, such as
reading materials, consumption and purchasing preferences, dress
fashions, movies, and, to a great extent, a hierarchy of social values.[2]

Given this intensive and extensive Americanization of the Philippines, how does one explain the rapid dismantling of these long-
nurtured institutions? Some have argued that the transplant never
took hold in the first place or that the imported American institutions never worked as expected in Philippine political culture.
Hence, in this view, martial law only dispelled the naïve pretense
that American-style government could or should work in the Philippines. It also created the opportunity for Filipinos to shake off their
lingering "colonial mentality" and seek a genuine national identity
based on indigenous culture. Others argue that American influence
is stronger than ever; that neocolonialism has increased Philippine
dependence on the United States; and, indeed, that several public
agencies and private enterprises of the United States had an instrumental role in implementing the martial law regime. Which view is
correct? Does martial law represent a defeat for American ideals
abroad or a victory for American interests at home?

Finally, the transition to authoritarian government in the Philippines also provides a test case for many important theoretical questions. Is President Marcos correct when he argues, as many Third
World leaders have, that the loss of civil liberties and representative
government is the necessary price that must be paid by developing
countries to achieve political stability and economic growth? How
does the case of the Philippines illuminate the following issues: In
general, what internal and external conditions lead to the creation
of an authoritarian regime such as the Philippines under martial
law? To what extent does an authoritarian political system depend
on external sources of support for its maintenance in power? Is
this type of government more or less likely to implement socioeconomic reforms than a competitive, democratic one?

Explanations of Martial Law

In response to all these questions about Philippine martial law,
participants and other observers have offered a range of interpretations wide enough to permit a taxonomy of opinion.

2. O. D. Corpuz, *The Philippines* (Englewood Cliffs, N.J.: Prentice-Hall, 1965),
p. 69.

The Official View

The official explanation for the necessity of martial law is formally stated in Proclamation No. 1081, signed by President Marcos on September 21, 1972. In brief, it argues that the country was "in urgent danger of violent overthrow, insurrection, and rebellion." Communist subversives, right-wing oligarchs, Muslim rebels, urban terrorists, student demonstrators, labor unrest, economic setbacks, and natural disasters—all these necessitated the regrettable but temporary imposition of martial law to restore order to the country. Proclamation No. 1081 emphasizes the immediate right-wing and left-wing threats to the Philippines. No change of government was intended. On the contrary, President Marcos states explicitly both in Proclamation 1081 and in its accompanying statement that martial law did not mean a military takeover of civilian government and that he was acting strictly in accordance with the existing constitution and laws of the Republic of the Philippines.

Other presidential statements, however, offer a longer-term justification for the continuation of martial law and the drastic change of governmental structures: namely, that it was necessary to achieve urgent socioeconomic reforms, to create the New Society. Government reorganization, agrarian reform, sustained, long-run economic growth, and the creation of a new system of popular representation based on *barangays* or "citizens' assemblies" were the initial major proposals in the New Society program. The reform proposals, especially the administrative and economic reforms, were particularly important in mobilizing the commitments of the technocrats of the public planning sector and the entrepreneurs of the private business sector to the New Society.

Democracy Failed

Others maintain that the crises of the moment were only symptoms of a deeper flaw. They argue that the system as a whole broke down, that Western-style democracy simply failed in the Philippines. The governmental structures of the republic were increasingly inadequate to deal with the fundamental crises facing the country. Reform measures only postponed the inevitable collapse. Hence, one American correspondent observed that it had never occurred to U.S. colonial officials that "our essentially Protestant tradition established in an underpopulated vast land and based on English legal habits might not serve as a necessarily useful model to a Catholic country of mixed Iberian and Malay culture, relatively overpopulated, small and poor." One durably prominent Filipino statesman, Carlos Romulo, lamented that "we never had the substance of democracy. . . . The old system was in chaos." The new system was "an attempt to find middle ground, an effort to restore national discipline."

The difference between these two explanations is only one of emphasis on short- or long-term factors. Both place great emphasis on the maintenance of social order and political stability as the fundamental prerequisite for other government objectives. Both explanations are widely accepted and espoused within the military and among government officials. Both serve to justify the existing New Society regime. However, two other explanations, starting from essentially the same facts, lead to sharply divergent conclusions.

Democracy Never Existed

The left-wing, radical critique rejects the official view and the democracy-failed view and argues that true democracy never really existed in the first place in the Philippines. Martial law was only the "end of an illusion."[3] Nominally democratic institutions had long been subverted by indigenous oligarchs and foreign imperialists. Hence, martial law did not fundamentally change the basic structure of power in the country. On the contrary, the Filipino ruling elite could now increase their oppression and exploitation of the masses without formal restraint.

On the far left, the New People's Army found some value in this "unmasked tyranny." Its Fourth Anniversary Statement of March 29, 1973, proclaimed that martial law "has more than ever made the situation excellent for armed struggle."

The national united front has greatly broadened and has become ever more firmly anchored on the necessity of armed struggle. . . . Even the most backward sections of the population are roused to the spectacle of the ruling clique tearing to shreds every semblance of bourgeois democratic process. The ruling system has hopelessly cracked up from top to bottom. No amount of cloaking it as a "new society" will conceal its

3. From the title of an early but thorough radical critique of martial law: *The Philippines: End of an Illusion* (London and Stockholm: Association for Radical East Asian Studies and Journal of Contemporary Asia, 1973).

bankrupt and decadent condition; it is unmitigatingly the old society becoming ever more oppressive and exploitive.[4]

Democracy Was Succeeding

One further explanation maintains that Filipino political institutions, despite their flaws, were improving rapidly. Necessary reforms were forthcoming, but martial law aborted the process. Increasing local political activity and nationalist pressures in the years before martial law are cited as evidence that democracy was succeeding in the Philippines. Urban workers, plantation laborers, and subsistence farmers were being organized into unions, federations, and cooperatives to pursue their mutual interests. Various groups within the church had joined the progressive reform movement. Economic policy and foreign policy were steadily acquiring a nationalistic outlook. All of these newly articulated and organized interests came together in the late 1960s in a call for a major overhaul of the 1935 constitution. After extensive debate and elaborate preparations, a Constitutional Convention was opened on June 1, 1971, to consider a broad range of social and political reforms.

Exponents of this view argue that the reform movement was perceived, perhaps correctly, as a grave threat to the dominent elites of the country, who reacted accordingly with intimidation, bribery, violence, and, finally, martial law in order to protect their interests. One prominent figure in the reform movement, Reverend Bruno Hicks, an American Franciscan missionary, asked rhetorically, "Could this have been the reason why martial law was declared: because democracy was just beginning to work [and] the grievances of the masses were finally getting organized, getting aired, bringing pressure to bear on the political institutions?"[5]

This explanation comes with its own variations, depending on how the dominant elites of the country are defined. In its simplest form, martial law is viewed as essentially a one-man coup by a

4. Fourth Anniversary Statement of the New People's Army, *Ang Bayan* (Eng. ed., Mar. 29, 1973), p. 1.
5. This view is amplified in Hicks' U.S. Congressional testimony before the Fraser Subcommittee: "Human Rights in South Korea and the Philippines: Implications for U.S. Policy," Hearings before the Subcommittee on International Organizations of the Committee on International Relations, U.S. House of Representatives, May and June, 1975. These hearings also contain testimony exemplifying the alternative explanations of martial law.

power-hungry dictator. President Marcos is just another Asian strongman, who plotted and prepared for several years to seize power unconstitutionally, imprison or neutralize all his opponents, and thereby avoid the constitutional two-term limit on his presidential tenure. Another variation argues that martial law was more than a one-man affair; that it represents a major realignment of elite factions, resulting in a sharp concentration of power and wealth within the national elite. It is based on the premise that the family remains the crucial unit of capital accumulation and investment and that fewer families are acquiring greater and greater economic and political power. Hence, martial law indicated the dominance of the elite family alliance headed by Ferdinand Marcos and his wife, Imelda Romualdez Marcos, over the other rival national elites and the more traditional local elites.

Yet another variation argues that the antireform alliance extends even further, to foreign, principally American, interests. In this view, the U.S. government wanted to maintain its military bases; multinational (principally American) corporations wanted to maintain their access to supply and demand; and both these groups provided support to the Marcos administration to install a regime friendly to foreign enterprise and American security interests.

Analyzing Martial Law

These explanations indicate the wide range of answers to the question of why martial law was declared. The purpose of this book is to try to narrow this range.

The basic question of how the distribution of power and wealth was affected by the martial law government is discussed in Chapter 1 by Jose Veloso Abueva. As a former dean of the College of Public Administration of the national University of the Philippines and as the former executive secretary to the Constitutional Convention, Abueva has a highly advantageous perspective from which to describe how New Society goals were formulated and implemented. His analysis provides a general introduction to the specific case studies and theoretical issues discussed in the subsequent chapters. Drawing upon a wide range of scholarly analysis and opinion, he provides a general account of how the doctrine of constitutional authoritarianism was enacted in public policy. Tax collection and other fiscal reforms, bureaucratic reforms, land reform, investment, trade, and other economic policies are surveyed. Abueva describes the increase in influence of the military and the civilian technocrats paralleled by the decline in influence of the courts, the press, and other autonomous political groups. Evaluating the early results of the New Society program, Abueva examines five aspects of government performance: daily public management, socioeconomic reforms and development, short-term government power and authority, long-term government power and authority, and the reform of government leadership and administrative functions. He finds that the Marcos administration has been largely successful in the latter three areas, but much less impressive in the first two. According to Abueva's analysis, Marcos now faces the "reformer's predicament." Having strengthened his rule and achieved some notable reforms, he may be increasingly reluctant to pursue further major reforms for fear of disturbing his present ruling coalition. Abueva concludes that "even assuming his sincerity about reforms, not until he can change the composition of his grand alliance, now still dominated by the biggest economic interests and the newly privileged groups under him, will he dare to risk all to make the 'Democratic Revolution, the authentic revolution.' "

In Chapter 2, Rolando V. del Carmen begins by discussing the constitutionality of martial law. By examining legal precedents and the interaction between the president and the supreme court, he finds that the declaration of martial law did indeed have constitutional and legal sanction. However, the new constitution, with its controversial provisions on the transitional government, was not ratified by any proper constitutional or legal procedure. Del Carmen discusses in detail the disputes surrounding the framing and ratification of the new constitution and the major court challenges to its implementation. He finds that the assumption of "constitutional authoritarianism" by President Marcos has severely eroded the rule of law and the independence of the judiciary in the Philippines. It is a classic case of political realities outweighing legal niceties. The political reality of an omnipotent executive led the Philippine Supreme Court to circumvent potential conflict with President Marcos and thereby avoid the fate of the now-defunct Philippine Congress. "Like the proverbial Oriental bamboo," del Carmen concludes, "the court has understandably chosen to bend with the wind in an effort to survive." Under current circumstances, the court will survive as long as President Marcos finds it tractable and useful to his rule.

Despite its dubious constitutionality, the New Society of President Marcos has often been justified as the only form of government capable of implementing meaningful social reform. The most important of these reforms, according to repeated Marcos administration statements, is that of land reform. Presidential Decree No. 27 of October 21, 1972, announced "The Emancipation of Tenants from the Bondage of the Soil." It was one of the earliest and most publicized of martial law reform measures. On the first anniversary of the declaration of martial law, President Marcos reviewed his government's achievements and again declared that "easily the most meaningful reform in the society is the emancipation of the farmer from his age-old bondage to the soil." Shortly thereafter, on the first anniversary of Presidential Decree No. 27, he further emphasized that "the land reform program is the only gauge for the success or failure of the New Society. If land reform fails, there is no New Society." In addition to these public statements, considerable government effort and international assistance have been devoted to studying the problem.

These priorities and efforts are the subject of Benedict J. Kerkvliet's analysis in Chapter 3. Despite the increased attention and high priority accorded to land reform, Kerkvliet finds that many agrarian problems of the Old Society persist in the New Society program. Contrary to its nominal objective of "the emancipation of all tenant farmers," Kerkvliet's analysis shows that the immediate objective of the New Society land reform program is "to protect the regime from rural unrest rather than to redistribute substantially wealth and political power to villagers." He demonstrates how the land reform program has been limited in scope and how legal, financial, and marketing obstacles prevent tenants from acquiring the land they till. Kerkvliet concludes that the combined opposition of agribusiness and the landed elite and middle classes make it unlikely that President Marcos will achieve his ostensible goal of social equity for the rural peasantry.

Since the declaration of martial law in September, 1972, few Philippine institutions have been transformed as drastically as the mass media. Before martial law was declared, the Philippine press was widely regarded as one of the freest in Asia. Since then, the press and all other mass media have come under the strict control of the government. This transformation challenges several old assumptions about the status of civil liberties in the Philippines. For example, given its long tradition of freedom of expression, how did the Philippine press lose its liberties so swiftly and with so little popular protest? What are the political costs and benefits of a government-censored press? What should be the role of the news media in a developing society? These are the questions explored by David Rosenberg in Chapter 4.

The answers are roughly categorized into two major, alternative views. The Marcos government has argued that the loss of civil liberties is the necessary price that Filipinos have to pay, if only temporarily, to achieve political stability and economic growth. According to this view, freedom of the press never really existed before martial law; rather, it was abused and subverted by Communists and oligarchs from within and without. Hence, it was deemed necessary under martial law to regulate the mass media in order to assure their responsible role in the development program of the New Society.

The alternative view holds that the defects of some pre-martial law news media did not warrant the wholesale restrictions imposed by the New Society. According to this view, President Marcos found it necessary to silence the free press in order to reduce the influence of his political opponents and prevent any criticism of his martial law regime. Rosenberg examines the evidence for these two alternative views and finds little evidence to support the Marcos administration's charges of subversion. Some abuses of the pre-martial law news media have been curtailed, but the New Society news media have their own problems of credibility, according to Rosenberg. "The people are asked to accept and actively support a regime purely on the basis of proclamations and decrees, without any knowledge of the factors involved, the priorities assessed, the arguments for and against, or the determination of national interest." Rosenberg concludes that in the absence of an effective and legitimate means of expressing a diversity of public opinion, both the government and the people are likely to be increasingly ignorant of and dissatisfied with each other.

In the concluding Chapter 5, Robert Stauffer provides a theoretical synthesis of the contending interpretations of Philippine martial law, based on the substantive findings of the previous chapters as well as on his own analysis of the political economy of refeudalization. Refeudalization, according to Stauffer, refers to the decline of autonomous groups within a political system and the increased dependence of the dominant groups within that political system on external sources of support. As applied to the Philippines, this variation of dependence theory maintains that growing pressures for increased nationalist autonomy (i.e., defeudalization) were reversed by martial law. Stauffer asserts that "a small group of Filipinos representing groups closely allied with American and other foreign interests overthrew the existing political system and imposed authoritarian controls over the rest of Philippine society." He indicates the theoretical conditions and specific events that led to the imposition of a dependent-authoritarian regime: the increasing popularity of the idea that strict discipline and technocratic government are essential for Third World development; the increasing nationalist threat to foreign, principally American, economic interests and to the increasingly strategic American military bases in the Philippines; the rise to prominence of a technocratic government elite and a national business elite, two groups that generally shared the views and policy preferences of foreign investors; the development of extensive personal linkages between Americans and Filipinos in such major Philippine institutions as education, research, government planning, industrial and trade associations, and the military and police; and, finally, the reorganization and expansion of government coercive institutions such as the military, paramilitary forces, and the police. The cumulative effect of these factors, according to Stauffer, was "to undermine the existing political structures, to greatly expand the power of the authoritarian agencies, and to make the coup simple to execute and sustain—and certainly also more probable." Stauffer further describes how the New Society regime consolidated its rule after martial law and promoted the refeudalization of the country with the assistance of foreign powers, a process he refers to as "the formalization of a U.S.-Japan Greater Southeast Asia Co-Prosperity Sphere." His analysis emphasizes the theoretical importance of conceptualizing the factors—in particular, the international factors—which facilitate the creation of an authoritarian regime. His evaluation provides support for the proposition that powerful industrial nations find competitive political systems undesirable in poor Third World nations in which they have important interests.

The appendixes provide several important documents and official statements relating to the analyses in the text. These materials do not give equal emphasis to all the points of view on Philippine martial law. Instead, the coverage emphasizes, first, the major governmental decrees relating to the declaration and consolidation of martial law rule and, second, the major opposition statements, which are not readily available to the general reader. Appendixes 1 and 2, containing the first two public statements of President Marcos after the declaration of martial law, provide what are still perhaps the most extensive and detailed justifications for his actions. Appendixes 3–10 indicate the major governmental decrees relating to the structuring and consolidation of the New Society institutions. Appendix 11 contains the Report of the National Committee for the Restoration of Civil Liberties in the Philippines (NCRCLP). The NCRCLP was founded in the United States by a group of Americans and expatriate Filipinos on the same day that martial law was declared. The material included here is drawn from its U.S. Congressional testimony on American foreign relations with the Philippines. It is an early and notable example of the now numerous anti-martial law activities emanating from the United States. Appendix 12 provides a statement from one of the most important anti-martial law groups operating within the Philippines, the Civil Liberties Union of the Philippines (CLUP). Its importance is due in large part to the composition of its editorial board, which consists of several still-prominent former senators and supreme court justices of the Philippines. This statement is one of several that the CLUP has published and distributed within the Philippines, all of which argue for the lifting of martial law and the holding of competitive elections. Appendix 13 and Appendix 14 supplement the scope of this volume by describing the changing role of the church under martial law. Although the church has generally been considered to be a politically conservative force in the Philippines, it has dramatically changed its position to become one of the few surviving pre-martial law institutions that afford public criticism of the Marcos administration. The Overview and Chronology outline the major stages and events in this reorientation.

The scope of the present volume has left untreated several major

issues which deserve further attention for a fuller understanding of
the dynamics of Philippine martial law. Foremost among these
issues is the war that the Marcos administration has been waging
against Muslim rebels in the southern Philippines. The death and
destruction arising from this conflict clearly present a major threat
to the internal stability of the martial law regime and to its foreign
policies. The fighting became intense in October 1972, suggesting
that the declaration of martial law was its principle cause. Warfare
was indeed intensified by three major policies of the new regime:
the centralization of power within almost exclusively Christian
groups; the suppression of dissenting views for greater autonomy;
and the regime's attempt to disarm the civilian population.[6]

For many Muslims, however, the origins of the war go back as far
as the sixteenth century. The current rebellion under the nominal
aegis of the Moro National Liberation Front (MNLF) can also be
seen as the most recent episode in a seemingly endless conflict against
central authority by a long-standing, highly autonomous cultural
minority. Despite the antiquity of the dispute, relatively little is
known about the objectives, organization, strategies, and resources
of the current secessionist movement. Further research is needed on
these competing demands for integration and autonomy under the
New Society.[7]

Additional research is also needed on the roles of the Communist
Party of the Philippines, the New People's Army, and the Philippine military forces under martial law. These are all obviously
difficult subjects for scholarly research; however, in the absence of
any widely accepted channels for expressing legitimate dissent, they
are increasingly critical to a fuller understanding of the New Society.[8]

6. For further development of this argument, see Lela Noble, "The Moro National Liberation Front" (San Jose State College [mimeograph], 1977).
    7. A good place to begin would be with Noble's manuscript mentioned above as
well as her "Ethnicity and Philippine-Malaysian Relations," *Asian Survey* XV (May
1975), 453–72; Peter G. Gowing, "Muslim Filipinos between Integration and Secession," *Southeast Asia Journal of Theology* XIV:2, p. 66; Robert Stauffer, "The 'Development' of Mindanao," *Pahayag* no. 30 (June 1975), pp. 3–7; and Leon Ma. Guerrero, *Encounter of Cultures: The Muslims in the Philippines* (University of the
Philippines, Asian Center Library, n.d.).
    8. For those intending to pursue research on these and other aspects of Philippine
martial law, the following are particularly recommended: Tom Walsh, *Martial Law
in the Philippines: A Research Guide and Working Bibliography,* University of
Hawaii, Asian Studies Program, Southeast Asia Working Paper No. 4 (1973);
Shiro Saito, *Philippine Research Materials and Library Resources,* University of
Hawaii, Asian Studies Program, Southeast Asia Working Paper (1974); and "A

Problems and Prospects of the New Society

Although each chapter of this volume focuses on a different aspect of martial law, several common findings of these analyses can be observed. Foremost among these is that the New Society has produced a sharp increase in the concentration of political power within the central government, especially in the urban areas. President Marcos and his closest allies share this power with the technocrats who increasingly control and direct the economy and with the military and national police who are in charge of the major enforcement agencies. Centralization of power has considerably facilitated "effective administration" and "rational planning," which appear to be the key catchwords of leadership.

Political order and economic growth are widely cited as the major achievements of the New Society. Private armies and crime syndicates have been disbanded, and thousands of unlicensed guns have been confiscated. Government reorganization efforts have led to the dismissal of many corrupt officials. Fiscal and monetary policies have been significantly improved. Reformed taxation policies have increased government revenues. The rate of inflation has declined. On the whole, the Philippines enjoys a higher credit rating now than before martial law. Foreign investment has increased substantially, as has domestic capital formation. Tourism has also increased. The planning and implementation of development projects has been considerably improved, especially in the public-sector areas of roads, ports, transportation, power, and land reclamation.

The gains that have been achieved, however, have led to a concentration of power and wealth within the economy similar to that within the political system. By actively pursuing policies to create "an attractive environment for foreign investment," the Marcos administration has greatly favored large firms in the industrial and

Radical Bibliography of Sources on the Philippines in English" (Providence, R.I.: Committee of Concerned Asian Scholars, Philippine Committee, August 1973; rev. ed., January 1977). Abundant economic data and analysis, especially for the period 1950–72, is contained in *Sharing in Development: A Programme of Employment, Equity and Growth for the Philippines* (International Labor Office, 1974). Event data is comprehensively reported in the biweekly *Philippine Times* (Chicago). A particularly valuable resource for hard-to-document events is the Honolulu monthly *Pahayag*. See its final issue, "Index to *Pahayag*: Nos. 1–52, December, 1972–April, 1977." Current research activities and materials are regularly reported in the *Philippine Studies Bulletin* of the Association for Asian Studies, Southeast Asia Regional Council.

trade sectors of the economy, many of which have become the local junior partners of multinational corporations. One consequence has been that the Philippines has increased its already high dependence on the world market to sell its major exports—minerals, sugar, coconut products, and timber—and to obtain the necessary inputs—oil, technology, and capital—for the New Society development program. Many of the early economic successes and reversals of the martial law government may be more accurately attributed to changes in the world prices of its key commodity exports and imports rather than to government management of the economy.

While the Marcos administration has been praised by some for increasing economic growth, it has been criticized by others for not distributing the benefits of this growth widely enough. Despite the prominent themes of discipline and austerity in the New Society, there is still ample evidence of conspicuous consumption and extravagant affluence. Economic reforms or social welfare policies such as land reform have been implemented only to the extent necessary to mitigate extreme duress, avoid open rebellion, and secure at least passive acceptance of the New Society.

The problem of increasing class differentiation in the economy is paralleled by the problem of legitimacy in the political system. The thorough centralization of economic and political power has greatly reduced political activity in the New Society. The role of local and provincial government has been sharply reduced. Other, nongovernmental, autonomous groups have been banned or placed under strict central government controls. The Marcos administration has made only perfunctory experimental attempts to mobilize popular support or encourage mass participation. Despite the many pronouncements, the New Society does not have a systematic or explicit ideology; major decisions are made on a pragmatic basis. There are no political parties or other coherent political organizations to explain, guide, or rally support to the New Society. The few participatory institutions that have been proposed—the system of citizens' assemblies or the legislative advisory assembly—are more symbolic than instrumental. The New Society is principally directed through the highly personalistic rule of Ferdinand Marcos. Indeed, so personalistic is his rule that no provisions for presidential succession have been announced.

The continuing lack of legitimacy and the government's inability or unwillingness to do anything meaningful about it raise questions about how much popular support there is for the New Society. Considerable support apparently comes from the business community, the urban middle class, landlords, and the military and civilian bureaucracies; at present, however, there are no reliable and accurate indicators of mass public opinion. Nevertheless, there are other signs of a growing disillusionment with the martial law regime. Crime and corruption are reported to have achieved or even surpassed pre-martial law levels. Strikes and demonstrations, although illegal, still occur. Underground resistance and open protest against the Marcos administration have grown steadily since martial law began.

The New Society has dealt with dissent in a number of ways. Centralized control over the economy and all government agencies as well as a compliant mass media are sufficient to ensure widespread compliance with the regime's peace-and-order policies. Arbitrary arrests and intimidations continue, but large-scale coercion has been used only selectively. However, local military units, often beyond the effective control of the central government, have frequently been accused of committing arbitrary violence. In order to control his own government bureaucracy, President Marcos has resorted to a system of informants, frequent dismissals, and personnel changes. Outside of government, he wins and maintains friends and allies through the strategic distribution of economic rewards. As long as economic performance is high, this brand of payoff politics is adequate to reinforce the ruling alliance and minimize significant dissent.

Nevertheless, there remain several sources of real or potential dissent within the country, including the Moro National Liberation Front, the Communist Party of the Philippines (CPP), the New People's Army (NPA), several groups within the church, urban intelligentsia, expatriate Filipinos, former members of the Federation of Free Farmers, some old elite families, even junior officers of the army, off fighting the secessionist movement in the south while their superior officers help President Marcos to run the country. Assassination or coup d'etat are no longer inconceivable; they have both been tried and they are still predicted by some. Under current government priorities and policies, dissent, however well smothered, can be expected to remain volatile. There are no institutionalized safety valves in the New Society; no opportunities to express dissent, however legitimate. As inequalities increase and grievances accumulate, the costs of repression can be expected to mount. With considerable foreign aid, the Marcos administration has so far been able to pay this increasing cost and maintain its rule.

Hence, the end of martial law is not in sight. Nor is there any realistic alternative immediately in view. Even the critics of the New Society seem unenthusiastic for a return to the Old Society of pre-martial law days. Very few of the pre-martial law institutions have survived with any significant degree of public trust or commitment of leadership.

Only the military has the means to change the regime; in such an event, it would seem unlikely that they would be more willing or able to implement the difficult reforms targeted by the New Society. The CPP and the NPA do not really have the means at present to overthrow the regime; and if they did, it is doubtful that a people's republic would permit any greater autonomy than presently exists. The MNLF appears more concerned with securing its own independence than with regaining the liberties of its northern brothers. And because of all the differences in ideology and personality, a united front among these groups against the New Society seems improbable.

Despite the lack of visible alternatives, the New Society cannot be said to be a stable political system. The heightened vulnerability of an economy increasingly dependent on the world market, the unresolved conflicts embedded in the secessionist movement, and the miscalculations of an uninformed bureaucracy all threaten the stability of the system. The most fundamental threat is the regime's lack of legitimacy. It would be premature to dismiss the principles of self-determination and representative government from any consideration of Philippine martial law. Filipinos were the first among Asians to demand these rights and to declare their independence from an authoritarian colonial regime, almost a century ago. These principles were again firmly established by Filipinos under the American Commonwealth in the Philippines. They continue to find expression underground, abroad, and increasingly in the open, in the Philippines. The hypocrisy of New Society attempts to gain popular support is the homage that vice pays to virtue.

The Philippines, like many developing countries, is undergoing profound social changes in social structure and world view. The New Society itself is formally dedicated to achieving revolutionary changes in a peaceful and orderly fashion. However, the current commitment of the Marcos administration to political order and economic growth at the expense of social equity and human rights only assures that social changes, when they do inevitably demand political accommodation, will be violent. At present, there are simply no institutions to provide for the peaceful accommodation of new and diverse interests and opinions. An authoritarian regime, installed to achieve political order, has been seen to contain its own inherent tendencies toward disorder.

1. Ideology and Practice in the "New Society"

JOSE VELOSO ABUEVA
UNITED NATIONS UNIVERSITY

How have power and wealth been shaped and shared in the Philippines since martial law was imposed by President Ferdinand E. Marcos on September 21, 1972? Proclaimed as a "revolution from the top" or "from the center," martial law in the Philippines was intended, among other things, "to save the nation" or to prevent or abort what the president saw as the gathering revolution from below in which the "leftists" were joined by the "rightists" in fomenting an upheaval. The other avowed goal was "to institute reforms" in a political, economic, and social system marked by an increasing concentration of power, wealth, and opportunities for advancement caused by and resulting in the rule of oligarchy.

The rhetoric of the New Society raises two major questions: How are power and wealth to be restructured or "democratized"? And what are the discernible effects of the changes and reforms that have been introduced? In due course, historians and social scientists will evaluate to what extent and under what conditions the new political elite, under a regime of "constitutional authoritarianism," are willing and able to redistribute their tremendous governmental and economic power in order to realize the avowed "revolutionary" goals of the regime. Meanwhile, it remains to be seen whether a "revolution from the top" is feasible in the Philippines.

Goals of the Democratic Revolution and the New Society

In 1971, a year before he imposed martial law in the Philippines, President Marcos published his diagnosis of Filipino society and his

Before its substantial revision this chapter was presented at the 30th International Congress of the Human Sciences for Asia and North Africa, Mexico City, August 3-8, 1976.

ideas for the "Democratic Revolution" and the "New Society." In his book *Today's Revolution: Democracy*, Marcos concluded that the fundamental defect of Filipino society is that it tends to be oligarchic: "The economic gap between the rich and the poor provides the wealthy few the opportunity of exercising undue influence on the political authority."[1] He observed that the "oligarchic elite manipulate the political authority and intimidate political leaders," while "the masses," because of their poverty, dependency, and lack of organization, "perpetuate a populist, personalist, and individualist kind of politics." One result is that "corruption at the top is matched by social corruption below."[2] Moreover, oligarchic control of the mass media "has perpetuated the simplistic politics that have been obstructive of meaningful change, . . . institutional change [and] the restructuring of society." In the end, the disillusioned and desperate "masses will just have to take power into their hands."[3]

Meanwhile, the crescendo of lawlessness, particularly in the urban areas; the strident cries and disruptive demonstrations for change by radical groups in Metro Manila (since 1976, the term for Manila and its surrounding three cities and thirteen municipalities); and the reports of increasing activity of Communist rebels and Muslim secessionists had heightened the people's fears and anxieties, as had the apparent inability of the government to cope with the anarchic situation. New political groups arose, reacting to perceptions of the government as a corrupt, unresponsive, and ineffective social institution in the face of worsening mass poverty, income inequalities, political elite competition, and the violence spawned by "political warlords." Demanding change, they advocated ideologies that ranged from mild reforms to outright revolution: the Welfare State of Diosdado Macapagal, the Social Democracy of Raul Manglapus, the Socialism of the Socialist Party, the National Democracy of the Kabataang Makabayan, and the Democratic Philippine Society of the Movement for the Advancement of Nationalism. The outlawed Communist Party of the Philippines was no longer alone in espousing a radical ideology.[4] In 1970, Congress and the president passed a law calling for the election of delegates to a Constitutional Convention that would initiate basic reforms—a governmental response

1. Ferdinand E. Marcos, *Today's Revolution: Democracy* (Manila, 1971), p. 96.
2. Ibid., p. 99.
3. Ibid., pp. 103–4.
4. Jose Veloso Abueva, *Filipino Politics, Nationalism and Emerging Ideologies* (Manila: Modern Book Company, 1972).

that elicited approval by 82 percent of the population in a national survey.[5]

On August 21, 1971, terrorists bombed the final campaign meeting of the Liberal Party in Manila. Opposition senatorial and other candidates and leaders present were hospitalized. President Marcos suspended the writ of habeas corpus, and speculation was rife that he would declare martial law. The election of six out of eight Liberal candidates to the Senate was an indication of the people's disapproval of the leadership of Marcos, who had campaigned actively on the issue of his performance.[6] The terrorists were never apprehended, and there would be more unsolved bombings in Metro Manila. Some opposition leaders suspected that Marcos was preparing for the imposition of martial law in the event that he could not extend his rule beyond his second and final term under the 1935 constitution.

In the same book, Marcos said: "I believe that in this troubled present, revolution is a fact, not merely a potential threat, and that if we value our sacred rights, our cherished freedoms, we must wrest the revolutionary leadership from those who would, in the end, turn the democratic revolution into a totalitarian regime."[7] He deemed it his duty "to revive the atrophied will of the political authority . . . the will of the sovereign people," and affirmed his belief that "a reorientation must proceed; society must be revolutionized."[8] He was determined to "democratize wealth and property" to make "equality of opportunity for all" a fact, to "revolutionize society for the sake of man, not for the sake of the State," to make the "Democratic Revolution, the authentic revolution," work: in short, to establish "the New Society" by a "Democratic Revolution" which is "constitutional, liberal and nationalist"[9]—"a continuing revolution by constitutional means."[10]

The president wrote that "unlimited democracy" and the "free enterprise" economy were both the causes and consequences of a social and economic setting marked by glaring gaps in wealth and power and by oligarchic dominance and mass subordination. It was

5. *Opinion Survey* (Manila: Research Center Philippines, 1971).
6. Editorial, *Philippines Free Press*, Sept. 11, 1971.
7. Marcos, *Today's Revolution*, p. 139.
8. Ibid., p. 104.
9. Ibid., p. 64.
10. Ibid., p. 63.

a system that must be changed. But, he added, "because the political culture abets the status quo, that too has to be radically changed."[11] Once more, in his own words, "Our populist, personalist and individualist culture must give way not only to collective responsibility, but beyond that to our historic responsibility."[12]

Hence, Marcos foresaw an all-embracing change in values and behavior that would be required of all Filipinos by the Democratic Revolution and the New Society. It would be a change away from an exclusively self-centered orientation to an inclusive one in which personal advantage would be linked with the good of others, of the whole nation, now and even beyond one's lifetime into the indefinite future. The intended changes are summarized in the term *disiplina* ("discipline"), which was the ubiquitous early exhortation and warning of martial law authorities. *Disiplina* has since been used in the New Society to change Filipino political culture and behavior through a variety of ways: presidential decrees, proclamations, general orders and instructions, new rules and regulations, old laws and codes, the flag, the national anthem, indoctrination, New Society songs, slogans, maxims, proverbs, citizen campaigns, presidential awards, commemorative ceremonies, varied applications of force and coercive sanctions customary in democracies, and calculated violations of human rights characteristic of authoritarian systems.

In addition to articulating his design for "a revolution from the top" as early as 1971, the president repeatedly warned his critics that he "would not hesitate to proclaim martial law if the situation demanded it," in order that they might "not go beyond the limits of legitimate dissent."[13] But few heeded the drastic implications of these warnings. When, on September 21, 1972, Marcos declared martial law over the entire country through Proclamation 1081, he did so with the loyal and effective support of the military in enforcing his decisions and actions as commander-in-chief and as president. On the night of September 22, 1972, under presidential orders, the army closed down all radio and television stations and newspaper offices and arrested prominent publishers, journalists, and commentators critical of the president, including a few who were

11. Ibid., p. 115.
12. Ibid., p. 89.
13. Ibid., p. 123.

allegedly involved in a conspiracy against him and the government; several opposition senators, a number of opposition delegates to the Constitutional Convention, a governor, and a congressman known to be close to the president but suspected of arms smuggling; labor leaders; and thousands of activists and protesters. Notorious criminals at large were rounded up. Checkpoints were established, and soldiers inspected all vehicles, padlocked the Congress building, and guarded the schools, which were closed down for a few weeks. The Philippine Constabulary's Camp Crame and the Philippine Army's Camp Aguinaldo, both in Metro Manila, and other detention centers in the country, soon to be inhabited by some 30,000 detainees, became instant symbols of the new martial law regime.[14]

The army next cracked down on the so-called "political warlords" and their "private armies" all over the country. A thorough and effective campaign for the surrender of privately held firearms yielded over half a million weapons, according to the president and the military. Military tribunals were created to process the martial law detainees. For months, news and rumors circulated about the arrest of suspected subversives and criminals. Heavy penalties were imposed for defiance of the criminal laws. To dramatize the seriousness of law enforcement by the authorities, a convicted Chinese drug pusher was executed by a firing squad. Presidential decrees, orders, proclamations, and instructions issued forth in rapid succession, as if to underscore the will of the president, with the assistance of the military, to strengthen their control on the conduct of the citizenry. Some agencies, including a few strategic private enterprises and public utilities, were placed under military direction or supervision. Military intelligence spread its surveillance far and wide, especially in the colleges and universities, which had been well known for their radicalism. By 1976, more than a thousand presidential decrees had been issued, in lieu of statutes that might have been passed by a legislature, as well as hundreds of other presidential edicts.

The Shaping and Sharing of Power

Martial law overtook the Constitutional Convention, which had been called to frame a new Filipino constitution responsive to the

14. *Report of an Amnesty International Mission to the Republic of the Philippines, 22 November–5 December 1975* (London: Amnesty International Publications, 1976), p. 4. The number of detainees swelled to 50,000 before it rapidly declined. By 1975 it was estimated that some 6,000 or more remained in detention camps.

demand for reforms in a period of mounting ideological confrontations.[15] The 1935 constitution, written by Filipino delegates under American colonial rule, was deemed inadequate for an independent country struggling for political, economic, social, and cultural development because of its colonial taint, its emphasis on civil rights to the neglect of social and economic rights and citizens' duties, and its restrictive concept of private property. The view prevailed that the old constitution somehow had resulted in the ills of Filipino democracy: oligarchical rule, political abuses, corruption, worsening social injustice, persistent underdevelopment. In a society dominated by lawyers, such a legalistic view has led to the traditional Filipino reliance on laws for solving national problems—despite their well-known violation in practice, often by the lawmakers themselves.

Among the most controversial issues of the Constitutional Convention from its inception in June 1971 was the proposed shift from a presidential form of government, under which President Marcos would not be allowed to seek a third term as president, to a parliamentary system that would allow him to continue in power by election as prime minister. So strong were the anti-Marcos forces in the convention that the proposed parliamentary government initially had few supporters. Moreover, even some delegates who favored a parliamentary government were disposed to include provisions in the new constitution that would disqualify both the president and Mrs. Marcos from ever becoming chief of state or head of government. Until the eve of martial law, the anti-Marcos delegates were able to prevent approval of draft constitutional provisions that would allow the continuation of Marcos' power in any form of government.

Although the Congress could not meet after martial law was declared and its building was locked upon presidential orders, the Constitutional Convention continued its sessions, minus some dozen opposition leaders who were detained. The convention was asked to hasten its historic task. In seventy days the delegates fully complied by adopting a new constitution. The document proper, consisting of a preamble and sixteen articles, is liberal, socially oriented, progressive, developmental, and nationalistic.[16] It provides for a parliamentary form of government. However, the transitory provisions that were tailored to the requirements of the martial law

15. See Abueva, *Filipino Politics.*
16. Jose Veloso Abueva, "Some Outstanding Characteristics of the New Constitution" (Quezon City [mimeographed], 1973).

regime enable President Marcos to enforce the constitution selectively. One such provision provides for an interim National Assembly to be convened by President Marcos to act as a transitional
legislature. Another would ensure the legal validity of all presidential decrees and other acts even beyond the period of martial law.
A third provision empowers the president to remove and replace
any official or employee in the executive or the judiciary.[17]

In January 1973, Marcos hastily called a referendum on the new
constitution through citizen assemblies, instead of through the
plebiscite required under the then existing 1935 constitution and
under the new one that he had already scheduled and then postponed indefinitely. Referendum voting was by *viva voce* or acclamation in citizen assembly meetings, not by secret voting supervised
by the Commission on Elections. The 1973 constitution was proclaimed ratified by the president on the basis of a report that 95
percent of the voters had favored it.[18] Marcos also declared that the
interim National Assembly would not be convened and that martial
law would continue for an unstated period.[19]

By a vote of six to four, the Supreme Court voted that the constitution had not been validly ratified by the people. Chief Justice
Concepcion voiced the majority opinion on this issue: "Indeed, I
cannot in good conscience declare that the proposed Constitution
has been approved or adopted by the people in the citizens' assemblies all over the Philippines when it is, to my mind, a matter of
judicial knowledge that there have been no such citizens' assemblies
in many parts of the Philippines."[20] However, bowing to the fait
accompli, the Supreme Court also declared that "there is now no
further obstacle to the new constitution" being considered in force
and effect because only four, not six, justices voted for its outright
unconstitutionality.[21] By *pakikisama* ("going along to get along"),
the Supreme Court avoided a frontal clash with the president and
the possible institution of a revolutionary regime, among other
consequences.

The imposition of martial law that began the transformation of
the Philippine political system resembled the bloodless palace coup

17. Constitution of the Republic of the Philippines, Article XVII, Secs. 1, 3 (2),
9, and 10.
18. Proclamation No. 1102, Jan. 17, 1973.
19. Proclamation No. 1103 and Proclamation No. 1104, Jan. 17, 1973.
20. *Javellana* v. *Executive Secretary, et al.*, L-36162, Mar. 31, 1973.
21. See comments of Rolando V. del Carmen, Chapter 2, below.

d'etats in Latin America insofar as the military was crucially involved. However, an elected civilian president was at the helm of government and no tanks and armor ever rumbled through Metro Manila. In most places outside Mindanao and the rebel-infested provinces of Luzon and east Visayas, the uniformed military became less visible if more powerful after September 1972.

Yet the military have continued to play a prominent and strategic role as the president's power base and right arm in law enforcement, counterinsurgency, containment of civilian opposition, civic action, and developmental activities, as well as in reinforcing the people's orientation toward the national community. One spokesman, Adrian Cristobal, explains the salience of the military thus: "Since we [in the Marcos administration] have adopted *discipline* as a necessary element of national progress, and since discipline has long been associated in our minds with the military way of life, it is but natural that the military now looms so vividly in our thinking."[22]

Under martial rule, the secretary of national defense and the top military leaders work directly and intimately with the president. The power, prerogatives, emoluments, and prestige of the military establishment have never been greater. This is true even though blatant abuses and corruption attributed to some officers and soldiers have made many citizens regard them with fear and hatred.[23] The military now enjoy a larger share of the government budget than ever before: the allocation for the military rocketed from P880 million in 1972 to P4 billion in 1976, or an increase of about 500 percent in four years. In 1977, the military and police will receive 18 percent of the total government outlay, the largest single allocation among all departments. The military establishment is being expanded from 60,000 in 1972 to a projected 250,000 in 1978. U.S. military assistance increased from $60.2 million in fiscal years 1970-72 to $118.7 million in fiscal years 1973-75, or an increase of about 200 percent,[24] a dramatic rise that has been interpreted as U.S. support of the Marcos martial-law regime.

22. Adrian E. Cristobal, Preface to *Guiding Principles of the New Society* (Fort Bonifacio, Rizal: Philippine Army Civil Relations and Information, 1976).
23. See Association of Major Religious Superiors in the Philippines, *Political Detainees in the Philippines* (Mar. 31, 1976), and *Report of an Amnesty International Mission, 1975.*
24. "Development News," *Philippine Development* IV:9 (Sept. 20, 1976), 38. Comparative figures in the FY 1977 budget are: defense and maintenance of peace and order, P5 billion or 18.2 percent; utilities and infrastructure, P8 billion or 29.2

Freed from their previous subordination to the national legislature and provincial governors, military officers have availed themselves fully of their enlarged opportunities to maintain peace and
order and enforce the laws as they see fit. For this contribution to
political stability and the president's continuing rule they have been
amply rewarded in status and power. While the generals and
colonels have joined the new political elite, junior officers and enlisted men have simply received their long-delayed due in equity,
given their low incomes, high risks, and heavy duties.

Alongside the officers of the armed forces, civilian technocrats
exercise delegated presidential authority as cabinet members and
heads of departments, agencies, or government corporations. Drawn
from the University of the Philippines and other educational institutions, as well as from business firms and the military, the technocrats act as presidential advisers, government executives, drafters
of presidential decrees, and advocates and defenders of the New
Society. Responsible only to the president and appointed by him,
they serve at his pleasure. They assist him in the exercise of his
tremendous executive and legislative powers, uninhibited by elected
representatives or by a critical press. Their common outlook might
be described in Robert Stauffer's words: they share "an ideology of
modernization, an aversion to politics, a belief in the free enterprise
system and yet a need for government planning, an elitist view of
society, and a commitment to development."[25]

Given unusual opportunities to test their developmental ideas and
apply their professional expertise—and responding to the allure-
ments of power, prestige, and material advantages—the technocrats
willingly assume the risks of success or failure in their high positions and in their commitment to the martial law regime. As
Remigio Agpalo has observed, "they all believe in the goals and
dreams of the President, for they have shared with him in forging
the strategies and tactics of carrying them out; they have no solid

percent; education and manpower, P2.8 billion or 10.2 percent; agriculture, fishery
and forestry, P2.1 billion or 7.7 percent; health and nutrition, P1.1 billion or 4
percent; industry, Po.6 billion or 2.2 percent; housing, Po.4 billion or 1.5 percent.
Figures on U.S. military assistance from "Military Assistance to the Government of
the Philippines," U.S. Congress, Subcommittee on International Relations, House
Foreign Affairs Committee, June 1975. See Friends of the Filipino People, *The
Logistics of Repression and Other Essays* (Washington, D.C., 1977).

25. Robert B. Stauffer, "Philippine Authoritarianism: Framework for Peripheral
'Development' " University of Hawaii [mimeograph], 1976), p. 8.

political base which was the principal attribute of the well-known oligarchs of the pre-martial law political system; and the incentives of working devotedly and faithfully with the President do not only involve the fear of losing honor, life and fortune were the martial law administration to fail, but also the joy and pride of fathering the birth of a new society."[26]

As for the judiciary, the president has publicly acknowledged that it has "in a great and substantial nature maintained the political stability of the country . . . by its prestige, trustworthiness, fairness, good name and reputation."[27] In fact, the Supreme Court has upheld the president or at least deferred to him each time that his status and acts have been challenged before it. As provided by the 1973 constitution, the Supreme Court now has administrative supervision over all lower courts. Until 1975, the time limits in the adjudication of legal disputes were generally observed, resulting in a speedier judicial process. Combined with improved peace and order, one effect is that property rights, essential to a free enterprise economy, are relatively secure in most parts of the country. But in late 1976 the chief justice complained about the slowing down of the courts and the resulting huge backlog of cases.

The judiciary has, however, lost a considerable part of its autonomy. The president has ultimate power over the entire judiciary because he may remove any judge or official in the Department of Justice. All decisions of the military tribunals become final only upon his approval. In addition, the suspension of certain civil and political rights in the 1973 constitution, the shrinkage of civil court jurisdiction, and the existence of several military courts—(at one time there were about twenty military commissions and forty provost courts)—all tend to undermine official assertions of judicial independence. In its report on "the State of the Nation after Three Years of Martial Law," the Philippine Civil Liberties Union observed, "For many, it is futile to invoke the rule of law. . . . The administration of justice is muddled." The CLU report also noted: "Veteran judges of long service have been dismissed through court notices of acceptance of their compulsory resignations."[28] In the

26. Remigio E. Agpalo, "The Political Elite in a Post-Traditional Society: The Case of the Philippines," *Elites and Development*, Friedrich-Ebert-Stiftung, Workshop Series VI (Bangkok: May 1975), p. 59.

27. *Philippines Daily Express*, Jan. 6, 1976.

28. "A Statement of the Civil Liberties Union of the Philippines on the State of

judgment of a mission of Amnesty International, "the judiciary . . . has become totally ineffective in preventing the violation of human rights which were detailed in [its] report. The rule of law under martial law is authoritarian presidential-military rule, unchecked by constitutional guarantee or limitations."[29] The fate of the Philippine judiciary probably illustrates "the fact that . . . a determined Chief Executive, acting under real or imagined national crisis and confident of military support, can effectively neutralize the judiciary as a constitutional watchdog or reduce it to virtual impotence if he so wishes."[30] In its weakened and subordinate state, the judiciary, headed by the Supreme Court, has survived by adapting to its new martial-rule environment. Indeed, it would seem that the Supreme Court has gone beyond legal compliance and mere pragmatic acquiescence to affirm the proposition that: "as commander-in-chief and enforcer of martial law, the incumbent President can promulgate proclamations, orders and decrees during martial law essential to the security and preservation of the Republic, to the defense of the political and social liberties of the people and to institute reforms to prevent the resurgence of rebellion or insurrection or secession or threat thereof, as well as to meet the impact of the worldwide recession, inflation or economic crises which presently threatens all nations.[31]

From the first days of martial rule, sanctions were imposed on all public servants to make the bureaucracy loyal and responsive to Marcos, and efficient and honest. The government was reorganized and purged of scores of politically unreliable or corrupt officials. Office heads were given blanket authority to separate, without an investigation, any employee deemed to be "notoriously undesirable." Several persons facing administrative or criminal charges were subject to summary dismissal. Moreover, official discretion in the purge of the bureaucracy was facilitated by requiring practically all government workers to submit their undated letters of resignation to the president. Many others not weeded out by this swift process

the Nation after Three Years of Martial Law" (Manila: Civil Liberties Union, Sept. 21, 1975).

29. *Report of Amnesty International Mission,* p. 54.

30. Del Carmen, "Martial Law," p. 32.

31. *Aquino* v. *Commission on Elections,* 62 SCRA 275, Jan. 31, 1975, as cited in Victoriano A. Hipe, "The Legal Aspect of Martial Law in the Philippines: Negotiating Between Precedents and Innovations" (Manila: College of Public Administration, University of the Philippines, September 1976), p. 13.

were to be removed by cost-saving reductions in personnel during the reorganization. Under the 1973 constitution, the president can fire any government official by the expedient of appointing a successor. Even Supreme Court justices can be dismissed by presidential decree or by the appointment of their successor.

The enormously enlarged powers of the government to induce the compliance and cooperation of the citizens was well exemplified in the intensified collection of taxes. This resulted in many more people, including those in arrears, paying their taxes promptly and honestly. The government mounted an extensive tax-information campaign, promising that increased revenues would go to constructive public projects and threatening severe penalties for tax delinquency. The penalties included fines, forfeiture, arrest and imprisonment, revocation of licenses and permits (which were made renewable in shorter periods), withholding of government salaries and fringe benefits, outright dismissal, and disqualification from transacting business with the government. At the same time, from 1973 to 1975 partial tax amnesties were granted on undeclared incomes and so-called "hidden wealth," and those who availed themselves of the amnesties were guaranteed immunity from any investigation or prosecution by the government. Again, the people were told that the expected revenues would finance the country's planned development. As a consequence of tax reforms and greater compliance the national revenues from taxes increased almost four times, from P5.3 billion in 1972 to P19.2 billion in 1976. Total government receipts rose over three times, from P5.7 billion in 1972 to P20.7 billion in 1976.[32]

The mass media of the Old Society were faulted for being negative, irresponsible, corrupt, and subservient to the oligarchs who controlled them, if not downright subversive. To reform and control the media, the martial law authorities initiated several moves. As mentioned earlier, several publishers and journalists were immediately arrested and detained, although all of them were subsequently released, without being tried for any offense. The *Manila Times,* the *Manila Chronicle,* and the *Philippines Free Press* were "sequestered," never to resume publication. Other journals, like the *Nation* and the *Graphic,* simply stopped publishing. Radio and tele-

---

32. *Five-Year Development Plan, 1978–1982* (Manila: National Economic Development Authority, September 1977), pp. 356–357.

vision stations belonging to the family of Eugenio Lopez, businessman brother of Vice President Fernando Lopez, who also published
the *Manila Chronicle,* were permanently closed, presumably because
their owners were believed to have conspired with the family of
Senator Sergio Osmeña, the defeated presidential rival of President
Marcos in 1969, to assassinate the president, in order to install Lopez
as president of the republic.

It was said that ownership of the mass media would be broadened to prevent their ever becoming the "tools of the oligarchs."
Censorship and licensing of the media were soon introduced, while
recalcitrant journalists were "invited" for interrogation by the military. Moreover, relatives and friends of the Marcos family set up
their own newspapers and radio and television stations. The government also established a Department of Public Information to
expand its own informational programs and oversee the various
communications media. Gradually, official censorship was lifted and
representatives of the private mass media were asked to institute a
self-regulating system consistent with the stringent reporting norms
of the New Society. But given the restrictions on free speech and
assembly, the press has been understandably timid and partial to
the regime, cautious and uncritical, preferring to be on the safe side.
Criticism of certain subjects seems taboo by tacit understanding;
these include the President and Mrs. Marcos, the regime, the military, and, earlier on, even the New People's Army and the Muslim
rebellion, unless clearance was obtained from the military officers
concerned. In a manifesto published in October 1976, critical citizens
stated: "The media's principal function is to flatter [the martial law
regime] no end, smear and discredit those who disagree with them,
hide or distort the truth, and manipulate public opinion."[33] Nevertheless, since about 1974 the media have occasionally carried criticisms of particular policies or agencies and general official behavior.
Rarely do Malacañang Palace (the president's office and residence)
or the Department of Public Information dictate headlines, although
they control some sources of news. Unlike the situation earlier,
foreign correspondents are again free to write and dispatch their
stories, on the theory that these are for foreign consumption and

33. "Manifesto on Martial Law and the Referendum of October 16, 1976," by
a Representative Group of Filipino Citizens (Makati, Rizal: Sept. 21, 1976), p. 7.
Printed material says it was signed by 170 persons whose names are listed on pp.
15 and 16.

would not easily be circulated inside the country, and that suppressing them would be counterproductive. Filipino reporters are less wary of the Media Advisory Council or the Department of Public Information than of the military, who seem to have the ultimate authority in determining what constitutes subversive behavior.

Some Catholic and Protestant clergymen and laymen have been the most forthright and courageous source of complaints and pressure concerning official abuses and injustice, especially against political prisoners, labor groups, squatters and ethnic minorities, and members of the church themselves. Militant religious leaders use the pulpit, Masses, prayer meetings, processions, their own radio stations, and mimeographed bulletins, which, though not enjoying mass circulation, reach significant numbers of the intelligentsia beyond religious circles. Special church commissions and liaison committees deal with the military and certain government agencies. Following serious confrontations and controversies between the church and the government, leaders from both sides have met with the president.

At best, however, the church has attempted to influence officialdom through moral suasion, which the government, in the absence of elections and a free press, can easily deflect whenever it wishes. In addition, the impact of religious resistance to government excesses is weakened by the division of church leaders, not unlike the laity, into militants, moderates, and conservatives, and by the vulnerability of the Roman Catholic clergy itself to countercharges of authoritarian rule, institutional wealth, and unconcern for the poor. The militant Catholic clergymen repeatedly assert "the right and duty of the Church to stand up in the defense of human rights and to support the just struggles of the poor and oppressed . . . whenever and by whomsoever they are being trampled upon."[34] They declare that "martial law is a regime of coercion and fear, of institutionalized deception and manipulation; and our people do not enjoy the ordinary human and civil liberties that are basic to the proper exercise of their rights of suffrage and to their free participation in government."[35]

34. Letter of twenty-one bishops and clergy to the editors of the *Daily Express*, the *Times Journal* and *Bulletin Today*, Sept. 20, 1976.
35. "A Declaration for Human Dignity at the Polls," Sept. 11, 1976, signed by fourteen Catholic bishops.

The moderates, best represented by Cardinal Jaime Sin, Archbishop of Manila, "give the authorities the benefit of the doubt." They tend to view controversies and clashes between religious spokesmen and the government as isolated cases not directed against the church itself, an established global institution that will survive all manner of abuse or persecution. When sufficiently provoked, the cardinal can openly disagree with the president, as when the former said: "This country doesn't belong to him [Marcos] alone. It belongs to all of us. So we should continue constructive criticism."[36] Whereas the militants believe that the church must play an activist, humanistic role in order to ameliorate life, enhance Christianity, and raise the people's awareness so that they can strive for their welfare, the majority of the eighty bishops are paternalistic and tend to treat the people "as children who should not be subjected to the rigors of martial law politics."[37]

In a sense, the conservative religious majority accommodate to "constitutional authoritarianism" in much the same way that the vast numbers of educated Filipinos do. Very few would follow Bishop Francisco Claver in "speaking the truth out at all times even when it leads to conflict with the government's policy of suppressing the truth."[38] Among these few are the more than 300 signatories of the published "Message of Hope to Filipinos Who Care,"[39] the members of the Civil Liberties Union who published "The State of the Nation after Three Years of Martial Law," and some scholars whose objective and dispassionate studies appear in academic journals and papers.

In 1975, the third year of martial rule, the authorities relaxed their control of public criticism and the media, possibly because of several factors: the increasing confidence of martial law authorities concerning their power and popular support; their sense that continued repression of free speech was counterproductive because the news media lacked credibility and legitimacy; the pressure of criticism from the foreign press, including the expulsion of the Philippines from membership in the International Press Institute; and

36. *Far Eastern Economic Review,* Dec. 10, 1976.
37. Ibid.
38. Bishop Francisco Claver, "Witnessing to the Truth: A Pastoral Letter of Concern" (Malabalay, Bukidnon, Nov. 23, 1976).
39. Horacio de la Costa, Jovito Salonga, and others (over 300 signatories), Manila, Oct. 1, 1976.

the reaction of some American officials and citizens, which might threaten continued U.S. assistance to the Philippines and hurt the international reputation of the president and the martial law regime. However, in 1976 the government again tightened its control of dissent. It detained editorial staff members of the student publication at the University of the Philippines, deported activist foreign priests and a foreign correspondent, closed two Catholic radio stations in Mindanao, and stopped the publication of the *Signs of the Times* by the Association of Major Religious Superiors and of the *Communicator* by the Jesuits. Official actions against the radio stations were purportedly undertaken because of their links with the Communist New People's Army in the south. Although the halted periodicals were said to be subversive in character, no formal charges were filed in court against the persons and organizations involved in their publication. Meanwhile, the defense establishment had warned against the resurgence of an antigovernment alliance among the Communist and Muslim rebels, the "Christian left," and rightist elements. Other government officials anticipated economic troubles due to the rising cost of oil imports and the weakening of export prices.

A second referendum was held on July 27–28, 1973. The official results indicated that 90 percent of the voters wanted "President Marcos to continue beyond 1973 and finish the reforms he has initiated under Martial Law."[40] The results also showed overwhelming disapproval of the holding of elections or the convening of the National Assembly. In a third referendum, on February 27–28, 1975, it was reported that 92 percent of the votes cast "want the President to continue exercising his powers under martial law and the Constitution."[41] By a reported 90 percent majority in a fourth referendum (and plebiscite) that was held on October 16–17, 1976, the voters again approved the continuation of martial law.[42]

Common citizen perceptions of these referendums are supported by sample studies conducted at the University of the Philippines (U.P.). According to De Guzman and Associates, the two 1973 referendums were "managed affairs" that "gave a semblance of

40. "The Concerns of the Filipino People: An Analysis of the Results of the National Referendum of July 28, 1973" (College of Public Administration, University of the Philippines [typewritten]).
41. Ibid.
42. *Bulletin Today*, Oct. 20, 1976.

citizen participation in public affairs," which was "necessary to
provide legitimacy to the martial law regime." Absent were "certain
minimum conditions" for authentic public participation: "free press,
public discussions of the issues and questions, freedom from fear
and insecurity, and adequate procedural safeguards," including "lack
of material time" for understanding the questions posed.[43] An
analysis of the official voting statistics on the 1975 referendum published by the Association of Major Religious Superiors showed
several inconsistencies that cast doubt on their accuracy.[44] A U.P.
study of the October 1976 referendum-plebiscite confirmed official
reports of high voter turnout and approval of the referendum as a
means of popular participation. The study also discovered a lack of
time for citizens to study the issues at stake, various factors that dis-
couraged intelligent and responsible participation, and "the absence
of safeguards to maintain the privacy and sanctity of the ballot."[45]
Some religious and citizens groups advocated the boycott of these
referendums, even in the face of official warnings that penalties
would be meted out for not voting.

President Marcos has carefully murtured his civilian political
base by his control of the bureaucracy and local governments. He
integrated all local police forces into one national police force under
a national commission and the Philippine Constabulary. The 1975
referendum gave the president additional basis for appointing or
replacing provincial, city, and municipal officials whose elective
terms had expired in December 1973. By this direct control of their
tenure, by restructuring local government boards and councils down
to the *barangay* (village government unit), by establishing a Department of Local Government and Community Development to
assist him in exercising his supervision and control of local government, and by consolidating local jurisdictions to form Metropolitan
Manila and placing this region under the governorship of Mrs.
Marcos, the president has effectively strengthened his nationwide

43. Raul P. de Guzman and Associates, "Citizen Participation and Decision-
Making Under Martial Law: A Search for a Viable Political System" (College of
Public Administration, University of the Philippines, March 1976), pp. 13 and 33.
44. "An Analysis of the Official Commission on Elections Data on the 1975 Referendums," *Signs of the Times*, Mar. 8, 1975.
45. "A Study of Political Participation: October 1976 Referendum" (Manila: College of Public Administration, University of the Philippines, Dec. 8, 1976), pp.
67–71.

power base, which also serves to legitimize his rule and to balance his dependence on military support.

Most citizens have become even less politically participant than in previous years. This is not surprising, given the preoccupation of most people, especially in the small towns and the rural areas, with the struggle for subsistence, their limited knowledge and information about public affairs (particularly under martial law), their seeming indifference to legal issues, their dependence on such governmental assistance as may reach them, or their desire simply to be left alone by the government. The absence of elections, of an open press, or of effective criticism of the government contributes to this situation. Besides, the martial law regime is able to obtain citizen acquiescence or acceptance and support through its guarantee of peace and order in most places, the expansion of public works and other governmental employment, the extension of credit to rice farmers, and the availability of rice and other essential commodities at regulated prices, as well as by its control of public information.[46]

As stated earlier, Marcos also closed down the once powerful Congress, which was in recess when martial rule began. Attempts by some legislators to convene were quickly frustrated. The president's assumption of legislative power and his virtual abolition of Congress epitomized his determination to transform the political system, consolidating all governmental powers within his person in the name of political stability, societal reforms, and accelerated national development. Until the advent of martial law, the Congress was a multifaceted symbol of an elite representative system and countervailing legislative power, as well as of horse trading and patronage, privilege and corruption, outside the executive branch. Congress assembled some of the best and also some of the worst political leaders in the nation. It was the training and recruiting ground for presidents. Although relatively few lamented its demise in view of its eroded reputation, despite the presence of the nation's best leaders in its ranks, it may be noted that authoritarian regimes in Indonesia, Singapore, Malaysia, Burma, South Korea, India, Taiwan, and China did not entirely dispense with their legislatures.

Under "constitutional authoritarianism," President Marcos may

---

46. For other perceived positive changes under martial law, see Jose V. Abueva, "Filipino Democracy and the American Legacy," *The Annals,* 428 (November 1976), 129.

rule indefinitely, as the constitution, the laws, and the referendum issues have been worded and interpreted. However, in his desire for legitimacy and with a view to "the judgment of history," not to mention his own appreciation of what is in the national interest under the circumstances, he has occasionally remarked that the crisis government was only transitory to a parliamentary democracy as intended in the 1973 constitution. Early in 1976 he convened the National Federation of Provincial and City Sangguniang Bayans (Local Legislative Councils), then created the national advisory body called the Batasang Bayan (National Advisory Legislative Council), which met in September, and, finally, issued a decree that established a Batasang Pambansa (National Assembly) in the same year. The body was composed of cabinet members and other administration officials and of representatives from the various councils and federations of local councils, including the federation of youth *barangay* councils (those of the barrios, or lowest government units). Full media coverage of the sessions enabled citizens to witness the orderly and dutiful conduct of the members under the president as presiding officer.

The brief government-dominated campaign on the referendum-plebiscite of October 16–17, 1976, was timed to coincide with the hosting by the government in Manila of the annual meeting of the International Monetary Fund and the World Bank. The public consultation had been endorsed by the Batasang Bayan at its session marking the fourth anniversary of martial rule, and was hailed by the media as a milestone in the transition to parliamentary government. It was reported that the plebiscite approved by a 90 percent vote the amendments to the constitution that would set aside the interim National Assembly that was never convened and establish an interim Batasang Pambansa as the "parliament," with President Marcos continuing to exercise the constitutional powers of prime minister under the 1973 constitution and of the president under the 1935 constitution. One amendment would also authorize him to act outside the "parliament" when he deemed it necessary. The Batasang Pambansa would continue to be composed of cabinet and other officials appointed by Marcos and those to be elected in 1977 or later. The effect of this fourth referendum was explained by Joaquin G. Bernas in a lecture on December 4, 1976:

Up until October 16, 1976, we could console ourselves with the thought that authoritarianism would be a very temporary affair and that when it finally ends it might take another generation before we are once again favored with a similar phenomenon. But on October 16, 1976, an amendment was approved which reads: "Whenever in the judgment of the President (Prime Minister), there exists a grave emergency or threat or imminence thereof, or whenever the interim Batasang Pambansa or the regular National Assembly fails or is unable to act adequately on any matter for any reason that in his judgment requires immediate action, he may, in order to meet the exigency, issue the necessary decrees, orders or letters of instructions, which shall form part of the law of the land" (Section 6.).

This is, as you can see, a declaration of distrust of any legislature, now or in the future, and at the same time an unconditional act of faith in the Presidency, now and forever. This is no longer temporary. This is a permanent arrangement.[47]

On August 20, 1977, on the eve of the international World Peace through Law Conference hosted by the administration in Manila, about 1,000 persons held the Filipino People's Convention on Human Rights. Jointly sponsored by the Alliance for Human Rights and the Philippine Organization for Human Rights, its leaders included Salvador Lopez, Jovita Salonga, Calixto Zaldivar, Diosdada Macapagal, and Cirilo Rigos. The Convention called for the immediate lifting of martial law, the removal of one-man rule, and the holding of elections. It adopted a program of government called "The People's Alternative" which emphasized the protection of human rights in the pursuit of reform and development. The convention established the Katipunan ng Bayan Para sa Kalayaan (The People's League for Freedom). However, the entire event was ignored by the media.

After Marcos announced that a fifth referendum would be held on December 17, 1977, to allow him to continue in office as president and be prime minister of the interim Batasang Pambansa, four human rights organizations issued "The Citizens' Manifesto." This documented the consequences of martial rule, analyzed the meaning of the referendum and urged its boycott so that elections might be

47. Cited in *The Decline of Democracy* (Geneva: International Commission of Jurists, 1977), p. 20.

held. It also commended to all Filipinos the thoughtful reading of
"The People's Alternative."

The Commission on Elections reported that about 90 percent of
the votes cast in the fifth referendum favored the president's proposition. With this confirmation that he could indefinitely continue
as president and also become prime minister of the yet to be formed
interim Batasang Pambansa, Marcos was set to call for the first
national election under martial law.

Clearly, one of the major changes of the New Society has been
the removal of the large and fragmented political elite of the pre-
martial law era which nevertheless allowed intra-elite competition,
a two-party system and alternation in power of the two major parties
through popular elections, and the general observance of civil and
political rights. Under the influence of the old political elite structure, according to Remigio Agpalo, "public policies were mangled,
reforms aborted, budgets delayed, feelings of frustration and cynicism aroused, and social unrest enkindled."[48] Undoubtedly, national decision making has been simplified and can be expedited by
the concentration of governmental powers in the president. As called
for in the 1973 constitution, the creation of the National Economic
Development Authority, with the president as chairman, can ensure
better coordination than in the past in both planning and implementation. Fiscal and budgetary processes do not have to contend
with a legislature.

Two economists at the University of the Philippines commented
approvingly on these changes and possibilities. According to Agustin
Kintanar, "these improvements . . . which substantially shortened
the time and reduced the costly bargaining between divergent political factions and vested economic groupings, have, on the whole,
led to the more efficient and rational allocation of scarce government
resources. These improvements . . . gain greater significance considering the absolute amount of government resources, as well as
the share of the government sector in GNP, which has been increasing substantially since 1972."[49] Commenting on the president's
flexibility in policy making and other features of the process, Mahar
Mangahas in an article on land reform observed: "The gestation

48. Agpalo, "Political Elite in a Post-Traditional Society," p. 59.
49. Agustin Kintanar, "Recent Fiscal Reforms in the Philippines," lecture at the
School of Economics, University of the Philippines, July 14, 1975.

period between stimulus and government response has been remarkably shortened, such that the interaction between government and
the general public can be seen more distinctly. . . . Policy can be
fine-tuned in the sense that legislation can be issued in a series of
steps, with modifications and amendments easy to insert in later
steps, depending on the public's reaction to the earlier ones."[50] The
merits of the present political system were described by President
Marcos himself in a speech in January 1975 in terms of its "crisis
government that had the real power to make quick decisions and
to implement them without obstruction from any source . . . to
attack problems with immediacy and directness . . . to deal with
both the unknown, the uncertain and the unexpected, and to adjust
with swiftness, adequacy and efficiency to unprecedented situations."[51]

However, in practice, the supposedly greater potential of the New
Society government structure for policy formulation and execution
that are at once speedy, synchronized, coordinated, as well as
rational and effective, is not readily realized. This is so because of
some priorities dictated by the requirements of authoritarian leadership, and the consequences of haste, secrecy, faulty knowledge,
bureaucratic politics, and inertia. Raul de Guzman and Associates
studied the policymaking process involved in the enactment of
presidential decrees on foreign investment, the local tax code, and
reorganization. They concluded that "the decrees . . . were prepared
by the technocrats . . . and adopted in a short span of time without
much benefit [of] public discussion of the issues and without ample
opportunity for those affected to ventilate their views."[52] The authors
noted "stray decrees," signed by the president, which indicate lack
of thorough staff work or interagency coordination.

Unlike the past, when interested citizens could be heard through
local councils or directly by their representatives in Congress, the
new *barangays* "did not have any . . . meaningful participation in
the decisionmaking process,"[53] the same authors said. "The curtailment imposed on the freedom of expression nullifies meaningful
participation. When there is fear of reprisal, citizens cannot freely

50. Mahar Mangahas, "Equity and Institutional Change: The Case of Land Reform in the New Society" (Los Baños, Laguna: International Rice Research Institute,
December 1976), p. 5.
51. Ferdinand Marcos, speech, Jan. 12, 1975.
52. De Guzman and Associates, "Citizen Participation and Decision-Making,"
p. 34.
53. Ibid., p. 30.

discuss their views as well as those of the administration. These are critical areas that are not open to discussion or criticism. . . . Policies are set above. Through the barangays, citizens are mobilized in the implementation of these policies."[54]

Some organized and urban-based interest groups are able to comment on certain pending decrees and to suggest policy changes when asked, such as when they invite the president or one of his technocrats to deliver a speech at one of their meetings. But often the president is in a rush, and consultations, if made, are necessarily hurried and inadequate. A trisectoral meeting of government, business, and labor called by the administration to consider minimum wages ended up leaving the decision to the president. At the two-day meeting of the Batasang Bayan, the P27.4 billion national budget for 1977 was passed in two hours without substantive amendments.

In concluding her study of personnel policies and administrative behavior under martial law, Ledivina Cariño notes how good intentions are being derailed by poor implementation: "Our findings show positive changes, particularly in the area of policy and institution of new programs. However, something breaks down at the level of implementation, due to unclear or inadequate criteria, bureaucratic inertia, impingement of particularistic values on the conduct of government activities, and the sheer bulk of tasks expected to be done by the same group of people who could not deliver the smaller package of services during pre-martial law days."[55] And in his evaluation of policymaking under martial law, Santiago Simpas reached this cautious conclusion:

The danger lies in the possibility that present policy-making has been reduced to "a conspiracy of friends." Policy-makers are accountable to only one man [President Marcos] whose knowledge of the situation in the field might be flawed and limited to what his close associates feel would conform to his wishes. The function Congress once performed—that of maintaining accountable officials—now lies in the Executive Office. The set-up is thought to be quite self-serving. Without newspaper exposés and criticisms, without investigations, without public hearings before the elected representatives of the people, the call [of politically conscious citizens] for "accountability" could be easily ignored. That the

54. Ibid., pp. 32–33.
55. Ledivinia V. Cariño, "Personnel Policies and Bureaucratic Behavior under Martial Law" (Manila: College of Public Administration, University of the Philippines, September 1976), p. 26.

government should evaluate itself reduces the "accountability" to the bootlicking sort of devotion to one's job. The public seems to have been left out.[56]

In sum, President Marcos—with the fullest collaboration of Mrs. Marcos, who as First Lady, Governor of Metro Manila, and diplomatic troubleshooter, is the president's alter ego and de facto assistant president—is the undisputed head of a new national power structure or grand coalition. It consists of: the military; cabinet members, technocrats, and the bureaucracy under them; persons close to the president or Mrs. Marcos, whether relatives or loyal friends and former politicians; local officials, who also hold office by presidential appointment; and several big businessmen who enjoy the political stability and economic incentives which the administration provides. At the base of this political pyramid are the millions whose welfare is the avowed aim of the New Society, in whose name change and reform are being initiated, and whose support or acquiescence provide the regime with legitimacy through referendums, citizen assemblies, and the local *sangguniang bayans* and *barangays*.

Gone are the old pluralist power structure, based on local leaders and factions, the two major political parties, and the new minor parties and political movements. Only one nationwide, nonparty political coalition is allowed to exist, and it functions without an adversary press, loyal opposition, or open academic criticism. In contrast to the large and fragmented political elite of the Old Society, the new elite is small, cohesive, and effectively under the president's command. In theory it is responsive to what it believes to be good for the people without the participation of their elective representatives. As Jeffrey Race put it: "There is a façade of citizen participation masking, in this case not very well, that there are intended to be no autonomous institutions under the New Society by which citizens can make their wishes come about—just an atomized public facing a newly strengthened central government."[57] Whenever the regime wants, it can ignore the views of those who disagree with or oppose it. Excluded from meaningful participation,

56. Santiago S. Simpas, "Policy-Making under Martial Law" (Manila: College of Public Administration, University of the Philippines, 1976), p. 23.
57. Jeffrey Race, "Whither the Philippines" (New York: Institute of Current World Affairs, Nov. 30, 1975), p. 10.

the opposition is isolated and immobilized. In a polarized society, where the "outs" have no foreseeable hope of replacing the "ins," the latter decide the rules of political participation and the limits of dissent, and serious oppositionists can only court detention, go underground, or stay abroad if they can.

The election on April 7, 1978, of 165 regional representatives to the interim Batasang Pambansa did not alter the basic political structure of "constitutional authoritarianism." Marcos formed the Kilusang Bagong Lipunan (New Society Movement) which fielded candidates in all regions, headed by cabinet members and others loyal to the President. In Metro Manila the KBL candidates were led by Mrs. Marcos. The former opposition Liberal Party boycotted the elections, alleging that elections under martial law were incongruous and absurd and would only allow Marcos "to create the facade of a democracy."

Only in Metro Manila did an organized opposition—the Lakas ng Bayan (People's Power), or Laban (Fight) in short—contest the elections. Laban was led by former Senator Benigno Aquino, who campaigned from his prison cell where he had been kept since martial law began. Sentenced by a military tribunal to death by firing squad for subversion, murder, and illegal possession of firearms, the one-time political rival of the president became a rallying symbol of anti-martial law citizens. During the elections opposition candidates openly denounced the president and his martial rule. They urged the end of martial law and the restoration of democracy. On election eve people in Metro Manila joined in a massive noisy demonstration organized through a chain letter by Aquino.

Given the results of the referendums, the victory of nearly all KBL candidates came as no surprise. But the total defeat of the Laban candidates in the metropolis, the stronghold of opposition to martial law, was followed by opposition charges of wholesale rigging of the elections and tampering of ballots. A postelection demonstration against the alleged "death of democracy" led to the arrest of its leaders, including some Laban candidates, and about 600 protesters. The reaction of the foreign press to the elections and the arrests was highly critical. The *Japan Times* mildly observed: "The election campaign permitted a public outcry against martial law and demands for restoration of basic freedoms. It will be difficult and unwise to silence this dissent now" (April 18, 1978).

The interim Batasang Pambansa that met for the first time on June 12, 1978, the eightieth anniversary of Philippine independence from Spain, was heralded by the administration as another step in the return to parliamentry democracy. In addition to the 165 elected members, the body has thirty-five members appointed by the president and fourteen representatives of functional sectors of society chosen by their organizations. However, Marcos as prime minister and president with indefinite tenure dominates the body. He can still legislate by decree, veto measures approved by the interim Batasang Pambansa, or dissolve it altogether. The body cannot remove the prime minister-president, ratify treaties, or repeal or modify any decree or edicts of the president. In short, it is not what its English translation would suggest—an interim National Assembly or Parliament with lawmaking powers, as provided in the original constitution. The interim body will last as long as Marcos wants. And no regular elections can be held independently of his will. However, the shocks of the first elections under martial law may well foster increased opposition even under severe odds, especially because a few anti-Marcos leaders from the Visayas and Mindanao were elected to the interim Batasang Pambansa.

The Expansion and Sharing of Wealth

In its declaration of principles and state policies, the 1973 constitution commits the nation-state to the principle of social justice and equity: "The State shall promote social justice to ensure the dignity, welfare, and security of all the people. Towards this end, the State shall regulate the acquisition, ownership, use, enjoyment, and disposition of private property and equitably diffuse property ownership and profits."[58] For his part, President Marcos has declared "the conquest of mass poverty" and the "democratization of wealth and property" to be among the major aims of the New Society. He has therefore sought popular approval and legitimacy for his "constitutional authoritarianism" or "crisis government," not only via the referendums, Supreme Court decisions, and the government-controlled mass media, but also particularly through policies and programs avowedly intended to strengthen the national economy, expand and improve government services to the people, effect land reform, and redistribute incomes and opportunity.

58. Article II, Sec. 6.

The administration has sought to help poor employees, farmers, laborers, and other citizens by simultaneous measures calculated to raise their productivity and incomes, to reduce their losses from the severe inflation that the country experienced from late 1973 through 1974 with the start of the worldwide oil crisis, and to provide employment for the jobless and underemployed. The multiple measures taken range from price support of agricultural products to subsidies of farm inputs, from salary increases and fringe benefits to price controls, from expanded infrastructure programs to Medicare hospitalization for government and business employees, from manpower training to agrarian reform, from direct hiring in the government to job placement abroad, from new and increased taxes and improved collection to greater government expenditures in the rural areas, from heavy foreign borrowing to the vigorous attraction of foreign investments into the country, and from crash rice-production schemes to the systematic promotion of exports.[59]

Under martial law, President Marcos has instituted far-reaching fiscal reforms which might have been impossible under the separation of powers and the checks and balances of the old political system. Tax reforms and improved tax information and administration increased the revenues sharply. From fiscal year 1964 until 1972, national government revenues were between 9 and 10 percent of GNP. In 1972 the revenues totaled P5.3 billion. Between 1973 and 1976, they rose by an annual average of 32.8 percent: from P8.2 billion in 1973, or 13.4 of GNP, to P19.2 billion in 1976, or 14.6 percent of GNP. Reflective of the expanded role of the government in development, national government expenditures expanded more rapidly than revenues: from P9.3 billion in 1973, or 15.2 percent of GNP, to P22.5 billion in 1976, or 17.1 percent of GNP. On the average, about 30 percent of the yearly deficits, P3.3 billion in 1977, have been financed by foreign borrowing.[60]

The number of people who filed their income taxes increased four times during the first two years of martial rule. The fiscal changes affect the basic structure and institutions of taxation and promise to become progressive and self-sustaining. The administra-

59. Ferdinand E. Marcos, "The President's Report to the Nation," Sept. 21, 1975, and Sept. 21, 1976. Also "Efforts Geared toward Human Welfare," *Times Journal*, Sept. 21, 1976.

60. *Five-Year Development Plan, 1978–1982*, pp. 355–356.

tion aims to disperse infrastructure and other resources of the government on a more equitable regional basis. Through use of increased revenues and maximum foreign borrowing, a greater share of GNP is being allocated to capital formation, including highways, irrigation and electrification. Staples—rice, sugar, and cooking oil—are sold at much lower than international prices. The redistributive effect of the Medicare program and the family-planning program may be also seen as a fiscal reform.

In the euphoria of the first year's achievements under martial law, the administration spoke of another economic miracle in Asia taking place in the Philippines. On the third anniversary of the New Society, the president asserted: "Judged by any of the known indicators for economic growth, the conclusion points to a high level of performance of the national economy." He said that during the three years of the New Society, GNP rose by an annual average of about 7 percent, and spoke of "unprecedented prosperity in the rural areas, an obvious upsurge in the purchasing power of the Filipino farmers, and a general air of confidence and optimism in the countryside."[61] He cited the administration's success in "bringing the government closer to the people." Indeed, government statistics showed that employment levels rose by an average of 3.8 percent from 1973 to 1976 and unemployment fell to 5.2 percent in 1976, from 7.0 percent in 1972.[62]

Compared to about $200–$300 million at the start of the New Society, international reserves rose to $739 million a year later, leaving a balance of payments surplus of $612 million. By September, 1975, the international reserves stood at $1.17 billion, indicating the strength of the national economy in spite of widespread international "stagflation."[63] However, because of the sharp decline in trade since 1975 due to the depressed market for exports, the merchandise trade surplus of $95 million in fiscal year 1974 shifted to a deficit of $801 million in fiscal year 1975[64] and to $879 million in 1976.[65] Accordingly, aggravated by the price of crude oil imports, the balance of payments position declined from the fiscal year 1974 surplus of $437

61. Marcos, "President's Report," Sept. 21, 1975.
62. *Five-Year Development Plan, 1978–1982*, p. 24.
63. Marcos, "President's Report," Sept. 21, 1975.
64. Ibid.
65. *Business Day*, Jan. 3, 1977, p. 4.

million to a deficit of $352 million in 1975, which then fell to $150 million as 1976 ended.[66] While prices of major exports dropped drastically, receipts from merchandise trade grew by 11 percent in 1973 and then dropped from 1975 to 1976, and nonmerchandise trade improved from 1973 to 1975 and dropped in 1976. Buttressed by larger borrowing, these movements somewhat checked the declining balance of payments which resulted in a surplus of $164 million in 1977. The international reserves were $1.64 billion at the end of 1976 and $1.52 billion at the end of 1977, compared to $549 million in 1972.[67]

Other indicators point to the New Society's economic upsurge at aggregate levels, not considering the issue of equity and distribution of benefits and income to the people, most of whom are poor and live in the rural areas. The economic growth of 6.9 percent from 1972 to 1977 was accompanied by high capital formation indicated by a yearly average rise of Gross Domestic Capital Formation of 12.6 percent; this meant an increasing investment-output ratio ranging from 20.8 percent in 1972 to 30.1 percent in 1977.[68] During fiscal year 1975, paid-in capital of newly registered business firms expanded by about 30 percent to a level of P1 billion. Investments in registered firms grew by 34 percent, primarily because of a 192 percent increase in local business investments. In the first three years of martial law, 13,300 corporations were established with a total paid-up capital of P2 billion.

The aggressive attraction of foreign investments of diversified origin drew over P365 million into the country, or more than double the record of a similar period before September 1972.[69] The regional headquarters of some 35 multinational corporations have relocated in the Philippines. The number of tourists increased by almost three times. Consequently, fears of foreign business domination have been heightened and some ill effects of the tourist influx are beginning to be felt.

The impact of the more impressive statistics of economic advance upon various segments of the citizens is varied and has been the subject of conflicting evaluations, depending partly on which segments are considered, on the time-horizons involved, the develop-

66. Ibid., p. 4, and Marcos, "President's Report," Sept. 21, 1975.
67. Securities Registration Statement, Republic of the Philippines, 1978.
68. Securities Registration Statement.
69. Marcos, "President's Report," Sept. 21, 1976.

ment strategies favored, or the political views of the analysts. To
begin with, the 6.9 percent increase in GNP from 1972 to 1977 is
the average of the yearly increases: 9.6 percent in 1973, 6.3 percent
in 1974, and 5.9 in 1975, 6.7 percent in 1976, and 6.1 percent in
1977.[70] Prior to martial law, from 1967 to 1972, the average growth
rate was a respectable 6.25 percent.[71] Per capita GNP (at 1972 prices)
rose from P1,517 in 1973 to P1,667 in 1976. Without considering
the equity of its distribution, this represents an appreciable net increase against a decline in population.[72] The external debt by the
end of 1975 was $4 billion, or 37.4 percent higher than the previous
year's, and as 1976 closed, the external debt had reached $5.55
billion.[73]

Even President Marcos admits to the setback caused by recession
and inflation and the evident vulnerability of the national economy
to international economics, especially because of its newly bolstered
export orientation. In his September 1975 public review of the
first three years of the New Society, Marcos acknowledged "serious
problems . . . shadowing our economic life." He noted: "We cannot escape the feeling here of being perpetually engaged in a race
with problems and crises, regardless of our response at any given
period." He did not mention that it was also despite the advantages
of the nearly absolute power he wields in an authoritarian regime.
Significantly, on the same occasion he announced a dramatic purge
of some "two thousand undesirables in the national government,"
devoting twelve out of the total of twenty-seven pages of his speech
to its details. This prompted critics and oppositionists to suspect
that he did not have much real progress to report to the nation
after three years of martial rule and was therefore diverting the
people away from the shortfalls in his reforms and development
efforts. (In the ensuing months, many of those purged would be
reinstated and several never left their posts, causing public misgivings concerning the sincerity of the president and the competence
of his staff.) As if to preempt the judgment of his detractors, the
president admitted: "Now underneath these surface impressions of

70. *Securities Registration Statement.* The figure for 1977 is an estimate.
71. National Economic and Development Authority, "National Income and Gross
National Product, CY 1946 to CY 1972," Oct. 10, 1973.
72. *Five-Year Development Plan, 1978–1982,* p. 20.
73. Marcos, "President's Report," Sept. 21, 1976; Licaros, "Report of the Central
Bank"; and *Philippines Daily Express,* Jan. 4, 1977.

vitality and stability, there are profound problems that embattle our New Society. The general signs of national strength and progress somehow do not yet completely translate into realities sufficiently relevant to the ordinary individual. . . . Growth is rendered in statistics and changes in the landscape, changes in the cities, in the roads, in the infrastructures. But more than this we need a new vigorous climate of confidence and hope."[74]

In his address on the fourth anniversary of the New Society, in September 1976, the president was much more assertive, confident, detailed, and comprehensive in reporting what he saw as the achievements of his administration and the country. He claimed that more had been achieved in three years than in the previous thirty. He stressed that under martial law "we undertook bold programs to create and redistribute both wealth and opportunity, to dismantle the system of privilege that favored the rich and the powerful, and to encourage the productive participation of millions." He related his programs of social services and reforms to "a total vision of social and economic equality." In his view, "we can certainly say that our people have not been denied equity in growth and participation in productive labor, equal opportunity in education."[75]

What did the people think about the president, the New Society, the problems they faced, the government programs intended to solve those problems and improve their welfare, and the quality of their lives in the New Society? As has been stated, official returns from the four referendums were overwhelmingly favorable to Marcos' continued rule under martial law, or against holding national or local elections. Remarks written on their ballots by one-tenth of the voters during the July 1973 referendum were analyzed by faculty members in the College of Public Administration, University of the Philippines. Voters' comments on various economic aspects of the government's development programs varied. Those concerning economic conditions in general were 50 percent favorable and 34 percent unfavorable. But on specific issues, 90 percent complained about high prices, 93 percent worried about low salaries and wages, and 90 percent were unhappy about the short supply of prime commodities. The following received mostly unfavorable comments: transportation (73 percent), infrastructure (70 percent),

74. Marcos, "President's Report," Sept. 21, 1975.
75. Marcos, "President's Report," Sept. 21, 1976.

electricity (64 percent). Agricultural reforms in general elicited almost equal percentages pro and con (about 22 percent), with as many as 55 percent of the comments being neutral or ambivalent. Land reform also obtained almost equal approvals and disapprovals (about 42 percent). Most negative remarks on land reform showed dissatisfaction with its implementation rather than opposition to it.[76]

Against the regime's claim to identification with the poor, its goals of "democratization of wealth," income distribution, and improved levels of living, it is important to assess relevant indicators. One such set comes from survey research conducted by the Institute of Philippine Culture for the Philippine Social Science Council from November 1973 to April 1974, a period of relatively high levels of achievement under martial law. Asked to compare their lives at the time of the survey (more than a year after martial law began) to the year earlier, 52 percent said their lives were about the same, 28 percent were happier, and 20 percent were not quite so happy. Rural residents had a "greater proportion of status-quo persons (56 vs. 49 percent) and fewer who [said] they were happier in late 1972 or early 1973 [soon after martial law] than they were at the end of 1973 or the beginning of 1974."[77]

Most survey respondents perceived changes in their communities compared to five years earlier (1968–69). However, more "respondents report emphatically that there is now less money available than five years ago (50 percent 'agree' vs. 42 percent 'disagree'), fewer jobs to be had (50 vs. 38 percent), fewer chances for advancement (47 vs. 42 percent), higher prices to contend with (54 vs. 42 percent)." A slight plurality said "there are better houses available in their communities (44 vs. 41 percent)."

Other scholars agree that, despite the greatly intensified efforts of the government to improve the economy, it will take at least another generation, or twenty-five years, to significantly redistribute income in a country where the upper 20 percent of the people earn 50 percent of total family incomes while the lower 50 percent receive less than 20 percent. Measured by an "index of inequality," the

<hr>

76. See "The Concerns of the Filipino People . . . 1973."

77. Emma Porio, Frank Lynch, and Mary R. Hollnsteiner, *The Filipino Family, Community and Nation: The Same Yesterday, Today, and Tomorrow?* (Quezon City: Institute of Philippine Culture, Ateneo de Manila University, 1975), p. 41. Based on a sample of 3,487 respondents living in and near the nation's largest urban areas or the "middle range of Filipino households."

Philippine score from 1956 to 1971 was 50, in a range of approximately 20 to 65 among various countries around the globe. In other words, the country belongs to the upper 20 percent of the world's most inequitble societies.[78]

Reviewing the period from 1965 to 1971, the first six years under the Marcos presidency and the last ones of the "Old Society," a study of the Development Academy of the Philippines disclosed that "poverty . . . clearly worsened" and that there was "no meaningful narrowing of the gap between rich and poor."[79] The latter trend dated back to the mid-1950s. The number of Filipinos "below the food threshold grew from 11.6 million in 1965 to 16.6 million in 1971." The average income ratio of the highest 20 percent to the lowest 20 percent (the "gap between the rich and the poor") was 12 to 1 in 1956, 13 to 1 in 1961, 16 to 1 in 1965, and 15 to 1 in 1971.[80] The salutary feature of this otherwise bleak picture is the reduction in the last generation of the gap between the highly schooled and the least schooled and of the gap in education between males and females. Since 1972 the government has increased its scholarships for poor students and has built more schools in the countryside and for cultural minorities.

Although the government's expenditure structure appears to favor the poor, "the poor pay, in effect, for the benefits they receive directly from the government."[81] In fact, most expenditure programs have benefited the big cities more, especially Metro Manila. Higher-income people have better access to and receive a higher value of benefits from government expenditures as in many developing countries. The three dominant regions—Metro Manila, Southern Tagalog, and Western Visayas—have continued to contribute more than one-half of total domestic output, increasing at the expense of the three lagging regions—Cagayan Valley, Bicol region, and Central Mindanao.[82]

78. Mahar Mangahas, "The Income Distribution Problem from an Academic Viewpoint" (Institute of Economic Development and Research, University of the Philippines, Dec. 15, 1975).

79. *Measuring the Quality of Life: Philippine Social Indicators* (Manila, 1975), pp. 11–13.

80. Ibid., pp. 12–13. "The 'gap between the rich and the poor' is roughly measured by the ratio of the average income in the richest 20 per cent of families to average income in the poorest 20 percent."

81. Mangahas, "Income Distribution Problem," p. 3.

82. *Five-Year Development Plan, 1978–1982*, pp. 49, 52.

Through the martial law years, the overall inequality score does not appear to have improved despite improvements in some places. The reasons cited by Managahas are:

First, there are some family income data from small surveys conducted since 1971 by market research firms, which indicate this. Second, in a national survey conductetd in late 1974 by the Philippine Social Science Council, 3500 respondents were asked what they felt about the social equality of people in 1974 compared to 1969. Fifty-five per cent of the respondents said conditions seemed worse in 1974. Seventeen per cent said they seemed the same, and only 28 per cent said they seemed better in 1974. Third, there has been very rapid inflation in the last few years (40 per cent in 1974) with the consequence that real wages of skilled and unskilled workers are lower today than they were back in 1950, even though, since then, real per capita GNP has about doubled.[83]

During the first ten years of Marcos' presidency (1965–1975), the wage rate indexes, in real terms (or purchasing power), decreased by 35.5 percent for skilled labor and 27.5 percent for unskilled labor.[84] Significantly, the government cites the lower wages in the Philippines as a comparative advantage in attracting foreign capital even as labor's right to collective action for their economic welfare, including the right to strike, has been reduced by presidential decrees.

Other obstacles to the government's avowed goal of income distribution may be cited. The tax structure is regressive relative to income (because of its reliance on indirect taxation) and therefore is heavier on the poor than on the rich. The rate of return to corporate equity, which favors the affluent families, is high and rising. The interest rate policy is "definitely antiequity."[85] The greatest beneficiaries of the credit extended to farmers are the rural bankers, whose gross income nearly doubled from 1972 to 1974.[86] More of the well-to-do are able to lease public agricultural land, forest land,

83. Mangahas, "Income Distribution Problem," pp. 2–3.

84. Also see Edita A. Tan, "Income Distribution in the Philippines," in Jose Encarnacion, Jr., et al., *Philippine Economic Problems in Perspective* (Quezon City: Institute of Economic Development and Research, University of the Philippines, 1976), and *Taxation, Government Spending, and Income Distribution in the Philippines* (Quezon City: Institute of Economic Development and Research, University of the Philippines, 1975), pp. 37–42.

85. Mangahas, "Income Distribution Problem," p. 11.

86. David Wurfel, "Philippine Agrarian Policy 1976: A Preliminary Overview" (Institute of Philippine Culture, Ateneo de Manila University, 1976), p. 11.

mineral, and fishpond areas at nominal rates. Moreover, manufacturers continue to be overprotected by the government, "resulting in inefficiency, low production runs, high domestic prices, and lack of exports,"[87] to the detriment of the public and the country. In short, the New Society has perpetuated the inequities of the Old Society that it has supposedly replaced.

Among all government programs, land reform probably has the greatest potential for improving equity.[88] It was for this reason, and because of its symbolism for reforms in the New Society, that the president issued a handwritten decree abolishing tenancy in rice and corn land soon after he imposed martial law. He also declared that the success of the New Society hinged on this particular program of transfer of ownership of rice and corn land from landlord to tenant, resulting in the latter's "emancipation from the bondage of the soil." The government has accomplished much more recently than in all previous years, through Operation Land Transfer. As of January 1978, the Marcos administration claimed that it had issued 360,477 certificates of land transfer to 258,974 farmers in sixty-seven provinces, involving a total area of 446,795. Through the Land Bank, the government had paid P637 million to 2,582 land owners of 90,087 hectares in forty-five provinces, cultivated by 46,959 tenants.[89]

But, as David Wurfel has reported, the administration has tolerated much evasion and resistance of landlords, is compensating them liberally, has not provided the program with adequate budgetary support, and has done little to enhance the status and the low morale of personnel in the DAR. Land reform policies and rules are confusing and decisionmaking is inordinately slow. Among tenant respondents in a survey conducted by the U.P.'s Agrarian Reform Institute, the most frequent and widespread grievances were landowners' insistence on high lease rentals, eviction of tenants, and landlords' refusal to shift from share tenancy to a leasehold system. "Against the DAR, the tenants' most serious grievance (10.7 percent of all grievance-responses made) was the delay in the distribution of Certificates of Land Transfer."[90] Contrary to the claim

---

87. "Manila: Attack on Tyre Profits," *Far Eastern Economic Review,* Dec. 31, 1976.
88. Mangahas, "Income Distribution Problem," p. 10.
89. Land reform in rice and corn lands was instituted under Presidential Decree 27, Oct. 20, 1972. The data are from *Opposition Claims and the Facts in the IBP Elections* (Manila, April 7, 1978), p. 5.
90. Wurfel, "Philippine Agrarian Policy," pp. 4–9; Agrarian Reform Institute, University of the Philippines, *An Analysis of Land Reform Grievances and Resolving Procedures* (Los Baños, Laguna, Mar. 1, 1976), pp. iv–vi.

of the DAR, Wurfel estimates that at the 1976 rates of accomplishment it would take the DAR eighteen years to distribute land-transfer certificates to all tenant beneficiaries. The Land Bank would need more than twelve years simply to compensate the tenants who have already received certificates, and it would take nearly fifty years to complete all the payment of all landlords who would lose their rice and corn lands.[91]

Moreover, since the government has required corporations with more than 500 employees to produce or import rice, more than 150 corporations have chosen to engage in rice farming. While this measure produced more rice, another consequence was the physical eviction of small cultivators from about 50,000 hectares of agricultural land, an even larger area than that gained by tenants through land reform by 1976.[92] Cultivators displaced from rice plantations, as well as from those planted to banana and pineapple, as in Mindanao, must wonder what the government means by its policy of "democratization of wealth and property."

The sixty-one page "Message of Hope to Filipinos Who Care," written and edited by former senator Jovito Salonga and Jesuit historian Horacio de la Costa and signed by more than 300 persons, concluded in October 1975 that "the undue concentration of wealth in a few hands has become compounded. Political power is now monopolized by one man. Wealth is increasingly concentrated in the hands of persons who either exercise martial law authority, or are their relatives, associates, cronies, or patrons."[93] The Civil Liberties Union in its report concluded: "The two striking features of the economy are that: (1) Notwithstanding the record growth rates officially claimed by the government and the sector of big business, the overwhelming majority of our people, composed of working men and fixed-income groups, have been considerably impoverished; and (2) the economy has become even more dependent than it has ever been on external factors, on foreign creditors, and foreign capital."[94]

The Philippines is only one among many countries that have recently experienced double-digit inflation, although it had one of the world's highest rates in 1974. The government claims to have

91. Ibid., pp. 3–4.
92. Ibid., p. 17.
93. De la Costa et al., "Message of Hope," p. 26.
94. "Statement of the Civil Liberties Union," pp. 27–28.

succeeded remarkably in reducing the inflationary rate, even as it repeatedly blamed recession abroad and the oil crisis for the domestic inflation and its effects on prices and levels of living. In contrast, studies show that the "imported inflation" accounted only for a relatively small part of domestic inflation: not more than 10 percent, according to the National Economic Development Authority and the Communications Research Center; not over 16 percent, according to the Central Bank.[95] On the basis of these figures and his own study, Vicente Valdepeñas concluded that "90 percent of the inflation is really due to the mismanagement of monetary and fiscal policy of the Philippines. . . . Spending has been increasing by almost 18 percent every year, whereas our output has been increasing by something like 5 to 6 percent." While praising the restoration of law and order and the administration of justice as positive for economic development, Valdepeñas pointed up certain weaknesses of the government in its development efforts. These were "the inability to make socialized pricing work" and "the tendency of the industrial program . . . to go into fairly ambitious capital intensive projects which will take generations to pay off . . . and to spawn industrial processes that have little to do with the resource endowments of the country and will therefore continue to be dependent on large, imported energy consumption."[96]

The Reformer's Dilemma

President Marcos has made clear his awareness of the unfinished, in fact unending, tasks of societal transformation faced by the Philippines. "In our own country," he has said, "the accumulated experience of the past three years promises more challenges, rather than relief. For once we set our program of reform in motion, there is no alternative but to prosecute it to its legitimate end."[97] Similarly, in his New Year's message for 1977, the president stated: "All that we have done and achieved during the last four years has inexorably thrust us into tasks of greater magnitude and responsibilities requiring the utmost of each of us."[98] When Marcos imposed martial law, with the critical support of the military, he justified his desperate

95. Vicente Valdepeñas, "Philippine Economic Problems in Perspective," U. P. School of Economics Lecture Series, Dec. 4, 1975.
96. Ibid., p. 9.
97. Marcos, "President's Report," Sept. 21, 1975.
98. *Bulletin Today*, Jan. 1, 1977.

move in terms of saving the republic from anarchy or a leftist-rightist overthrow, and of remaking the Filipino society, polity, and economy. It is therefore legitimate for any serious inquirer to ask, as D. Weintraub did: "To what extent is the change primarily politically oriented—that is, calculated to maintain the center institutionally and personally; or else does it indeed propose to tackle the basic societal issues . . . ?"[99]

This question must be seen in the proper context of the characteristic, sequential, or simultaneous concerns of political leaders almost everywhere, and therefore of Ferdinand Marcos himself. It is said that political leaders are typically confronted with five kinds of problems of incumbency: how to *cope* with their social and economic environment from day to day, how to *change* their social and economic environment, how to *maintain* their authority in the present, how to *ensure* their continuance in power and authority in the future, and how to *adapt* their political and administrative infrastructure for effective leadership.[100] The first may be called the day-to-day problem of public management; the second represents the unending challenge of development and socioeconomic reform; the third is the problem of personal and official legitimacy, credibility, and efficacy; the fourth, the problem of continuity and self-succession in power; and the fifth concerns the improvement, if not remaking, of the structures and institutions of governance. The listing does not suggest their priority in importance or sequence in urgency, because these attributes of the problem vary depending on particular leaders and their circumstances.

However, it may be hypothesized that when at any time the foremost political leaders in a country decide that most if not all these problems require urgent and drastic solutions, it is highly probable that a personal and national crisis is perceived by them. This perception could lead them to institute radical changes in the power structure. Usually, this would be accompanied by a justification of the sudden changes made and the introduction of new values, goals, and prescriptions of behavior for political rivals and the citizenry at large.

99. D. Weintraub, *Development and Modernization in the Philippines: The Problem of Change in the Context of Political Stability and Social Continuity* (Beverly Hills: Sage Publications, 1973), p. 22.

100. Warren Ilchman and Norman Uphoff, *The Political Economy of Change* (Berkeley: University of California Press, 1971), p. 33.

Even if no violent and successful revolution takes place, because this is rare in history, usually a new constitution soon symbolizes a new order that tends to be more authoritarian than the one it has displaced. Often the array of changes introduced is justified in terms of pulling off a long-delayed or frustrated true "revolution" aimed at realizing "the substance of democracy" and rejecting its empty form. The new leadership would wish to do no less than to redesign the whole political structure and culture. Political experience, whether indigenous or imported, as well as applied social science and technology, provide the new leadership with the ideas and techniques of social control in inducing the desired behavior of other leaders and of the ruled. This scenario seems to fit the Philippines both when martial law was declared and thereafter. In this context, the consequences of martial law for the twin reform objectives of democratizing power and wealth can be conclusively analyzed.

In his *Notes on the New Society*, President Marcos pinpointed "equality" as the "central problem . . . of the revolution from the center." Consequently, he concluded, "the fundamental task of drastic political reform is to democratize the entire political system."[101] In fact, however, political power is much more concentrated now than before martial rule. The breadth and depth and range of political participation are defined by the president, who exercises executive, legislative, military, and administrative functions. Many objective observers would agree with David Rosenberg's observation that "the most clear-cut political change is the increasingly pervasive strength of the Marcos regime. Political and economic initiative continue to come from the center. Not only is the Marcos regime concentrating and mobilizing wealth, it is also concentrating and mobilizing other instruments of political power, in particular, the military, the mass media, and foreign resources. These instruments of political power constitute a technologically modernized form of elite domination. In this fashion, elite rule persists. Indeed, the ruling elite now possesses greater power than ever before."[102] Three years after he declared martial law, Marcos himself observed:

101. Ferdinand E. Marcos, *Notes on the New Society of the Philippines* (Manila, 1973), p. 70.
102. David A. Rosenberg, "Conclusion: Premonitions of Martial Law," in Benedict J. Kerkvliet, ed., *Political Change in the Philippines* (Honolulu: University Press of Hawaii, 1974), pp. 257–58.

"Among some of the poor, there is still the nagging fear that they have, again, been left behind, and that we have liquidated an oligarchy only to set up a new oligarchy . . ."[103] The fact is, according to Jeffrey Race, "Despite President Marcos' assurances that his moves are intended to abolish the oligarchy of great families that previously controlled Philippine politics . . . martial law and what it has brought in tow represent the breakthrough of one segment of that oligarchy, which has now gone on to abolish the rules by which the oligarchs jointly dominated the country in the past."[104]

Concluding his review of the evolving political concepts of President Marcos as validated by the Supreme Court, Victoriano Hipe warns: "The view that martial law can be an instrument to *change* society for the better—thus a martial law to end future martial laws—, that a new Constitution can be validly ratified under martial law, and that a Constitution can ratify past as well as future acts of the martial law administrator as 'a part of the law of the land,' are dangerous precedents to future Filipinos living in a democratic society."[105] The record-breaking example set by Marcos that the continuation in power of a head of government and chief of state can be achieved through constitutional changes effected under martial law would be an irresistible temptation to his successors in office.

As the rules and practices of authoritarianism have begun to be institutionalized by Supreme Court decisions and the recent constitutional amendments, politically concerned Filipinos have ample reason to doubt Marcos' written assurance in 1973 that "it should be apparent to the responsible citizen that when a democratic government takes strong measures to preserve itself, it is not for the purpose of concentrating power in the hands of one man."[106] Cardinal Jaime Sin, Archbishop of Manila and titular head of the Catholic Church in the Philippines, has expressed his fears about the future of the country if martial law is continued: "I am afraid of the future. I have always conveyed this fear. The security of the country is based on the Constitution. The Constitution should be above the President. At the moment he controls the Constitution. He says it is the people who change the Constitution, but I don't believe the

103. Marcos, "President's Report," Sept. 21, 1975.
104. Race, "Whither the Philippines," p. 1.
105. Hipe, "Legal Aspects of Martial Law," p. 16.
106. Marcos, *Notes on the New Society*, p. 133.

people know what is happening."[107] As 1976 ended, seventeen militant Catholic bishops summed up the condition of human rights and justice by stating: "Under martial law . . . our people have been deprived of rights that are theirs simply because they are human: rights to freedom of speech, of association, rights to due process, to meaningful participation in decisionmaking processes, to meaningful processes touching their common welfare, rights to truth and information, rights even to their dignity as thinking men and women."[108] The viewpoint of certain political prisoners and victims of abusive treatment, and of their relatives and concerned friends, is expressed by Amnesty International as follows: "In reality, at least up to [December 5, 1975], the only rule of law in the Philippines under martial law has been the unchecked power of the executive branch and the military."[109]

On New Year's Eve, 1977, a colonel in the armed forces "chided some government officials in both military and civilian agencies who continue to follow Old Society practices of graft, corruption, and immorality, using influence to commit such acts,"[110] while a newspaper columnist expressed the popular belief that "it is no secret that some high officials seem to be more interested in self-aggrandizement than in service to the people."[111] On March 23, 1978, *Times Journal* columnist Ernesto O. Granada wrote: "The sad observation of many is that the New Society has not cleansed the bureaucracy of undesirables. To cite only the more visible faults, so many in the civil service still treat the public they are supposed to serve as mud. And are on the take. . . . Indeed, [a] purge should start with some of the highest in the bureaucracy. Possibly, with the cabinet."

One of the salient and demoralizing features of martial rule is the seemingly widespread belief, whether true or false, that it has enabled the Marcoses themselves to accumulate vast riches because of the absence of countervailing powers and effective public scrutiny. However, such belief might be mitigated by the common if not cynical assumption that most powerful officials are dishonest, by

107. *Far Eastern Economic Review,* Dec. 10, 1976, p. 11.
108. *"Ut omnes unum sunt,"* *Far Eastern Economic Review,* Dec. 10, 1976.
109. *Report of an Amnesty International Mission,* p. 53.
110. Florencio Magsino, Superintendent of the Philippine Military Academy, in *Bulletin Today,* Jan. 1, 1977.
111. *Bulletin Today,* Dec. 31, 1976.

the suspicion that rumored allegations of aggrandizement by the Marcoses is exaggerated by opponents who are unable to counter their nearly absolute power, by the denials of the president and his closest friends, and by the media that always extol the virtues of the ruling family and taboo the dissemination of any information that questions its integrity.

Indeed, the New Society may be regarded as a tradeoff: political authoritarianism for development and equity. Inasmuch as the former is a reality, it is in order to determine how much of the latter has taken place.

The expansion of wealth—in terms of volume of production of goods and services, higher productivity, accumulation of capital stock, availability of more capital for investment, greater corporate activity, and larger foreign exchange reserves—is a verifiable fact. It also seems true, however, that the new economic gains are going mostly to the capitalists, entrepreneurs, and managers, to the larger producers of export products, and to urban-based businessmen, professionals, and merchants, some of whom also share in the exercise of the president's powers.

Given the high if slightly falling population growth, continuing inflation at close to 10 percent, the still regressive taxation, the drop in real wages, and the obstacles to regional development land reform and public management, the new wealth and incomes are, as indicated above, not being redistributed any better than before martial law. On the other hand, this observation would be disputed by administration officials. And it also may be argued that most capitalist or private-enterprise economies take a long time to "take off," and that, in the Philippines, the bases for such growth are being laid with greater vigor, determination, and rationality than ever before. But how long will the "democratization of wealth and property" take?

The Philippines, in the view of Mangahas, follows the trend hypothesized by the economist Simon Kuznets, that income inequality typically first rises until it reaches a peak before it falls.[112] If the government's GNP growth target of 7 percent per year is attained indefinitely, it is estimated by the U.P. School of Economics[113] that income inequality will "rise by a few more points

112. Mangahas, "Income Distribution Problem," p. 5.
113. Mindanilla Barlis, "Preliminary Projections of GNP and Income Inequality

during the 1980s, from the present score of 50, and will drop to
perhaps 46 to 47 points by the year 2000. By the latter date, some
6 to 8 million families out of a total 17.8 million would still be
below the food poverty threshold (computed on a minimum
diet)."[114]

In contrast to the country's persistent problems in achieving development and equity, certain qualified gains deserve to be emphasized. The New Society has improved peace and order, compared
to the chaotic situation in the sixth and seventh years of the Marcos
presidency or the eve of martial law. The exceptions are the rebel
areas of Luzon and Mindanao and urban areas where crimes against
property appear to have increased. Government revenues and expenditures have substantially increased. Both food production and
infrastructure construction have been boosted as never before, with
massive injections of foreign financing. Indeed, the government has
raised large foreign loans for development, attracted foreign investments, promoted and expanded exports, and developed tourism.
The continuing search for oil has been intensified and three major
oil strikes have been reported off Palawan. Even though several
serious problems have slowed down land reform on rice and corn
lands, the record of the New Society exceeds all previous efforts.
A measure of citizen discipline and social order has been instilled,
although complaints of "backsliding" are often heard and long-term
political stability is not assured. Export markets have been diversified to lessen the country's dependence on the United States and
Japan, but these two countries still account for 58 percent of
Philippine exports and 45 percent of imports, and the Philippines
still face depressed prices for its traditional exports. Diplomatic and
trade relations have been opened with China, Soviet Russia, Vietnam, and other socialist states. Philippine sovereignty is being
asserted in the operation of U.S. military bases in the islands.
Greater support has been given to research in science, agriculture,
technology, and even the social sciences. Given its pragmatic ends
and norms, which do not necessarily coincide with its publicized
ideology, the government in the New Society has introduced relatively greater rationality and a long-range perspective in its planning

---

in the Year 2000," U.P. School of Economics, PREPF Phase I Report (August 1975),
as cited in Mangahas, ibid.

114. Mangahas, ibid.

and management.[115] The population growth rate is reported to have fallen from 3.2 percent to 2.8 percent.[116]

In view of his paramount role in national development, President Marcos' self-assessment of martial rule is crucial for what can and what cannot be done, allowing for slippage and resistance because of political and bureaucratic factors and the people's responses. When asked by *Newsweek* if he was satisfied with the results of martial rule, Marcos replied: "Would I do it all over again? Yes. Although naturally there are areas where I would seek some improvements or emphasize other areas of development. But no matter what the critics say—and some accuse me of everything from becoming the richest man in Asia to having sex orgies in the presidential palace—*we are on the right track. Not only theoretically but factually.* Look at the mess we were in and where we are now! Look at our nation's economic and social progress! What is the American expression? The proof of the pudding is in the eating. Well, there it is [emphasis added]."[117]

The taste of the pudding also depends on who eats it. As the differing evaluations presented in this chapter, especially those of objective analysts and candid citizens, clearly show, the president's viewpoint is far from thoroughly informed and unbiased, although he seeks improvements and changes in emphases in his policies and programs. Despite his desire for honest feedback, the tendency is for his political associates and technocrats and the guided media to feed him the kind of "reality" that they think would please him and Mrs. Marcos. For all its imperfections the Old Society was characterized by intra-elite competition, protest movements, exposés in the "oligarchic" media, and periodic campaigns and elections— all of which enabled the incumbent leaders to know what various groups felt about their leadership and performance. Because a reliable feedback mechanism and the imperative of public accountability are now lacking, because the Marcos regime is so powerful and entrenched that it may expect to rule indefinitely, and because the president's security limits his mobility and domestic exposure

115. For an earlier assessment of the New Society, see Jose Veloso Abueva, "Filipino Demorracy and the American Legacy," *Annals of the American Academy of Political and Social Science* 428 (Nov. 1976), 127–33.

116. Marcos, "President's Report," Sept. 21, 1976. The corrected estimate of current population growth rate is 2.8 percent.

117. Richard Z. Chessnoff, "Conversation in Manila," *Newsweek,* Aug. 9, 1976.

outside Metro Manila, sycophancy and self-deception now peren-
nially surround and insulate the regime's highest leaders. The
veteran journalist and weather vane of the New Society, Teodoro
Valencia, writes nostalgically about the time when reporters published annual summaries of the performance of government offices.
In contrast, he says, "now . . . they're written by the public officials,
usually self-praises and glowing accounts fed to the public."[118]

Undue reliance by Marcos on civilian and military technocrats
who lack political sensitivity recalls David Halberstam's account of
how "the best and the brightest" got America into the Vietnam
quagmire by their alienation from the people's concerns, their being
too sure of their own judgments, and their all-too-human oppor-
tunism. The cult of personality and the histrionics and ostentation
in the highest circles of the New Society have no equal in modern
Philippine history. Too often, moreover, some of those who wield
power confuse their own identities and interests with those of the
government, the nation, the state, or the society as a whole.

There are also varied perspectives and criteria for evaluating long-
range progress in building the New Society, whose ideology—if not
all of its practice—would be acceptable to most loyal, concerned,
and patriotic Filipinos. From the mundane and meaningful viewpoint of the average Filipino, President Marcos himself has provided a five-way test of societal transformation: "(1) If we can
really free the small man from the chain of poverty that has
shackled his ancestors to the land they tilled for others, (2) if we
can locate him at the center of increasing opportunity for himself
and his family, (3) if we can produce enough, and (4) pay our
workers enough, so that their labor can assure them of a better
quality of life, (5) if we can provide the proper machinery of government so that no one is deprived of an efficient administration of
justice, then we can remain firm in our hopes that we are building
a New Society."[119] How, when, and to what extent some 35 million
less fortunate Filipinos could be so advanced is a staggering challenge before the nation.

Apparently, as the third year of martial law, the sanguine hopes,
if not euphoria, of the Marcos regime were shared by diminishing

---

118. "Over a Cup of Coffee," *Philippines Daily Express,* Jan. 5, 1977.
119. Quoted in "Development for the New Society" (Manila: Bureau of National
and Foreign Information, Department of Public Information, 1974).

numbers of people, even among those who had benefited under the new dispensation. The energy crisis that began in 1974 and the world recession that followed in its wake, causing the prices of Philippine exports to tumble and domestic prices to rise with the double-digit inflation, demonstrated how dependent the national economy is on the world economy. New events and old structures continue to mark the limits of even Marcos' concentrated governmental powers in stimulating economic growth and arresting inflation, let alone stopping social inequities or reversing the tides of the international market. It has taken huge deficit financing and more than $5 billion of international borrowing, in addition to bilateral and international assistance, to stop another peso devaluation and steeper inflation. As the triple crises of lower export earnings, still higher oil costs, and the Communist and Muslim rebellions threaten the country, the vaunted advantages of "constitutional authoritarianism" over the old order become increasingly unconvincing.

Despite the claim of the National Economic Development Authority that from 1973 to 1976 self-sufficiency in rice had been attained, government credit and resources had been mobilized for food production, rural household income had expanded, and the pattern of income distribution between rural and urban areas had improved, the planning agency concluded in 1977: "However, farm productivity is still generally low and underemployment is high; the diffusion and assimilation of technological innovations in small farms have been slow; infrastructure facilities are still inadequate. The process of agrarian reform and farmer institutional development has yet to overcome administrative, financial, and managerial constraints."[120]

In presenting the administration's long-range plans (for 1978–1982, 1978–1987, and to the year 2000), the National Economic Development Authority acknowledged with scholarly objectivity "the following urgent problems and challenges":

Inadequacy in Basic Needs. The increase in the real per capita GNP of more than three percent per year in the last four years has not appreciably alleviated the condition of the urban and rural poor who comprise more than half of the total population. A relatively large segment of the population especially in the rural areas continues to want in the basic

120. *Five-Year Development Plan, 1978–1982*, p. 105.

needs in life, i.e., food, clothing, shelter and minimum education. To a large extent this may be attributed to the severity of the various crises that confronted the country in recent years. The problem remains severe notwithstanding government subsidy in rice, fuel, transport, basic wage goods, housing and other social services.

Income Inequality. Limitations in the purchasing power of most Filipinos exist in spite of the marked growth of the country's economy. This indicates the personal and geographical maldistribution of income and wealth in the country. Preliminary data on family income distribution in 1975 revealed that the top 30 percent of income recipients in the country account for 63.9 percent of total income. The middle 40 and lowest 30 percent of families received only 26.4 percent and 9.7 percent of income, respectively. Although improvement over the 1971 distribution was registered, future development efforts will have to be decisively directed toward a more equitable dispersal of the benefits of economic progress.

Unemployment and Underemployment. As of August, 1976, the unemployment rate for the whole country was 5.2 percent of the labor force or 790,000 people. This seemingly low unemployment rate is negated by a large underemployment rate of 10.7 percent of the total employed or 1.6 million persons. This indicates the shortage of productive employment in the country. In most instances, even the income of those employed is not enough to raise them above the level of poverty. More and better income-earning employment opportunities must therefore be created to raise the general standard of living and to effect a more equitable income distribution in the country.

Heavy Pressure of a Rapid Population Growth. Although fertility has begun to fall in recent years, the most optimistic projection still places population growth at 2.3 percent in the next decade. . . . Unless reduced to a more manageable level, rapid population growth will compound problems currently facing the country and make solutions more difficult to reach.

Balance of Payments and Price Instability. The reforms instituted since 1972 contributed to the relatively stable performance of the economy at the height of adverse external events. However, being a highly open economy, the Philippines will continuously be affected by disturbances in the external sector. . . .

Energy Constraint. The smooth sustenance of the country's growth momentum is continuously threatened by an unstable supply of energy. About 90 percent of the country's energy requirements are based on imported petroleum. Thus, an upsurge in oil prices strains the country's balance of payments and pushes up production costs in a wide area of economic activities.

Environmental Problems. The rapid expansion of human settlements and accelerated development activities in agriculture, mining, forestry and manufacturing have resulted in a number of environmental problems. These problems are apparent in drying lakes and rivers, soil erosion, floods, and other pollution problems. . . .

Regional Growth Disparities. A number of regions in the country lag behind the more developed ones in terms of growth, employment and provision of basic services to their growing population. These depressed regions especially the rural areas became the seat of discontent in many instances in the past.

The rapid migration of population to a few urban areas of more developed regions resulted in serious employment, housing, health and other congestion problems. This premature migration made urbanization more an aspect of poverty than a symbol of growth.

Accordingly, the administration would direct development efforts in the next ten years principally toward the solution of the above problems by aiming for these development goals:

(1) Promotion of social development and social justice through: creation of productive employment opportunities; reduction of income disparities; improvement of the living standards of the poor; and enrichment of social and cultural values;

(2) Attainment of self-sufficiency in food and greater self-reliance in energy;

(3) Attainment of a high and sustained economic growth;

(4) Maintenance of an acceptable price level and improvement in domestic resource mobilization and balance of payments position;

(5) Increased development of lagging regions especially rural areas;

(6) Improvement of habitat through development of human settlements and proper management of environment; and

(7) Maintenance of internal security and harmonious international relations.[121]

From a long-range analytical view, Weintraub asserts that "what is crucial for development is . . . the extent to which the system is capable of generating ongoing change at all levels, in the sense of increasing societal openness and flexibility, of purposive exposure to and ability to solve problems of growing complexity; of 'absorbing' difficulties and reverses; and of creating novel opportunities. Essential, in other words, is a legitimation of or an institutional

121. Ibid., pp. 6–8.

potential for a continuous rearrangement of existing commitments, and for an unimpeded flow, exchange and mobilization of all social goods."[122] Pre-martial law Filipino society probably lacked such generation of "ongoing" change at all levels. It remains to be seen whether Filipino society under the Marcoses or after them would be able to acquire that self-sustaining capacity.

In the short run, President Marcos and the New Society regime he heads may be evaluated anew in terms of the five typical concerns of statesmen alluded to above: (1) daily public management, (2) fostering socioeconomic reforms and development, (3) maintaining their authority in the present, (4) continuing in power and authority in the future, and (5) reforming the political and administrative structures to enhance their leadership and the capacity of the government for performing its functions. Which of these have been emphasized and satisfied the most since September 21, 1972?

It would appear that the New Society leaders have accorded highest priority to, and therefore succeeded most, in their third and fourth concerns, that is, in assuring power and authority in the present and the foreseeable future, barring unforeseen events. With respect to the fifth, they have been quite successful in obtaining the kind of constitution and Supreme Court validation that provides them with a suitable political structure. They claim to have broken the back of Communist dissidence and Muslim secession, and to this extent perhaps they have "saved the nation," which was the president's first justification for imposing martial rule. On the twin rationale of "instituting reforms," the record shows that Marcos has achieved the opposite of "democratizing the entire political system."

It may be that before the promised democratic and egalitarian structures of the New Society can be established, there has to be consolidation of power at the top, or at the center, in the hands of Marcos, who had risen to the pinnacle of power in the Old Society that he led for seven years until he finally decided to transform it in the image of the New Society under one-man rule. After all, five years is a very short time in any nation's political development, or for shifting from competitive elite politics to authoritarianism and then out of it. It may be that such a monopoly of power is indispensable for instituting basic land reform, tax reform, and other

---

122. Weintraub, *Development and Modernization*, p. 22.

redistributive programs, administrative reforms, the control of rebellion and lawlessness, and so on. It may be that "constitutional authoritarianism" as a form of "guided democracy," "crisis government," or "benevolent dictatorship" is being used in a transition to the parliamentary democracy envisaged in the 1973 Constitution. The president publicly regarded his original Batasang Pambansa (National Assembly) and now the Interim Batasang Pambansa as major steps in that direction. In politics, timing is essential, and who among his contemporaries would understand timing better than Marcos?

However, the case of land reform under the New Society does not support the optimism that underlies the above suppositions. A thorough and expeditious land reform affecting agricultural and urban land would be not only one of the best ways to attain equity in Philippine society, but also, by the same token, the most telling measure of the political will, security, and sophistication being mustered by Marcos as a social reformer. For without attaining extraordinary success in socioeconomic reform and development, he is likely to be remembered mainly for his extraordinary ability to survive the longest as a Filipino president or head of government, and for the resulting public sacrifices and political system that would be his legacy to future generations. Instead of concentrating land reform in rice and corn lands, evidently for some practical political consideration, he could shift to a strategy of vigorous implementation and the extension of land reform to land planted to other crops as well as to high-priced urban land. If and when he does this, he will give credibility to all his reform undertakings. He might also justify the powers he has accumulated under the New Society at the cost of human rights and many human lives.

On the other hand, Marcos may feel that full-scale reforms on several fronts might threaten the coherence of his present ruling coalition and further endanger his life. In this case, in the near future it would seem more likely that less painful incremental changes will continue to be made in the social and economic structure. Political self-preservation, the democratic heritage of the past three generations, the basic conservatism of Filipino society, and the so-called "politics of integration and not of conflict,"[123] calculated to

123. Quoted phrase from Marcos, "President's Report," Sept. 21, 1976. The influence of American liberal democracy, Spanish Catholicism, and Filipino traditions is discussed in Abueva, "Filipino Democracy," pp. 118–33.

unify the nation and to preserve the new political structure, would combine to dilute the outward revolutionary zeal of Marcos into more rhetoric and moderate change. Even assuming his sincerity about reforms, not until he can change the composition of his grand alliance, now still dominated by the biggest economic interests and the new privileged groups under him, will he dare to risk all to make the "Democratic Revolution, the authentic revolution."

The Marcos regime has yet to prove that its concentrated, pervasive political and economic strength can and will be utilized to make fundamental changes in the political and economic structure of society. Yet such change is needed for the achievement of a shared and sustained development—brought about by a people-oriented, rather than a "trickle-down" strategy—and an effective and truly participatory democracy. It is problematical whether the "Democratic Revolution" can be mounted by Marcos from the center or the top, thus preempting for good, as he has intended, the Jacobin type of revolution from below. It remains to be seen whether a grand coalition, newly established, will soon forego its powers and privileges. Indubitably, the Marcos regime has manifested its capacity for structural changes that have enlarged and consolidated its power. It has also initiated other institutional innovations deserving of implementation and development: tax reforms, long-range planning through the National Economic and Development Authority, regionalization, integrated area development, metropolitan government, farmers' cooperatives, increased agricultural credit, rice-production schemes, electric cooperatives, water resources management. Thus, if it genuinely wants to, its capacity for power accumulation could be utilized in institutional reforms that would benefit the common man.

Even if the Marcos regime fails to fulfill its promises of societal reforms, it could last for many more years through a combination of modest improvements here and there and the continuation of "constitutional authoritarianism," provided the peace and order situation and the livelihood of most people and the national economy do not deteriorate to the point where a military faction, perhaps backed by elite competitors, would feel justified in taking over. This could be the case even if Race's prediction comes true and the future does bring the country more corruption, more purges, more cynicism, more cult of personality, and more scapegoatism.[124] Under comparable conditions, the longevity of authoritarian rule in many parts of the world is a historical fact.

Some of the vocal critics of Marcos who demand a return of liberal democracy sincerely, if naïvely, and for good reasons base their arguments on the defects of martial rule, others, hypocritically demanding the same, simply wish to recoup their lost elite status. Unfortunately, like Marcos before he imposed his one-man rule, many opposition political leaders were not known for their reformist ideas and zeal when they were in power before martial law, although among them are persons of impeccable integrity who have learned from the dialectics of pre-martial law politics and the Marcos authoritarianism. No other than Marcos, who has developed a comprehensive ideology of societal change, now has the power to initiate such a process in earnest or, alternatively, to forfeit a historic opportunity in national development that has been paid for dearly in loss of democratic values, the polarization of Filipino society, and untold public sacrifices, for all their consequences for nation building and development, not to mention for Marcos' final place in history.

As a result, some nonpartisan citizens have believed with Marcos and his partisans that the premature holding of national elections for parliamentary government, before society has been restructured, would resurrect the evils of the Old Society without exorcising the ills of the New. Recent memories can lead one to ask the "chicken or the egg" question: "What is the meaning of competitive elections of the very few who are wealthy and powerful by the votes of the great majority who are poor, dependent, vulnerable, and manipulable, and whose circumstances in life had not improved through the many elections in which they had participated?"[125] These considerations add to many people's tolerance, if not acceptance, of "constitutional authoritarianism" for its perceived advantages and despite all its visible flaws, for they see no realistic alternative as yet.

Indeed, the dilemma of the reformer has been made clear by William Overholt: "Marcos and his [civilian and military] techno-

124. Race, "Whither the Philippines," pp. 12–13.
125. Question from Jose V. Abueva, review of Carl H. Landé, *Southern Tagalog Voting, 1946–1963: Political Behavior in a Philippine Region,* in *Journal of Southeast Asian Studies* VI (September 1975), 224.

crats now face both the dangers of under-correcting and oversteering. And the irony is that they will find themselves doing both if they are not careful: they could so negate normal political processes and expectations that they create a united front against themselves and yet not succeed in creating the social discipline and governmental efficiency that they seek. Such an outcome is by no means inevitable, but the dangers must not be underestimated either."[126]

Other observers do not discount the potential for a bloody upheaval, such as the Communists may have long wanted to bring about, with only limited success, if "constitutional authoritarianism" fails. "So long as resources and power continue to be lodged in a few in this otherwise enlightened age," writes Mary Hollnsteiner, "the potential for grassroots movements looms ever greater."[127] In Robert Shaplen's view, "the Philippines has not yet had its real revolution. At some point, despite the easy going ways of the Filipinos, the underlying explosive social and economic discontent will burst forth."[128] The failure of the New Society's reform program, according to Salvador Lopez, "will convince the people that there is no option left but the forcible seizure of political power in order that the goals of the social revolution which for centuries they have striven to achieve but which have repeatedly eluded them may finally be realized."[129]

"In the longer run," David Wurfel predicts, "the pattern of Philippine political development is likely to resemble that of Indonesia, Vietnam, or one of the various political sub-types in Latin America."[130]

126. William D. Overholt, "Martial Law, Revolution and Democracy in the Philippines," *Southeast Asia Quarterly* II (Spring 1973), 2.
127. Mary R. Hollnsteiner, "People Power: Community Participation in the Planning and Implementation of Human Settlements," *Philippine Studies* 24 (1976), 5–36.
128. Robert Shaplen, "Southeast Asia—Before and After," *Foreign Affairs* 53: 3 (April 1975), 546.
129. Salvador P. Lopez, "The Philippines under Martial Law" (Quezon City: University of the Philippines Press, 1974), p. 21.
130. David Wurfel, "Martial Law in the Philippines: The Methods of Regime Survival," *Pacific Affairs*, 50: 1 (Spring 1977), 29.

2. Constitutionality and Judicial Politics

ROLANDO V. DEL CARMEN
SAM HOUSTON STATE UNIVERSITY

The Philippines became an American territory in 1898 after the signing of the Treaty of Paris between Spain and the United States. By law, the new regime established a judicial system that preserved the court structure of the Spanish period but whose procedures were patterned after those of the U.S. federal courts. Hierarchically, it originally consisted of the Supreme Court, the courts of first instance, and the justice of the peace courts. The courts of first instance were located throughout the country and exercised original and appellate jurisdiction over cases specified by the legislature. At the base of the judicial ladder were the justice of the peace courts, which were found in the municipalities (the smallest unit of government) and whose jurisdictional reach was limited.[1] By statute, the Congress of the Philippines later created other courts, notably the Court of Appeals, which was composed of a presiding justice and seventeen associate justices.[2]

The political system before martial law was patterned institutionally after that of the United States. There were the traditional branches of government, the separation of powers, and a system of checks and balances. The judicial power was "vested in one Supreme Court and in such inferior courts as may be provided by law."[3] The Supreme Court was composed of a chief justice and ten associate justices who were appointed by the president with the

---

1. At the time of the adoption of the new constitution, the judicial system in the Philippines basically consisted of the Supreme Court, Court of Appeals, courts of first instance, municipal courts, and other special courts created through specific legislation. For a discussion of the historical background of Philippine courts, see M. Gamboa, *An Introduction to Philippine Law* 6th ed. (Rochester, N.Y.: The Lawyer's Cooperative Publishing Co., 1955), pp. 469–75.

2. Republic Act No. 296, Sec. 33, as cited in Gamboa, p. 472.

3. Article VIII, Sec. 1 of the old constitution.

consent of the Commission on Appointments and held office until they were seventy years old. It enjoyed independence from and co-equal status with the two other branches in a tripartite system of government. As the nation's highest tribunal, the Supreme Court deservedly held great prestige and eminence and was considered to be the "most important legitimizing institution" in the country.[4]

As a U.S. territory, the Philippines was ruled for almost four decades through executive decrees and congressional statutes. In 1934, a Constitutional Convention was called upon authorization from the United States Congress.[5] The convention drafted a consti-tution for the Philippines which became effective in 1935 after approval by the President of the United States and an overwhelm-ing endorsement in a nationwide plebiscite. After enjoying com-monwealth status for about a decade, the Philippines obtained independence from the United States in 1946. The 1935 constitution continued as its basic charter with only minor amendments. In the late sixties, however, agitation for revision mounted. The constitu-tion was viewed by an increasingly militant segment of the popula-tion as anachronistic and a relic of a colonial era, adopted as it was when the Filipinos were American subjects and owed allegiance to the United States. In 1971, a Constitutional Convention was called and immediately began deliberations.

On September 23, 1972, while the Constitutional Convention was in the final stages of its protracted endeavor, President Marcos an-nounced martial law. In a speech delivered on nationwide radio and television, he said: "The proclamation of martial law is not a mili-tary takeover. I, as your duly elected President of the Republic, use this power implemented by military authorities to protect the Re-public of the Philippines and our democracy."[6] He went on to say that "the judiciary shall continue to function in accordance with its present organization and personnel," subject to certain limitations. Four months later, addressing the Consultative Council at Mala-cañang Palace, the President pledged that the government would

4. Jean Grossholtz, *The Philippines* (Boston: Little, Brown, 1964), p. 127.
5. Embodied in the Tydings-McDuffie Independence Law of 1934, Sec. 1 of which provided: "The Philippine Legislature is hereby authorized to provide for the election of delegates to a constitutional convention which shall meet in the hall of representatives in the capital of the Philippine Islands . . . to formulate and draft a constitution for the government of the Commonwealth of the Philippine Islands, subject to the conditions and qualifications prescribed in the Act."
6. *Philippine Times,* Sept. 30, 1972, p. 2.

be based on constitutionality and reiterated that he had declared martial law legitimately on the basis of the old constitution. "I have not grabbed power," the president said at a news conference. He described the new government as one of "constitutional authoritarianism," and added that the broad powers he wields are subject to checks and balances by the country's Supreme Court.[7]

These and similar statements by high Philippine officials collectively paint the image which the government wishes to portray to observers at home and abroad: that the declaration of martial law was constitutional; that despite the realities of a one-man rule, constitutional procedures have not been abrogated; and that the judiciary as an institution is alive and well. In order to evaluate these claims, it is necessary to inquire into the current status of constitutionalism in the Philippines, to assess the nature of the interaction between the president and the Supreme Court under martial law conditions, and to identify the changes that have been brought about by the new constitution insofar as these changes affect the judiciary.

The Constitutionality of Martial Law

Despite strong arguments to the contrary, and long before the case was eventually decided by the Supreme Court, the preponderantly tenable position appeared to be that the declaration of martial law by President Marcos enjoyed constitutional sanction. Article VII, Section 10, paragraph 2 of the 1935 constitution states that: "In case of invasion, insurrection, or rebellion or imminent danger thereof, when the public safety requires, he [the President] may suspend the privileges of the writ of habeas corpus or place the Philippines or any part thereof under martial law." "There is no doubt in everybody's mind," the president asserted on September 23, 1972, "that a state of rebellion exists."[8] His critics, on the other hand, point out that when martial law was proclaimed, Congress was in session, the Supreme Court and inferior courts were open, the Constitutional Convention was in session, and none of the provincial governments was under Communist control.[9] All this may have been true, but as far as President Marcos and his legal advisers

7. *New York Times*, Jan. 21, 1973, p. 1.
8. *Philippine Times*, Sept. 30, 1972, p. 2.
9. For extensive arguments against the constitutionality of the martial law declaration, see *U.S. Congressional Record—Senate*, April 12, 1973, pp. S 7309 ff.

were concerned, the issue of constitutionality had been settled by the court nine months earlier in the case of *Lansang v. Garcia.* In a unanimous decision penned by the then Chief Justice Roberto Concepcion, the Supreme Court upheld the president's suspension of the privilege of the writ of habeas corpus, which he had imposed three months earlier after the mass killing during the political rally of the Liberal Party in Plaza Miranda. The court ruled that the president did not act arbitrarily, but in fact had substantial basis for declaring that a state of rebellion existed and that public safety required the suspension of the writ of habeas corpus. The court, after examining available evidence, concluded: "We entertain . . . no doubt about the existence of a group of men who have publicly risen in arms to overthrow the government and have been and still are engaged in rebellion against the government of the Philippines."[10]

Aside from its immediate impact, the decision was significant in that the supreme court in *Lansang* abandoned the doctrine of non-inquiry into the factual basis for the president's suspension of the privilege of the writ of habeas corpus, a doctrine which the court had used in previous cases and which was justified on the basis of the separation of powers. The *Lansang* case, though it involved the suspension of the writ of habeas corpus, did have definitive implications for martial law because, as quoted above, the conditions for the suspension of the writ of habeas corpus and the declaration of martial law are exactly the same. Thus the court in effect removed a possible roadblock to the declaration of martial law, particularly because in the intervening months the peace and order situation in the country suddenly deteriorated. Had the court refrained from making any pronouncement concerning the existence of a rebellion, there could have been grounds to argue later that the Supreme Court could not constitutionally countenance such a danger-laden move as the imposition of martial law despite prevailing conditions. Without this prior court imprimatur, the public would perhaps have viewed the Marcos takeover with a jaundiced eye and a lot of misgivings. Unwittingly, therefore, the court gave the president the green light for martial law and may in fact have emboldened him to impose it. Aware of the credibility value of this court pronouncement, President Marcos specifically invoked the *Lansang* case in

10. *Philippines Free Press,* Dec. 25, 1971, p. 5.

his September 23, 1972, speech to support the constitutionality of his proclamation.[11]

The first set of cases brought before the Supreme Court immediately after martial law were petitions for habeas corpus filed by thirty prominent detainees, among whom were former senators Diokno and Aquino, the erstwhile chief critics of the president. After a curious two-year delay, which saw other important cases promptly decided, the Supreme Court held that President Marcos' declaration of martial law was indeed constitutional. The multifaceted 537-page decision gave a clear judicial endorsement of martial law, but at the same time held that the court had the power to scrutinize the acts of the government to determine whether they had resulted in manifest transgressions of liberty.[12] Seven of the twelve justices found that President Marcos, exercising the constitutional prerogative to declare martial law, had done so in an emergency situation and without arbitrariness. Predictably, the Supreme Court cited the 1971 case of *Lansang* v. *Garcia,* concluding that they were convinced that a state of rebellion then existed, and still exists, in the country.[13] Thus for jurisprudential purposes, the issue of the constitutionality of the martial law proclamation has been sealed and settled. But the rationale and motivation for the Supreme Court decision will be argued in private legal circles in the Philippines for years to come.[14]

11. The president said: "This danger to the Republic of the Philippines and the existence of a rebellion has been recognized even by our Supreme Court in its decision in the case of Lansang v. Garcia, dated December 11, 1971. . . . Since the Supreme Court promulgated this decision, the danger has become graver and rebellion has worsened or escalated." *Philippine Times,* Sept. 30, 1972, p. 2.

12. *Philippine Times,* Oct. 1, 1974, p. 7.

13. Another justification given by the court was the ratification of the president's acts by the referendums of January and July 1973.

14. Opponents of the president can point to the "bootstrapping" nature of the court's decision. While they admit that a state of rebellion involving Muslims in the south does exist, such came about because of martial law. Moreover, the rebellion has been played down by the government through media claims that conditions in the country have in fact returned to normal since martial law. In a speech before the Makati Rotary Club Feb. 25, 1975, former senator Francisco Rodrigo, referring primarily to the legality of the impending referendum which the supreme court was asked to ban, summarized the stand taken by the Marcos critics:

1. President Marcos holds no public office—he is not president under the 1935 or 1973 Constitution. His term under the 1935 Constitution expired on December 30, 1973. He is neither President nor Prime Minister under the 1973 Constitution because this specifically provides that such positions be filled by means of an election by the National Assembly, which to date has not been convened.

2. President Marcos holds no legal transitory powers: the 1973 Constitution

The real reason for the president's consolidation of power has been the subject of extensive speculation and emotional debate. But intent is highly subjective and difficult to isolate. There is one aspect of the debate, however, which is particularly germane to the issue of constitutionalism. Whatever may have been the president's motivation, there is no question that under the old constitution, he could not have stayed in office longer than December 30, 1973. The old constitution was explicit: "No person shall serve as president for more than eight consecutive years."[15] The same section further provided that the president's term "shall end at noon on the thirtieth day of December," four years after his election, and that the term of his successor "shall begin from such time." Whether this inevitably swayed the president's decision in any manner is, to be generous, conjectural. What is certain, however, is that the above provisions have since undergone drastic revision such that under the new constitution the president can stay in office in various capacities for virtually as long as he wishes.

Framing and Ratifying the New Constitution

At the time martial law was imposed, the Constitutional Convention had almost completed the process of revising the 1935 constitution. It was a long and lively task, punctuated by charges of manipulation and bribery hurled against President Marcos by some

has not been legally ratified, hence there is no legal transition from one constitution to the other.

3. Even if the 1973 Constitution is in force, President Marcos is not empowered to call a referendum because said Constitution provides that amendments to the Constitution can be effected only through elections or plebiscites.

4. The calling of the referendum is not within the power of a martial law government—the power to declare martial law is granted by the Constitution but also is limited by the same Constitution. A martial law government can only act legally on matters relating to cases of "invasion, insurrection or rebellion, or imminent danger thereof."

5. Consultative referendum violates the concept of sovereignty—the referendum is a "consultation with the people." This violates the principle of sovereignty of the people because President Marcos cannot be found by the results of a "consultation" as he would by that of an election or a plebiscite.

6. Referendum question violates the 1973 Constitution. The question: "How do you want your local officials selected, by election or appointment by the President?" clearly violates the spirit and letter of the 1973 Constitution which clearly mandates the election of several local officials.

The 1975 referendum was held constitutional by the Court. *Philippine News*, Mar. 13, 1975, p. 1.

15. Art. VII, Sec. 4.

convention delegates.[16] The major controversy centered on the proposal to change from the American-patterned presidential form of government to a parliamentary one similar to that of Great Britain. The merits or demerits of the proposal, however, took a back seat to acid accusations that the president wanted a parliamentary government so he could perpetuate himself in office as prime minister. Charges understandably ceased after martial law was declared. The convention did finish its task two months thereafter. It adopted a parliamentary form of government with a strong prime minister.

The new constitution, by virtue of circumstances alone, is a controversial and innovative document. Its most maligned provision was, and still is, the article on transitory provisions[17] which is purportedly designed to effect an orderly transition from martial law and the old constitution to the new one. The article starts with the provision for an interim National Assembly which is to consist, among others, of those members of the existing Congress who would express in writing their option to serve therein, and the delegates of the Constitutional Convention who voted affirmatively for the transitory provisions.[18] Those who voted otherwise (and there were 15 out of the 317 delegates who voted negatively) would of course be excluded! Given the fact that the members of the interim National Assembly were to receive a windfall of P216,000 per year for salary and expenses, the attractiveness of this self-induced offer must have been more than the most patriotic of delegates could resist.

In essence, the transitory provisions validated all proclamations, orders, and decrees issued by President Marcos under martial law and made all government officials removable from office through the expedient of considering their positions vacated upon the appointment and qualification of their successors. But controversial though these provisions were, more acute apprehensions centered on Section 3, which stated that the incumbent president "shall continue to exercise his powers and prerogatives under the 1935 Constitution

16. For detailed accounts of these charges and countercharges, see the early 1972 issues of the *Philippines Free Press,* a then influential weekly newsmagazine.
17. Philippine Constitution (1973), Art. XVIII.
18. Art. XVII, Sec. 2 provides, inter alia: "The members of the interim National Assembly shall be . . . and those delegates to the nineteen hundred and seventy-one Constitutional Convention who have opted to serve therein by voting affirmatively for this Article."

and the powers vested in the President and Prime Minister . . . until he calls upon the interim National Assembly to elect the Interim President and Prime Minister." Since no definite date for such election was set, the president could call it within twenty days or twenty years—whichever was sufficient to enable him to create the New Society. Delegate Pacifico Ortiz, a Jesuit priest and former president of the Ateneo de Manila University, who resigned that post to run for the Constitutional Convention, summed up the fears of his colleagues when he moaned that "it took Kemal Ataturk 15 years to lay down the foundation of Modern Turkey, 20 years for Mussolini to create Fascist Italy, 12 years for Hitler to forge the Third German Reich, 10 years for de Gaulle to bring about the resurrection of France, and in Spain, after 40 years of transition government, the people are still waiting for Franco to restore the Spanish Monarchy."[19]

Apprehensions notwithstanding, the new constitution was overwhelmingly approved by the Constitutional Convention and signed by the delegates on November 30, 1972. Immediately thereafter, President Marcos issued a decree allowing various segments of the population to freely debate the charter provisions and called for a plebiscite to take place on January 15, 1973.

The atmosphere of free debate was not to last for long. Three weeks later, the president announced that the holding of a plebiscite was postponed to an indefinite date. The decision to postpone, according to the president, was the result of a pulse-taking of various sectors of society. He claimed that the Filipinos had slipped back into their old habits and that the enemies of the state were taking advantage of the debate to foment anxiety, confusion, discord, and subversion. Martial law was reimposed in full force, free debate was banned, and the spreading of false rumor was made punishable by death. In place of the scheduled plebiscite, nationwide "citizens assemblies" were organized for an informal referendum. Five questions were originally to be submitted to these groups for consideration, but six were later added.[20]

19. Speech by Delegate Pacifico A. Ortiz, submitted in explanation of his vote on the proposed Constitution, Dec. 1, 1972 (mimeograph).
20. *New York Times,* Jan. 11, 1973, p. C5, reports that the eleven questions were submitted to the citizens assemblies:
"Do you approve the organization of the citizens assemblies as the basis of popular government to decide the issues affecting the country?
Do you approve the proposed new Constitution?

The validity of the ratification procedure through the use of citizens assemblies instead of the constitutionally prescribed process was swiftly challenged and labeled a "farce" by the president's critics.[21] In his arguments before the Supreme Court impugning the regularity of the proceedings, former senator Jovito Salonga summarized what he perceived to be blatant flaws in the procedure.[22] His allegations have been supported by other individuals, including a former close advisor of President Marcos who has since defected from Marcos' official family. In an interview in San Francisco, Primitivo Mijares claimed that the whole referendum was "rigged" and that he was one of three individuals who had a hand in the scheme. "There was really no nationwide gathering of voters," Mijares claimed, "but we somehow had to produce referendum results."[23] Allegations of irregularity (if the referendum were to be based on the old constitution) were officially confirmed in the joint concurring opinion of Justices Makalintal and Castro in the new constitution cases when they said that "the Citizens Assemblies were not limited to qualified, let alone registered, voters, but included all citizens from the age of fifteen, and regardless of whether or not they were illiterates, feebleminded, or ex-convicts." The justices went on to state: "In short, the constitutional and statutory qualifications were not considered in the determination of who should participate. No official ballots were used in the voting; it was done mostly by acclamation or open show of hands."[24]

Do you want a plebiscite on it?

Do you want an election to be held in November, 1973? [This had been prescribed under the old constitution.]

If there is no election in November, 1973, when do you want elections to be conducted?

Do you want martial law to continue?

Do you approve of the New Society?

Do you approve of the reform measures under martial law?

Do you think that Congress should meet again in regular session?

Do you want a plebiscite later on the new Constitution?

Do you like the way President Marcos is running the Government?"

21. See letter from Rev. Fr. Francisco Claver to President Marcos as published in *Philippine Times,* Mar. 31, 1973, p. 4.

22. For a verbatim transcript of Salonga's arguments, see *Philippine Times,* Mar. 15, 1973, p. 9.

23. Ibid., Mar. 1, 1975, p. 7.

24. The decision went on to say: "No official ballots were used in the voting; it was done mostly by acclamation or open show of hands. Secrecy, which is one of the essential features of the election process, was not therefore observed. No set of rules for counting the votes or of tabulating them and reporting the figures was prescribed or followed. The Commission on Elections, which is the constitutional

Undaunted by all this and armed with a 95 percent positive mandate from the citizens assemblies, President Marcos issued three proclamations on January 17, 1973. The first one announced the outright ratification of the new constitution, hence dispensing with the scheduled plebiscite.[25] The second declared the abolition of the interim National Assembly provided for in the transitory provisions.[26] This must have caused immense dismay and consternation among the members of the Constitutional Convention, who were looking forward to reaping the benefits of their dubious affirmative votes. The third proclamation mandated the continuation of martial law for an unstated period.[27]

Immediately after the president set January 15 as the date for a nationwide plebiscite, ten identical petitions were filed with the Supreme Court to stop it, based on a variety of constitutional grounds. But while the court was hearing oral arguments on these petitions, President Marcos stunned his opponents by suspending the plebiscite and thereafter declaring the new charter ratified through the citizens assemblies. This constitutionally marginal but tactically effective move must have taken the Supreme Court by surprise, but at the same time afforded it a convenient way out of a legal dilemma. By a nine to one vote, the court dismissed the petitions as "moot and academic" in view of the presidential proclamation. But the decision expressly kept open the avenues for other actions on the proclamations if raised in proper cases. This was an open invitation and thus set the stage for the new constitution cases which promptly occupied the attention of the court.

The New Constitution Cases

The most dramatic set of cases perhaps ever to be decided by any Philippine court came in the form of four identical suits filed immediately after the dismissal of the plebiscite cases. The suits

body charged with the enforcement and administration of all laws relative to the conduct of elections, took no part at all, either by way of supervision or in the assessment of the results." Joint opinion of Justices Castro and Makalintal (mimeograph), p. 7.

25. Proclamation No. 1102, "Announcing the Ratification by the Filipino People of the Constitution Proposed by the 1971 Constitutional Convention."

26. Proclamation No. 1103, "Declaring that the Interim National Assembly Provided For in Article XVII [Transitory Provisions] of the New Constitution Be not Convened."

27. Proclamation No. 1104, "Declaring the Continuation of Martial Law."

were initiated by the president of the National Press Club, two private citizens, and five senators, who collectively asked the court to declare the new constitution void and to prohibit key government officials from carrying out its provisions. They pleaded with the court to "save the Republic from the stark reality of a dictatorship." The petitioners did not reject the provisions of the new charter. What they asked for was a new plebiscite in accordance with the provisions of the 1935 constitution. In reply, the government cautioned against judicial intervention and maintained that the use of citizens assemblies represented "substantial compliance" with the provisions of the old constitution. Appearing as counsel for respondent officers of the now defunct Philippine Senate, Senator Tolentino, one of the country's most respected constitutionalists, surprised legal circles by supporting the government's position—saying that the Marcos revolution was, as Tolentino called it, a "real revolution which had the distinction of being achieved without bloodshed."[28] It should, he said, be regarded as having succeeded since it appeared to have the support of the military and there was no proof that a majority of the Filipinos did not support it. This position advocates the interesting but dubious doctrine that one who impugns the constitutionality of an official act must also carry the burden of proving that the act does not enjoy popular support, a formidable task under martial law conditions!

The court's historic decision,[29] announced on April 2, 1973, is long, complex, and strongly reminiscent of Justice John Marshall's judicial technique employed in *Marbury* v. *Madison,* where that great chief justice adroitly obtained pragmatic legal results without unduly provoking powerful enemies or forthrightly forsaking idealistic allies. In summary, the court held that "there is now no further obstacle to the new constitution," thus refusing to invalidate the president's assumed power to rule the country indefinitely or

---

28. *New York Times,* Feb. 17, 1973, p. C6.

29. Ibid., Apr. 3, 1973, p. L3. The supreme court, in a 245-page decision, divided the issues involved in the cases into five and voted on each issue separately. The issues were: (1) Whether the court had jurisdiction over the validity of proclamation that declared the charter ratified by the people. The vote was four no, six yes. (2) Whether the constitution was validly ratified with substantial compliance of the people. Vote: six no, four yes. (3) Whether the Filipino people had acquiesced in the new constitution. Vote: three no, four yes, three abstentions. (4) Whether the petitioners were entitled to relief by an injunction against the executive branch. Vote: six no, four yes. (5) Whether the new charter was in force. Vote: two no, four yes, four abstentions due to lack of judicial certainty.

until new elections are held. But this apparent legitimation of the
status quo was misleading, because the court also held by six to four
(there was one vacancy in the court) that the new constitution had
not been ratified in substantial compliance with applicable constitutional and statutory provisions. On the issue of whether
the Filipinos, without a valid ratification, did in fact acquiesce in the
new constitution, the vote was indecisive—four voting in the
affirmative, three opposed, and three abstaining. If the new constitution was not validly ratified and if the court could not get enough
votes to say that the Filipino people acquiesced in it, how then could
it be in force and operation? The ultimate result was dictated by a
procedural twist which worked in this manner: Two of the six
justices[30] who voted against a valid ratification also said that there
were considerations other than judicial ones which were relevant
and unavoidable and which were beyond the competence of the
court to determine—referring to the "President's own assessment of
the will of the people as expressed through the Citizens Assemblies
and the importance of the 1973 Constitution to the successful implementation of the social and economic reforms he has started or
envisioned."[31] Therefore the court voted six to four to dismiss the
petitions. The court then concluded that "there were not enough
votes to declare that the new Constitution was not in force [note
the double negative wording]"[32] since procedurally the votes of at
least six justices were needed to declare the ratification process
unconstitutional.[33] In the instant case, only four voted for outright
unconstitutionality. Therefore, since the constitution was de facto
in operation, it continues to be in force not because it is valid but
because the necessary six votes could not be obtained to throw it
out.[34] It is here that Marcos' unilateral ratification proclamation of

30. Justices Fred Ruiz Castro and Querube Makalintal.

31. Joint opinion of Justices Makalintal and Castro, p. 15 (mimeograph).

32. The various opinions of the court on the five major issues raised in the cases
were summarized by Chief Justice Concepcion in a seventy-eight page opinion. He
then concluded that the overall result was that "there were not enough votes to
declare that the new Constitution was not in force."

33. It is of interest to note that the government argues that under the 1935
constitution, eight votes were necessary, pursuant to Art. VIII, Sec. 10, to declare
the ratification proclamation invalid. The court rejected this interpretation, holding
that this applied only to "treaty or law" and that therefore the votes of six members
of the court would have sufficed for nullification.

34. Two weeks after the Supreme Court decision was made public, counsels for
the petitioners filed a *constancia* (pleader's comment and observation on a court's
decision) with the same tribunal on the ground that "the dispositive portion of the

last January 17, 1973, assumes the proportion of a farsighted antici-
patory legal strategy.

Over the past years, the Supreme Court has been called upon to
decide cases of major significance and impact to the martial law
regime, but none equals the critical nature of the new constitution
cases. Their importance was both substantive and symbolic. Until
that time, the court had not been forced to face up to the challenge
of having to define its own role and place under martial law.
Through a blend of judicial parsimony and strategic timing by the
president, the Supreme Court had managed to postpone any authoritative pronouncement on the Marcos takeover. In the new constitution cases, the court had to confront that challenge. Its response
was to shift from its former stance as a strict and uncompromising
watchdog over the actions of the other departments of government
to that of a pliable institution that recognizes the exigencies of a
given reality and adapts to it. Once that bridge was crossed and its
self-defined role made public, subsequent cases became easier for the
court to resolve and for the citizenry to predict.

The position on the new constitution cases may be difficult to
glorify jurisprudentially and taxing to analyze legally, but its pragmatic wisdom is clear. Ultimately it was a victory for the president
in that it legitimized a fait accompli. The president lost the battle
but won the war. On the other hand, his critics also had reasons for
satisfaction. The rebuke given the president concerning the use of
an unconstitutional procedure and the court's assumption of jurisdiction despite contrary presidential directives gave them a valid
claim to a moral triumph. But the biggest beneficiary of the decision
has been the Supreme Court itself. For while sparing the president
the embarrassment of a major legal setback, it mustered enough
courage to rebuke him, albeit gently, as if to remind the president
that, martial law and the demise of Congress notwithstanding,
checks and balances still existed through the judicial branch of
government. The uncompromising posture taken by the then Chief
Justice Roberto Concepcion[35] and Justice Calixto Zaldivar against

---

Supreme Court decision was not supported by the substantive findings of the
majority members of the Tribunal." *Philippine Times,* June 15, 1973, p. 7. In a
major decision in September 1974, the court expressly ruled that the declaration of
martial law was constitutional.

35. Concepcion's decision in the new constitution cases proved to be his
valedictory. He resigned from the court a short time thereafter, two months before his

the president on all five major issues raised in the cases, and the majority vote against the president on the issue of the valid ratification of the new constitution, gave the country's constitutionalists reasons to applaud and keep their faith in the court—or at least in some of its members.

The atypically fluid and passive role taken by the court in the new constitution cases is perhaps best understood in the context of viable alternatives. Viewed realistically, what would have been the consequences of a decision adverse to the government? The decision would have had to mandate the holding of a nationwide plebiscite under conditions envisioned in the old constitution—which means voting by secret ballot, participated in only by those at least twenty-one years old, and devoid of any free-speech restraints. President Marcos would have found this difficult to accept, since it was what was originally envisioned under the January 15, 1973, plebiscite, which he had earlier postponed. Chances were that the new constitution would have been approved even under this procedure, but perhaps by a majority much smaller than the president wanted. If this was unacceptable, would the president then have risked defiance of the court's order in an effort to protect the higher interests of the New Society?

In a statement allegedly made to the American press,[36] President Marcos is reported to have said that even President Abraham Lincoln at one time during the Civil War failed to comply with the order of Chief Justice Roger Taney, obviously referring to ex parte *Merryman*.[37] In that case, decided in 1861, Taney wrote an opinion holding unconstitutional Lincoln's suspension of the privilege of the writ of habeas corpus and directed the clerk of court to send a copy to the president. The chief justice then said: "It will remain for that high officer, in fulfillment of his constitutional obligation, to take care that the laws be faithfully executed, to deter-

---

compulsory retirement at age seventy, which led to a host of speculations. One source maintains that the chief justice "quit because he could no longer withstand the outside pressure on the High Tribunal without compromising its independence and integrity." *Philippine Times,* May 15, 1973, p. 4. Poor health was given as the official reason for the resignation. Concepcion himself has not come out with further comment. This resignation set the stage for the president to reorganize the court in accordance with the provisions of the new constitution, which state that "The Supreme Court shall be composed of a chief justice and fourteen associate justices" (Art. X, Sec. 2, Par. 1). However, as of the latter part of 1975, there were only twelve justices in the supreme court, most of them Marcos appointees.

36. *Philippine Times,* Mar. 15, 1973, p. 6.
37. 17 Fed. Cases 144 (1961), No. 9487.

mine what measures he will take to cause the civil process of the United States to be respected and enforced."[38] These words fell on deaf ears as Lincoln continued anyway to exercise the power that Taney had held unconstitutional. A realistic appraisal of the relationship between the president and the Supreme Court under emergency conditions was perhaps best articulated by Clinton Rossiter when he said that "in a condition of martial necessity the President has the power to suspend the privilege of the writ of habeas corpus. The most a court or judge could do is read the President a lecture based on Ex Parte Merryman."[39] This realism was echoed by Justices Castro and Makalintal in their joint opinion when they said that "if a new government gains authority and dominance through force, it can be effectively challenged only by a stronger force; no judicial dictum can prevail against it."[40]

On a more basic level, consider the alternatives available to the president if the decision were unacceptably adverse to him. Under the new constitution, which would have been in operation de facto, the number of supreme court justices was increased from eleven to fifteen.[41] The government could then conceivably have asked for a rehearing while five new justices were appointed and sworn in. With a solid pro-Marcos bloc of four then in the court,[42] this would have assured him of at least a nine to six vote in his favor.[43] Here again, he can cite an American precedent. For did not President Franklin Roosevelt attempt to pack the U.S. Supreme Court in the 1930s when he was convinced that he had something bigger at stake than the independence of the court? But even more significantly, the transitory provisions of the new charter state that "the incumbent members of the Judiciary may continue in office until they reach the age of seventy years, *unless sooner replaced* [emphasis added]."[44] One might conjecture that the ominous message of this provision

38. As quoted in Clinton Rossiter, *The Supreme Court and the Commander in Chief* (Ithaca: Cornell University Press, 1951), p. 23.
39. Ibid., p. 25.
40. Joint opinion of Justices Castro and Makalintal (mimeograph), p. 10.
41. Art. X, Sec. 2.
42. Justices Antonio Barredo, Felix Makasiar, Felix Antonio, and Salvador Esguerra voted consistently for the government's stand in all the five major issues raised in the new constitution cases.
43. This statement is based on the factual situation prevailing at the time the cases were decided. Since then, the chief justice has resigned and President Marcos has appointed a new chief justice and other justices to the court.
44. Art. XVII, Sec. 10. Five of the six justices who said that the 1973 constitution has not been validly ratified later joined the others in taking a new oath of office under the new constitution.

may not have been lost upon the members of the Supreme Court when deliberating on the new charter cases.

The New Constitution and the Judiciary

The new constitution is a "mixed bag" for the judiciary. On the one hand, it contains innovations designed to accommodate public needs, strengthen control over the judiciary's internal operations, clarify ambiguous provisions, and expedite the disposition of cases. But it also introduces sections that hamper the flexibility of the judiciary, threaten its independence, and by conscious design relegate that body to a subordinate position vis-à-vis the two other branches of government.

To begin with, the new constitution basically preserves the judicial structure that has been in existence since the American regime. But it also introduces certain modifications. Membership in the Supreme Court has been increased from a total of eleven to fifteen. The number of justices cannot be increased or reduced by legislative fiat, thus precluding the possibility of a court-packing scheme.[45] The Supreme Court is the only judicial body of constitutional creation. All other courts are established by law and exist only at legislative discretion. Since the National Assembly has not to date been convened, there has not been any opportunity for the legislative body to effect any structural changes in the judicial setup. It must be noted, however, that the president during the transitory period also exercises the powers of the National Assembly. He can therefore revamp the judicial department or abolish it if he so desires through the expedient of an executive order.

The one significant innovation in the judicial structure is the creation of the Sandiganbayan.[46] This special court, to be established by the National Assembly, is to have jurisdiction over civil and criminal cases involving graft, corruption, and other offenses committed by public officers and employees, including those in government-owned or -controlled corporations in relation to their office, as may be determined by law. A related provision creates the office of the Tanodbayan, the Ombudsman.[47] This administrative agency receives and investigates complaints relative to public office, includ-

45. Phillippine Constitution, Art. X, Sec. 2 (1973).
46. Ibid., Art. XIII, Sec. 5 (1973).
47. Ibid., Sec. 6 (1973).

ing those in government-owned or -controlled corporations. It makes appropriate recommendations and, in case of failure of justice as defined by law, files and prosecutes cases in court.

Under the new constitution, no person may be appointed to the Supreme Court unless he is a natural-born citizen of the Philippines, at least forty years old, and has for ten years or more been a judge of a court of record or engaged in the practice of law in the Philippines.[48] The new legislative body—the National Assembly—is to prescribe the other qualifications of judges in all other courts, provided that they be natural-born citizens and members of the Philippine bar.[49]

Members of the judiciary, under the 1935 constitution, were appointed by the president with the consent of a joint congressional body—the Commission on Appointments.[50] In contrast, the 1973 constitution eliminates any form of legislative check and vests the power of appointment solely in the country's new chief executive, the prime minister.[51] The 1935 constitution was silent on the process of legislative removal of inferior court judges, but by law such was vested in the president, who in turn acted upon recommendation of the Supreme Court.[52] The new constitution takes this power away from the chief executive and lodges it solely in the Supreme Court. Justices of the Supreme Court are guaranteed tenure in office during good behavior until they reach the age of sixty-five (the retirement age was seventy under the old constitution), and can be removed only by impeachment.[53]

The jurisdiction of the Supreme Court is expressly provided for in the new constitution, while that of inferior courts is precribed by the National Assembly.[54] The highest tribunal is given the power to "exercise original jurisdiction over cases affecting ambassadors, other public ministers, and consuls" and to "review, revise, reverse,

48. Ibid., Art. X, Sec. 3 (1) (1973).
49. Ibid., Sec. 3(2) (1973).
50. Art. VIII, Sec. 5, of the 1935 constitution stated: "The members of the Supreme Court and all judges of inferior courts shall be appointed by the President with the consent of the Commission on Appointments."
51. Philippine Constitution, Art. X, Sec. 4 (1973), provides: "The members of the Supreme Court and judges of inferior courts shall be appointed by the Prime Minister."
52. University of the Philippines Law Center Constitutional Revision Project (Dilliman: University of the Philippines, 1970), p. 503.
53. Philippine Constitution, Art. VIII, Sec. 9 (1973).
54. Ibid., Art. X, Sec. 1 (1973).

modify, or affirm on appeal or certiorari, as the law or the rules of
the court may provide, final judgments and decrees of inferior courts
in specified cases."[55] These judgments and decrees include all cases
in which the constitutionality or validity of any treaty, executive
agreement, law, ordinance, or executive order or regulation is in
question; all cases involving the legality of any tax, impost, assessment, or toll, or any penalty imposed in relation thereto; all cases in
which the jurisdiction of any inferior court is in issue; all criminal
cases in which the penalty imposed is death or life imprisonment;
and all cases in which only an error or question of law is involved.[56]

The Supreme Court is expressly given the power to declare a
treaty, executive agreement, law, ordinance, or executive order unconstitutional.[57] This authorization for judicial review was also
incorporated in the 1935 constitution, which stated that "no treaty
or law may be declared unconstitutional without the concurrence of
two-thirds of all the members of the Court."[58] The new constitution
provides that "all cases involving the constitutionality of a treaty,
executive agreement, or law shall be heard and decided by the
Supreme Court *en banc,* and no treaty, executive agreement, or law
may be declared unconstitutional without the concurrence of at least
ten members."[59] The 1935 constitution provided only for "treaty or
law," hence raising doubts concerning the power of the court to
pass on the constitutionality of executive agreements. This should
now be considered settled through constitutional edict. Cases heard
by a division of the court requires the concurrence of at least five
justices in a division of seven or eight members. If the required vote
is not obtained, the case shall be decided *en banc* where the "rule of
eight" applies.[60] Cases are argued in open court, consultation is held
before reaching a decision, cases are assigned for the writing of a
majority decision, and any justice may write a concurrent or dissenting opinion.[61]

Presumably in response to persistent clamor from the public and

55. Ibid., Sec. 5 (1973).
56. Ibid.
57. Ibid., Sec. 2(a) (1973).
58. Ibid., Art. VIII, Sec. 10 (1973).
59. Ibid., Art. X, Sec. 2(2) (1973).
60. Ibid. Sec. 2, provides, inter alia: "All other cases, which under its rules are
required to be heard en banc, shall be decided with the concurrence of at least eight
members."
61. Ibid., Sec. 8 (1973).

the mass media, the new constitution gives to the Supreme Court the power of administration over all courts and their personnel.[62] It may discipline judges of inferior courts and order their dismissal by a vote of at least eight members. Although the 1935 constitution was silent on it, administrative supervision of inferior courts was previously given by statute to the executive department—a carryover of the practice during the American era when the Judiciary Division of the Department of Justice assumed extensive responsibility over court supervision.[63] The new constitution also empowers the Supreme Court to assign judges of inferior courts temporarily to other stations as public interest may require.[64] Previously the Supreme Court could only veto any temporary designation or transfer of judges to another district by the Department of Justice, but could not initiate such a transfer. A new provision also authorizes the Supreme Court to effect a change of venue to avoid a miscarriage of justice.[65] The power to promulgate rules concerning pleading, practice, and procedure in all courts has been given directly to the Supreme Court, with the proviso that such may be "repealed, altered, or supplemented" by the legislative branch.[66] In actual practice, this has resulted in an awkward overlapping of jurisdictional responsibilities and has occasionally been the source of friction between the judicial and legislative departments.

Perhaps taking a cue from recent statutes passed in state legislatures in the United States, the new constitution provides that "the maximum period within which a case or matter shall be decided or resolved from the date of its submission, shall be eighteen months for the Supreme Court, and unless reduced by the Supreme Court, twelve months for all inferior collegiate courts, and three months for all other inferior courts."[67] Should cases before the Supreme Court and intermediate appellate courts remain unresolved within

62. Ibid., Sec. 6 (1973).
63. See U.P. Law Center Project, p. 511.
64. Philippine Constitution, Art. X, Sec. 5(3) (1973), provides that the supreme court has power to "assign temporarily judges of inferior courts to other stations as public interest may require. Such temporary assignment shall not last longer than six months without the consent of the judge concerned."
65. Ibid., Sec. 5(4) (1973).
66. Ibid., Sec. 5(5) (1973), further provides: "Such rules shall provide a simplified and inexpensive procedure for the speedy disposition of cases, shall be uniform for all courts of the same grade, and shall not diminish, increase, or modify substantive rights."
67. Ibid., Sec. 11 (1973).

the prescribed period after submission thereof, the decision or resolution appealed from shall be deemed affirmed and the original
special civil actions or proceedings for habeas corpus dismissed.
Nothing is said about cases in the lower courts upon which no
action is taken within the prescribed time. If the above provision is
to be construed as mandatory, as it ought to be, then these cases
will have to be dismissed.

An analysis of the changes makes it evident that as far as the
judiciary is concerned, there has not been any radical departure from
the system previously in existence. The judicial setup has not undergone any major alteration, procedures are basically the same, and
the qualification requirements do not differ markedly from those
under the old constitution. Nonetheless, changes of potentially far-
reaching significance must be identified and briefly analyzed.

The creation of a special antigraft court, the Sandiganbayan, is an
obvious institutional response to persistent public outcries against
the endemic excesses of Philippine officialdom. Its actual results
must be seen, however, if it is to remove nagging doubts by the
public about the effectiveness of a governmental response to what
has been perceived as a traditionally political and social problem.
The new office of the Tanodbayan, or Ombudsman, formalizes a
function heretofore performed by politicians, albeit with dubious
results. Its potential for restoring public trust in the political process
will depend on its level of visibility and the confidence it can generate, through solid accomplishments, in a public that had learned
to regard government officials with a justifiably high degree of
suspicion.

The removal of any form of legislative control over the power of
appointment affords the prime minister the opportunity to pack
the court with his own protégés.[68] The change is of more than pass-
ing significance because it also reflects a conscious rejection in the
constitution of one of the salient features of the doctrine of checks
and balances. Jurisdictionally, Article X, Section 5(a), of the 1973
constitution provides that the Supreme Court shall have jurisdiction
over "all cases in which only an error or question of law is involved." This seemingly innocuous addition may in fact seriously
circumscribe the jurisdiction of the Supreme Court because now
cases which contain not "only" but "also" questions of law will have

68. Ibid., Art. VIII, sec. 2(5) (1973).

to be excluded from the jurisdiction of the Court. The new provision is certainly more restrictive in scope.

Procedurally, Article X, Section 2(2), of the new constitution states that "all other cases which under its rules are required to be heard *en banc,* shall be decided with the concurrence of at least eight members." A simple majority of those present would not suffice to decide the case. This is noteworthy because obviously the required eight votes for a decision would be difficult to obtain. Moreover, while this section specifies only one type of case—one involving the constitutionality of a treaty, executive agreement, or law—to be heard *en banc,* the court may add other cases to that category under its power to "promulgate rules concerning the pleading, practice, and procedure in all courts."[69] This carte-blanche provision insures elasticity and convenience. Without being suspicious, one can speculate on the types of cases which the court might later decide to add to the category when faced with strong internal ideological rifts and possible external pressures.[70]

The provision for an extraordinary majority of ten affirmative votes to declare a treaty, executive agreement, or law unconstitutional limits the flexibility of the court and further tilts the balance of power against the judiciary. It establishes a strong presumption in favor of the constitutionality of official acts and assures the country of a passive court on questions of national importance. In a government already characterized by the institutional predominance of the executive department and clouded by the realities of martial law, this requirement further curtails the effectiveness of the court as a constitutional watchdog.

The transfer of the power of supervision and discipline over inferior courts and their personnel from the executive department to the Supreme Court should enjoy popular endorsement and support. Under the former setup, suspicions abounded concerning undue influence on judges who were beholden to politicians for their appointment and promotion. There were pervasive charges of political favoritism and unholy alliances in the disposition of cases, particularly at the lowest court level. The new provision removes the

---

69. Ibid., Art. X, Sec. 5(5) (1973).
70. The decision in the new charter cases revealed a solid bloc of four pro-Marcos justices—Barredo, Antonio, Makasiar, and Esguerra. Four others tended to be independent—Concepcion, Zaldivar, Fernando, and Teehankee—while two were the swing men—Castro and Makalintal.

baleful effects of politics from the judiciary and places administrative control in the hands of officials who are presumably apolitical and deeply interested in preserving the integrity of that institution. The constitutional change mandating the speedy disposition of cases in all courts within a certain time will surely tax the resources and severely test the efficiency of the judiciary. Nonetheless, it should give a much-needed psychological boost to a citizenry that has recently gone through the trauma of mass arrests and experienced a more rigid, if not overzealous, implementation of existing laws. Whether or not the provision amounts to more than window dressing is still a matter of conjecture.

Three new sections in the new constitution strike a harsh blow to the already shrunken stature of the judiciary. Article X, Section 12, states that the Supreme Court, within thirty days from the opening of the regular session of the National Assembly, shall "submit to the President, the Prime Minister, and the National Assembly, an annual report on the operation and activities of the judiciary." This is indeed an undisguised attempt to relegate the judiciary to a subordinate position vis-à-vis the two other branches of government. This provision, more than anything else, constitutes the key to an understanding of the role the courts are programmed to play in the New Society.

Another section preempts the power of the judiciary to pass on the constitutionality of whatever the president did before the approval of the new constitution and pursuant to martial law. This provision states that "all proclamations, orders, decrees, instructions, and acts promulgated, issued, or done by the incumbent President shall be part of the law of the land, and shall remain valid, legal and binding, and effective even after lifting martial law or the ratification of this Constitution. . . ."[71] The approval of the constitution through the citizens assemblies therefore ipso facto validated all prior presidential acts regardless of constitutional merit and thereby deprived the Supreme Court of the power of judicial review over what must be conceded to be highly sensitive and controversial executive pronouncements.

To compound this institutional injury on the judiciary, a decree was issued by President Marcos immediately upon proclamation of martial law that removed from the jurisdiction of the judiciary all

71. Sec. 3(2) of the transitory provisions of the new constitution.

cases involving the validity, legality, or constitutionality of decrees, orders, or acts issued, promulgated, or performed by him or his designated representatives pursuant to his martial law proclamation.[72] The president also divested the judiciary of power to rule on crimes committed by public officials and those against the public order.[73] Interpreted broadly, this encompasses any and all crimes ranging from the most serious to the trivial, from subversion to vagrancy. The net result is a situation where, through executive edict, jurisdiction can be withheld from civilian courts at will and military tribunals are authorized to try anybody at any time for any crime, according to military procedures. Part of the above jurisdiction has been given back by presidential edict, but is withdrawable at any time "in the public interest."

The easy transfer of jurisdiction has led to a proliferation of military courts since martial law. Their existence has been facilitated by General Order No. 8, issued by President Marcos a few days after the martial law proclamation, which empowers the chief of staff of the armed forces "to create military tribunals to try and decide cases of military personnel and *such other cases as may be referred to them* [emphasis added]." Subsequent decrees authorize the military to assume jurisdiction over "those involving crimes against public order" and other specified crimes.[74]

The implications in the current situation deserve a further comment. By nature, military tribunals are structurally and procedurally constituted to try cases relevant to the performance of duties by members of the armed forces.[75] They are not designed to exercise jurisdiction over offenses committed by civilians—particularly when civilian courts are open, as they have been in the Philippines throughout the martial law period.[76] The inequities in a military

72. General Order No. 3. See Appendix 4 for the full text.
73. General Order No. 3 was in effect disregarded in the supreme court when it continued to assume jurisdiction over cases plainly covered by its provisions.
74. General Order No. 12, dated Sept. 30, 1972. Also General Orders Nos. 12-A, 12-B, and 12-C.
75. These military commission and provost courts are headed by a president and have one law officer each and five other members of at least the rank of a major. Each has a trial counsel, an assistant, and a prosecutor from the Department of Justice. Making up the defense panel are one defense counsel and an assistant. The accused, however, can avail himself of the services of civilian lawyers. Trials are held continuously if litigants are prepared; otherwise, postponements for one week are granted. *Philippine News,* Oct. 4, 1973, p. 16.
76. Extensive arguments impugning the constitutionality of trials by military courts of civilians have been presented in the petition filed by former senators

trial when extended to civilians should be readily apparent. Of prime concern is the fact that a military tribunal is under the president's control as commander-in-chief. By decree he may reverse, modify, or completely disregard its decision at will. This certainly emaciates the due process guarantee in the constitution.[77] Moreover, the existence of military courts with power to assume jurisdiction over any designated set of cases at any time upon order of the chief of staff or the president is nothing less than an outright takeover by the executive department of the duties and prerogatives of the judiciary. Neither the old nor the new constitution authorizes such preemption of functions, and both, in fact, affirm the existence and power of civilian courts.[78] It stands to reason that, given implicit infirmities, the creation of military tribunals with power to try nonmilitary-oriented offenses committed by civilians is at least presumptively unconstitutional. The above considerations notwithstanding, the Supreme Court on May 9, 1975, upheld the jurisdiction of military commissions to try the case against former senator Aquino. A majority of the eight justices ruled that the commission had been lawfully constituted and validly vested with jurisdiction to hear cases against civilians.[79]

Debatable though the above situation may be, the most damaging sections in the new constitution are those contained in the transitory provisions. Section 10 states that "the incumbent members of the Judiciary may continue office until they reach the age of seventy years, *unless sooner replaced in accordance with the preceding section* [emphasis added]." The "preceding section" referred to provides that "all officials and employees in the existing government . . . shall continue in office *until otherwise provided by law or decreed by the incumbent President of the Philippines. . . .*

Lorenzo Tanada and Jovito Salonga, principal counsels for former senator Benigno S. Aquino, Jr., with the supreme court seeking an injunction to stop the military tribunal from trying the criminal cases against Aquino. The arguments cite extensive Philippine and American precedents for support. See *Philippine Times,* Sept. 15, 1973, pp. 7–9.

77. Article IV of the new constitution contains the bill of rights. Section 17 states: "No person shall be held to answer for a criminal offense without due process of law." A similar provision was contained in Art. III, Sec. 1(15), of the old constitution.

78. Philippine Constitution, Art. X, Sec. 1 (1973), states that "the judicial power shall be vested in one Supreme Court and in such inferior courts as may be established by law." Nowhere in the new constitution is there any mention of military courts.

79. *Philippine Times,* July 1, 1975, p. 2.

[emphasis added]." More than three years after the approval of the new constitution, the Philippines is still in a period of transition. Since the transitory provisions are operative for an indefinite length of time, a judge may be dismissed by the president at any time by appointment of his successor without the official being told the reason for his removal or without his being informed beforehand that he was to be removed. Hence, judges who were appointed under the provisions of the old constitution (this includes most of the present judges), and who have not been allowed to take a new oath under the new constitution, have become, to use a Filipino parlance, "casuals"—a decidedly derogatory label previously reserved for partisan manual laborers who somehow managed to find temporary political employment during the height of the pork-barrel season! In his 1973 Annual Report, former justice J. B. L. Reyes, president of the newly integrated bar of the Philippines, intimated that several judges have in fact been fired from office and have asked for help from the bar, but the organization cannot intercede on their behalf because the bar could not possibly know, in the absence of an explanation from whoever ordered the removal, whether it was arbitrary or for cause.[80]

The Survival of the Court

A close scrutiny of events in the Philippines since the imposition of martial law warrants the conclusion that constitutionalism is pale and anemic, although it is by no means dead. Labels of "constitutional authoritarianism" and protestations of a "smiling martial law" barely obscure the reality of a one-man rule; neither do they help dispel the grave dangers inherent in a political system where a single person, lofty of motives though he may be, simultaneously exercises the duties and prerogatives as president under the old constitution, prime minister and president under the new constitution, and a one-man legislative body for a virtually indefinite period of time.

One question deserves to be raised: Despite his apparent exercise of limitless power, why has President Marcos taken extra care to

80. A few months after martial law was imposed, President Marcos asked for and obtained courtesy resignations from all presidential appointees including judges, with the exception of justices in the Supreme Court and the Court of Appeals (Letter of Instruction No. 11). It is presumed that these letters of resignation are still valid and that the president can act on them at any time.

project the image of constitutional rectitude as a living and vital process in the country? One can suggest converging explanations. Obviously, the admission of a blatant power grab would be dysfunctional and impolitic, for foreign as well as domestic consumption. The specter of the Philippines, long ballyhooed as the showcase of American democracy in Asia, unreservedly repudiating constitutional niceties would be traumatic to Americans as well as to Filipinos. Rejection of the American brand of democracy—yes, but the total absence of a constitutional process—no. There is need for a grasp at constitutionalism for everybody's peace of mind—including perhaps that of the president. Images and symbols sometimes become more important than reality, particularly in the Philippines. There the government's claim of constitutionalism gains easier credence in view of President Marcos' reputation as a constitutional expert and a legendary lawyer—who graduated number one in his law class at the University of the Philippines, topped a difficult bar examination with a record-breaking score despite his having to review in prison because of a lower-court conviction for the alleged fatal shooting of his father's political opponent, and capped his then incipient legal career by arguing his own case on appeal before the Supreme Court and winning an acquittal.[81] In the mind of the masses, this legal lore gives the president the benefit of the doubt on constitutional questions and with it the presumption that he must know what he is doing.

What can be gained from the Philippine experience? If nothing else, it re-stresses certain basic realities that advocates of legalism may tend to take for granted. Foremost among these is the fact that in a developing nation, a determined chief executive, acting under real or imagined national crisis and confident of military support, can effectively neutralize the judiciary as a constitutional watchdog or reduce it to virtual impotence if he so wishes. Indeed, in times of national stress, such shibboleths as "judicial independence" and "checks and balances" can be swept aside and rendered substantively inoperative. Constitutionalism can and often does take a back seat to concerns of national stability and survival. All these steps may be effected with judicial acquiescence, presumably born out of

---

81. For an interesting biography of President Marcos, see Hartzell Spence, *For Every Tear a Victory: The Story of Ferdinand E. Marcos* (New York: McGraw-Hill, 1964).

necessity. For beneath its veneer of prominence, the judiciary is in actuality a weak and dependent institution that must lean on the executive for substance and support. In the traditional American tripartite system of government, the concept of coequal branches is less than a meaningful reality. It is merely a concept worth aspiring for. American history tells us that as far back as 1832, President Andrew Jackson, in a fit of anger over a Supreme Court decision that he strongly disapproved, was heard to have said (referring to the then chief justice): "John Marshall has made his decision; now let him enforce it."[82] When the chips are down, that disdainful statement becomes more than a classic joke told in political science classes. It becomes a reflection of reality.

From the Philippine experience, one also realizes that U.S. Chief Justice Charles Evans Hughes's dictum, about the constitution being what the judges say it is, is much more than a catchy constitutional adage. It can become a convenient vehicle for adaptation and improvisation. The art of interpretation, as lawyers well know, has many phases and lends itself to various techniques, including that which takes into account stark realism as opposed to abstract ideals at a given time. When that happens, the dilemma becomes one of balancing unpleasant alternatives. Must the judiciary adapt to insure survival, or should it stand unyielding and take the full measure of an omnipotent executive's wrath?[83]

82. See *Justice in America: Courts, Lawyers, and the Judicial Process*, by Herbert Jacob (Boston: Little, Brown, 1972), p. 214.

83. In a speech delivered before the Philippine Bar Association and Philippine Lawyers Association at the Manila Hilton Hotel Feb. 19, 1974, former chief justice Querube C. Makalintal (who together with Justice Castro tilted the balance in favor of dismissal in the new charter cases) made this interesting postscript: "It would be interesting, were it not so morbid, to speculate on what would have happened if the Supreme Court had refused to recognize the effectivity of the new Constitution and resolved to continue functioning pursuant to the oath its members had taken to uphold and defend the 1935 Constitution. *Considering the political situation at the time, the government conceivably could have become, in theory at least, a revolutionary one.* Even the wisdom of hindsight cannot now enlighten us as to the consequences that would have ensued: among others, in respect of our foreign relations; of the program of land reform; of the tax measures that have since been proven quite successful; of foreign investments; of the overall peace and order situation; *indeed, of the role of the entire judiciary in that government* [emphasis added]." *Philippine Times*, Mar. 31, 1974, p. 5. A more biased view of the Supreme Court's dilemma is given by Primitivo Mijares, a former close adviser and confident of Marcos who has since become a defector and a bitter critic of the president: "One of the means which the President has found most effective to bend the will of the Supreme Court to his liking is the scheme of his calculated leaks on his plans for the high court should he ever be rebuffed by the judiciary. Every time the

The Philippine Supreme Court has made its choice and, like the proverbial Oriental bamboo, it has understandably chosen to bend with the wind in an effort to survive. With its pinions clipped and its head slightly bowed in situational submission, the court can be said to have experienced and passed the apex of its institutional crisis. On the balance sheet, the court has done the president more service than disservice, more good than harm. As long as the court stays tractable, the president will find it in his interest to keep it open and operational. Travails and setbacks notwithstanding, the Philippine Supreme Court is there to stay. This is much more than can be said of the hitherto powerful Philippine Congress, which has long since been consigned by the president to an extended period of forced rest. Be that as it may, the ultimate concern is whether or not the president, given current circumstances, is operating under the "rule of law." That is a difficult question which only he can meaningfully answer, not through what he says, but through what he does in the difficult months, years, or perhaps decades ahead.

---

high court would be called upon to decide a suit against the President or the regime, he would mount a forum to warn the justices that an assertion of judicial independence would result in the loss of their jobs. The message is usually beamed in this wise: If the President did not draw the support of all sectors, *he might be compelled to dismantle the existing apparatus of martial law and give way to the inevitable establishment of a revolutionary government run by a military junta* [emphasis added]." *Philippine News*, Mar. 6–12, 1975, p. 2.

3. Land Reform: Emancipation or Counterinsurgency?

BENEDICT J. KERKVLIET

UNIVERSITY OF HAWAII

Standing in the crowded and richly decorated Maharlika Hall in the presidential palace, Ferdinand Marcos proclaimed "The Emancipation of Tenants from the Bondage of the Soil." At the climax of this Presidential Decree No. 27, he said, "Now, therefore, I, Ferdinand E. Marcos, President of the Philippines, by virtue of the powers vested in me . . . do hereby decree and order the emancipation of all tenant farmers as of this day, October 21, 1972." The date was exactly one month after the president had proclaimed martial law in the country. Flashbulbs popped, television cameras whirred, and the entourage of cabinet officers and other dignitaries smiled and applauded vigorously. Many people in the audience did, too, especially the young men and women who sat on the floor in front of the president and who looked more like students than farmers. But older men who were peasants, standing at the back of the room, appeared bewildered. As they returned in military trucks to their small homes in the countryside, they must have wondered: What does this decree really mean?

It is a legitimate question. My investigation, based on newspaper articles, government reports, scholarly studies of this and earlier Philippine land reforms, and studies of agrarian programs elsewhere in the Third World, has led me to the following findings. President Marcos' government has accomplished more land reform between 1973 and 1976 than it did during the preceding seven years. Its program, however, closely parallels previous land reform plans of Philippine governments. Those attempts brought little improvement for the peasantry, mainly owing to four conditions in Philippine politics, conditions that have persisted during martial law. First, the purpose of land reform is to protect the regime from rural unrest rather than to redistribute substantially wealth and political power to villagers. Second, Filipino elites design and administer the agrarian program with scarcely any participation from villagers, while landlords either resist its implementation or try to manipulate it in order to protect their own interests. Third, largely because of the first two conditions, the scope of land reform is narrow. Only a small fraction of all peasants can potentially benefit. Finally, many of those villagers who conceivably could benefit and own their land probably will lose out in the long run. In sum, the agrarian reform program in the Philippines seems headed for the same fate that has befallen other such programs in similar regimes—a little improvement for a few rural people but continued poverty and oppression for most.

Land Reform Accomplishments

President Marcos contends that his martial law regime is a "revolution from the center" to create the "New Society." A vital part of this revolution is land reform. "Mr. Marcos is building the new Filipino society on the bedrock of land reform," said a Sunday *New York Times* advertisement supplement paid for by the Philippine government.[1] On the first anniversary of Presidential Decree (PD) 27, Marcos put it this way: "The land reform program is the only gauge for the success or failure of the New Society. If land reform fails, there is no New Society." When he summarized his government's achievements after one year of martial law, Marcos stated that "easily the most meaningful reform in the society is the emancipation of the farmer from his age-old bondage to the soil."[2]

Marcos' "emancipation" announcement of October 21, 1972, and various other decrees and official documents furnish the outline of the program.[3] Agrarian reform promises a "family size plot" of land to all tenants farming rice and corn. Although official estimates vary as to how many tenant families this includes, the commonly accepted figure is 1 million who farm between 1.3 million and 1.5

1. "Philippine Prospects," advertisement supplement, *New York Times*, June 10, 1973, p. 4.
2. *Daily Express* (Manila), Oct. 23, 1973, p. 1; Sept. 22, 1973, p. 6.
3. The major presidential decrees and related documents regarding land reform through July 1973 are published in F. D. Pinpin, comp. and ed., *Philippine Laws on Agrarian Reforms* (Manila: Cacho Hermanos, 1973). Others since then are printed in several volumes under the general title *Proclamation No. 1081 and Related Documents*, with the same compiler and publisher.

million hectares (1 hectare equals 2.47 acres). "Family size plot," according to PD 27, means three hectares of irrigated land or five hectares of unirrigated land. Before actually owning land, however, tenants must: pay for the land within fifteen years; join a government-sponsored cooperative and contribute to a fund that will guarantee the amortization payment of any member who defaults; adopt modern farming practices (including high-yielding varieties of seed); and pay real estate taxes on the land.[4] The former landowners will be compensated either by the tenants in fifteen yearly installments plus 6 percent interest, or through one of several other plans in which the government acts as a middleman and banker.

Lined up behind the Office of the President to administer the program is the Department of Agrarian Reform (DAR). Its 5,400 employees, 88 percent of whom are divided into 200 agrarian reform teams across the country, oversee projects ranging from land surveys by aerial photography to the distribution of "land-transfer certificates" to tenants. Working with the DAR on agrarian programs are numerous agencies, including the Department of Agriculture, Department of Local Government, and the Central Bank. Also assisting, with money and advisors, is the Manila mission of the United States Agency for International Development (USAID).

The government chose a "programmed," multistage approach rather than a large-scale, single-stage approach to redistribute large landholdings. It focused first on landlords who owned over 100 hectares, and then on owners with 24 to 50 hectares. Least affected thus far are owners with less than 24 hectares, although technically speaking all landowners with more than 7 hectares farmed by tenants lie within the scope of land redistribution. The government's principal yardstick to measure achievement is the number of tenants who have received land-transfer certificates. As of November 1975, 206,146 tenants farming 363,238 hectares had received these certificates.[5] In early 1974, a few of these peasants began to pay for their lands.[6] In order to assure that landlords are adequately reimbursed

4. As outlined by Conrado F. Estrella, Secretary of the Agrarian Reform Department, in *Bulletin Today* (Manila), Oct. 23, 1973, p. 10.

5. Philippines, Department of Agrarian Reform, "Summary: Operation Land Transfer, as of November 3, 1975" (Quezon City: 1975), p. 1.

6. For accounts of early payments and compensation to landlords, see *Bulletin Today*, Mar. 22, 1974, p. 1, and May 30, 1974, p. 1.

for their land, the government established the Land Bank with an authorized capital stock of P3 billion.[7]

Land reform, however, is but one part of the government's "integrated" approach to rural development. According to DAR publications, other components of the "reform package" include easy loans to small farmers, agricultural extension services, infrastructure improvements such as irrigation systems and feeder roads, and government-sponsored rural cooperatives. The major example of the other components is "Masagana-99," under which 600,000 rice farmers have borrowed between P600 million and P1 billion each year between 1973 and 1975. The figures far surpass previous similar government loan programs. With these loans, rice growers purchase chemical fertilizers, insecticides, and other additives. Their average crop yields have risen from 60 to 78 cavans per hectare (1 cavan equals 110.2 pounds).[8] By integrating land redistribution with other rural projects, the government expects peasants' living conditions to improve and the country to become self-sufficient in rice and corn. By 1976, the government predicted that the Philippines would have its first rice surplus in years.[9]

The Marcos government realizes that it cannot independently finance land reform and related projects; it has sought assistance especially from the United States and the World Bank.[10] In keeping with a five-year (1974–1979) agricultural development plan it drafted with the Philippine government, the United States, for instance, has financed over P75 million for agricultural loans to farmers each year since 1973, underwrites a P528 million irrigation project in Central Luzon, pays a large share of a multimillion-peso rural development scheme in the Bicol region of Luzon, and sub-

7. Conrado F. Estrella, "A Comprehensive Report to the President of the Philippines" (Quezon City: Department of Agrarian Reform, Oct. 2, 1973), p. 7.

8. *Bulletin Today*, Nov. 28, 1973, p. 20; *Times Journal* (Manila), Jan. 7, 1974, p. 16; *Wall Street Journal*, Nov. 18, 1974, p. 1; *Manila Journal* (international edition), Apr. 26, 1975, p. 12. The name "Masagana-99" comes from the project's goal to increase participating farmers' yields to 99 cavans per hectare.

9. *Honolulu Star Bulletin*, Dec. 25, 1975. For an analysis skeptical of the government's claims to rice self-sufficiency, see Philip Bowring, "Rice Self-Sufficiency Claim May Be Premature," *Far Eastern Economic Review*, Mar. 28, 1975, pp. 43–45.

10. See, for instance, "Financial Aspects of Land Reform," memorandum from the Central Bank of the Philippines, c. early 1973; and *Bulletin Today*, July 24, 1974, p. 18. The memo estimates the government will need foreign assistance for 60 percent of its rural infrastructure projects.

sidizes a nationwide rural electrification program costing more than P400 million through 1977.[11]

Government officials acknowledge weaknesses in the land reform program. "Five major problems" Secretary of Agrarian Reform Conrado Estrella cites are sluggish agrarian courts, too few cooperatives, too few DAR field teams, an inadequate number of lawyers to assist tenants, and low wages for DAR employees who often take higher-paying jobs elsewhere.[12] The DAR field staff, for instance, is spread thinly; each person is responsible, on the average, for 245 hectares and 200 tenants.[13] Estrella and his colleagues contend these limitations are small, however, compared to the accomplishments outlined above. Under martial law, they say, the government has achieved more land reform than all previous administrations combined.

True enough, pre-martial law governments all but ignored the numerous agrarian laws dating from the 1930s. Several reasons explain why the laws were weak and unenforced and why agrarian reforms have never substantially improved villagers' lives. Judging from available evidence, however, the same major reasons continue to apply during martial law.

Land Reform as Counterinsurgency

Previous agrarian reforms were never intended to reduce significantly the chasm between peasants and elites. Instead, the purpose of land redistribution and related programs was to undercut existing or potential agrarian unrest. This was as true for President Manuel Quezon's "Social Justice" program in the 1930s, when peasant activism was sweeping Central Luzon, as it was in the 1950s, when Filipino officials and American advisors were desperately trying to halt the Huk rebellion. As one scholar concluded from official Filipino policy in the early post-World War II years,

11. Interview with a USAID official, State Department, Washington, D.C., Jan. 29, 1974; *Bulletin Today*, Sept. 30, 1973, p. 12; *Business Day International* (Manila) Aug. 11, 1975, p. 16; *Bulletin Today*, Nov. 6, 1973, p. 1; *Times Journal* (international edition), Mar. 2, 1974, p. 1; *Business Day International*, Apr. 7, 1975, p. 18.
12. Paul Strauss, "Manila's Mixed Results," *Far Eastern Economic Review*, Sept. 26, 1975, pp. 49–50, 52.
13. J. Eliseo Rocamora and Corazon Conti-Panganiban, *Rural Development Strategies: The Philippine Case* (Quezon City: Institute of Philippine Culture, Ateneo de Manila University, 1975), p. 113.

"There was no desire on the part of the government to transform the structure of agrarian society; . . . [Presidents Roxas and Quirino] wanted to reduce unrest without changing the system."[14] A principal architect of Ramon Magsaysay's agrarian programs in the 1950s candidly described the resettlement programs (EDCOR), artesian well projects, and "civic action" as parts of the "psych war aimed at the soft core of the Huk movement."[15] Although President Magsaysay and some others in the government may have become more interested later in land reform as a means to significant changes, most Filipino politicians and U.S. State Department advisors intended to concede only enough legislation and funding for agrarian projects to keep rural discontent to a manageable level.[16]

The Marcos regime's intentions are the same. The justification for martial law in the first place was to counter an allegedly dangerous threat of revolution by the New People's Army and other "Communist" groups. Emphasizing land reform, therefore, became an obvious choice because, as Marcos and his cabinet members have frequently said, antagonistic relationships between tenants and landlords cause agrarian revolts. Roy Prosterman, an American who advised the Marcos government on land reform, put it in this way: "Land ownership [through land reform] is the one thing that stops insurgents cold."[17] If the government can stop or at least reduce rural unrest, it will have avoided a major source of instability.

Political stability is necessary not only to stay in power but also to attract large amounts of foreign investments. One keystone of the Marcos administration's policies since martial law has been to prime economic development with foreign investments, and a principal

14. David O. D. Wurfel, "The Bell Report and After: A Study of the Political Problems of Social Reform Stimulated by Foreign Aid" (Ph.D dissertation, Cornell University, 1960), pp. 440–41.

15. Interview with Jose Crisol, Secretary of Defense during the administration of President Magsaysay, Quezon City, Philippines, Dec. 15, 1969.

16. For more details and substantiation on this point, see Frances L. Starner Magsaysay and the Philippine Peasantry (Berkeley: University of California Press, 1961), esp. pp. 186–98; John L. Cooper, The Philippine Agricultural Land Tenure Study (Manila: USOM-FOA, March 1954); James P. Emerson, Land Reform Progress in the Philippines 1951–1955 (Manila: U.S. International Cooperation Administration, 1956); and Al McCoy, "Land Reform as Counter-Revolution," Bulletin of Concerned Asian Scholars 3 (Winter-Spring 1970), 27–30.

17. Quoted in Jack Daughty, "A Call for U.S. Aid to the Philippines," Seattle Post-Intelligencer, Nov. 13, 1972, p. 1. Also see Roy L. Prosterman, "Land Reform as Foreign Aid," Foreign Policy 6 (Spring 1972), 121–41.

attraction for foreign businessmen is the government's steps to assure "peace and order" in the cities and countryside.[18]

Similarly, the government uses land reform to disarm its critics. This is the first time the republic has known martial law. Political and economic power have been concentrated in even fewer hands than before, the military have assumed a major role in national and local government, civil liberties are nearly dead, and foreigners permeate the economy more than before.[19] None of these things would have been possible prior to martial law, certainly not without an uproarious national debate and broad-based dissent. But government programs like land reform, which the government-controlled media publicize uncritically, have persuaded many people, inside and outside the Philippines, to support the regime or at least not actively oppose it. A USAID official captured this sentiment when he said, "I'm not too hot on supporting dictatorships, although we [the U.S. government] seem to be doing this more and more. But it makes it easier to do so when they have programs like the land reform that the Philippine government has."[20]

Land reform, therefore, is a means the government uses to maximize stability and its legitimacy with minimum concessions to the rural masses at the expense of wealthy elites and foreign investors. This is the reform's major political goal. It implies that the regime will push land distribution only far enough to keep unrest below a tolerable level or until the reform jeopardizes higher priorities. The president's previous record on land reform, the government's attitude toward reform advocates, and the pace of implementation support this argument, as does the reform's narrow scope, which will be discussed in a later section.

18. Corporate Information Center (CIC) of the National Council of Churches of Christ, USA, *The Philippines: American Corporations, Martial Law, and Underdevelopment* (New York: IDOC/North American Edition, no. 57, November 1973), pp. 28, 31.

19. Among available studies that have compiled evidence that supports this contention are the chapters by David A. Rosenberg and Robert B. Stauffer in this book; Association of Major Religious Superiors in the Philippines, "Summary of National Survey [to investigate Martial Law]" (mimeograph, Nov. 26, 1973), portions published in *Pahayag* (Honolulu) no. 14 (January 1974) and in *Philippine Times* (Chicago), Dec. 31, 1973; Charles F. Thomson, five-part story on the Philippines, *Philadelphia Evening Bulletin*, Jan. 20–24, 1974; and Civil Liberties Union of the Philippines, *Three Years of Martial Law* (Makati, Rizal: 1975).

20. USAID official, interview, Jan. 29, 1974.

Marcos' Record

Because of his record, it is difficult to believe President Marcos will emancipate all tenants and destroy the landed elites. He was president of the country for nearly seven years (1966–1972) before martial law, and basically the same land reform laws were on the books then as now.[21] And on many occasions he promised land reform. In 1966, for example, he said, "There is no turning back, I will not hesitate to use military funds if necessary to push through the land reform program."[22] And in August 1970 he was still saying, "Land reform . . . will be the central program of the government under this administration. . . . It shall be the central point, the beacon towards which all programs of government must converge. The other programs must provide support to land reform."[23]

Yet the evidence shows that the President's actions were far weaker than his words. For example, a study for USAID reports, "When President Marcos became President in 1966, he announced that he would convert 350,700 tenants into leasees by the end of 1969. As of September 30, 1968, 13,377 farmers had obtained lease-hold contracts and on December 31, 1969, 28,616 farmers had such contracts."[24] Another USAID report concluded that by the end of 1970, "the land reform program was found to be in its seventh year of operation with fewer than 2 percent of the nation's small farmers having received any tangible benefits from the program."[25] One year later the president had designated only 236 of the nation's 1,506

21. All major components of the martial law land reform program—the Department of Agrarian Reform, the Land Bank, the conversion of rice and corn tenants to small landowners, the government-sponsored cooperatives, and the expansion of credit services—are contained in the Agricultural Land Reform Code of 1963 (Republic Act 3844), as amended in 1971 (RA 6389), and supporting laws. In some respects those laws were stronger from the peasantry's viewpoint than the current decrees. For example, they allowed tenants twenty-five years to buy their land rather than only fifteen, and they protected the peasants' right to collective bargaining and to form their own unions. For the text of RA 3844, see Philippines, The Agricultural Tenancy Commission, *The Land Reform Primer* (Manila: Bureau of Printing, 1965). For RA 6389, see Pinpin, *Philippine Laws on Agrarian Reforms*, pp. 63–155.

22. Cited in Conrado F. Estrella, *The Democratic Answer to the Philippine Agrarian Problem* (Manila: Solidaridad, 1969), p. 79.

23. Cited on the cover of a Philippine government and USAID publication "Land Reform: Integrated Development Program for Nueva Ecija" (Manila: c. 1971).

24. Harold D. Koone and Lewis E. Gleeck, "Land Reform in the Philippines," *USAID Spring Review of Land Reform, Country Papers* (Washington, D.C.: June 1970), p. 47.

25. Philippine government and USAID, "Land Reform," p. 7.

municipalities as "land reform areas."[26] Of the 180,000 shares tenants in those 236 municipalities, only 53,000 were actually affected; and 69 percent of them were in one province, Nueva Ecija (thirty-one municipalities), where USAID and the Philippine government had concentrated a land reform "pilot project" beginning in 1971.[27]

After declaring martial law and abolishing the Congress, Marcos claimed that the legislative branch had obstructed his land reform program by refusing to appropriate sufficient funds. The record, however, shows that even though the amount appropriated between 1965 and 1972 was small (P1.3 billion) the amount that the executive branch actually released for spending was even smaller—less than P52 million or 32 percent of the appropriated amount.[28]

Frances Starner, who carefully studied earlier land reform efforts, reports that even in the 1950s, Marcos, who was then a congressman, was one of the most vocal critics of the agrarian reform legislation of the Magsaysay administration.[29] Today he is also one of the largest landholders in the country. Reportedly, among the agricultural lands of Marcos and his family are 20,000 hectares in Cagayan Province, 10,000 hectares in Isabela Province, the Carlota sugar estate and sugar centrals in Negros Occidental, and several hundred hectares in Davao, other parts of Mindanao, and Panay. But the land reform program that Marcos now affirms, does not touch these holdings. In fact, reliable reports say that the president and his family use the courts to take land for themselves from small owners.

Attitude toward Reformists

The government that espouses radical land reform has also imprisoned outspoken advocates of land redistribution—leaders of large peasant unions such as the Malayang Samahang Magsasaka (MASAKA) and Federation of Free Farmers (FFF), Senator Jose Diokno, Father Edward Gerlock, and Father Edicio de la Torre,

---

26. Philippines, National Land Reform Council, *Accomplishments of Land Reform Project Administration: Terminal Report, June 1964–September 1971* (Manila: c. 1971), p. 19.

27. Ibid.; and Basilio N. de los Reyes, "Can Land Reform Succeed?" in Frank Lynch, ed., *View from the Paddy* (Quezon City: Institute of Philippine Culture, Ateneo de Manila University, 1972), p. 84.

28. National Land Reform Council, *Accomplishments of Land Reform*, p. 30.

29. Frances Starner, "The Waterbug Psyche: Philippines," *Far Eastern Economic Review*, Jan. 21, 1974, p. 31.

to mention only a few. When Gerlock was arrested, for example, he was helping peasants in Mindanao oppose large banana producers who, he said, had "bulldozed people right off the land."[30] In addition, the government allows villagers to join only its own peasant organizations; all other peasant unions are illegal. And by presidential decree the government has outlawed demonstrations, labor strikes, and similar actions. Yet, from as far back as the 1930s to the most recent land reform law in 1971, peasant organizations and their marches, court cases, strikes, and pickets provided the major impetus for land reform in the Philippines. The belief that agrarian reform was possible through legal and nonviolent means was largely due to the continued political activities of peasant organizations. For example, Akira Takahashi, well known for his studies in Central Luzon, wrote in 1971 that even though the landed class would react strongly against agrarian reform, "This response can be contained by the legislative framework and the posture of the judiciary, and, *more basically, by peasant organizations and movements* [emphasis added]."[31] Even the current secretary of the Department of Agrarian Reform wrote in 1969 that the positive conditions to balance off numerous obstacles to land reform were "free assembly, free speech, and a free press."[32] These freedoms, however, do not exist under martial law.

Pace of Implementation

Inconsistencies and delays in implementation reflect the government's desire to enjoy a reputation for distributing land without doing much of it. DAR officials and Marcos himself have vacillated on such significant points as the guidelines for implementing the reform, the number of hectares landlords may retain, the amount of land tenants will get, and the completion date. In early 1973 the government announced that the "rules and regulations" which detail the mechanics for implementing reform had been formulated. But not until July 1975 were they actually completed.[33] Originally Marcos also vowed that landowners might retain up to 7 hectares if

30. *Washington Star-News*, Nov. 25, 1973, p. A15. Diokno and Gerlock are no longer in prison, but government police keep them under surveillance.
31. Akira Takahashi, "The Peasantization of Kasama Tenants," in Lynch, *View from the Paddy*, p. 133.
32. Estrella, *Democratic Answer*, p. 62.
33. *Manila Journal* (international edition), July 19, 1975, p. 2.

they farmed the land themselves. Within a few months, however, he changed the amount to 50 hectares and then later to 24 hectares. Only in late 1974 did the government return to the 7-hectares limitation, but it eliminated the self-cultivation stipulation. The owner could now keep tenants to farm his land. In 1972, Marcos decreed that all tenants would own between 3 and 5 hectares of land. But, DAR officials later admitted, this is arithmetically impossible because only 1.5 hectares of rice and corn land exist for 1 million tenants. Officials then announced that they would make amends for insufficient land by transferring tenants to virgin or underused lands in Mindanao and elsewhere. But aside from the unlikelihood that such resettlement is feasible, the scheme is already compromised because Marcos and other officials have said that "landowners whose big estates have been expropriated under the agrarian reform program would be given the first crack at the exploitation of these virgin agricultural lands."[34] In 1973, government officials promised that all rice and corn tenants would own land by the end of that year. Later they revised this to 1975. But in 1975, they said they needed until late 1977 to distribute all land-transfer certificates (not titles) to qualified tenants.

Indeed, if the rate at which the DAR distributed certificates in 1975 continues, it will take another fourteen years before less than half of the 1 million tenants get them.[35] The 206,000 tenants with certificates as of late 1975 represented less than a quarter of all rice and corn tenants and less than half of approximately 440,000 tenants farming for landlords with over seven hectares. A large number of these recipients live in Central Luzon, scene of the Huk rebellion twenty years ago, where the government has concentrated its reform activities.

Because, as one observer sympathetic to the reform has noted, the certificates "are almost meaningless until land has been valued and amortization has begun," the number of tenants paying for their

34. *Bulletin Today,* May 16, 1973, p. 1. Also see report in Bernard Wideman, "The New Society at Home: Philippines," *Far Eastern Economic Review,* Dec. 31, 1973, p. 18.

35. Strauss, *Far Eastern Economic Review,* Sept. 26, 1975. Strauss provides a table showing monthly printings of certificates for 1973–1975. Also see Tsutomu Takigawa, "A Note on the Agrarian Reform in the Philippines under the New Society" (Quezon City: Discussion Paper No. 74-17, Institute of Economic Development and Research, School of Economics, University of the Philippines, Oct. 5, 1974), pp. 17-25.

lands is a better indication of implementation.[36] After three years, October 1972 to November 1975, 15,400 tenants had begun to pay for the 29,000 hectares to which they held certificates.[37] They represent less than 2 percent of all rice and corn tenants, and 3.5 percent of those tenants whose landlords own more than 7 hectares. At this rate, eighty-five years will pass before all qualified tenants begin to amortize. In the meantime, they continue to pay rent to their landlords. The number of landowners compensated as of November 1975 was 550—less than .2 percent of the roughly 350,000 owners of rice and corn lands or 1.5 percent of the 38,000 landlords with more than 7 hectares of rice and corn lands.[38]

DAR officials sometimes attribute the unmet deadlines and sluggish implementation to landlords' resistance to reform redistribution. Because the Marcos government prides its reform for being "compassionate" to landowners, it cannot push them too hard, too fast. Meanwhile, the piecemeal approach and the fluctuating exemptions give "the owners time and incentive to backdate their titles and to parcel out their holdings illegally to relatives in hopes that the loopholes . . . would eventually be sufficient to avoid losses."[39] Said one foreign land reform expert, "With a reform like this, time is of essence. The longer the reform drags out, the more difficult it is to implement, the more abuses and resistance there are, and the more negotiation and arbitration it takes."[40]

Landlord Opposition and Domination

Perhaps the most widely cited cause for the failure of previous land reform efforts in the Philippines is the control of the political

36. William Overholt, "Report of Meeting: Land Reform in the Philippines," Southeast Asia Advisory Development Advisory Group (SEADAG) seminar, Baguio, Philippines, Apr. 24–26, 1975, p. 25.

37. Department of Agrarian Reform, "Summary: Operation Land Transfer," Nov. 3, 1975, p. 1.

38. Ibid. The figures 350,000 and 38,000 come from *Bulletin Today* (Manila), Mar. 13, 1974, p. 24, and an open letter from Wolf Ladejinsky to Secretary Conrado F. Estrella, Oct. 7, 1974, first published in the *Wall Street Journal* and reprinted in the Association of Major Religious Superiors in the Philippines (AMRSP), *Various Reports*, Dec. 20, 1974, p. 2. Probably most of the 550 compensated landlords are among the 6,000 owning more than 24 hectares (and 40 percent of all tenanted land).

39. Joseph Lelyveld, "Despite Marcos Vow, Few Tenant Farmers Get Land," *New York Times*, Mar. 14, 1975. Lelyveld's article is also one of several sources for quotes from Secretary Estrella and other officials emphasizing that the government must show compassion toward landlords.

40. Quoted in Daniel Southerland, "Philippines On-going Land Reform," *Christian Science Monitor*, Dec. 17, 1975.

system by the landed elite.[41] Sometimes landed interests have blat-
antly obstructed agrarian reform, as when landed families in the
countryside use private armies to harass tenants who advocate land
reform or join peasant unions. More commonly, though, elite Filipinos have been more subtle. For example, land reform laws have
typically included provisions that work to the advantage of even
the largest landowners—provisions such as the retention limit of 500
hectares in the 1956 law or the "self-cultivation" clause in the 1963
law that permitted landowners to replace tenants with machinery
and wage laborers. Previous land reform laws and administrative
guidelines have also left considerable interpretation to the courts
and bureaucracies, which the landed interests, with their sophistication, education, political pull, and wealth, could use to their advantage much more readily than most villagers could. Agrarian reform
agencies, too, have generally remained in the hands of the elite, with
little or no input from the peasantry.

Under martial law, large and medium-size landlords continue to
obstruct agrarian reform. Some resist outright. Shortly after Marcos
issued PD 27, the DAR reported: "We have received reports that
there are many landowners who are ejecting their tenants in violation of the . . . order of the President." Some landowners forced
tenants to sign on as farm laborers to evade PD 27; others filed
"criminal charges against their tenants to coerce them to leave";
and they used other methods "too many to list." That was in January 1973. Violations continued the following month and included, for example, "physical acts of dispossession like bulldozing
of farms, demolition and/or burning of houses, manhandling, maul-

41. See, for example, for pre-World War II, Jim Richardson, "Does Grass-Roots
Action Lead to Agrarian Reform?" in Lynch, *View from the Paddy*, pp. 143–50;
Loretta M. Sicat, "Quezon's Social Justice Program and the Agrarian Problem"
(master's thesis, University of Philippines, 1959); and Benedict J. Kerkvliet, "Peasant
Society and Unrest Prior to the Huk Revolution in the Philippines" *Asian Studies* 9
(August 1971) 172–204. For post-World War II, see Edison I. Cabacungan, "A
Study of the Philippine Land Reform Code of 1963" (Ph.D. dissertation, Virginia
Polytechnic Institute, 1969); Estrella, *Democratic Answer*; Jeremias U. Montemayor,
"Progress and Problems of Land Reform in the Philippines," in James Brown and
Sein Lin, eds., *Land Reform in Developing Countries* (Hartford, Conn.: University
of Hartford, 1968), pp. 199–222; Francis J. Murray, Jr., "Land Reform in the
Philippines: An Overview," in Lynch, *View from the Paddy*, pp. 151–68; Starner,
Magsaysay; Gerald C. Wheelock, "Structural Determinants of the Distribution of
Rural Credit Institutions in the Philippines, 1950–1970" (Ph.D. dissertation, Cornell
University, 1972); Wurfel, "The Bell Report"; and Kerkvliet, *The Huk Rebellion:
A Study of Peasant Revolt in the Philippines* (Berkeley: University of California
Press, 1977), Chapters 4–5.

ing, intimidation, etc."[42] Despite DAR warnings, the landlords persisted. A religious group's national survey in October 1973 found that "landowners throughout the country resist the implementation of the land reform program. There have been numerous accounts of harassments and threats [and] outright evictions of tenants . . . throughout all eleven regions of the country. . . . Politicians and government officials are generally not in favor of land reform."[43]

President Marcos finally announced a decree (PD 316) in October to prohibit the evictions. But they continued. In December 1973, Secretary Estrella asked landowners to "desist from filing charges against their tenants" and ejecting them; he did the same thing six months later.[44] In October 1974, a researcher wrote: "The resistance and sabotage offered by the landowners to the agrarian reform program have become stronger and [have] taken various forms today. . . . The most common practice used by the landowner is to file criminal charges against his tenants to the local courts, whatever the reasons may be. After this, it often happens that the tenants are arrested and put in jail by the police."[45] Despite these violations, no landowners have been arrested.

Subtle resistance to land redistribution is even more pervasive. Among the landowners' methods are subdividing their farms among their children in order to break large holdings into small ones but keep them in the family, converting rice and corn lands to sugarcane and other crops not covered by PD 27, turning lands into subdivisions for residential lots, mortgaging their lands to associations or corporations not affected by land reform, or charging rents on tenants' house lots.[46] Most of the day-to-day implementation of agrarian reform is left to the DAR agents in the provinces, who, in addition to probably being underpaid and undertrained,[47] also

---

42. DAR Memorandum from Secretary Conrado R. Estrella to All Regional Directors, Jan. 9, 1973; and Agrarian Department Memorandum, Circulars No. 2 and 2-A from Secretary Conrado F. Estrella to All Regional Directors et al., Feb. 14 and 15, 1973. Reprinted in Pinpin, *Philippine Laws on Agrarian Reform*, pp. 37–43.

43. Major Religious Superiors, "Summary of National Survey," p. 2.

44. *Bulletin Today*, Dec. 18, 1973. Also see Wideman, *Far Eastern Economic Review*, Dec. 31, 1973, p. 18, and *Times Journal* (international edition), June 29, 1974, p. 2.

45. Takigawa, "A Note on Agrarian Reform," p. 71.

46. Ibid., esp. pp. 75–84; Lelyveld, *New York Times*, Mar. 14, 1975; and David Wurfel, "Preliminary Report on Research into Philippine Agrarian Policy in 1974," paper presented to the Institute of Philippine Culture, Ateneo de Manila University, Quezon City, August 1974.

47. A study of land reform administration in the Philippines during 1970–1971

have to get along with local elites, most of whom are landowners themselves. Not surprisingly, therefore, a nationwide study in October 1973 found that while DAR agents rarely side openly with the landlords, "they are accused of tolerating the abuses of the latter and giving into political pressure. They are very often blamed for making amicable settlements between landlords and tenants, disadvantageous to the tenants."[48]

DAR agents also have to cooperate with local detachments of the military, which help to administer numerous projects that previously were considered civilian, including land reform. Not only do some officers own land (especially in the seven to thirty-hectare range), but the Philippine Constabulary (PC) and army detachments have historically been allied with local elites and only rarely have been known to side with the peasantry. Consequently, reports of the military aiding local landlords, businessmen, and politicians to skirt land reform are understandable, as are numerous incidents of the military abusing villagers even when they are only asking for what the government has promised.[49]

Finally, the direction of the agrarian reform program's planning and decisionmaking is from the top down. Government technocrats in the DAR and related agencies, together with consultants from USAID and elsewhere, decide what the program is supposed to be. Out in the countryside, lower-echelon administrators try to carry out the plans. Peasant participation is minimal. Instead, the government tells the villagers what they should do. Even the Philippine Federation of Land Reform Farmers is DAR-instigated.

The government's rural cooperatives illustrate this top-down approach. Although only a fraction of these cooperatives (Kilusang Bayan) and barrio associations (Samahang Nayon) have formed thus far, PD 27 and related reform laws require that all tenants eventually become members. Whatever nongovernment cooperatives villagers might have already do not count. This rule and the other stipulations for members came from the central government, not

---

found that the provincial agents of the various land reform agencies at that time were the lowest paid and most abused of all other administrators in the program. Lilia C. Panganiban, "Land Reform Administrative Procedures in the Philippines: A Critical Analysis" (Land Tenure Center, University of Wisconsin, LTC No. 82, c. 1972), pp. 30, 31, 34, 38.

48. Major Religious Superiors, "Summary of National Survey," p. 3.

49. Ibid., pp. 3, 7, 9–11; Wideman, *Far Eastern Economic Review*, Dec. 31, 1973, p. 18; Major Religious Superiors, *Various Reports*, Apr. 25, 1975, pp. 54–55.

the villagers.[50] Similarly, the April 1973 decree that outlined the cooperative program creates councils composed of high-echelon bureaucrats from such agencies as the Central Bank, Philippine National Bank, and DAR. They will control the finances and training programs for cooperative leaders. Evidence indicates that these leaders are from business, the professions, and government, not from the peasantry.[51] Moreover, the cooperatives can have non-peasant members, including landowners who still have tenants. Judging from the experiences of similar cooperatives, whatever power the government leaves them, the better-off members, especially the larger landowners, will take.[52] In addition, the cooperatives rely on rural banks for credit. Yet these banks remain in the hands of the local wealthy persons. As USAID found out in 1972–1973 in Nueva Ecija, these local elites resist any efforts by small farmers to buy into the banks in order to influence banking policies.[53] Given this situation, one can understand why peasants seem skeptical of the government's cooperatives and sometimes oppose them, as they have opposed earlier ones.[54]

50. This even offended Jeremias Montemayor, one of the few pre-martial law spokesmen for peasant unions who has supported Marcos' land reform. Jeremias U. Montemayor, "Progress and Problems of Philippine Agrarian Reform Under Martial Law," paper presented to the Rural Development Panel Seminar on Land Reform in the Philippines, SEADAG, Apr. 24–26, 1975, Baguio, p. 33. One researcher argues that the reform's foremost shortcoming is its failure to delegate "substantive authority and functions to the local level." Duncan A. Harkin, "Strengths and Weaknesses of the Philippine Land Reform," SEADAG paper 75-5, 1975, p. 13.

51. Reflected in newspaper accounts of government-sponsored seminars, meeting, and training sessions for the cooperative program: *Liwayway Balitang Maynila*, Nov. 20–27, 1972, p. 49; *Bulletin Today*, May 28, 1973, p. 11; Sept. 30, 1973, p. 24, and Dec. 30, 1973, p. 1. The last news item, for example, describes a "work-shop-seminar" on cooperatives for government officials, private business leaders, and consultants from the Friedrich-Ebert Foundation of West Germany to plan the cooperative program outlined in PD 175, which met at the Sulo Hotel, a high-class hotel in Quezon City. No peasants attended.

52. A conclusion reached by several studies of previous government-encouraged cooperatives, the most famous of which were the Farmers Cooperative Marketing Associations, or FaCoMas, of the Agricultural Credit and Cooperative Financing Administration during the 1950s and 1960s. See, for example, Wheelock, "Structural Determinants," and Montemayor, in Brown and Lin, *Land Reform*. Villagers I knew in Nueva Ecija in 1970 had no use for FaCoMas because they involved too much red tape and were controlled by the local elite.

53. USAID, Office of Agricultural Development, "Status Report: Agricultural Credit and Cooperatives Program of the Nueva Ecija Land Reform Integrated Development Program" (Manila: July 1973), pp. 20–21.

54. Major Religious Superiors, "Summary of National Survey," p. 5; Wideman, *Far Eastern Economic Review*, Dec. 31, 1973, p. 18; and "Farmers Denounce 'Crash' Rice Production Program," *Pahayag* no. 10 (September 1973), p. 5.

Limited Scope of Reform

Even if previous land reforms had been fully implemented, they would have touched only a small proportion of the tenants. An even smaller percentage of all peasants would have been included because landless agricultural workers, who constitute a sizeable portion of the peasantry, were excluded. This limited scope of earlier efforts remains true today.

Land reform under martial law excludes tenants who farm crops other than rice and corn. It also excludes rice- and corn-farming tenants if their landowners have less than seven hectares. Therefore, if it were implemented fully and if affected tenants could pay for their lands within fifteen years, it would include 34 percent of all tenant farmers and only 8 percent of all peasants who owned no land as of 1972. These statistics require an explanation.

According to 1970 crop data, the Philippines had, in rounded figures, 3.1 million hectares planted in rice and 2.4 million hectares in corn. Together these two crops accounted for 62 percent of the 9 million hectares of crop area that year. Sugarcane with 370,000 hectares and abaca with 170,000 hectares were the two largest crops on the remaining land.[55] According to the 1960 census for agriculture, 78 percent of the 865,000 tenant farmers grew primarily rice and corn and 22 percent of the tenants farmed primarily other crops.[56] If we assume that these same percentages are true in the 1970s and if we take the government's recent figure of 1 million corn and rice tenants, then the Philippines in the mid-1970s has 1.28 million tenants, 280,000 (22 percent) of whom farm crops other than rice and corn. Excluding sugarcane, abaca, and other commercial croplands, therefore, excludes a large proportion of the country's tenants. (Because the crop area for rice and corn has decreased in recent years while the area for commercial crops—especially cane and fruits—has increased, 22 percent probably underestimates the proportion of tenants on these lands.)[57]

55. T. M. Burley, *The Philippines: An Economic and Social Geography* (London: G. Bell and Sons, 1973), p. 47.

56. Philippines, Bureau of Census and Statistics, *Census of the Philippines, 1960, Agriculture*, II, p. 13; 670,876 rice and corn tenants out of 864,538 total tenants. The 1971 Agricultural Census was not used because it does not give crops by tenure and its tenancy figures are much less than those from the Department of Agrarian Reform.

57. Three recent studies mention that the area for rice and corn has decreased while the commercial crop area has increased. Richard W. Hooley and Vernon W. Ruttan, "The Philippines," in R. T. Shand, ed., *Agricultural Development in Asia*

By omitting owners with less than seven hectares of rice and corn land, the reform excludes another 560,000 tenants (56 percent of 1 million).[58] Altogether, the reform excludes 840,000 tenants (66 percent) and includes 440,000 (34 percent). This is not to say that all tenants want to own their land and be rid of their landlords. Many may not. The point here is that the government's claim that its reform will "emancipate all tenant farmers" is false. Only a third of all tenants even qualify for the program.

Finally, land reform offers nothing to the largest group of peasants—the 4 million agricultural laborers.[59] Because of land scarcity and high unemployment in nonagricultural sectors of the nation's economy, the number of agricultural workers is increasing beyond population growth. Like tenants, they own no farmland; but unlike tenants, they also have no land to farm. They are wage laborers on such lands as the 7,800-hectare pineapple plantation of Dole Philippines in Mindanao, the 6,000-hectare banana plantation of Del Monte's Philippine Packing Company, and the numerous mechanized rice ranches of several hundred hectares each in Nueva Ecija, Tarlac, and other provinces. They also work for smaller landowners doing seasonal labor such as harvesting, transplanting, and hauling. Some are migrants, like the 36,000 sugarcane *sacadas* in the Bisayas; most live year round in one place. But all have in common low

---

(Canberra: Australian National University, 1969), p. 243; Jose Drilon, Jr., *Agri business Management Resource Materials,* II (Tokyo: Asian Productivity Association, 1971), p. 7; and Takigawa, "A Note on Agrarian Reform," pp. 80–84. Also see his discussion (pp. 76–78) of the difficulties one has when trying to interpret what lands are "primarily" rice and corn and what are "primarily" for other crops. It raises another point over which landlords who wish to resist land reform can haggle and use to their advantage.

58. The figure 56 percent appears in Ladejinsky's October 1974 letter to Secretary Estrella. It also jibes with a November 1974 Letter of Instruction from President Marcos, which said that 44 percent of all tenants farming rice and corn had landlords who owned more than seven hectares. That would leave 56 percent of these tenants with landlords owning less than seven hectares. Bernard Wideman, "New Lease on Life for Marcos' Estate Plan," *Far Eastern Economic Review,* Nov. 29, 1974, pp. 38–39.

59. Insufficient information prevents an accurate estimate for the number of landless peasantry. Nevertheless, census data report that in 1959, 5.4 million people were engaged in "agriculture, forestry, hunting, and fishing." (Philippines, Department of Commerce and Industry, Bureau of the Census and Statistics, *Yearbook of Philippine Statistics, 1966* [Manila: 1966], pp. 87, 193.) The vast majority were probably in agriculture. And 2.2 million of them were "farmers" who either owned the land they tilled or were tenants. The difference between these two figures is 3.2 million people, most of whom were probably agricultural laborers. On the basis of the nation's annual population growth of about 3 percent, the number is 4.5 million by 1970. I estimate that 4 million of these people are agricultural laborers.

wages and continual poverty. Wages that were generally below the legal minimum before martial law have declined since then because employers disregard previous wage levels and inflation has averaged 20 percent since 1972. Earlier laws, such as the 1971 land reform code, had guaranteed these agricultural laborers the right to organize their own unions, and whatever progress there was for better wages and conditions had come through collective actions such as the sugar workers' strikes in Negros Occidental in 1969–1972. The martial law regime, however, forbids such aggressive organizations. It encourages only those unions that either management or government can supervise.[60]

Adding 4 million agricultural workers and 1.28 tenants, one gets an estimated 5.28 million Filipino peasants who own no land. Whereas a comprehensive land redistribution program would include all these villagers, the Marcos government's program aspires to include only 440,000 of them—8 percent of the total.

Besides discriminating against most peasants while favoring only a few, this limited reform leaves untouched many of the country's largest landowners. Half of the nation's 500 millionaires, for instance, are sugar barons.[61] Land reform does not reduce the wealth and political power of these and other families with large sugar lands. Nor does it jeopardize landowners who use tractors, combines, and laborers to grow rice on ranches. Indeed, these landowners have a favored place in the New Society.

The same government that promises to break up large landholdings and emphasize small-scale farming also encourages land concentration and agribusiness. Using such incentives as tax credits and duty-free importation of farm machinery and airplanes, the government helps capital- and land-rich Filipinos to invest in agribusiness. These plantation and ranch owners, with assistance from government police and other authorities, often evict small farmers as they

60. For recent information on conditions for agricultural workers in one part of the Philippines and on repression by landowners and the government, see four reports prepared by the Association of Major Religious Superiors in the Philippines: "Case Histories of Sugar Workers' Struggles," Dec. 2, 1974, 52 pp.; "Structures in the Sugar Industry," Dec. 12, 1974, 30 pp.; "A Historical Sketch of Oppression in the Negros Sugarland," Dec. 22, 1974, 18 pp.; and "A Study of Sugar Workers in the Haciendas of Negros," January 1975, 22 pp. Also see articles in the Major Religious Superiors' weekly publications *Various Reports* and *Signs of the Times;* see, for example, issues of Jan. 16, Feb. 14, Feb. 21, and June 13, 1975.

61. F. Sionil Jose, "Memo to the United States Congress," *Solidarity* 6 (May 1971), 4.

expand.[62] Marcos has even waved aside previous laws prohibiting foreigners from producing food crops, and decreed in May 197: that they could engage "in the culture, production, milling, processing, and trading, except retailing, of rice and corn."[63] And since then the National Grains Authority and Marcos himself have urged American and other foreign investors into "the rice and corn industry," emphasizing in particular the development of "virgin lands."[6] One of the several benefiting companies is Standard Fruit Corporation (StanFilCo), an American-owned subsidiary of Castle and Cooke, Inc. It now has a 1,300-hectare rice ranch in Mindanao that is fully irrigated and highly mechanized. Seeding, fertilizing, and pest control are done by airplanes and harvesting by combines. The ranch employs only 100 workers. The first crop in 1975 averaged 100 cavans per hectare. Because it can grow about 2½ crops per year, the total production was about 300,000 cavans. StanFilCo planned to sell 30,000 of these to workers here and at its pineapple and banana plantations and canneries, and the remaining 270,000 cavans elsewhere.[65]

Major Obstacles for Prospective Landowners

Although previous land reform plans were never carried out fully, they did reach some villagers. Specifically, government agencies resettled a few thousand ex-tenants in Mindanao and other places, and they purchased a few thousand hectares of land that several hundred tenants began to pay for. The government even had plans as far back as the late 1930s to help the prospective land

62. President Marcos decreed in May 1974 (PD 440), for instance, that planes and their spare parts and accessories could be imported duty-free. This, he said, would hasten "farm development and production." *Times Journal* (international edition) May 25, 1974, p. 2. Regarding evictions and pressures against small farmers, see for example, *Various Reports,* Jan. 3, and Feb. 7, 1975, and *Signs of the Times* Sept. 12, 1975.
63. PD 194, "Authorizing Aliens, as Well as Associations, Corporations or Partnerships Owned in Whole or in Part by Foreigners to Engage in the Rice and Corn Industry, and for Other Purposes," May 17, 1973, in Pinpin, *Proclamation No 1081 and Related Documents,* II (PDs 108–227), p. 241.
64. *Daily Express,* Aug. 17, 1973, p. 10; *Bulletin Today,* Nov. 16, 1973, p. 1 and Purito Go, "Philippine Setback," *Far Eastern Economic Review,* Sept. 17, 1973 p. 40.
65. Bernard Wideman, "Philippine Rice Plan Pays Dividends," *Far Eastern Economic Review,* Oct. 10, 1975, pp. 57–58. Dovetailing with the government's encouragement to agribusiness is its request that all large companies, Filipino and foreign owned, provide rice and corn for their employees to buy. Some of these companies are merely purchasing rice from the world market, but as of April, 1975 seventy-nine had begun to grow their own on 19,700 hectares. *Manila Journa* (international edition), Apr. 19, 1975, p. 13.

owners on these government-purchased estates to form production and marketing cooperatives similar to those proposed in Marcos' current program.[66] And in the early 1950s the central government considered asking those tenants buying their lands to form "farmers' associations" that are similar to the "barrio associations" under the Marcos plan, including the responsibility of association members to pay the annual land payment of any member who defaults.[67]

Unfortunately, few among this small number of peasant families actually benefited in the long run. Take for example the Bahay Pare estate in the Central Luzon province of Pampanga. In 1940, the government decided to purchase this 2,000-hectare estate and then resell the land in parcels of 2 to 4 hectares to the tenants, hoping to calm the tumultuous agrarian unrest there. Today most of the villagers farming this land are still tenants. Only a handful ended up owning any land. By 1950 the problem was clear—many peasants could not pay for their land. Some began selling to other people, who, after buying several hectares, turned around and rented parcels to tenant farmers. Other potential owners lost out to incompetent or corrupt government officials in the Rural Progress Administration and Bureau of Lands.[68] This same pattern was true for the seven or eight thousand peasant families on the nearby Buenavista estate in Bulacan. Half, perhaps more, of the farmers of the 27,000 hectares there are still tenants. Many simply could not keep up with annual payments. Others paid for their land but never got titles because of gross impropriety among government agencies that became a national scandal. Some residents bought more land than they could farm, then rented to tenants. Only a handful of the original tenants became legal owners of their land parcels.[69]

The government claims that tenants with land-transfer certificates

66. "Proposed Plan of Activities in Connection with the Hacienda Buenavista," c. 1940 (National Library, Manila, Papers of President Manuel Roxas, Bundle 10, Buenavista folder).

67. Philippines, Office of Economic Coordination, *Report and Recommendations of the Advisory Committee on Large Estate Problems* (Manila: 1951), pp. 30–31.

68. Philippines, Bahay Pare Estate Investigation Committee, *General Report* (Manila: 1954). Philippines, Presidential Investigating Committee on Bahay Pare, *Memorandum for the President of the Philippines — Subject: Bahay Pare Report* (Manila: Aug. 29, 1955); *Memorandum Regarding Amendment to Recommendation "A" in the Memo on Bahay Pare Estate* (Manila: Jan. 20, 1956); and *Memo for Chairman, Land Tenure Administration — Subject: Bahay Pare Estate* (Manila: c. 1956).

69. Philippines, Committee to Look into the Condition of the Buenavista Estate in San Ildefonso, Bulacan, *Report of the Presidential Committee* (Manila: August 20, 1954); Primitivo D. Mijares, "The Buenavista Scandal," *The Manila Chronicle*, Aug. 29, 1970, p. 2.

will eventually own their land. Furthermore, according to the DAR
and Marcos, as these villagers switch from tenancy to landownership
they will become more financially secure and will join the middle
class.

Neither the government nor the large landowners, however, will
give away land. A land-transfer certificate is not a title. It is only
a paper promising the person it names that he has a right to purchase a particular piece of land. The tenant must pay for the land
within fifteen years, pay 6 percent annual interest on the balance
due, pay the annual land taxes, and give five pesos each month and
one cavan of grain per hectare to the government-sponsored cooperative. He must also participate in the government's "package program" to grow high-yielding varieties of corn or rice, and must use
the required fertilizers, pesticides, and other additives. If for some
reason he decided to quit farming or cannot make his annual payments, he cannot sell the land. His annual payments do not build
up equity, further evidence that the certificate is not a title and the
tenant is not a landowner. The owner of the land during the fifteen
years is either the original landowner or the government—specifically, the DAR and the Land Bank. If a tenant fails to pay his
annual installment, he can lose his right to purchase any land.

As in the past, tenants—with or without land certificates—will
need credit in order to survive from one harvest to the next. But
tenants with certificates will no longer have landlords to borrow
from. Instead, they must ask agencies such as the Agricultural
Credit Administration (ACA) at 12 percent interest, privately
owned rural banks (at the same rate of interest), or moneylenders.
Tenants frequently prefer loans from their landlords, even though
interest rates are higher, because they can get them more easily
and reliably.[70] To borrow from government agencies and banks,
they must submit documents, prepare forms, then wait for weeks
before knowing whether their applications have been approved.
Another problem has been insufficient money in the banking system.
In 1970, for example, this meant that many tenants and small landowners who qualified for loans from rural banks in Central Luzon
did not get them.[71] The amount of available credit in 1973, although

<hr/>

70. Interviews with villagers in Talavera, Nueva Ecija, 1970; Brian Fegan, "Between the Lord and the Law: Tenants' Dilemmas," in Lynch, View from the Paddy,
p. 120; and Panganiban, "Land Reform Administrative Procedures," pp. 33–34.
71. Interview with Treasurer, Rural Bank of Talavera, Nueva Ecija, June 25, 1970;

more than before, was also insufficient for the number of farmers needing loans for increasingly expensive fertilizers and other additives for high-yielding seeds.[72] In addition, because the rural banks and the government agencies want to be repaid, they loan money to "preferred risks"—those farmers most likely to repay. Because the ACA, for example, has a low percentage of repayment—33 percent in Nueva Ecija in 1972–1973—government agencies as well as rural banks will probably become even more selective about who will get these loans. This was an important theme of a 1973 USAID report on Nueva Ecija.[73] Naturally, the more successful peasants and the large landowners who farm with machinery and hired laborers will continue to get credit much more easily than others. Many tenants will have to borrow high-interest loans from moneylenders, who may then put a lien on their land-transfer certificates, thereby making their chances to own land even more improbable. Finally, tenant farmers, including those with certificates, can only get "production loans" from government agencies and banks. They must use the loans to buy seed, fertilizer, farm implements, and so on, or to pay a part of their annual installments. They cannot get loans for nonagricultural purposes such as funeral or medical expenses and other emergency needs.

Besides the problem of getting loans, tenants will probably have major difficulties making the required annual payments and meeting other obligations in order to own their lands after fifteen years. Villagers themselves have expressed this doubt. Tenants in Nueva Ecija, for example, were unsure in 1970–1971 about switching from share tenancy (*kasama*) to leasehold tenancy (*buwisan*). They worried that credit would be less reliable because landlords would no longer be obligated to give loans. They were also reluctant to assume the burden for all agricultural expenses, which under share tenancy they divide with the landowner but under leasehold they must pay themselves.[74] Filipino villagers, like most peasants around

---

interviews with villagers in Talavera, 1970; and Panganiban, "Land Reform Administrative Procedures," p. 30.

72. Major Religious Superiors, "Summary of National Survey," p. 4.

73. USAID, "Status Report," pp. 10, 12, 16, 19, 24. Also see Fegan, "Between the Lord and the Law," p. 120; Panganiban, "Land Reform Administrative Procedures," pp. 33–34; Wheelock, "Structural Determinants," p. 10; and Dalmacio A. Cruz, "A Comparative Study of Agricultural Cooperatives in Japan and the Philippines," *Journal of Agricultural Economics and Development* (Manila) 2 (January 1972), 263, 267.

74. Romana Pahilanga-de los Reyes and Frank Lynch, "Reluctant Rebels: Leasehold

the world, are risk minimizers, not profit maximizers—and for good reason. One bad year, due to poor weather, crop diseases, or any number of other calamities that can strike an individual family or a whole area, can be deadly.

The household budget in Table 3.1 and the land values in Table 3.2 illustrate how marginal the situation is for persons in one Nueva Ecija village, even if tenants have land-transfer certificates and begin to purchase land rather than rent.[75] A tenant family of six with only two hectares of rice land would net, roughly, only P200. If the family had three hectares, which is probably above average in the 1970s, the margin would be around P1,300. And this example does not include a number of reasonable expenses such as education costs for children and medical bills. Nor does it take into account the fees for the local cooperatives, which all certificate holders are required to join under the Marcos program. Finally, this budget does not take into account such extraordinary but plausible expenses as funerals, weddings, or replacing a dead carabao; nor does it consider what would happen when droughts, typhoons, or plant diseases damage or destroy the crops. On the other hand, the budget excludes possible additional household income from, say, larger crop yields or money that a tenant farmer, his son, or his wife might earn from part-time work. Although pluses such as these might happen to a few tenants for several years in a row or to many tenants once in a while, they are unlikely to occur for most tenants for fifteen years in a row. More likely, people will eventually fall too far behind in their payments, thereby postponing real ownership indefinitely or losing their option to buy.[76]

An additional reason to doubt that most tenants will be able to

Converts in Nueva Ecija," in Lynch, *View from the Paddy*, pp. 7–49; and Benedict J. Kerkvliet, "Agrarian Conditions since the Huk Rebellion: A Barrio in Central Luzon," in Kerkvliet, ed., *Political Change in the Philippines* (Honolulu: Asian Studies at Hawaii, University Press of Hawaii, 1974), pp. 1–76.

75. For other evidence showing marginal economic conditions of villagers see Cabungan, "A Study of Philippine Land Reform," pp. 82, 184; Fegan, "Between the Lord and the Law," pp. 113–28; Henry T. Lewis, *Ilocano Rice Farmers* (Honolulu: University of Hawaii Press, 1971); and Takahashi Akira, *Land and Peasants in Central Luzon* (Tokyo: Institute of Developing Economies, 1969).

76. Additional support for this argument comes from a recent study of tenants, leaseholders, and amortizing tenants in Nueva Ecija. It found that a high percentage of persons in all categories default on loans and amortization. (The amortizing tenants are a result of previous land reforms, not the current one.) Mahar Mangahas, Virginia A. Miralao, and Romana P. de los Reyes, *Tenants, Lessees, Owners: Welfare Implications of Tenure Change* (Quezon City: Institute of Philippine Culture, Ateneo de Manila University, 1974), pp. 72–80, 114–16, 148–49, 158.

Table 3.1. Representative household budget for a tenant family of six with either two hectares or three hectares of rice land, Barrio San Ricardo in Talavera, Nueva Ecija (c. 1973)

Household Budget	Pesos (P) 2 ha.	3 ha.
Agricultural income		
65 cavan/ha.; P35/cavan	4,550	6,825
Expenses		
Agricultural		
Seed: 1.25 ha./cavan; P35/cavan	56	84
Harvest: 6 cavan/ha.; P35/cavan	420	630
Thresher rental: 5% gross harvest	228	341
*Irrigation: P30/ha.	60	90
*Fertilizer: P30/bag; 3 bags/ha.	180	270
*Spray: P40/gal.; 1 gal./ha.	80	120
*Transplanting: P45/ha.	90	135
Plowing and related expenses[a]	150	150
Interest on loan for asterisked items: 12%	45	74
Subtotal	1,309	1,894
Payment for land per year (see Table 3.2)	1.081	1,622
Household expenses		
Rice: 6 cavans/person/year	1,260	1,260
Other: clothing, meat, fish, fruits, vegetables, home needs, misc.[b]	720	720
Subtotal	1,980	1,980
Total expenses	4,370	5,496
Net return		
(Agricultural income — total expenses)	P180	P1,329

[a] Villagers could give only a very rough estimate for expenses in this category.

[b] In 1970, villagers' estimates for this category worked out to be about P1.50 per day for this size household. People said, however, that this would be a minimum estimate. In order to reflect the increased cost of living in 1973, I have used P2.00 per day per household for this table.

Source: Derived from household budget data from twenty-three households and several other interviews with residents in San Ricardo in 1970, and revised to reflect 1973 price increases reported for Nueva Ecija in general and the Talavera area in particular. For more details, see my "Agrarian Conditions since the Huk Rebellion: A Barrio in Central Luzon," in Kerkvliet, ed., *Political Change in the Philippines: Studies of Local Politics Preceding Martial Law* (Honolulu: Asian Studies at Hawaii, University Press of Hawaii, 1974).

win in the long run is the "green revolution." The demands for cash expenditures in order to cultivate high-yielding seeds are tremendous. These "miracle" seeds are more productive than local varieties only if the farmer irrigates well, uses chemical fertilizers, and applies pesticides. These inputs require cash, which small landowners and tenant farmers often must borrow. For maximum productivity, capital needs eventually include modern grain driers,

Table 3.2. Calculated Land value and annual payment for fifteen years for representative rice land in Barrio San Ricardo, Talavera, Nueva Ecija (c. 1973)

Rice Land	Land value (P)[a]	Amortized annual payment (P)[b]
1 ha.	5,250	540
2 ha.	10,500	1,081
3 ha.	15,750	1,622

[a] Formula for calculating land value: A × B × 2.5 = land value (according to PD 27), where (A) is based on the average of previous two normal harvests: 60 cavans (the median range for average yield in San Ricardo, Talavera, in 1965-1970 was 60-64 cavans; this is above the nation's average), and (B) is based on peso equivalence of P35/cavan palay (the government guarantees this price; it could be higher, depending on the outcome of negotiations between landlords and tenants).

[b] Based on amortizing tables in the *Realty Bluebook* (San Rafael, California: Professional Publishing, 1969).

mechanized granaries, tractors, more research for more productive seeds, and improved fertilizers and pesticides. This type of agriculture is not only ecological Russian roulette because of continuous applications of chemicals, but also it runs counter to small-scale farming. As one author has argued, "It was inherent in the design of the new varieties of rice that where private enterprise prevails, the rich farmers will be made richer and the poor farmers poorer."[77]

Supporting this argument is evidence from many Third World countries, including the Philippines.[78] Small Filipino farmers themselves are skeptical of these methods; they suspect irreparable damage to the land and they fear going into debt so often and for increasingly large sums. As one Nueva Ecija tenant explained to me in 1970, "It is better to plant local seeds and be more confident of having enough to eat than it is to gamble by taking on large loans for lots of fertilizer and so forth to plant miracle rice. The gamble could be lost; then you not only have a poor crop but a big debt. The gamble with miracle rice is even greater than usual because those seeds catch more diseases than local seeds."

Yet tenants holding land-transfer certificates are required to use

77. Marvin Harris, "How Green the Revolution," *Natural History* 81 (June-July 1972), 30.
78. See, for example, Keith Griffin, *The Political Economy of Agrarian Change* (Cambridge, Mass.: Harvard University Press, 1974); Harry W. Blair, "The Green Revolution and 'Economic Man': Some Lessons for Community Development in Southeast Asia," *Pacific Affairs* 44 (Fall 1971), 353–67; Mahfooz Ahmed, "Green Revolution, Productivity, and Income Distribution: An Assessment of Implications for Rural Development in Developing Countries in ESCAP Region," in *Approaches to Rural Development in Asia* (Kuala Lumpur: Asian Centre for Development Administration, 1975), pp. 73–108; Erich H. and Charlotte F. Jacoby, *Man and Land: The Essential Revolution* (London: André Deutsch, 1971), Appendix IV.

high-yielding seeds and follow the government's package program of agricultural methods. Recent fertilizer shortages alone suggest hardship for these small farmers. The Philippines imported 50 percent of its fertilizer needs in 1973, 75 percent in 1974, and 80 percent in 1975. Prices rose from $50 per ton in 1972 to $225 per ton in 1974—a 450 percent increase.[79] Big landowners, agribusinesses, and some small landowners can afford these prices. Least able to pay, however, are other small landowners and tenants, including those with land-transfer certificates.

A final observation supports the doubt that even those few tenants included in the land reform program will benefit. Those who get small plots of land will still be at or close to the bottom of a terribly lopsided distribution of wealth and political power in the Philippines. Even if the agrarian program could "break up the big landholdings," as Marcos has vowed,[80] it will not alter the large landowners' economic position. Tenants included in the program will remain tenants for at least fifteen more years while they pay for land. Meanwhile, former landlords will get a good price for their lands, 6 percent interest on unpaid principals or earnings from preferred shares of stock, and other benefits and tax exemptions. As one USAID official volunteered, the landlords will be "very well compensated; they will end up with more per hectare than . . . the tenants will be paying."[81]

PD 27 stipulated a formula for tenants, landlords, and the DAR to calculate prices of redistributed land. Subsequent decrees and administrative orders in 1972–1973 explained methods for paying landlords those prices. Nearly 98 percent of the compensated landlords as of March 1975 preferred the method whereby the government's Land Bank paid them 10 percent of the price in cash and the remaining 90 percent in Land Bank bonds.[82] (The bonds are tax free, earn 6 percent interest and mature in twenty-five years. They can be used to purchase property and equipment, and can be collateral for loans.) With that formula and this favorite method of compen-

---

79. *Bulletin Today*, Nov. 24, 1973, p. 18; *Philippine Times*, Dec. 31, 1973, p. 8; *Times Journal* (international edition), Oct. 12, 1974, p. 13; and "Fertilizer Situationer: Why the High Prices," *Signs of the Times*, Jan. 30, 1976, p. 22. The last article notes that between 1972 and 1974, profits for the world's eight largest fertilizer producers increased between 30 and 65 percent.

80. Cited in Edward R. Kiunisala, "Land Reform: Its Concept," *Bulletin Today*, Jan. 20, 1974.

81. USAID official, interview, Jan. 29, 1974.

82. Overholt, "Report of Meeting: Land Reform in the Philippines," p. 15.

sation, the minimum effective compensation to landlords is 92 percent of their land's agricultural value. It is probably closer to or
exceeding 100 percent if the market for Land Bank bonds, which
are negotiable, rises as expected.[83] As a consequence of this compensation and the previously mentioned limited scope of the reform, its
impact on the country's distribution of wealth will be infinitesimal.[84]

That impact will be even smaller now because the government
has replaced the pricing formula in PD 27 with negotiations between landlords and tenants. Most observers agree that this change
is a concession on the government's part to landlords, and it will
mean higher prices for redistributed land. Rather than the P4,500
to P5,000 per hectare officials and researchers expected, had the
formula been used, the average price for compensated land as of
late 1975 was nearly P6,500 per hectare.[85]

These attractive compensations are essential, according to both the
Marcos government and USAID, "in order to get landowners involved in land reform. It's a quid pro quo sort of thing."[86] In fact,
one theme that Marcos and others have stressed is that land redistribution is advantageous to large landowners because they can put
the money previously tied up in land into more profitable investments. Under these conditions, consequently, some large landowners
have been willing to sell their lands.

The end result of this kind of redistribution is no change. Those
few landowners who are affected by land reform will not "lose"
their land; they will be selling it for a handsome return that the
government guarantees. The rich, in short, will remain rich—if not
richer—and powerful, while the poor will remain poor, be they
landless or landed peasants.

Comparison with Other Land Reform Programs

Since declaring martial law, the Marcos government has enjoyed
the image of redistributing land and thereby being an ally of the

83. Harkin, "Strengths and Weaknesses of the Philippine Land Reform," pp.
18–19.
84. United Nations, International Labour Office, *Sharing in Development: A
Programme of Employment, Equity, and Growth for the Philippines* (Manila:
International Labour Office, 1974), pp. 490–92.
85. Overholt, "Report of Meeting," p. 14; USAID official, interview, Jan. 29,
1974; Department of Agrarian Reform, "Summary: Operation Land Transfer," Nov.
3, 1975, p. 1.
86. Interview with a USAID official, State Department, Washington, D.C., Jan.
30, 1974.

peasantry, while simultaneously doing nothing to benefit tenants at the landlords' expense. It reimburses the few owners whose lands are affected, but requires tenants to pay for the land and shoulder other costs. While making concessions to other landlords who resist the reform, it makes peasants suffer the consequences of a prolonged implementation during which time owners squirm through the reform's loopholes. Only a small fraction of the landless peasants even qualify for land; an even smaller number are likely to get any. Yet the reform probably has helped to reduce unrest, which was the government's intention anyway. By distributing a handful of land-transfer certificates each month and reaching a small number of peasants through other agrarian projects, the government has kept alive its promise to emancipate all landless villagers. This effect, coupled with the overtly repressive measures of martial law, can minimize agrarian revolt, although probably not indefinitely.

One can push the analysis one step further by briefly comparing Philippine land reform to other land reform programs. The Marcos government is only one among many which has vowed that land reform will redistribute wealth and political power, substantially improve the peasantry's well-being, and increase agricultural production.

The most comprehensive study to date of agrarian reform over time was published in 1965 by Elias Tuma. After examining twelve cases in all parts of the world from the early Greeks until the 1950s, Tuma concludes that there are two broad classes of agrarian reform. Most agrarian reform efforts are in what he calls "Class I." Advocates of Class I reform, Tuma says, premise the reform on private property, individual land holdings, and inequality of wealth and income. Consequently, when expropriation is necessary, compensation is paid for the property surrendered. "Given these basic premises, when these reformers introduce reform they tend . . . to undertake only limited redistribution of land, to maintain private individual ownership and operation, and to keep farms on a small, uneconomical scale. They also tolerate concentration of ownership and inequality as well as class differences and conflict."[87]

The results of Class I reforms, Tuma finds:

. . . are usually only a reduction of the original problems rather than

---

87. Elias Tuma, *Twenty-Six Centuries of Agrarian Reform* (Berkeley: University of California Press, 1965), p. 225.

their solution. In fact, the potential danger of new conflict remains, since the institutions from which conflict arose in the first place remain. . . .

[A] western type of reform (Class I) tends to be of limited impact, since it does not reach to the foundations of the system as do socialist reforms. This type of reform has not averted revolutions or created democracies, nor is it capable of doing so. It may, as in the past, create short-term stability, delay violent eruption of hostilities between tenure groups, and recruit support for the reformer government. Therefore, if the reforming countries desire such short-term achievements, reform may be quite helpful. But if they genuinely desire a fundamental change, they should either institute fundamental changes in the tenure structure or utilize means other than land tenure reform.[88]

Similar to Tuma's typology is a more recent analysis by Keith Griffin. He argues that the rural programs he studied in numerous Third World countries fall along a continuum. At one end is a "technocratic strategy," at the other is a "radical strategy," and in between falls the "reformist strategy."[89] The technocratic strategy emphasizes increased agricultural production, encourages competition among producers, allows large landholdings (plantations, agribusinesses, ranches) to dominate total production, permits property owners to benefit from technical changes and higher output, and concentrates agrarian policymaking and implementation in the central government. The reformist strategy distributes land to peasants while also encouraging capital-intensive farming on large holdings, tries to benefit both "middle peasants" and large landowners, and emphasizes redistribution of income to some sectors of the peasantry but not all. Governments following this strategy, Griffin writes, "tend to vacillate in their choices of policies" and frequently proclaim one thing while actually doing another.

Neither strategy benefits peasants much. Governments tending toward a technocratic strategy welcome inequities because they assume "that the rich will save a large proportion of their extra income and thereby contribute to faster accumulation and growth. In other words, the concentration of income and wealth is one of the ways whereby the output objective is expected to be achieved." Whatever redistribution occurs in the reformist strategy results primarily from upper income groups giving to the middle. "Those in the lowest deciles of the income distribution may receive higher

88. Ibid., pp. 225–26, 241.
89. Griffin, *Political Economy of Agrarian Change*, pp. 198–203.

earnings, e.g., because of greater employment opportunities, but they are unlikely to improve their relative share—or to increase their political influence."

Contrasting with Class I, technocratic, or reformist strategies are Class II reforms in Tuma's analysis and the radical rural development strategy in Griffin's study. Class II reforms reject private ownership of land, do not compensate former landowners for expropriated property because such compensation would mean no redistribution of wealth and income, and advocate an equitable distribution of economic and political resources. The radical strategy, too, prohibits private property, fosters communal farms, and encourages local levels to plan and implement agrarian programs. Its objective is first to achieve rapid social change and a redistribution of political power, next to redistribute wealth and income, and third to increase production. "In short, the objectives are greater mass participation, economic equality and faster growth."

Whether Class I or Class II or technocratic, reformist, or radical, all land-redistribution and related agrarian programs have political purposes. Governments use them to legitimize their power or win to their side additional supporters. What distinguishes the programs, in political terms, is the degree to which they make concessions to peasants at the expense of large and medium-sized landowners. Governments with radical or Class II strategies cast their lot with tenants, agricultural laborers, and small landowners. They require large property owners and other elites to pay the economic and social costs of development. At the expense of these owners and elites, peasants improve their economic and political conditions until former landlord and former tenant become more or less equal. Governments following Class I, technocratic, or reformist strategies, however, are closely tied to the propertied classes and only loosely to the peasantry. At most they ask both the landed and the landless to bear the burden of development. At best they seek only to modify the excesses of wealth and political power of the elite. With these strategies, the peasantry's conditions may improve slightly, but significant inequities of wealth and power continue.

The Philippine government's land reform and related agrarian programs fit rather snugly in Tuma's Class I type and somewhere between Griffin's technocratic and reformist strategies. Based on information he collected prior to martial law, Griffin considers that the Philippine government's rural programs lean toward the technocratic end of the continuum.[90] Perhaps in recent years the government has shifted slightly toward the reformist strategy. But by no means has it moved toward Class II or a radical strategy. This comparison gives us further grounds for expecting the Marcos government's agrarian program to benefit peasants only slightly.

Erich Jacoby, who for years has studied agrarian conditions around the world, drew a pessimistic conclusion in 1971 about land redistribution in most countries: "In the truly underdeveloped countries is has as yet had only a limited effect and it remains to be seen to what extent it is at all feasible within the socio-economic framework where powerful vested interests dominate the administration and control the very machinery designed for implementation." Furthermore, he says, the only possibility short of revolution whereby land reform might be beneficial for villagers is if two conditions exist: first, if peasants are free to develop a movement that attempts to level out social and economic differences and that will represent the peasants' interests at the highest political levels; and second, if technical assistance from governments concentrates on changes in the socioeconomic structure of these countries.[91] Included in the second condition is the proviso that the United States and other Western governments stop economic, political, and military support to the vested interests in these countries. In the Philippine case, neither of these conditions exists. Nor are they likely to arise during martial law.

90. Ibid., p. 204.
91. Jacoby, *Man and Land*, pp. 213–14.

4. Liberty versus Loyalty: The Transformation of Philippine News Media under Martial Law

DAVID A. ROSENBERG

MIDDLEBURY COLLEGE

Virtually every country in the world endorses the principles of freedom of expression and freedom of the press. This is true of Western liberal-capitalist countries, Communist countries, and developing countries alike. Whatever the ideological or political differences among nations, there appears to be almost universal agreement on the principles of freedom of expression. Freedom of the press is guaranteed in almost every constitution of the world. Obviously, however, there are some striking differences in practice. For example, most Americans would say that the Soviet press is not free, politically. However, most Soviets would say that the American press is not free, economically. In short, the concept of freedom of the press is defined differently and practiced differently in different countries. The conclusion to be drawn from this rather straightforward observation is that the term "freedom of the press" is so highly generalized that it has relatively little informational content; therefore, because it has so little specific meaning, it can achieve universal endorsement.

A second conclusion is that each country provides its own operational definition of freedom of the press. In more practical terms, every nation decides how much autonomy to grant to its communications media. In terms of policy, every government controls its media, in one way or another, according to its needs and resources. The question is not *whether* to control the press or not; the real question is *how* to control the media. Countries with liberal-democratic political cultures tend to employ a system of *professional control*; that is, a system of independent self-regulation based on professional standards of practice. But journalism is not just or not

145

completely a profession; it is also a craft and an art. Hence, it is difficult to define and enforce standards of practice. Furthermore, the press is also a business; that is, an economic enterprise in the pursuit of profit, and therefore subject to *economic control*. Under this system of control, freedom of the press is limited by the publisher's interest in maintaining sufficient sales and advertising revenues to ensure his property rights of ownership. In all countries, freedom of the press is also limited by a system of *legal controls*. There are laws on libel, privacy, censorship, national security, and copyrights, to name but a few, all of which place restrictions on freedom of the press. Legal and judicial controls also govern conflicts between freedom of the press and other freedoms, for example, the right to a fair trial. Lastly, the press is also subject to *social control*. Cultural norms, social criticism, patronage and support from a constituency of readers all provide a diffuse boundary around the concept of freedom of the press. Hence, there are many ways in which a society may control its media: professional controls, economic controls, legal controls, and social controls. Typically, most countries have a mixture of these various types of controls, and the mixture changes as their historical experiences change. The exact pattern of control at any given time is determined by public policy. In other words, the pattern of controls is primarily determined by political considerations.

The concept of freedom of the press generally refers to a particular pattern of control in which legal and governmental constraints are at a minimum. Historically, it is a relatively recent development. The first mass media which came into being in Western Europe around the beginning of the eighteenth century were introduced under strict authoritarian control. The privilege of publication was extended by permit or decree only to those who were politically "safe." They enjoyed this privilege only as long as they refrained from criticizing the regime in power. In fact, it would be more accurate to say that these early mass media were clearly expected to preserve the regime in power. This pattern of control, more arbitrary than legal, was protested by the bourgeoisie and urban intelligentsia, and some reforms were achieved. Anyone who had the means to post a bond could apply for a license to publish. In this manner, economic controls on the media were introduced. The classic, liberal-democratic concept of freedom of the press did not come into being until the revolutions of the late eighteenth and nineteenth centuries. It was vividly expressed in the French Declaration of the Rights of Man, written in August 1789, one month after the fall of the Bastille: "The unrestrained communication of opinion being the most precious right of man, every citizen may speak, write, and publish freely" (Article 11). Based on the philosophy of the Enlightenment and a belief in the natural rights of man, it held that any rational man, given the facts, could distinguish right from wrong, truth from falsity. As opposed to the earlier "authoritarian" view of the media, this became known as the "libertarian" view.

Given this ideological environment, the mass media flourished. Within a very short period of time, the relationship between the government and the press was almost precisely reversed. Instead of existing by sufferance, as long as it supported and advanced government policy, the press now became independent of government. Its new role was to represent and guard the public interest. In time, this libertarian pattern of control offended the Victorian sensibilities of the postrevolutionary order. A reaction set in. It was in response to this late-nineteenth-century threat of government censorship that professional associations of journalists were first organized. Their task was to restrain their ranks in order to preserve their recently acquired autonomy. Toward this end, codes of ethics, statements of purpose, courses of instruction, and schools of journalism began to appear. It is only in the twentieth century that professional norms have come to predominate over other forms of media control, primarily in Western liberal-capitalist democracies. However, the pattern of control continues to evolve in response to changing circumstances. For example, the pattern of control over the electronic media—radio and television—tends to be more authoritarian than the print media.

The purpose of this brief historical review is to show that the concept and practice of freedom of the press has been evolving continuously in response to changing social circumstances. The noble phrase "freedom of the press" should not obscure the fact that all societies control their media in one way or another, and the pattern of control changes as social circumstances change.

For all governments, the basic issue of public policy is how to establish a pattern of control of the mass media that provides both freedom of the press, which is by now an almost universally stated objective, and responsibility of the press, in which the press has the ability to respond to what its government sees as its national objectives. If a society is undergoing rapid social change, or if its government is committed to major social reforms, then the problem of balancing the freedom of the press with the responsibility of the press is especially difficult. These difficulties are clearly evident in most developing countries today.

Colonialism, Nationalism, and the Mass Media in Southeast Asia

There is little precedent for the institutions of the mass media in traditional precolonial Southeast Asia. In most cases, the origins of the mass media were colonial and Western in terms of personnel, format, language, and editorial outlook. Their content was originally limited to official news and decrees addressed to a relatively small, exclusive, urban audience. They were not, in fact, mass media; they were elite media.

The indigenous press of Southeast Asia grew out of a pervasive spirit of anticolonial nationalism at the end of the nineteenth century. In many countries, one could observe a close relationship between a nationalist movement and a literary movement, especially in their early, intense stages. The same people were often involved in politics, journalism, and literature; for example, Adam Malik in Indonesia, Jose Rizal in the Philippines, U Nu in Burma, Rabindranath Tagore in India. All were involved in a variety of ways in seeking to express what they perceived as their country's national destiny. The early indigenous press was largely created and employed by these leading nationalists as an instrument for public enlightenment, social reform, and political action. As a result, the early indigenous press of Southeast Asia was primarily a partisan press. Journalism began as a by-product, a political calling, a literary avocation. The language of the press was, on the whole, the language of the metropolitan country, and, as a consequence, it seldom had a large audience within the colony. Its elite, rather than mass, orientation was also limited by high costs of production, low levels of literacy, and, in several instances, by deliberate colonial policy. It was not national in scope, but it was nationalist in outlook. There was only one major news story throughout the late colonial period: independence. In advocating independence, the indigenous, nationalist press often flaunted colonial law, a tendency which often led to its suppression. In many cases, however, it preferred to remain opportunist, and went underground. In sum, the press under colonial rule in Southeast Asia was divided into two parts: a colonial press, Western in origins and orientations, and an indigenous press, partisan, nationalist, elitist, and oppositionist.

This was the situation on the eve of independence. However, institutions nurtured under colonial auspices were often found to be inappropriate to nationalist aspirations after independence. After generations of restrictions and suppression, most of the newly independent governments of Southeast Asia initiated a period of relative freedom of expression. There were very few legal restraints on what could be said or published. In the Philippines, Indonesia, Malaysia, and Burma, the excitement of national independence generated a tremendous growth of the mass media. The press was free to the point of being licentious. And, on the whole, this period of libertarian control did not last very long.

As the newly independent governments of Southeast Asia consolidated their positions in power, they became progressively less tolerant of what they saw as the conflicting, confusing, and overly critical views of the press. Increasingly, they saw this freewheeling press as a potential threat to the rather fragile sense of national unity they were attempting to strengthen. A libertarian pattern of control of the media, it was argued, would only exacerbate potentially dangerous ethnolinguistic and social differences. As a result, most Southeast Asian governments evolved a policy toward the media that responded to their immediate fears of disunity and threats of chaos, rather than the long-term needs of national integration. They felt the media should contribute, to the fullest extent possible, to the nation-building struggle. And so, with one notable exception, the mass media in Southeast Asia were mobilized or nationalized or socialized. Call it what you will, the newly liberated press of Southeast Asia quickly lost its autonomy from government and legal control.

The one notable exception was the press of the Philippines. For two and a half decades after independence, the Philippine press remained largely unencumbered by government constraint. According to many observers, it was the freest press in Southeast Asia. As one observer put it, "The Filipino journalist, unlike his colleagues in so many neighboring countries, could go about his profession without fear of arrest or harassment from the authorities." Columnists and editorial writers were remarkably outspoken and the government was remarkably tolerant of the steady stream of abuse and criticism it received. Indeed, in the first quarter-century of independence, freedom of the press had become a major part of Filipinos' claim to democratic government.

This situation lasted until September 1972, when President Marcos declared martial law throughout the country. At the same time, he shut down almost every newspaper, radio, and television station, except his own, and imprisoned his most outspoken critics.

Seldom in Southeast Asia has there ever been such a drastic change in the status of the media. As one delegation of Asian journalists noted, "The Philippine Government's actions against the mass media have no parallel in the whole of Asia. A complete shutdown of media has not been attempted in Park Chung Hee's Korea, Ayub Khan's Pakistan, Thanarat's Thailand, Sukarno's Indonesia, or Lee Kuan Yew's Singapore."[1] There are two general considerations that help to explain this abrupt transition. The first has to do with the historical experience of the Philippine media; the second, with the pattern of oligarchic control that dominates political life in the Philippines. It is worth examining these factors in greater detail in order to understand what may lie ahead for the Philippine press.

Discontinuities of Media Development in the Philippines

The historical experience of the Philippine media can be described as very uneven, at best. Under colonial rule, the media experienced several long periods of suppression, punctuated by relatively brief periods of permissiveness. Whenever a favorable political environment existed, the press flourished. When restraints were lifted, during Spanish Republican rule, toward the end of the Spanish colonial period, during the revolution of 1896, during the Commonwealth period under American rule, and during the postwar period, the number and circulation of periodicals rose dramatically.[2] These

---

1. T. J. S. George, "The Party's Over," *Far Eastern Economic Review*, Nov. 18, 1972, p. 14.
2. For a full discussion, see David A. Rosenberg, "The Development of Modern Mass Communications in the Philippines," doctoral dissertation, Cornell University, 1972.

alternating periods of suppression and proliferation have had peculiar consequences. There has been little continuity of development; publications and press associations seldom survived from one period of permissiveness to the next. In general, whenever freedom of the press has been permitted, Filipinos have defended it with passion. Whenever it has been prohibited, they have complied with government regulation with obsequiousness.

During the post-World War II period of independence, from 1946 to 1972, press freedoms were formally guaranteed in Article III, Section 8, of the Constitution of the Republic of the Philippines (1935), which clearly linked freedom of the press with its public advocacy role, stating: "No law shall be passed abridging the freedom of speech, or of the press, or the right of the people peaceably to assemble and petition the Government for redress of grievances." In this environment, the news media were generally aggressive in "fiscalizing" the activities of government and in scrutinizing the private behavior of public officials and other prominent figures.

Freedom of the press, however, was not always balanced with responsibility. For example, libel suits against offensive journalists were frequent, but convictions were very rare. The libel laws were never rigorously enforced. A libeled or slandered person might threaten suit, but was more likely to find a sympathetic newspaperman to publish a denial or countercharge. Hence, libel bred more libel. Legal controls did not establish veracity as a rock-bottom standard of news reporting.

During the 1960s, increasing criticism of vituperation in the press led to the first major attempt to control the news profession. In 1965, the Philippine Press Council (PPC) was established by the Philippine Newspaper Publishers Association and the National Press Club in order to head off external regulation and act as a policing body for the press. The PPC attempted to do what the government, the public, and journalists were not able to do: define, maintain, and enforce standards for the freedom and responsibility of the press. The PPC recognized that "there have been violations on the part of some newspapers and newspaper workers of the accepted norms of ethical practice," and that "there has been no adequate recourse to seek remedy for abuses of the press other than the courts of justice and in most cases judicial action is long, tedious and expensive. Moreover, some persons who have legitimate grievances against the press do not want to sue or file a criminal complaint but want only some kind of disciplinary action." The PPC also admitted that "the great power wielded by the press sometimes leads to tyranny."[3]

The PPC adopted a code of ethics and set up a procedure for registering complaints. It also required a statement from plaintiffs that "resort to the Press Council entails the obligation of not referring the case to a court."[4] The Council could enforce press responsibility in a number of ways: "An offending newspaper may be warned, may be required to publish a correction or retraction of apology, or required to publish in full the findings of the Council against it. In the case the offender is a newspaper worker, the Council may ask the publisher to discipline him by a fine or a dismissal."[5]

It is difficult to evaluate the efforts of the PPC to enforce its code of ethics on Filipino journalists. Few complaints were received and the council had only a brief history. It was the first and, so far, the only significant attempt to establish a system of professional control of the mass media.

Oligarchy and Ownership

The second general consideration in seeking to understand Philippine mass media has to do with the nature of the oligarchy. In the Philippines, the communications media are important instruments of political and social control. Hence they generally reflect the power structure of society. The same elite groups that dominate the political, economic, and social institutions of the country also dominate its media. This was true before martial law and is still true today. The major difference is that before martial law the oligarchy was large and dispersed; while today it has been contracted and consolidated. Before martial law, each major elite faction maintained its own media outlet to espouse and defend its primary economic interests. As long as the oligarchy was divided into these factions and no single faction dominated the others, an effective system of freedom of the press resulted, by default, if not by design. Freedom of the press, in this sense, meant freedom for one elite faction to

3. *The Philippine Press Council* (Manila: Philippine Press Institute, 1965), p. 1.
4. Ibid., p. 2.
5. Ibid., p. 3.

espouse its views without restriction by another. There were some other benefits to this pattern of control. The competition among publishers spurred a rapid expansion of the media. Several innovations were also introduced, both editorial and technological. But this competitive environment did not provide much support for professional career development or responsible standards of news reporting. In a sense, the press of the Philippines grew too fast; it outpaced attempts at institutional integration. Publishers had become too competitive, even jealous and suspicious of one another, to cooperate on behalf of professional development. Thus while this pattern of stalemated competition among elite factions provided an effective form of freedom of the press, it did not provide the necessary support for the establishment of an independent news profession.

From Civil Liberty to Government Loyalty: Precipitating Factors

Three major factors broke the stalemate and produced the situation that now exists. The first was the steady politicization of the news media throughout the 1960s. This can be appreciated by examining Table 4.1, which outlines the major economic interests of Philippine publishers as of 1969.

Table 4.1. Major economic interests of Philippine publishers before martial law

Family ownership	Major newspapers	Major economic interest
Elizalde	*Evening News, Philippine Sun*	Mining, insurance, import-export, iron and steel, paint and oils, rope, sugar, distillery
Lopez	*Manila Chronicle*	Meralco, sugar, finance, lubricating oil
Menzi	*Manila Daily Bulletin*	Mining, shipping, agriculture, lumber, school and office supplies and equipment
Roces	*Manila Times, Taliba, Daily Mirror*	Publishing
Soriano	*Philippine Herald*	San Miguel (food and beverages, containers, sand and glass, aluminum, plastic), mining, paper, oil development, copper products, insurance, finance

Source: This at best partial listing has been compiled from the institutional advertisements of the groups themselves as well as such listings as "Chronicle Special Report: Top 100 Corporations," *Manila Chronicle,* Sept. 22, 1969.

Table 4.1 indicates one major exception to the big business domination of the media. For the Roces group, publishing was a big business in itself. Their other interests were relatively minor. The Manila Times Publishing Company, which included the *Times,* the *Daily Mirror, Taliba,* their supplements, and *Weekly Women's Magazine,* as well as the Associated Broadcasting Corporation (a television station and six radio stations), ranked high among Philippine corporations. Data for the other newspapers were not generally available, but none boasted a profit; nor did they need one. The media subsidiaries of Soriano, Elizalde, Lopez, and Menzi all received a variety of direct and indirect subsidies and internal transfers. For example, the *Manila Chronicle,* which never reported a profit, satisfied its foreign exchange requirements from Meralco, the Manila Electric Company, also owned by the Lopez family.

It became increasingly apparent throughout the 1960s that newspapers were valuable political instruments. According to one scholar, "The newspapers are operated to support the vested interests of the owner."[6] A Filipino editor observed that "most newspapers here are extensions of business empires. We are a country where, unfortunately, keeping a newspaper is a good defense weapon for big business."[7]

The issue of freedom and responsibility of the press must be understood in the light of this pattern of ownership and control. Publishers, representing the major elite factions, competed against each other with little constitutional, legal, or professional restraint. Their news media became their political instruments.

The second major factor was the concentration of media ownership and the establishment of politically powerful multimedia or trimedia networks. The election campaign of 1969 provided the impetus for these developments. A. Soriano y Cia acquired control of the Radio Mindanao Network and the Inter-Island Broadcasting Network, comprising one television station and sixteen radio stations, in addition to its other economic and print media interests. Elizalde interests expanded to include the Manila Broadcasting Company and the Metropolitan Broadcasting Company, comprising one television station and thirteen radio stations. By far the biggest multimedia network was controlled by the Lopez family through the ABS-CBN Broadcasting Corporation. It included four television

6. John A. Lent, "The Philippines," in John A. Lent, ed., *The Asian Newspapers' Reluctant Revolution* (Ames, Ia.: Iowa State University Press, 1971), p. 207.
7. Amadeo Dacanay, former editor of the *Evening News,* in ibid.

stations, two television relay stations, and over twenty radio stations. In 1970, it also acquired Sarmiento Telecommunications Network, with its twenty-four microwave relay stations, worth over P20 million. ABS-CBN had control over television transmission from Manila to Negros, Cuby, Bacolod, Cagayan de Oro, and Davao.[8]

The third factor was the increasing determination of President Marcos to inhibit criticism of his administration. As it turned out, he was far more sensitive to public criticism and far more determined to control it than any of his predecessors. It should be pointed out that ever since the founding of the Republic, Filipino national politicians have generally felt it necessary to directly own, or indirectly control, at least one major news outlet. Manuel Roxas, who won the presidential election in 1946, ran the *Daily News* and *Balita* as virtual organs of the new Liberal Party. The defeated candidate, former Commonwealth President Sergio Osmeña, then published the *Morning Sun*. Several years later, President Ramon Magsaysay employed the media extensively and systematically as an instrument of governance. Magsaysay's experiences strongly influenced subsequent government-media relations. Virtually all competitors for national political office have sought or recruited allies from the media. When in office, Filipino leaders have continued this alliance. They have also attempted to neutralize criticism from media belonging to other elites, often under the rationale of curbing the excesses and abuses of freedom of the press. On the whole, relations between government and media were characterized not by detachment and mutual respect, but rather by collaborating or feuding.

During his first term in office, President Marcos made repeated attempts to establish a Department of Public Information, which would centralize the press relations activities of his administration. Although he never received congressional approval, he managed to achieve almost the same result through internal reorganization and a greatly expanded budget. The Public Information Office coordinated public and private resources in his 1969 reelection campaign with great success. It is estimated that Marcos spent ten times as much on print media publicity as did his opponent, Senator Sergio Osmeña, the Liberal Party candidate.

After Marcos was reelected in November 1969, government-media

8. All data from *Philippine Mass Media Directory: 1971* (Manila: Philippine Press Institute, 1972).

relations quickly changed. Marcos had won reelection by a very wide margin and he expected widespread support. But he was in no position to fulfill his many campaign promises. The government treasury was nearly exhausted and a team of examiners from the International Monetary Fund had arrived to prescribe emergency measures. In order to satisfy the government's international creditors, Marcos had to devalue the peso and institute a national austerity program.

On January 16, 1970, university students demonstrated against these measures at the gates of Malacañang, the presidential palace. The President's Guard reacted violently and several students were shot and killed. Another, larger confrontation followed on January 20. This time, students were joined by striking workers in a mass demonstration against the Marcos government. Again there was violence, reported widely in the mass media.

President Marcos very much wanted the press on his side in this confrontation, and he went to great lengths and expense to win them over. He invited the publishers to a luncheon after the January student-worker demonstrations, and asked for their cooperation and support. But the publishers did not, on the whole, acquiesce. Joaquin P. Roces, head of the Manila Times Publishing Company, remarked, "We still have in our ranks a number of dedicated aggressive reporters whose allegiance is to the truth."[9] Many prominent journalists supported the students and the workers. They also charged Marcos with gross financial mismanagement, which they attributed to election bribery. Most offensive to these journalists was what they saw as a heavyhanded effort of the president to "capture the press." Relations between the president and the press deteriorated very rapidly after this. It is ironic that President Marcos, after applying more resources to public relations than ever before, after winning an unprecedented reelection campaign by a record vote, became so unpopular so fast, at least on the editorial pages. He reacted with bitter disillusionment. One quote is especially revealing. At one of the Gridiron dinners of the National Press Club in Manila, he complained, "You elect a President, award him the mantle of authority, make him the symbol of sovereignty of the people, and after that— you shoot him down with every weapon you have."[10] He went on

9. "Two Views of the Press," *Press-Forum*, March 1970, p. 9.
10. Ibid.

to accuse his critics—in the same speech and in a number of subsequent public confrontations—of being "whiners," "time-wasters," "fault-finders," "skeptics," "nihilists," "defeatists," "naïve," "uninformed," "inveterate gripers," and "insufferably arrogant."

The press responded with a pooled editorial which appeared under the same banner headline in every major newspaper. It was "An Appeal to the President" to crack down on graft and corruption—in the Marcos government! Then the conflict went beyond verbal exchanges and took a more threatening turn. Quintin and Rizal Yuyitung, publisher and editor of the *Chinese Commercial News,* were abruptly deported to Taiwan, on charges of spreading Communist propaganda. The charges were hardly credible. The newspaper was published in Chinese; it had a very small circulation; and its publisher, Quintin Yuyitung, far from being subversive, was president of the prestigious Manila Overseas Press Club. The only evidence the government offered was an Associated Press news item on Mao Tse-tung, which was carried by several Manila newspapers. Finally, the government announced that the Yuyitung brothers were not actually deported, but rather extradited by the Taiwan government.

Following these events, in March 1970 the administration made its own publishing debut with *Government Report,* a weekly distributed free of charge from the Office of the President. Few people outside the government read the paper. But its very first issue carried an ominous headline: "Can Publishers Foment Disorders?" The new weekly complained that "the national press can no longer be trusted," and therefore, the government had to tell its own story. Marcos also placed the Philippine Broadcasting Company and the Radio-TV-Movie Office directly under his office. The Voice of America radio station was acquired by the National Media Production Center (NMPC) and renamed the Voice of the Philippines. Started as a USAID communications development project, the NMPC eventually became the publicity center for the President's Public Information Office. The budget of the NMPC went up from P9.1 million in fiscal year 1970–1971 to P12 million in 1971–1972. Close friends of the Marcos family also acquired a radio network and began a daily newspaper to further represent administration policy. "Marcos strikes back," wrote one columnist, and many others wondered whether the government was launching a full-scale at-

158　　　　　　　　　　　　DAVID A. ROSENBERG

tack to discredit the press. These suspicions were heightened by large increases in government spending for public relations, media production, indirect subsidies, and verbal assault. One columnist complained, "What the almighty cannot buy or seduce, will be cowed and silenced by threats, or drowned out by an organized chorus of hosannas."[11]

The charges and countercharges polarized relations between Marcos and his critics. Journalists found it difficult to maintain any objective neutrality. "You can only be very friendly or very hostile to Marcos," said one newspaperman. "If you're friendly, then the other newspapermen accuse you of being bought; if you're hostile, then Marcos accuses you of lying."

On the eve of martial law, government-media relations were highly unstable and highly polarized. Two major alternatives emerged from the clamorous debate on the proper role of the press. One side emphasized the freedom of the press as a fundamental civil liberty; the other side emphasized the social responsibility of the press as an instrument for national development. The former advocates were confronted with a number of problems. A variety of structural factors limited the press to a relatively small, upper-class, urban audience. This market was insufficient to sustain an independent media industry. Moreover, most publishers had other economic interests. Journalists were often undertrained and underpaid. It was extremely difficult for most reporters to survive solely on their newspaper salaries. Newspapermen were susceptible to or attracted to other pursuits, including national politics, where the prevailing style of communication further impeded objective reporting. Substantial efforts at internal reform had been made by the Philippine Press Institute through training programs, research, and the establishment of the press council. But far more programs were necessary in order to have a significant impact on the quality of the news profession. The increasing threat of intervention in the freedom of the press did create pressure for internal reform, but not enough to preserve institutional autonomy.

Others were highly critical of the "unbridled freedom of the press." Many journalists themselves complained about the tendencies of the press toward divisive and irresponsible exposés, scandalizing

11. Alfredo R. Roces, "Vulnerable, That's Why," *Manila Times*, May 17, 1970, p. 5.

and hyperexpressiveness. Some newspapermen began organizing a "Second Propaganda Movement," one that would commit the press and other media to the service of national unity and development. Other journalists called upon the government to nationalize the press. They argued that only a strong sense of social responsibility among journalists could ensure the proper exercise of freedom of the press. Unbridled freedom, they argued, often ended up as "national self-flagellation," "a reminder of our colonial mentality," and a "disgrace to the nationalist sensibilities." Within the news media, sentiment for some form of nationalization grew. This trend had little organizational coherence or direction, but it was a clear indication of the basic vulnerability of the press.

President Marcos capitalized on this vulnerability in the week before martial law by accusing the press of "fomenting disorder" and "harboring Communists and Communist sympathizers." His accusation resulted in vitriolic countercharges in the columns of the major dailies. Eddie Monteclaro, president of the National Press Club and secretary-general of the Movement of Concerned Citizens for Civil Liberties (MCCCL) protested the administration's charges and called for a mass rally in Plaza Miranda on Thursday, September 21, 1972. The MCCCL was an ad hoc coalition of over thirty civic, religious, labor, student, teacher, and political-activist groups formed to protest the suspension of the writ of habeas corpus a year earlier. The MCCCL's chairman was Senator Jose Diokno. The principal speaker at the rally was Senator Benigno Aquino, Jr., the chief surviving Marcos opponent in the Liberal Party. One after another, the speakers accused the president of attempting to impose martial law, of instigating the rash of bombings, of increasing foreign intervention in the economy, of raising domestic prices, and of attempting to capture the press. About 30,000 people attended the rally in Plaza Miranda. It received national radio, television, and press coverage. That night, the martial law decree was enacted. The first major action of President Marcos was to shut down every newspaper and radio and television station except his own. In the following few days, a number of opposition leaders were arrested: senators, congressmen, Constitutional Convention delegates, journalists, writers, professors, students, labor union leaders, peasant union leaders, the leaders of almost every other institution that had opposed Marcos. No specific charges were entered for any of these arrests. However, the president did issue a statement that the government would arrest anybody who "had consciously or unconsciously taken part in the conspiracy against the government, given aid and comfort to the forces of insurgency and subversion and have either directly supported, or aided and abetted the subversion of our established values and traditions."

Marcos accused the press specifically of publishing "rumormongering, inflammatory, and libelous news items and commentaries." It can probably be admitted that there were in fact a lot of "rumormongering, inflammatory, and libelous" journalists in the Philippines. But those journalists who landed in jail were generally among the most respected and most professionally responsible ones in the country. They were both influential and critical. These journalists did not accept the administration's claim that Communist terrorists were responsible for the bombings, or for the attempted assassination of Defense Secretary Juan Ponce Enrile, or for the mass assassination attempt on the Liberal Party leadership in Plaza Miranda the previous year. The primary reason they were arrested was to silence their anticipated criticism of the declaration of martial law. It is significant that only one major publisher was arrested at the outset of martial law, Joaquin Roces. He was the only publisher for whom newspaper work was a central concern and not a sideline, the one who had most to lose from the end of the freedom of the press, and consequently the most strongly opposed to President Marcos' policies. This was not the case with Elizalde, Menzi, Soriano, or Lopez. Their other political, economic, and managerial resources are still considerable. Toward these powerful families, President Marcos has adopted a twofold policy: secure their compliance with the provisions of the New Society, or reduce their economic and political influence.

The Charge of Communist Subversion

At the very outset of martial law, all of Manila's daily newspapers, several weeklies, all television channels, and all radio stations were shut down by the national police. Foreign news agencies and cable and telegraph offices were also closed. Many journalists were arrested, including several of the most prominent in the country. Freedom of the press came to a very abrupt halt.

Only one newspaper (the *Philippines Daily Express*), one television station (Kanlaon Broadcasting System's Channel 9), and the government-owned radio station (Voice of the Philippines) were permitted to resume operations in order to broadcast the president's announcement of Proclamation No. 1081, the declaration of martial law. Among other things, Proclamation No. 1081 provided the "general orders for the Government to control media and other means of dissemination of information." Initially, this control over the country's media was exercised by a small committee, consisting of three representatives from the Malacañang Press Office and three representatives from the Department of National Defense. Co-chairmen of the committee were Press Secretary Francisco Tatad and Defense Secretary Enrile. Enforcement was entrusted to a group of army officers in the military's Office of Civil Relations.

The harsh treatment of the media was widely noted by foreign observers. While many were willing to give President Marcos the benefit of the doubt in his handling of domestic violence, few approved of his treatment of the news media. Why did the president resort to such drastic measures? Undoubtedly, he was infuriated with a few newspapermen who were particularly critical of his administration. But he also accused the press, in general, of tolerating attempts "to distort or slant news if not resort to outright falsification."[12]

Three different explanations have been offered by President Marcos for his extensive curtailment of press freedoms under martial law. Originally, he accused the press of "harboring Communists and Communist sympathizers." Therefore the press had to be "controlled and cleansed of these subversive elements."[13] He explained to foreign newsmen that "we did not pick them up on mere mischievousness or vengeance or vindictiveness . . . they were locked up, not because they were critical of me but because they participated in a conspiracy, a conspiracy of the communist party and . . . we got the goods on them."[14]

Hence the first rationale for the sharp curtailment of freedom of

12. "Liars," *Manila Chronicle*, Sept. 17, 1972, p. 3.
13. "NBC-TV Interview with President Ferdinand E. Marcos," Oct. 3, 1972. The text of the interview was published in "NBC-TV Presents Marcos on FM," *Ningas-Cogon*, October 1972. The Communist plot theory was also detailed in a presidential speech to the top officers of the Philippine armed forces, as reported in "Every Citizen Has a Right," *Philippines Daily Express*, Sept. 28, 1972.
14. "Every Citizen Has a Right," p. 6.

the press was that Communist subversion threatened the nation and the media had been infiltrated and subverted by Communist propagandists. In a speech to top officials in the armed forces on September 26, 1972, Marcos explained that the takeover of the news media was a preventive measure:

The enemy uses the weapons of modern revolution, the media—newspapers, television, and radio—to promote anything that assaults and destroys the foundation of society. Therefore the commander-in-chief must meet this threat not only with modern artillery, tanks, bullets, and rifles, but with the most sophisticated weapons of preventive operations, of even media.

This is the rationale for the arrest of some in media who participated in subversion by allowing consciously or unconsciously the printing, publication, dissemination, and spreading of stories to undermine the system in which we live; strengthened the morale, or gave aid and comfort to the enemy.[15]

Such broad charges—against conscious or unconscious participation in subversion—invited skepticism. Marcos, however, promised that the imprisoned newsmen would receive a fair trial and that newspapers which did not participate "openly and frankly in subversion, or participated least, or without malice . . . would be permitted to operate later on."[16] However, none of the detained newsmen ever had a trial of any kind. Nor were formal charges ever made against any of them. No evidence of subversion was offered to justify the detentions. The accusations were quietly dropped; the detained newsmen were gradually all released; and no official explanation has ever been offered. It is difficult to dispel the conclusion that the wholesale clampdown of the press and the rapid arrest of Joaquin Roces, Maximo Soliven, Theodore Locsin, Napoleon Rama, and others was a punitive action against hostile publishers and outspoken political enemies.

Rules of Public Information under Martial Law

Strict government control of the mass media was established within hours of the enactment of martial law. On September 22, 1972, in "Letter of Instruction No. 1," President Marcos ordered Press Secretary Tatad and Defense Secretary Enrile to "take over and control

15. Ibid.
16. Ibid.

or cause the taking over and control of all such newspapers, magazines, radio and television facilities and all facilities and all other media of communications, wherever they are, for the duration of the present emergency."[17] Shortly thereafter, "Letter of Implementation No. 12" created the Department of Public Information. Press Secretary Tatad was appointed the new Secretary of Public Information with the immediate task of preparing guidelines for local and foreign news censorship. The guidelines appeared in Department of Public Information Order No. 1 on September 25. All news media were ordered to "print and broadcast accurate, objective, straight news reports of positive national value, consistent with the efforts of the government to meet the dangers and threats that occasioned the proclamation of martial law and the efforts to achieve a 'new society.' "

The news media were prohibited from carrying "any editorial opinion, commentary, comments or asides, or any kind of political, unauthorized, or objectionable advertising." The new regulations also expressly prohibited:

4a. Materials that tend to incite or otherwise inflame people or individuals against the government or any of its duly constituted authorities.
  b. Materials that undermine the people's faith and confidence in the government or any of its instrumentalities.
  c. Materials that are seditious, not based on facts, or otherwise without definitely established and well-identified verifiable sources, or based on mere allegation or conjecture.
  d. Materials that downgrade or jeopardize the military or the law enforcement authorities, their work and their operations.
  e. Materials that abet, glorify, or sensationalize crime, disorder, lawlessness, violence.
  f. Materials that destroy or tend to destroy public morals as well as morale.
  g. Materials that foment opinions and activities contrary to law.
  h. Materials that sow or generate fear, panic, confusion, ignorance and vulgarity among the people.

The same regulations applied to domestic and foreign news reporting. Similar regulations applied to photographic materials. In

17. Letter of Instruction No. 1, Sept. 22, 1972.

all cases, all material for publication had to be cleared by the Department of Public Information.

Some of the regulations were particularly vague; for example, "No foreign dispatch will be filed from the Philippines which impugns, discredits, questions or criticizes any positive effort of the government." In case of any ambiguity or misunderstanding, however, the rules could be amended or modified, without prior notice.

The effect of such drastic censorship was to eliminate almost all news, except for official releases and statements. This news was disseminated in the few media which, according to Information Secretary Tatad, "have not participated in the communist conspiracy." Tatad also indicated that he was examining the records of the media that remained shut down to determine whether they had "participated willingly or unwillingly, consciously or unconsciously, in the conspiracy against government."[18] There were no provisions for enforcement or penalties; Tatad only said that his department would "act according to our findings."

Although domestic dissent was silenced, foreign criticism increased. A delegation of journalists from India, Japan, and Indonesia arrived in Manila in early October 1972 to confer with officials of the Asian Press Foundation on efforts to loosen the news censorship and to obtain the release of detained newspapermen. The head of the Asian Press Foundation, Joaquin Roces, was himself still under arrest. The delegation met with President Marcos on October 4, and received his assurance that a "Press Consultative Panel" would be organized to "work toward the lifting of censorship and the possible release of detained journalists."[19] In another interview with foreign correspondents, Marcos explained that the Press Consultative Panel would include both media representatives and government representatives. "They shall establish their own rules and they can determine exactly who should operate."[20] A number of journalists were released, but not Roces or several other prominent journalists. Censorship of foreign news was loosened a bit, but domestic controls remained stringent. The visiting delegation of journalists left the Philippines with an agreement under which they would restrain criticism of Philippine martial law in

18. "Reopening of Other Media Establishments Still Being Studied," *Philippines Daily Express,* Sept. 29, 1972, p. 4.

19. "Clashes with Reds Reported," *New York Times,* Oct. 6, 1972, p. 7.

20. "NBC-TV Presents Marcos on FM," p. 24.

the foreign press for a period of fifty days in exchange for government efforts to liberalize the media and free the remaining imprisoned journalists. This was a major victory for President Marcos in his early attempts to neutralize foreign press criticism of his martial law declaration.

The Charge of Oligarchic Conspiracy

The Press Consultative Panel never went into operation. Instead, on November 2, 1972, President Marcos issued Presidential Decree No. 36 which provided a new rationale for government censorship: it was necessary to dismantle the oligarchic structure of ownership of the media. The "Old Society" press was "too sick to heal"; it was "beyond reform," said the president. It had to be replaced completely with a "New Society" press. Public Information Secretary Tatad explained that, under the old society system of freedom of the press,

there were no private rights, where it concerned the newspaperman's curiosity; there were no rules about accuracy, fairness, taste, or intelligence that could not be turned upside down, more or less permanently and without relief. The situation in which commonly fallible men had come to believe themselves infallible and almighty, in all things and to all people, was a situation that had to be cured, whether or not the society came to that point which culminated in the proclamation of martial law. Public decency or intelligence, outraged beyond what it could take, would sooner or later have cried out, and we'd like to believe that official intervention only made this sooner, rather than later.[21]

Official intervention was necessary, said President Marcos, because "the old freedom of the press meant nothing more than the freedom of the elite few to impose their ideas and their rule on the rest of the citizenry."[22] Under the New Society, said Primitivo Mijares, "press freedom is for the people and not for a few self-anointed publishers, who are in the business and not in the vocation of media."[23] These were the reasons why it was necessary to break up the structure of ownership of the old media, explained Secretary

21. Francisco S. Tatad, Speech to the Symposium on Philippine Development, Hyatt Regency, Manila, June 28, 1973.
22. "The Purpose of Man," *Philippine Daily Express*, May 20, 1973, p. 6.
23. Primitivo Mijares, "Freedom Not for Publishers," *IPI Report*, July/August, 1973, p. 7.

Tatad." "It is also the reason why the government has initiated the launching of community newspaper networks all over the country. Eventually, all the people will be reading newspapers which they themselves own and put out."[24]

The major targets of the new decree were the media owners who had previously been hostile to Marcos. The decree cancelled all the existing franchises granted by the Philippine Congress to media owners whose facilities "have remained unused by their holders and those that have violated the terms under which they were issued."[25] As interpreted by Information Secretary Tatad, this meant the permanent closing of the news media that had been shut down at the outset of martial law. The president stated that he would no longer tolerate private monopoly in media ownership.[26]

The decree also created the Mass Media Council, chaired by the secretary of public information and the secretary of national defense. Its executive secretary was retired Brigadier General Ceferino Carreon. Despite the new title, the basic structure of government control remained as before. The Mass Media Council was authorized to review applications for permission to operate any mass media; however, only the president could certify the authority to publish. Certificates of authority were valid for six months, when they would be reviewed by the council.

In a separate statement, Tatad said that foreign news agencies were exempt from the six-month renewal limit. Also, foreign dispatches no longer had to be submitted for "prior clearance," provided that foreign correspondents adhered to the government guidelines contained in Department Order No. 1. Domestic news media were permitted to publish editorials and opinion columns, but only after consulting with the department on who would write the commentaries.

The establishment of the Mass Media Council was an attempt to restore some semblance of normality to the mass media. Appearances, however, were deceptive. After forty-one days the censorship of foreign dispatches had been lifted, but a set of vague guidelines remained. Publications which the military regarded as subversive

24. Tatad, Speech to the Symposium.
25. See report of Pablo Y. Barretto, "Rigid Rules for Media Operations Bared," *Philippine Times*, Nov. 15, 1972, p. 3.
26. "Manila Dooms Some Papers, Networks," *New York Times*, Nov. 3, 1972, p. 6.

or conspiratorial had been permanently banned. Publications which had been allowed to resume or start operations were all very reluctant to risk printing any possible offensive news or commentary. They were given certificates of authority to publish because— in the words of one official—"they've agreed to write positive news."[27] It had been expected that President Marcos would relax his harsh policy toward the media, but there was little evidence of any liberalization from the Mass Media Council.

The first fatality of the new policy was the Manila Times Publishing Company, publisher of the *Manila Times, Taliba,* and the *Daily Mirror.* Its publisher, Joaquin Roces, sent out over 1,600 termination notices to employees as one of the oldest and most respected news organizations in Asia was formally dissolved by its management. A similar fate met the *Manila Chronicle,* owned by Eugenio Lopez, an industrialist, and Ferdinand Lopez, the former vice-president; the *Philippines Herald,* owned by the Soriano family; and the *Evening News,* owned by the Elizalde family.

Eventually, these newspapers were officially terminated under the so-called "normalization" rules issued in November 1975. At the same time, several other publications of the pre-martial law period were also officially terminated, including the *Philippines Free Press,* the *Chinese Commercial News,* and the *Fookien Times.* All of these publications were declared to be "sequestered" papers; that is, they were not permitted to resume activities because, it was claimed, they were associated with subversive or criminal activities. In fact, no charges against these publications or their owners were ever made public. Government plans to replace these publications with "community newspaper networks" were quietly shelved.

By the end of 1972, only three daily newspapers had been allowed to operate. Of these, the *Philippines Daily Express* was by far the largest in terms of circulation. The paper was financed by friends of President Marcos, including Roberto Benedicto, who was appointed Philippine Ambassador to Japan, and Enrique P. Romualdez, who is a cousin of the President's wife, Imelda Romualdez Marcos. It began publishing in May 1972, before martial law was declared. At ten centavos per copy, it was widely regarded as a losing proposition; but after martial law was declared, it became the sole

27. "Foreign Correspondents Face Censorship Perils," *New Orleans Times-Picayune,* Jan. 7, 1973, p. 36.

surviving newspaper. Over the following year, its circulation surpassed half a million, its advertising rates went up 350 percent, and it became a highly profitable enterprise.

The first publisher of the *Daily Express* was Juan A. Perez, Jr., a veteran journalist, who had previously been a public relations advisor to the President at Malacañang. The chief editorial writer was Primitivo Mijares, formerly the head of the palace press corps and also the first president of the revived National Press Club. Hence, from its origins, the *Daily Express* has had very close ties to President Marcos. Not surprisingly, therefore, its editorial and news policy is very proadministration, and it is widely regarded as the quasi-official news organ of the President.

Two other daily newspapers appeared in Manila during the first year of martial law, both backed by close friends of President Marcos. The *Times-Journal*, financed and managed by Edmundo Ongsiaxko, was the first to appear under the new rules. It is published by Philippine Journalists, Inc., which includes most of the principal staff members of the newspaper. Headed by Manuel B. Salak, formerly of the *Manila Times*, most of the staff was drawn from now-defunct newspapers. Secretary Tatad gave his assurances that the *Times-Journal* was "not a house organ of a vested interest and commercial interest." Lorenzo J. Cruz, the assistant secretary of public information, said that the staff had been investigated and had been found to be respectable journalists not involved in corruption or subversion.[28]

The third newspaper to appear in Manila was the *Bulletin Today*. Apart from a slight name change, it is basically the same paper as the pre-martial law *Manila Daily Bulletin*. Its publisher, and principal owner, is H. M. Menzi, a long-time friend and former senior military advisor to President Marcos. He still holds the rank of brigadier general. The top editorial staff includes Ben F. Rodriguez, Teddy Owen, Jr., and Pat Gonzales, all of the former *Daily Bulletin* staff. Probably the oldest newspaper in the Philippines, its durability is due to its small, faithful audience, primarily in the commerce and shipping community. Another business-oriented daily, *Business Day*, continued publication without interruption by martial law.

These newspapers, all close to the Marcos government, covered

28. Henry Kamm, "Marcos Approves New Newspaper," *New York Times*, Oct. 17, 1972. For further details, see "New Daily OK'd," *Business Day*, Oct. 17, 1972.

the daily news in Manila in the immediate post-martial law period. They also provided the main daily outlets for commercial and government advertising. This afforded them a substantial source of revenues, reported the Press Foundation of Asia, "to a point where they can even afford to turn down some [advertisements]. The suspicion of many press people is that the Administration will allow its friends to take advantage of this situation."[29]

For many observers, the "oligarchic conspiracy" might have been a more plausible rationale for regulating the press than "Communist subversion." But in practice, the oligarchic structure of media ownership was not dismantled; rather, it has been contracted. The official policy was to take control of the media away from the oligarchy and broaden public ownership. Just the opposite has happened. Media ownership is now concentrated among a few elite factions, all of them either close friends or relatives of the Marcos family.[30]

The Media as Instrument of Social Change

By the beginning of 1973, President Marcos had weathered the storm of protest, both domestic and foreign. Another, presumably more durable rationale for regulating the press was announced in a presidential decree: the media were to become "an effective instrument in the attainment of social change."[31] They were to become committed to the tasks of nation building and development.

Attention was first turned toward the expansion of the government's information services. The Department of Public Information was reorganized to coordinate the Presidential Information Office, a bureau of broadcast, and a national news service. Information Secretary Tatad requested the peso equivalent of about $17 million for the entire operation. A considerable portion of this was intended to absorb some of the many journalists who had been unemployed since the beginning of martial law. A number of regulatory committees were spawned within the department: the Bureau of Standards for Mass Media, the Bureau of National and Foreign

---

29. George, "The Party's Over."
30. For more information on the Marcos family and their relationship with current media activity, see John A. Lent, "The Philippine Press under Martial Law," *Index on Censorship*, Spring, 1974; and Ruben Diario, "Managing the Media Filipino Style," *Bulletin of Concerned Asian Scholars*, January-March, 1974.
31. Presidential Decree No. 191, May 11, 1973.

Information, the Bureau for Research, Evaluation, and Special Operations, and several other bureaus. The department became the major manufacturer of news, press releases, books, radio and television programs, and even an LP album, *No Shade but Light,* a recording of excerpts of presidential speeches.

By March 1973, the government was sufficiently self-confident to permit the National Press Club to resume its activities. President Marcos himself inducted the new officers of the organization and instructed them to avoid "publicity-making and image-building" and "to write and talk about positive things with excellence as their only criterion." He also said that he has "specifically directed that the private sector should be represented in the Mass Media Council" and that "the government would stay away from their self-regulating activities."[32]

A highly qualified form of self-regulation did finally evolve when President Marcos decreed the removal of direct government supervision of the mass media. On May 11, 1973, he abolished the Mass Media Council and created instead the Media Advisory Council, composed of representatives of the media and headed by the president of the National Press Club. In Presidential Decree No. 191, Marcos took note that, under his martial law rule, the mass media "have shown willingness to institute a system of self-regulation and international discipline within their ranks to the end that no part of media may ever again, consciously or unconsciously, engage or take part in any conspiracy against the Government." Failure to do so would again bring government intervention, he noted.

However, government supervision of the mass media was not removed; it was only supplemented by the Media Advisory Council. The council could review licenses to operate media, but they were only valid with the president's approval. The council could issue guidelines and rules for the mass media, but again, they were only valid with the president's approval. The president could also appoint his own representatives to the panel. Finally, all news media employees had to secure work permits, which were only granted after security clearance from the military.

In practice, the Media Advisory Council worked closely with the Depratment of Public Information. The work of drawing up guidelines was done within the Department's Bureau of Standards for

32. "Media Is Asked: Regulate Selves," *Bulletin Today,* Mar. 8, 1973, pp. 1, 7.

Mass Media (BSMM), headed by Andres Cristobal Cruz. The BSMM formed a series of committees, consisting of representatives from the bureau and the private sector, which produced a forty-five page document entitled "Policies, Objectives, Organizational Set-up, Code of Ethical Conduct, Guidelines, Rules and Regulations for Mass Media." The regulations begin by acknowledging that "freedom of the press is one of the most fundamental human rights," but then go on to list several chapters of qualifications. For example: "Under the present conditions of emergency, the media should be encouraged to work closely with the government in attaining maximum stability," and "It is the responsibility of all media men . . . to see that their writing or broadcasting may not endanger the program of national consolidation or confidence in government," and "News should be avoided that will bring into hatred or contempt, or excite disaffection towards the government as well as the various instrumentalities under it."

The council further required all mass media operators to sign an "instrument of adherence" promising "wholehearted support" of the regulations. Despite all these efforts to clarify "the role of press as an instrument of social change," the government often found it necessary to provide supplementary instructions. In one memorandum, the news media were told to "refrain from reporting the results of studies ordered by the President . . . unless they are first cleared by the Office of the President." In another, they were told to "refrain from reporting on any statement made by certain public officials seeking to heap the blame for certain allegedly irregular situations on another official or government agency." In yet another, they were told to "refrain from giving publicity to any stories on crime or alleged epidemics that tend to create the wrong impression here or abroad."[33] In sum, the council lacked credibility as an independent, civilian, self-regulatory agency of the mass media.

The role of the Philippine news media "as an instrument for the attainment of social change" remains ambiguous. What topics can be discussed? What opinions can be expressed? What news reported? What is permitted and what is prohibited? There are no clear-cut answers to these questions. As long as there is no writ of habeas corpus, Philippine newspapermen are going to be extremely

---

33. For further details, see "More Curbs for RP News Media" and " 'Sunshine' News Guidelines" in *Philippine Times*, June 30, 1973, p. 12.

172   DAVID A. ROSENBERG

cautious. They are subject to arrest without warrant, and to detention for an indefinite period without charge. There have been
several cases of arrest and detention. Consequently, journalists have
been reluctant to report even the most objective criticism of government policies. They have virtually nothing but praise for the Marcos
family and their close associates. The credibility of the press is so
low, according to Sidney Schanberg of the *New York Times,* that
it has become a mere publicity machine, and therefore an embar-
rassing liability of the government.[34] President Marcos himself has
admitted that the press has become too sycophantic and obse-
quious.[35] His press secretary, Francisco Tatad, has also complained
that the press is "excessively conformist."[36] The press, he claimed,
"went from too much criticism in the old society to excessive, incompetent praise" in the new society.[37] He encouraged more in-
depth reporting and evaluation of government policy. The press,
however, has been understandably reluctant to venture out of
bounds. Former columnist and ambassador J. V. Cruz called the
situation a "national scandal and disgrace."[38] These criticisms come
from the proponents of a guided press for the Philippines, from the
government itself. Through their own criticisms, they have undermined this third explanation for ending freedom of the press. The
news media now lack both credibility and legitimacy. It is not now
"an effective instrument in the attainment of social change." It is
more of a handicap in the government's attempts to win popular
support.

The Actual Bases for Government Control

Three different explanations for restricting the freedom of the
press have been offered by the martial law government of President
Marcos: the need to cleanse the media of Communist subversion,
the necessity to dismantle the old oligarchic conspiracy, and the role
of the press as an instrument of social change. However, as we have
seen, there is little evidence to support any of them. In each case,
there has been a large discrepancy between the declared official

34. Sidney H. Schanberg, "FM's Thorn: His Publicity Machine," *Philippine Times,*
July 15–31, 1974.
35. Ibid.
36. Bernardo Ronquillo, "Cloud over the Sunshine Press," *Far Eastern Economic
Review,* Apr. 16, 1973.
37. Ibid.
38. Derek Davies, "Traveller's Tales," *Far Eastern Economic Review,* May 27,
1974.

policy and the actual pattern of government control. What other explanations can be offered? The evidence presented here suggests that there have indeed been a few significant changes in government policy toward the mass media; however, these can best be explained as attempts of the Marcos administration to establish and strengthen its powers under a martial law regime of dubious constitutional legitimacy. The changes that have occurred can be explained in terms of three major factors. First, the initial policy of closing down virtually the entire mass media was intended to silence the anticipated criticism of the declaration of martial law. Second, after martial law was imposed, President Marcos attempted to provide some semblance of legitimacy and normality through a selective loosening of controls over the news media. Third, as the government acquired some meaure of voluntary support, Marcos moved to weaken permanently the influence of his political opponents. These three factors deserve to be discussed in turn.

The real motive behind the initial policy is clearly demonstrated in the wholesale closings and arbitrary arrests of publishers and journalists known to be critical of President Marcos. The policy had strong support among several army officers who viewed the news media as being directly responsible for the growing discontent of past years.[39] Marcos responded to these views by placing the job of censorship in the army's Office of Civil Relations. The army has remained extremely sensitive to any adverse publicity or criticism of government policy, however valid. Even rumors and the spreading of rumors were banned as subversive activities, ipso facto. Brigadier General Fidel Ramos, chief of the Philippine Constabulary, declared that "rumor-mongers and those who thrive on fishing out false information inimical to the public welfare or that would tend to make the people unduly worried or jittery will be arrested and detained."[40] In this instance, the rumors alleged that the constabulary was conducting house-to-house nighttime searches in various "zones" around Manila, a practice reminiscent of the Japanese Occupation. The rumors were subsequently confirmed—but not in the Philippine news media.[41]

Secondly, in an effort to provide a semblance of legitimacy and

39. For further details, see T. J. S. George, "Media Moderation," *Far Eastern Economic Review*, Dec. 2, 1972, p. 14.

40. *Times-Journal*, Oct. 27, 1972.

41. Henry S. Hayward, "Night Raid in Manila," *Christian Science Monitor*, reprinted in *Philippine Times*, Dec. 15, 1972, p. 5.

normality in the Philippine media, President Marcos had made several tactical concessions to placate foreign press criticism. Marcos, Enrile, and Tatad all had occasion to meet with delegations from the International Press Institute, and after each meeting a few more journalists were released from detention.[42] The first major interviews that Marcos granted after the declaration of martial law were with foreign correspondents from *Newsweek* and NBC. In general, control over foreign news correspondents has not been as strict as control over domestic news. In turn, almost all favorable foreign press comment is dutifully reported in the Manila dailies.[43] Government officials have pointed out that "the new measures taken to cure the affliction in the press have succeeded in giving the Philippines, for the first time, a more accurate, and therefore more favorable image in the foreign press."[44] The government also attempted to boost a more favorable image through special advertising supplements in foreign newspapers.[45]

In order to provide a further aura of legitimacy for his policy toward the media, President Marcos has also tolerated a certain degree of domestic criticism of his administration. An example of this occurred a month before the constitutional referendum of January 1973, when Marcos lifted the martial law restrictions on freedom of speech and freedom of the press. He ordered his departments of Information, Defense, and Justice to "see to it that all media give an opportunity to those opposing and favoring the ratification of the new Constitution to meet face to face in formal debate. You will direct that all printing presses print all forms of propaganda whether in favor or against the new constitution and see to it that all military personnel allow their open and free discussion."[46]

Criticism of the proposed constitution did indeed arise, in great volume. In addition, several petitioners, including Eddie Monteclaro, president of the old National Press Club, asked the Supreme Court

42. Negotiations detailed in "News of the World's Press: The Philippines," *IPI Report,* February 1973, p. 2.
43. For an example, see Maria Teresa Manuel, "How the World Learned . . . and What It Was Told," *Philippines Daily Express,* Sept. 26, 1972, p. 5.
44. Tatad, Speech to the Symposium.
45. For an example, see "Philippine Prospects," *New York Times,* June 10, 1973 (Section II). The thirty-two-page supplement, produced by the Department of Public Information, was subtitled "After Twenty-six Years of Democratic Stalemate, Dynamic Leadership Directs the Republic toward the New Society."
46. Tillman Durdin, "Manila Suspends Curbs on Debating New Constitution," *New York Times,* Dec. 21, 1972, p. 3.

to stop the plebiscite on the new charter on grounds that it was undemocratic, improperly drafted, confusing, contradictory, dictatorial, and could not be properly considered until full civil liberties were restored. This was a very strong indictment of the martial law regime and could not be tolerated by Marcos. The petitioners' presentations were barred from publication; the plebiscite was postponed; and harsh restrictions on public debate were reinstituted. Shortly thereafter, Marcos abandoned the idea of a plebiscite in favor of "citizen assemblies," which provided a way to manipulate public opinion in support of the new constitution.[47] Subsequently, the Supreme Court dismissed the petitioners' complaints as "moot."

The president's tolerance of criticism turned out to be very limited and brief. His repressive reaction created an atmosphere of fear and mute compliance in the media. Very few journalists were willing to report anything that could be construed as critical, even when given official sanction, for fear of reprisal.

The third factor, the attempts of President Marcos to weaken permanently the influence of his political opponents, is certainly not limited to the mass media, but it is clearly evident in that arena. The initial pattern of arrests and closings cannot be wholly explained in terms of a Communist conspiracy or an oligarchic one. None of the detained newspapermen was specifically accused or tried for conspiracy. What they had most in common was their known criticism of the Marcos administration. It can be speculated that the major reason so many of these people were arrested in the first place was to provide Marcos with bargaining leverage in order to force them to cooperate with his martial law regime. Marcos bargained with the press in the same manner that he bargained with the church, the Federation of Free Farmers, the sugar lobby, and other powerful groups in the country. Those who cooperated—Andre and Jose Soriano, Hans Menzi—were permitted to resume their activities. Those who did not—Eugenio Lopez, Sr. and Jr., and Joaquin Roces—were subjected to further harassment and dispossession of their interests. In the euphemistic words of President Marcos, "They have rejected their responsibility to assist in land reform and to remedy other injustices."[48]

47. Tillman Durdin, "Marcos Gets His Kind of Democracy," *New York Times,* Jan. 21, 1973.
48. Jack Foisie, "Marcos Stripping Power of Richest Families," *Los Angeles Times,* Apr. 19, 1973, pp. 1, 14.

One can not help being skeptical about Marcos' motives. Several elite families remain secure under martial law rule. However, the elite families who have been the target of Marcos' actions—Lopez, Osmeña, and Aquino—are all old political enemies. Marcos has taken the opportunity of martial law to dismantle their economic interests and put an end to this old feud in the oligarchy. For example, friends of the president are taking control of the idle Lopez media facilities.[49] The government has also removed Meralco, the Manila Electric Company, from Lopez ownership. Acquired by the Lopez family in 1961, Meralco became the biggest public utility in the country and the center of a conglomerate of companies engaged in manufacturing, construction, oil refining, and other activities. A government investigation into alleged mismanagement in Meralco led Eugenio Lopez, Sr., and Fernando Lopez to the decision to sell out their private interests.[50]

In summary, the official rationales for government control of the media have not been substantiated or applied consistently. Major discrepancies remain between official policy and actual government control of the mass media. The discrepancies can best be explained by the efforts of the Marcos administration to strengthen its position in power and weaken the influence of its political opponents.

Civil Liberties and National Development

The existing situation in the Philippine news media is not unusual in Southeast Asia, but is it necessary or desirable? Is it true, as President Marcos and his supporters assert, that "the loss of civil liberties is the necessary price that Filipinos must pay for political order and economic growth"? Is it possible that stable government is the first prerequisite for national unity and that a free and outspoken press is in fact a serious threat to both stable government and national unity? The Marcos administration has calculated that the national purpose is not well served by the free expression of conflicting, confusing, and often critical views. It may reason that the administration must strengthen itself before it can pursue national development effectively.

49. Ibid.
50. For further details, see "Offer Is Made to Sell Meralco," *Times-Journal*, Sept. 18, 1973, pp. 1, 8, and "Meralco Stocks Move Up," *Times-Journal*, Sept. 19, 1973, pp. 1, 8.

It can be seen in the Philippines, as elsewhere in Southeast Asia, that there are strong pressures against a libertarian pattern of control of the media. There is a widely recognized need to create a pervasive loyalty to the nation rather than to the family, the ethnic community, or the regional group. Strong, unified, ideological leadership is required to create this national consciousness. There is widespread popular support for economic development in the Philippines, but this support must be mobilized and harnessed. Social discipline must be instilled to generate capital and productive skills for the developmental effort. This also requires strong, unified leadership. The magnitude of the tasks confronting the Philippines is so great that the leadership demands and expects full popular support for its objectives. If most Filipinos gave their full support to President Marcos and his plans to build a New Society, they would probably find little value in diverse and divergent views of the press or in competing political parties. But this is not the case. There are large segments of the population that, for a variety of reasons, have withheld their support. Because of various religious, regional, and ideological differences, they are unwilling to work under the leadership of the Marcos government. Some groups, notably the Muslims and others in the south, are probably unwilling to accept any strong nationalist leadership from Manila. They still maintain active opposition, sometimes violent opposition, to the current regime. In such cases, their opposition is regarded as treason. Indeed, under the current regime, virtually any opposition is regarded as treason.

In the absence of an effective and legitimate means of expressing dissent or opposition, both the government and the people are likely to be dissatisfied with each other. The people are asked to accept and actively support a regime purely on the basis of proclamations and decrees, without any knowledge of the factors involved, the priorities assessed, the arguments for and against, or the calculation of national interest. This policy of noncommunication is not likely to strengthen loyalties to the nation. It is almost always more persuasive to hear many sides of the argument, rather than just the final decree.

In seeking to achieve a higher degree of government stability and national unity, the Marcos government has imposed a system of uniformity on the Philippine press. In doing so, it has successfully avoided any sustained criticism of its policies. But the long-term costs may soon outweigh the short-term benefits. The "captured press" of the Philippines has no credibility, even to its chief architects; how can they expect the rest of the country to believe it? National unity and popular participation in the nation-building effort would be better served by a spontaneous diversity of opinion, rather than an imposed uniformity of opinion. The existence of a diversity of opinion would provide a forum for the discussion, explanation, and debate of public policy. It would permit a means to assess popular response to government policy and to mobilize popular support for national unity. Without this opportunity for diversity, participation is meaningless.

The argument presented here for freedom of the press in the Philippines does not necessarily imply a restoration of the pre-martial law mass media. In general, Filipino journalists themselves neither expect nor desire a return to the situation that existed before martial law.[51] Nor do they desire a continuation of the lack of press freedom as exists under martial law. But they do not foresee any realistic alternatives.

There is one possibility that receives little attention, but which appears increasingly likely. The Marcos government itself may voluntarily grant greater press freedoms in order to better monitor and control its own bureaucracy and policies. This motive was evident in the appeal Defense Secretary Enrile made to the press and other groups to help him deal with military abuses of authority. His memorandum of August 12, 1975, offers the press some protection from military harassment; it provides that the military shall not "summon, arrest, or detain" any member of the news media without his prior clearance in writing.[52] A similar motive was evident in President Marcos' appeal for public support for his "sweeping and continuous" program of government reforms. In September 1975, he also asked for the help of all Filipinos, and in particular the press, in reporting all incidents of abuse of authority.[53] Some Manila newspapers responded with front-page stories on corruption and scandal

---

51. For more information on how Filipino journalists view their newspapers, see David A. Rosenberg, "Redefining Freedom: The Changing Ideology of Filipino Journalists," paper presented at the Midwest Association of Asian Studies, University of Ohio, Athens, Oct. 24, 1975.

52. *Bulletin Today*, Aug. 14, 1975.

53. Arnold Zeitlin, "High Society Crimes Put Strain on Marcos," *Bangkok Post*, Sept. 30, 1975.

in high circles and with editorial-page columns demanding greater press freedoms. But there is still considerable uncertainty on the extent of this new permissiveness of the regime.[54]

Unfortunately, these guarantees of press freedom, limited as they are, are only personal, not institutional. Marcos and Enrile could change their policies and clamp down again, as they have done on previous occasions. There are still no constitutional guarantees to support or extend these civil liberties. However, this recent turn of events does provide emphatic evidence that even an authoritarian government needs reliable public information for its own policies and an effective system of mass communication for public support. Mass communication is a two-way process; it involves both message and reply, information and feedback. Communication, literally, is the process of making a community. This is perhaps the best defense of freedom of expression: it is the best way to build a national community.

54. See account of Leo Gonzaga, "Where Timidity Is the Better Part of Valour," *Far Eastern Economic Review*, Oct. 3, 1975.

5. The Political Economy of Refeudalization

Robert B. Stauffer
UNIVERSITY OF HAWAII

The overthrow of the Philippine political system by President Marcos in September 1972 would have occasioned more serious intellectual attention than it has so far received, had it occurred a decade earlier, before such events had become commonplace in the Third World. At the time of the coup, America's impending defeat in Indochina totally overshadowed events in the Philippines and thereby contributed to this inattention. In the years since then, America's preoccupation with its Watergate-revealed political pathologies may well have dampened any ardor for seeking to understand the causal forces involved in the destruction of a competitive political system in yet another Southeast Asian nation, even if the one being destroyed had long been claimed—especially by Americans—as one of the few viable democracies in the Third World. This inattention deserves remedy. In this chapter I propose to make a beginning by describing the processes involved in the emergence of a coalition of interests—domestic and foreign—willing to overthrow the institutions of Philippine politics and to create an alternative administrative state system more congruent with its goals.

Among the three central problems to be addressed in this chapter, one will be the changes in the alliances supporting and opposing President Marcos during his administration and especially the creation under his aegis of a new coalition willing to overthrow the system. How the winning coalition proceeded to carry out its program will constitute the second theme, and the major portion of the chapter. My third concern is with the larger issues embedded in the coup, issues that should be made to contribute to our understanding of the causal forces associated with the creation and sustenance of authoritarian regimes in Third World nations and with the maintenance of underdevelopment.[1] This theme will be discussed first, since even a nonformalized model of the causal elements associated with the coup should assist us in understanding what took place and in relating the Philippine case to the larger body of theory dealing with authoritarianism in the Third World.

As the chapter title suggests, I begin with the assumption that Philippine martial law marks the emergence of tighter and to some extent new relationships with external systems,[2] and, by implication, the defeat of those groups urging the expansion of that degree of Philippine autonomy achieved in the pre-coup era. The local effect of the system change was the imposition of authoritarian controls over society and the dismemberment of democratic institutions. Much social science literature sees this type of move into authoritarianism as perfectly consistent with the predominant "lower class" makeup of a poor society such as that of the Philippines,[3] and certainly predictable on the basis of social and economic indicators[4] and of the reactions of systems under "stress."[5]

While a rather comprehensive body of theoretical literature exists on authoritarianism and on specific authoritarian regimes,[6] little

1. The term might better be "dependent development," since the current model advanced by most industrial nations for poor countries is to permit and even encourage a limited degree of industrialization in the Third World so long as it remains safely dominated from the metropolitan centers. Technological dominance assures this. See M. Merhav, *Technological Dependence, Monopoly and Growth* (London: Pergamon, 1969).

2. The post-coup New Society regime has moved to open diplomatic and trade relations with Soviet-bloc nations and with the Peoples' Republic of China. Despite this success in breaking out of an earlier Cold War set of constraints on Philippine international relations, these are only cosmetic changes. The significant modifications in Philippine relationships with the outside world have been of a type to increase Philippine dependence on, and to more firmly integrate the Philippines into, an American-Japanese-dominated sector of the world economy.

3. S. M. Lipset, *Political Man* (New York: Doubleday, 1963).

4. P. Cutright predicted that the Philippines, because its political institutions were "overdeveloped" for its social and economic base, could be expected to resolve the difference "by decreasing their level of political development." "National Political Development: Measurement and Analysis," *American Sociological Review* 28 (April 1963), 253–64, esp. p. 263. Also see J. S. Coleman, "Conclusion: The Political Systems of the Developing Areas," in G. A. Almond and J. S. Coleman, eds., *The Politics of the Developing Areas* (Princeton, N.J.: Princeton University Press, 1960).

5. D. C. Korten, "Situational Determinants of Leadership Structure," in G. D. Paige, ed., *Political Leadership* (New York: Free Press, 1972).

6. For an introduction to the literature, see citations in S. P. Huntington and C. H. Moore, *Authoritarian Politics in Modern Society: The Dynamics of Established One-Party Systems* (New York: Basic Books, 1970); J. J. Linz, "An Authoritarian Regime: Spain," in E. Allardt and S. Rokkan, eds., *Mass Politics: Studies in Political*

attention is given to causes for a turn to such political forms except to view them as natural for poor societies seeking rapid economic development. In fact, much of the accepted political development theory implicitly (and frequently explicitly) supports authoritarianism as the proper form of politics for underdeveloped polities as they face the "crises" of development and seek "stability."[7]

Theorists who work largely within a framework that views underdevelopment as symbiotically related to overdevelopment, and who deal with concepts of dependency and domination, imperialism, and center/periphery relations, also typically take as a given the fact that the Third World partners in these relationships will have authoritarian political systems.[8] But since the interesting theoretical problem to these analysts is not the political systems of the poor nations, their contributions, while central to any understanding of underdevelopment, are of less help in dealing with the issues associated with the creation of authoritarian regimes.[9]

Recent work, however, suggests that this gap is rapidly being closed. P. C. Schmitter in an essay titled "The 'Portugalization' of Brazil?" specifically links "protracted authoritarian rule" with "'de-

---

Sociology (New York: Free Press, 1970); and J. J. Linz, "The Future of an Authoritarian Situation or the Institutionalization of an Authoritarian Regime: The Case of Brazil," in A. Stepan, ed., *Authoritarian Brazil: Origins, Policies, and Future* (New Haven, Conn.: Yale University Press, 1973).

7. G. A. Almond and G. B. Powell, *Comparative Politics: A Developmental Approach* (Boston: Little, Brown, 1966); S. P. Huntington, *Political Order in Changing Societies* (New Haven, Conn.: Yale University Press, 1968); R. B. Pratt, "The Underdeveloped Political Science of Development," *Studies in Comparative International Development* VIII (Spring 1973), 88–112; and M. Kesselman, "Order or Movement? The Literature of Political Development as Ideology," *World Politics* 26: 1 (October 1973), 139–54.

8. Dependency theory is discussed by S. J. Bodenheimer, "Dependency and Imperialism: The Roots of Latin American Underdevelopment," *Politics and Society* 1 (May 1971), 327–58; also see A. G. Frank, *Capitalism and Underdevelopment in Latin America* (New York: Monthly Review Press, 1967); A. G. Frank, *Latin America: Underdevelopment or Revolution* (New York: Monthly Review Press, 1969); J. Galtung, "Feudal Systems, Structural Theory of Revolutions," *IPRA Studies in Peace Research* 1 (1970), 110–88, and "A Structural Theory of Imperialism," *Journal of Peace Research* 2 (1971), 81–118; L. R. Alschuler, "Satellization and Stagnation in Latin America," *International Studies Quarterly* 20:1 (March 1976); and J. D. Cockcroft, A. G. Frank, and D. L. Johnson, *Dependence and Underdevelopment: Latin America's Political Economy* (Garden City, N.Y.: Doubleday, 1972).

9. One important exception to this was the application of "linkage theory" to the support of authoritarianism in Brazil. See D. A. Chalmers, "Developing on the Periphery: External Factors in Latin American Politics," in J. N. Rosenau, ed., *Linkage Politics: Essays on the Convergence of National and International Systems* (New York: Free Press, 1969).

layed-dependent' development," and while he seems to assume that the original imposition of authoritarianism by the Brazilian military in 1964 was a "within-system" change, he argues that the "system could be in trouble" if "foreign capitalists, international civil servants, or United States officials lose confidence in the Brazilian military's capacity to guarantee stability."[10]

A study of the Philippine case might provide data for extending this body of theory to include conditions under which intersystem relationships contribute to the destruction of indigenous representative political institutions and to the creation of an authoritarian regime.[11] While few relatively democratic polities remain in the Third World to be transformed into authoritarian systems, a closer examination of the linkage mechanisms through which one was transformed will augment our knowledge about the day-to-day forces that work to maintain authoritarianism as the modal political form for poor nations. To the degree that empirical studies substantiate the existence of a symbiotic political relationship between the industrial and the poor nations, as has already been established to exist for their economies, and if that relationship typically consigns the poor nations to authoritarian regimes while reserving democratic ones for the developed nations, then important new questions will have been raised for political development theorists.[12]

In two related essays that have since become classics, Johan Galtung[13] constructed a general model to explain an important set of relationships (including the political) typically existing between developed and underdeveloped countries, relationships that sustain the asymmetrical distribution of values between the groups. This

10. P. C. Schmitter, "The 'Portugalization' of Brazil?" in A. Stepan, ed., *Authoritarian Brazil: Origins, Policies, and Future* (New Haven, Conn.: Yale University Press, 1973).

11. A. Lijphart provides a useful review of the uses to which a case study can be put, and a general defense of this type of work. This case study of the Philippines would fall largely within his "hypothesis-generating" category, A. Lijphart, "Comparative Politics and the Comparative Method," *American Political Science Review* 65 (September 1971), 682–93.

12. As long as no relationship is assumed to exist (beyond "international relations") between industrial and poor nations, developmentalists can advocate authoritarianism for developing peoples without experiencing cognitive dissonance. Should the connection between the types of political systems be established, then they would have to admit their preference for a global stratification system based on unequal distribution of both economic *and* political goods or construct a social science in which values are more openly integrated into theory and practice.

13. Galtung, "Feudal Systems"; "A Structural Theory."

model—and I will work with his "feudalism" version[14]—is stronger than those produced by *dependencia* and neo-Marxist imperialism theorists in that it is more general, can be applied to relationships between other than only capitalist nations, and has already been operationalized and tested.[15] A nonformal version of the theory states that a *feudal* relationship exists between two levels of units when "the interaction relation is highly asymmetric so that influence flows much *more* from high to low than vice versa and the exchange of value in general takes place on terms that favor higher strata *more* than lower strata. Further, there is *little* horizontal interaction relative to the amount of vertical interaction. And, there is *little* multilateral interaction relative to all the bilateral interaction there is."[16]

Defeudalization can begin when any one of these four relationships is reversed, and complete defeudalization would demand equalization of each. Political independence of colonies, for example, constituted a limited degree of defeudalization of one of the modes of foreign domination; gaining partial control over a national economy, as was done during the period of protectionism in the Philippines, represents a modest additional advance in the same direction. If the nationalists' demands advanced in the late 1960s and early 1970s in the Philippines had been even partially achieved, defeudalization would have been radically advanced.

Refeudalization,[17] however, can be imposed on any one of the feudal relationships, and Galtung argues that the probability of refeudalization "seems high" for units in the world system because, among other reasons, of the "great rank difference" (i.e., gross

14. Galtung's model of feudal relationships, which makes more formal the relationships that have been generalized from studies of feudal systems as they have existed in history, could be usefully employed in the study of any feudal system.

15. Galtung, "A Structural Theory"; N. P. Gleditsch, "Trends in World Airline Patterns," *Journal of Peace Research* 4 (1967), 366–408, where a portion of an earlier version of the Galtung theory was tested; J. Galtung, C. Beck, and J. Jaastad, "Educational Growth and Educational Disparity" (Oslo: Chair in Conflict and Peace Research, University of Oslo, 1975); R. D. Walleri, "The Political Economy of International Inequality: An Empirical Investigation of Economic Imperialism," Ph.D. dissertation, University of Hawaii, 1976.

16. Galtung, "Feudal Systems," p. 129.

17. The term is especially felicitous since it escapes certain conceptual difficulties that similar words suffer, e.g., "recolonization" or "neocolonization," or the wordiness found in one attempt to describe an aspect of the same process, Sunkel's "transnationalization of the capitalist system." (O. Sunkel, "A Critical Commentary on the United Nations Report on Multinational Corporations in World Development," *IDS Discussion Paper* No. 52 [June 1974], p. 2).

power differences) among units and the limited resources available for the types of interaction demanded if defeudalization is to be a success. As will be seen in the following pages, the changes instituted under martial law in the Philippines represent a reversal of earlier defeudalization trends and the acceptance of new forms of penetration and control from the outside. In short, the era since September 1972 is one during which refeudalization has occurred in the relationships of the Philippines to the larger world system.

The Refeudalization/Authoritarian Model

For refeudalization accompanied by a turn to authoritarian rule to take place in a previously democratic polity such as the Philippines, significant changes must precede the coup. While the following list may not be exhaustive, it contains the basic dimensions:

1. The ideological climate must have shifted in a manner to support authoritarianism as a proper political form for poor nations. The mass of political development theory produced during the 1960s gave this support by emphasizing nation building, rational development, and various linear models each tending to postpone issues of political rights and popular control of the political process until after relatively high levels of social and economic development have been reached.
2. There must be resources in the poor nation desired by the outside that are either threatened or have taken on new significance because of other changes in the world.
3. Before a system-changing coup can take place against a well-institutionalized representative government, the new developmental ideology must have penetrated key strata of the government. In a sense these strata—the technocrats—constitute a counterelite against the politicians whom they will replace in the new system.
4. A change to an authoritarian pattern of government requires a buildup of the police and the military, and the prior militarization of the society.
5. Such a change also requires support wider than that to be found only within the government. Since refeudalization will take place in relationships with nations and institutions in the capitalist world, important sectors of the business community will have to join the counter-revolutionary coalition.

6. Not one of these conditions takes place in isolation: each is intimately assciated with representative groups from industrial nations, and each rests on either new or newly strengthened ties based on relationships clearly structured along patterns of dominance/dependency.

Following the successful overthrow of a previously democratic polity, a *dependent-authoritarian* regime will perform certain tasks if refeudalization is to be institutionalized:

1. Political institutions through which nationalist demands were typically voiced must be suppressed and (at a later date) pliable substitutes created. At a minimum, this phase includes the elimination of parliament, political parties, an independent judiciary, and regional political institutions.
2. Leadership of the nationalist movement must be neutralized, and controls established to neutralize potential opposition activity.
3. Mass media must be placed under authoritarian control, and directed to promulgate the ideology of the new system.
4. The degree of autonomy permitted groups must be significantly limited in comparison with the system that was replaced.[18]

18. J. J. Linz includes in his comprehensive definition of authoritarianism the observation that such regimes typically permit a limited, controlled degree of pluralism ("Spain," in Allardt and Rokkan, p. 225). One of the main operational modes of authoritarianism—corporatism—is built on a rationalized model of pluralism. Corporatism, to use P. Schmitter's definition, is a "system of interest representation in which the constituent units are organized into a limited number of singular, compulsory, non-competitive, hierarchically-ordered and functionally predetermined categories, certified or licensed (if not created) by the State and granted a deliberate representational monopoly within their respective categories in exchange for observing certain governmentally imposed controls on their selection of leaders and articulation of demands and supports." In L. S. Graham, *Portugal: The Decline and Collapse of an Authoritarian Order,* Sage Professional Papers in Comparative Politics vol. 5, series no. 01–053 (Beverly Hills, Calif.: Sage Publications, 1975), p. 63. Also see his "The 'Portugalization' of Brazil?" p. 206. Linz and Schmitter drew their authoritarian/corporativist models from the empirical settings of Franco's Spain and prerevolutionary Portugal. Each recognizes the broader cultural ties of these political cultures to Latin America—and I would add by extension to the Philippines. Also see J. J. Wiarda: "Toward a Framework for the Study of Political Change in the Iberic-Latin Tradition: A Corporative Model," *World Politics* 36 (January 1973), 206–35; and "Corporatism and Development in the Iberic-Latin World: Persistent Strains and New Variations," *Review of Politics* 36 (January 1974), 3–33).

There is an extensive literature on the still broader appeal and appropriateness of the corporativist (fascist) model for developing countries—and for the developed. See P. C. Schmitter, "Still the Century of Corporatism?" *Review of Politics* 36 (January 1974), 85–131; A. J. Gregor, "Fascism and Modernization: Some Addenda," *World Politics* (April 1974), 370–84; A. J. Joes, "Fascism: The Past and the Future," *Comparative Political Studies* 7 (April 1974), 107–33; H. J. Turner, Jr., "Fascism

5. Changes will be made in the legal and institutional framework to facilitate the new position accorded representatives of the dominant nations, and to protect their interests. It goes without saying that the "psychological" climate will have also been altered to give the necessary affective supports to the foreign representatives resident in the polity.

Pre-Coup Anti-System Changes in the Philippines

Since our main concern is with the changes that have taken place in the Philippines subsequent to the imposition of martial law, we need pay only the briefest attention to the anti-system changes introduced during the late 1960s and early 1970s into the Philippine political system. Many, if not each, deserve fuller treatment if our understanding of the impact of highly developed nations on poor countries of the Third World is to be advanced.

By the early 1960s, an earlier, almost naïve expectation that the nations newly created out of colonial empires would develop along democratic lines had given way in the face of an increasing number of military coups and the demands of realpolitik to an acceptance of authoritarianism as the more likely form of government to expect. Increasingly the literature on development generated in the United States stressed the need to develop stronger and more efficient administrative instruments of rule, to increase the capabilities of political systems, and to cope with crises associated with development. The cumulative effect has been to denegrate politics, to eschew discussion of political development strategies that might tap into democratic participatory values, and to emphasize those placing reliance on Westernized elites who through their control over modernizing agencies could bring about development. Some openly argued that the Philippine political system was dysfunctional for economic development[19] and that the costs of Philippine elections, along with other costs related to politicians (who are charged with "misperceiving" the existential reality of the Philippines), were holding back Philippine development.[20] In fact, other changes to be

and Modernization," *World Politics* 24 (July 1972), 547–64; S. K. Smith, "Corporatism and the Garrison-Mangerial State," *Society* 12:4 (May/June 1975), 63–68; and B. Gross, "Friendly Fascism: A Model for America," *Social Policy* 1 (November/December 1970), 44–53.

19. F. H. Golay, "Some Costs of Philippine Politics," *Asia* 23 (Autumn 1971), 45–60.

20. The charge was made in H. Averch et al., *The Matrix of Policy in the*

reviewed below would not have been as likely had those who build the models of development not made this major intellectual shift to authoritarianism. The shift cut the ground from under those who would support a dynamic view of the potentialities of politics, of political parties, and of representative institutions, and prepared the way for a move to elite technocrats as the chosen instruments for development. Any reading of the Philippine media and of the pronouncements of key Filipino administrators during this period attests to the reality of this shift, as do statements of President Marcos himself.[21] They had come to view the political process as inhibiting development: the solution increasingly proffered was a turn to authoritarianism and technocratic rule.

The second dimension of change prior to the coup centered on the future of American interests in the Philippines. Two conditions were involved. The special protections and advantages given to Americans in the Philippines came increasingly under attack as the nationalist movement gained strength during the 1960s; these special rights—summarized in the Laurel-Langley Agreement—were due to expire on July 3, 1974. As that date became more imminent without a satisfactory solution for the post-1974 protection of American property and business rights in the Philippines, pressure from the United States mounted.[22]

Changes in the larger political setting of Southeast Asia as a consequence of the defeat of American forces in Vietnam and the promulgation of the Nixon Doctrine gave greater importance to the

---

Philippines (Princeton, N.J.; Princeton University Press, 1971). For two excellent critiques of the study, see B. J. Kerkvliet, "Critique of the Rand Study on the Philippines," *Journal of Asian Studies* 32 (May 1973), 489–500; and L. V. Cariño, "A Crisis of Reporting: A Critique of the Rand Report," *Philippine Journal of Public Administration* 14 (October 1970), 354–77. Both show that fundamental errors of judgment about the Philippines were facilitated by naïve faith placed in the sophisticated research methodology employed by the AID team.

21. F. E. Marcos, *Today's Revolution: Democracy* (Manila: 1971).

22. By the summer of 1972, if one is to believe the discussions appearing in the pages of the *Journal of the American Chamber of Commerce of the Philippines* (*JAACP*), several alternative formulas had been worked out by U.S. and Philippine authorities to protect property acquired under the parity amendment and the Laurel-Langley Agreement. Hardly had these formulas been agreed to than the Philippine Supreme Court upset all negotiations by its decision in the *Quasha* case (Aug. 17, 1972), which in effect stated that all lands acquired by Americans under the parity amendment had been gotten illegally and would revert to the Philippines July 4, 1974. A parallel case struck at multinational corporations in certain categories of economic activity by denying them the right to employ foreigners (*Lusteveco* case, decided Aug. 18, 1972).

massive military installations maintained by the United States in the Philippines. The added importance of these strategic American interests, coupled with extreme concern over the future of American holdings and opportunities in the Philippines, combined to provide powerful incentives for supporting system changes that would bring about the types of guarantees desired by Americans.[23] Further, the dramatic increase during the 1960s in the importance of the Philippines as a supplier of a number of mineral products especially to Japan, America's co-partner in the development of Southeast Asia, added weight to this dimension.

Although President Marcos was a consummate politician who managed the intricate relationships of party and legislature with brilliance and verve, he nonetheless proceeded as soon as he had gained the presidency to build new power into that institution, to transform old administrative agencies, and to create new ones that cumulatively would provide the executive branch with a greatly expanded capability for giving planned direction to public policy. To accomplish this, he brought into high executive office a group of young administrators most of whom had had graduate education in the United States in economics, law, or business administration and who shared a common set of values.[24] By the early 1970s these administrators had come to be clearly recognized as a coherent group and to be labeled the "technocrats," a term used both in opprobrium and in praise by those sensitive to changes taking place in the executive branch. The American Chamber of Commerce of the Philippines in general gave enthusiastic support to the policies being advanced by this group.[25] These policies included increased

23. After the coup, a U.S. Senate document included this statement: "We found few, if any, Americans who took the position that the demise of individual rights and democratic institutions would adversely affect U.S. interests. . . . U.S. officials appear prepared to accept that the strengthening of presidential authority will . . . enable President Marcos to introduce needed stability; that these objectives are in our interest; and that . . . military bases and a familiar [sic] government in the Philippines, are more important than the preservation of democratic institutions." U.S. Senate, Committee on Foreign Relations, 93rd Congress, 1st Session (1973), "Korea and the Philippines: November 1972. A Staff Report" (February 18), 45.

24. An editorial ended with the conclusion that the technocrats "share more or less the same orientation. As the present chairman of the NEC has put it, 'We speak the same language and understand each other well.' " *JACCP* (June 1971), p. 3.

25. Many lists of technocrats are available. *JACCP* welcomed the appointment of Dr. Gerardo Sicat as the new chairman of the National Economic Council as "part of the Administration policy to get more and more technocrats into the public service." The article went on to list "other technocrats now holding Government positions." Included were Finance Secretary Cesar Virata, Chairman Leonides Virata

reliance on private foreign investment, removal of restrictions to free trade and capital flows, removal of many constitutional restrictions against foreign dominance of key sectors of the Philippine economy, eager acceptance of new foreign-debt burdens and of the dependency such a policy dictates, support of an export-oriented type of industrialization with much of the initiative to be left in the hands of multinational corporations, and domestic austerity.[26]

As nationalist pressures mounted during the late 1960s and early 1970s, these policies came under attack from the rapidly expanding coalition opposed to the Marcos administration. The attack frequently centered on the technocrats themselves because of their putative role as promoters of American interests. One nationalist spokesman, after charging that the technocrats were furthering the neocolonization of the Philippines, argued that the basic problem was that these individuals were directly recruited into public service from foreign firms,[27] or were known prior to appointment as staunch advocates of economic development policies favored by foreign investors and foreign funding agencies, policies antithetical to those favored by nationalists.[28] With new nationalist successes in gaining adherents among legislators, in the mass media, and ultimately in the courts, the technocrats came to represent a beleaguered alternative to a government run by politicians and their allies. By the time of the second Marcos administration, these devel-

of the Development Bank of the Philippines, Chairman Vicente Paterno of the Board of Investments, Chairman-General Manager Roman Cruz, Jr., also of the Board of Investments, Executive Secretary Alejandro Melchor, and Agriculture Undersecretary Arturo Tanco. *JACCP* (August 1970), p. 36. Examples of the chamber's support include strong editorial praise for the work of Finance Secretary Virata in presenting the Philippine case for new loans to the "Consultative Group" in 1971 (*JACCP* [May 1971], p. 3); for the role Central Bank Governor Licaros and Treasurer Virata played in forcing antiinflationary policies on the Philippines in 1970 as part of the set of conditions before new loans would be forthcoming (*JACCP* [November 1970], p. 3) and for the general rationalizing effort of a number of government agencies concerned with the economy. As the *Journal* stated it, they were "all manned at the top echelon by technocrats or professional economists and corporate managers." (*JACCP* [June 1971], p. 3).

26. The basic outlines of the economic and social programs that were later to be put into force under martial law were already wrapped up in a unified package by the end of 1971, especially in the four-year plan (FY 1972–1975), a product of an interdepartmental committee headed by the NEC. The plan incorporated most of the policies outlined, although those prohibited by the existing constitution or resisted by relatively strong pressure groups could not be openly advocated, let alone implemented, until after martial law.

27. A. Lichauco, "The Lichauco Paper: Imperialism in the Philippines," *Monthly Review* 25 (July/August 1973), 65.

28. Ibid., p. 61.

opment administrators constituted a sizeable component of a counterelite dedicated to economic development methods other than those possible under the existing political system with its free press, periodic elections, and institutions for public control and examination of administrative actions.

The changes outlined in the three dimensions so far discussed would have remained in the blueprint stage, however, had other changes not been accomplished prior to the coup. One of the most important of these additional preparatory moves was the rapid expansion and retooling of the Philippine military and paramilitary forces. One of the earliest moves made by President Marcos in his first term as president was to develop the military into a force that could be more directly utilized as an agency of "development," a policy that led to his being able to claim in his campaign for his second term that as a result of the civic-action programs of the military he had provided more schools and roads for Filipinos than all previous presidents. This rapid expansion into civic-action work also gave the military experience in serving as an administrative arm of the chief executive, and helped integrate it into the American military's counterinsurgency and civic-action programs, an integration that was aided by the president's decision to dispatch a Philippine military unit to Vietnam and to rely increasingly on the American model in dealing with insurgents. This led to a reliance by the Philippine armed forces on the more sophisticated weaponry developed in Vietnam, which in turn has increased the dependency of that military on the United States for material and increasingly for direct field support (noncombat, largely, but with recurrent claims that advisors are involved in combat situations). As a result of these changes and of the new policies adopted, the Philippine armed forces were expanded and given a proportionately larger share of the public budget (a total increase of 400 percent) under President Marcos.[29]

Similarly, Marcos instituted radical changes in the training of the Philippine police. Shortly after assuming office in 1966, the president proceeded to work out with the American Embassy a program that would turn most of the training functions over to AID. The guiding document was prepared by Frank E. Walton, who had earlier, according to one report, "integrated and expanded the police forces

29. P. B. Daroy, "The Military Takeover," *Graphic*, August 2–9, 1972, p. 6.

of South Vietnam and mobilized them for counterinsurgency and paramilitary operations."[30] Since the inception of the program, AID has equipped and established nine regional police training academies, established thirty "Law Enforcement Communications Systems networks," and given technical advice and assistance to eight city police departments.[31] As of the end of fiscal year 1970, some 10,540 policemen had been trained, 60 communications technicians and 1,895 operators given special courses,[32] and some 50 police officials sent to the International Police Academy in Washington.[33] Despite the heavy emphasis in the program given to training for the control of urban protest activity, the larger portion of American aid to the Philippines during this period for purposes of strengthening the regime in the "internal security area" was given, according to the U.S. Senate report, as "support for the Philippine Constabulary as a part of the Military Assistance Program."[34]

The militarization of the Philippines under Marcos was clearly recognized by many long before the coup occurred. As early as 1968, Senator Benigno S. Aquino, Jr., denounced the "menace of militarism" associated with the civic action programs.[35] Popular periodicals contained many articles on the subject; one in 1970 reviewed the overall militarization of the rural areas as a result of executive policies culminating in the establishment of the Home Defense Forces.[36] By 1972, predictions in the mass media of a military coup were commonplace, and by summer, details about preparations being taken by President Marcos for the imposition of martial law were public knowledge. All that remained was for the new system to be called into action.

The fifth component of the pre-coup anti-system is the most difficult to unravel. The business community had grown rapidly following Philippine independence. The traditional export sectors flourished under Laurel-Langley, indigenous businessmen gained through "nationalization" (i.e., anti-Chinese) legislation, new industrialists appeared during a relatively short era of protectionism, and

30. B. H. Gillego, "Our Police Forces as a Tool of American Imperialism," *Ronin* 1 (October 1972), 13.
31. U.S. Senate, 1973 Staff Report, pp. 38–39.
32. Gillego, "Our Police Forces," pp. 12–13.
33. Senate, Staff Report, p. 39.
34. Ibid., p. 38.
35. *Philippines Free Press*, Feb. 17, 1968.
36. N. Roces, "The Civilian Guards in Different Clothing," *Graphic*, Jan. 7, 1970.

groups associated in one manner or another with foreign economic activities surged ahead. The radically different political economy basis of power of each sector naturally produced divisions within the business community. These were widened by the highly destructive effects of the two IMF-dictated decontrol and devaluation moves (1962 and 1970), which shifted benefits to the traditional export sector, significantly weakened the fledgling Filipino industrialists, and contributed new power to the foreign community and its Philippine allies.

The most dramatic result of these changes appears to have been a split in the business community that saw some entrepreneurs move into the nationalist camp and finally support the radical wing of the movement.[37] Others apparently became convinced that the development strategy offered by the technocrats, with their vision of growth through reliance on public and private external loans, on foreign private investment, and on dependent industrialization for export, was to their best interests. Both groups, however, joined on one line of policy: they opposed the power of the chief defender of the status quo, the sugar bloc.

It is extremely difficult to identify actors and positions clearly in these developments.[38] None of the business associations supported the nationalists, although individual businessmen belonged to such groups as the Movement for the Advancement of Nationalism (MAN), financed the various nationalist writers, and contributed to the many nationalist movements. At the same time, however, each of the associations on occasion printed editorials in their journals advocating mild nationalistic policies, only to argue simultaneously for policies that would, if adopted, weaken Philippine business vis-à-vis foreign business. What does appear clear from a reading of the journals of the Chamber of Commerce of the Philippines, the Chamber of Agriculture and National Resources, and the Philippine Chamber of Industries, in the period leading up to the coup, is that these groups largely accepted the need to rely heavily on foreign loans and investments (the Philippine Chamber of In-

---

37. J. Fast, "Imperialism and Bourgeois Dictatorship in the Philippines," *New Left Review* (April 1973), 69–96; and M. Meadows, "Colonialism, Social Structure and Nationalism: The Philippine Case," *Pacific Affairs* 24 (Fall 1971), 337–52.

38. This is not true for the sugar bloc, however. *Sugar News,* the publication of the Philippine Sugar Association, consistently maintained the position that a continuation of the status quo was in the best interest of the nation.

dustries at times had mild reservations on the latter point), and that the total system needed rationalization based on greater discipline, leadership, and less interference by politicians, especially those in Congress.[39] The development ideology had taken hold of the leaders in all these associations. A statement such as the following was common: "The modernization of the underdeveloped country is a revolutionary process. Like all revolutions, it means the overthrow of an old order and the installation of a new order. It needs its conspirators, who in turn need their revolutionary vision, their commitment and their method. . . . I ask the leaders of the business community to come up to the challenge posed to the modern businessman in the decade of the Angry Seventies."[40]

In sum, in the years leading up to the coup, the Philippine business community had become alienated from the existing institutions of politics and had come to opt either for a radical nationalism (a small minority) or for changes largely along lines defined by the developmental experts, the technocrats associated with President Marcos. While these policies promised to provide a great impetus to business, they also assured that expansion would take place within an economy integrated in much more complex ways than the earlier simpler colonial economy with the industrial nations, and that Philippine business increasingly would have to make its peace with the multiplicity of agencies and control mechanisms flooding in from the outside: the multinational corporations, the foreign banks, the representatives of the "international community"—the bankers from the Asian Development Bank (ADB) and the International Bank for Reconstruction and Development (IBRD) and the technical assistors from a multitude of public and private sources—as well as the omnipresent representatives of the U.S. government implanted throughout the Philippine system. By the early 1970s the

39. In 1970 the president of the Philippine Chamber of Industries was calling for a strong leader "to lead this country and its people out of our present crisis" (see the *Industrial Philippines* [May 1970], p. 3). In a later article in the same journal, an official of the chamber launched an attack on the press for creating a crisis of national identity by stressing "negativism in the Filipino national personality" (January 1972, p. 5). And an editorial in the *Journal of the Chamber of Commerce of the Philippines*, on "violent" youth and labor demonstrations, came close to predicting "the imposition of martial law sometime next year" (*Commerce* [January 1972], p. 2). All three groups repeatedly complained about the role Congress and the politicians were playing in slowing down development.

40. S. K. Roxas, "Social Responsibility of Businessmen," *Commerce* 68 (February 1971), 8–9.

great proportion of the Philippine business community had come to accept this model of development, a model of dependent industrialization falling somewhere between the Brazilian and South Korean models.

This development is related to the sixth hypothesized dimension of pre-coup change. The expansion of existing linkage relationships between Philippine and American groups, public and private, has already been discussed. During the decade prior to the coup, the impact of the antipolitics developmental package common to most American models began to take hold as more Filipinos returned to the Philippines from advanced study in the United States and as new lines of linkage were established. Critical examples include the American foundation-funded expansion of the College of Business Administration and the College of Public Administration of the University of the Philippines, the new Asian Institute of Management, and the near-total monopoly of positions in the economics departments of the prestigious universities, some backed up by resident American professors on long-term contracts. The same thing was occurring in Philippine government agencies as increasing numbers of foreign advisors became permanent adjuncts to the planning and administrative processes.[41] Certainly the expanded role assigned the military in internal security matters by the United States, ironically occasioned in part by the American experience in guiding the anti-Huk campaign in the early 1950s, resulted in new and expanded lines of interaction between the military of the two countries, with the United States providing the models, the equipment, the training, and the control.[42] The same can be said about the linkages in the police system, except that these tended to be newly created rather than expansions of older patterns.

The *Journal* of the American Chamber of Commerce of the Philippines recorded the constant strengthening of the links between the American and Filipino business communities as it published

41. An article on the relationships between personnel in the National Irrigation Authority and the UNDP that gives one example of these patterns is A. P. Varela, "The NIA-UNDP Groundwater Development Project: A Case Study in Transnational Development Administration" *Philippine Journal of Public Administration* 16 (April 1972), 186–203.

42. M. T. Klare, "Review of 'Open Secret: The Kissinger-Nixon Doctrine in Asia' by V. Brodine and M. Selden," *Bulletin of Concerned Asian Scholars* 5 (September 1973), 57–61; M. D. Wolpin, *Military Aid and Counter-revolution in the Third World* (Lexington, Mass.: Lexington Books, 1972).

accounts of new joint ventures, of success stories about Filipinos who had made it in the world of multinationals, and of the unlimited growth possibilities opened up by foreign investment and the technology and export markets provided by multinational corporations. The American Chamber relied quite frequently on Filipinos to articulate the demands for changes in the Philippine system to bring it in line with policies, constantly reiterated in the *Journal,* similar to those advocated by the Marcos administration's technocrats. These views were disseminated to the business community through the chamber's publications and through the Philippine Association, a private group of Filipino and American businessmen viewed by one nationalist as "perhaps the most flagrant organization in the private sector which serves as imperialism's instrument in this country."[43]

The *Journal,* moreover, constantly supported related policies that in turn necessitated a rapid expansion of the network of relationships between key Filipinos and multilateral funding agencies. The chamber gave considerable attention to a report prepared in 1970 by a World Bank official for a preparatory meeting of seven nations and four international organizations with the Philippines, to consider setting up a "Consultive Group" for the Philippines, as well as to later developments of that agency. The report praised the Philippine administration for its "commendable display of political courage" in forcing a high degree of austerity on the nation through devaluation and decontrol, and went on to advocate additional adjustments to assure a more rapid flow of private investment into the country. In discussing these proposals, the report warned that the existing favorable trend should not be reversed "by legislative or administrative action which would unduly restrict the scope for foreign investment in the country."[44]

Parallel support for building close dependency relationships with the multilateral funding agencies was enthusiastically provided by the Philippine Chamber of Industries, partially, it may be noted, because several high officers in that association in the years immediately preceding the coup were simultaneously officers in the Private Development Corporation of the Philippines. The PDCP is a corporation specifically designed to service the needs of foreign

43. Lichauco, "Imperialism in the Philippines," p. 79.
44. *JACCP* (November 1970), p. 42.

interests by providing intermediary functions between them and Filipinos interested in embarking on development projects mostly involving association with non-Filipinos. The corporation has some eighteen foreign banks or other financing concerns as shareholders including, among others, groups from the United States, Great Britain, Germany, Japan, and Hong Kong; the executive committee of the board of directors contains two non-Filipinos out of five.[45]

This overview of the growing web of relationships involving Filipinos in development projects largely determined by outsiders largely misses the seductive excitement accompanying that process. Undoubtedly there must be exhilaration associated with taking part in facilitating the building of a branch plant in the Philippines of a famous multinational corporation, of becoming part of the business bustle of a supermodern enclave like Makati and its smaller counterparts elsewhere in the nation, of providing jobs for unemployed Filipinos through the expansion of industry. Unfortunately, however, it is well recognized by now that such activity has its high costs. Despite all the talk about "social justice" in the New Society, evidence from other Third World nations further along on this route abundantly demonstrates that among the costs is an increase in the gap between rich and poor and an actual lowering in the standard of living of the latter, both urban and rural.[46] Typically, the bottom 40 percent of the population suffers an absolute, not alone a relative, drop in income; unemployment increases, despite a small increase in jobs in the modernizing sector of the economy; and the great wealth generated by development, and so proudly announced in the frequently spectacular GNP annual increases, is effectively channeled into the hands of a minute percentage of the population.

What is frequently overlooked, and never made explicit, is that this general "trickle down" developmental model requires increas-

45. *Industrial Philippines* (September 1970), p. 19.
46. F. H. Cardoso, "Associated-Dependent Development: Theoretical and Practical Implications," in A. Stepan, ed., *Authoritarian Brazil: Origins, Policies, and Future* (New Haven, Conn.: Yale University Press, 1973); I. Adelman and C. T. Morris, *Economic Growth and Social Equity in Developing Countries* (Stanford, Calif.: Stanford University Press, 1973); I. Adelman, "Growth, Income Distribution and Equity-Oriented Development Strategies," *World Development* 3 (February/March 1975), 67–76; H. Chenery et al., *Redistribution with Growth* (London: Oxford University Press, 1974); and C. Chase-Dunn, "The Effects of International Economic Dependence on Development and Inequality: A Cross-National Study," *American Sociological Review* 40 (December 1975), 720–38.

ing levels of internal violence against groups protesting their diminishing status in their own nations. As these protests are turned against the physical presence of external domination—the property and agents of multinational corporations, for example—a new wave of repression follows. These costs seem not to have been taken into account when the dominant portion of the business community opted to accept an associated, secondary position in the increasingly complex institutions for the development of the Philippines headquartered in the industrial nations of the world, which for the Philippines primarily means the United States and Japan.[47]

Martial Law: Consolidation of Dependent-Authoritarianism

It was not until he imposed martial law that President Marcos was able to attack directly the institutions standing in the way of a rational consolidation of refeudalization, whose planning he had so largely facilitated and whose implementation he had attempted to execute within the constraints imposed by the existing political system. It was this system that he proceeded to dismantle, once martial law had been decreed. He moved most rapidly to neutralize the institutional supports of the system, such as the various sectors of the media, the wide variety of student associations dedicated to a furtherance of national independence, and their many parallel organizations in other parts of society, and to silence key leaders of the nationalist movement. These included individuals from both houses of Congress, from the Constitutional Convention that was sitting at the time, and from elective offices at the provincial and municipal levels. It was, however, only after this neutralization of

47. Many articles favoring expanded reliance on Japan appeared in the business journals during this period, especially *Industrial Philippines*. Not until more than a year after martial law did Marcos move to overturn the long-standing opposition centered in the Senate against a commercial treaty with Japan. Once the treaty was "ratified," Japanese private investment began to flow in, to challenge what had been an undisputed monopoly by Americans and to assume for Japan a role commensurate with its position as the Philippines' primary trading partner.

While the United States stands to gain significantly through the refeudalization process (it will continue to enjoy old privileges flowing from domination and to benefit as its citizens participate in the "development" of the Philippines), Japan stands to gain the most. The new order gives Japan a legitimate role, a central position in the business of modernizing the Philippines, knitting it more intricately into the larger regional market system. Refeudalization seems to mean the formalization of a "U.S.-Japan Greater Southeast Asia Co-prosperity Sphere." The idea of regional subimperialism has been discussed by J. Galtung, "Social Imperialism," *World Indicators Program* No. 7 (August 1975); and H. Feith, "Southeast Asia and Neo-Colonialism," paper presented at a conference on Australia, Papua, New Guinea and Southeast Asia, Melbourne, May 9–11, 1975.

nationalist leaders and politicians associated with the movement[48] had successfully been carried out that Marcos, after having gotten a new constitution from the Constitutional Convention that assured him unlimited authority for an indefinite period, took the step of closing down Congress and thereby eliminating the central institutional support for the Philippine political system. By this move he struck not only at the power of the political elite, but also at the political parties and at the manner in which political power had been rooted in a nationwide network of congressional constituencies, the overwhelming majority of which were rural. This power base was destroyed, as was the ability of those enjoying its benefits to continue to dominate the larger system.[49]

The dismantling of the existing political system was accompanied by attacks on other aspects of the dispersed power base: police forces throughout the provincial cities were placed under central authority, many elected officials at the provincial and municipal levels were placed under arrest, local courts were bypassed on important cases by the emerging network of military courts, and provincial "warlords" were eliminated. Allies of the elective political elite in the bureaucracy were fired and some were jailed.

During the destruction of the representative system the Philippine Supreme Court, after handing down the two crucial pronationalist decisions mentioned earlier, moved solidly back into line and consistently decided cases during the early months of martial law in a manner to give legality to the coup. After the new constitution was promulgated, the court affirmed the legality of the new document and the legal packing of the court, thus ensuring its pliant subservience to the New Society.[50]

48. No comprehensive, balanced account of the remarkable rise and expansion quantitatively and geographically of the nationalist movement in the Philippines during the late 1960s and early 1970s has yet been written. A good case for the *timing* of the coup can be made placing it at the moment when nationalist pressures for a more independent and autonomous Philippines began seriously to threaten the counterdemands from the metropolitan nation(s). See R. B. Stauffer, "The Marcos Coup in the Philippines," *Monthly Review* 24 (April 1973), 19–27, and "The Political Economy of a Coup: Transnational Linkages and Philippine Political Response," *Journal of Peace Research* 11:3 (1974), 161–77.

49. See R. B. Stauffer, *The Philippine Congress: Causes of Structural Change,* Sage Research Papers in the Social Sciences, III: 90–024 (Comparative Legislative Studies Series. Beverly Hills and London: Sage Publications, 1975) for a more detailed analysis of the congressionally centered opposition to the development model being advanced by Marcos and his technocrats.

50. Illustrative is the statement by Chief Justice Fred Ruiz Castro in 1976, a month after some 500 new arrests had been made in an attempt to stamp out op-

These outlines of the processes by which the pre-coup political system was destroyed have been easy to follow. The same cannot be said in every instance for the types of institutions being created to give stability and permanence to the New Society. Some, of course, appear quite openly as cornerstones of the new order; others, still in the ambivalent stages of becoming, are more difficult to detect. Among the former, the military has emerged for the first time in modern Philippine history as a major component of the governing process. It has been dramatically enlarged, from approximately 60,000 at the time of the coup to an announced strength of more than 250,000 by the end of 1975. Military officers have been installed as provincial governors, heads of provincial development agencies, managers of industrial enterprises. Military tribunals have been given the right to try civilians for certain classes of crimes. The Philippine Constabulary—the national police component of the Philippine military—has been expanded and given control over the more than 1,500 previously autonomous local police forces in the country, police forces that had long served as the bases of power of rural political elites.[51]

This dramatic increase in the size, functional roles, and degree of centralization and politicization of the military and the paramilitary forces in the Philippines under martial law represents the single most important institutional development of the New Society. There has been a simultaneous expansion in the economic development planning agencies—centralized in the National Economic and Development Authority (NEDA)—and in all administrative agencies involved in "development," and an attempt has been made to create an administrative elite to give the total process more centralized direction.[52] These institutional modifications parallel those made in the military, and represent the fleshing out of the total military/bureaucratic package through which the Philippines is to be developed into a "New Society."

---

position to the regime, that "Filipinos are better off today than in any other time in Philippine history, insofar as recognition of human dignity and the enjoyment of the basic freedoms are concerned." He continued by claiming, "At present, liberty flourishes under the rule of law" (*Manila Journal*, Jan. 29–Mar. 7, 1976, p. 6).

51. See Merlin Castro, "Toward a Garrison State," *Pahayag*, May/June 1974, p. 2.

52. Through the training programs of the Development Academy of the Philippines, created after martial law. Its director has used the "steel frame" metaphor—from British India's administrative service—to describe the role its graduates will play in building the New Society.

What is surprising about the new order in the Philippines is that it has held back from building the other institutions typically associated with the authoritarian model, institutions to provide for a carefully controlled form of citizen participation. Except for the quasi-party "slate" in the 1978 elections, there has been no move made to create a government-sponsored political party or parties, even if it is the rare authoritarian state that has existed as long as has the "New Society" without such a transmission belt. Little has been done to utilize elections to knit together rulers and ruled in the new order. What had been done prior to 1978 was to hold an occasional plebiscite in which voters could vote simply yes or no, their single responses answering an undifferentiated cluster of questions (e.g., Do you approve of martial law? Do you approve of President Marcos' rule? Do you approve of your local officials? Do you approve of Philippine foreign policy?). Elections were held for the nonappointed representatives to an interim National Assembly (*Batasang Pambansa*) in April 1978 but led to a new wave of arrests and a tightening of repressive controls. The results indicate that the regime has not found a successful formula for utilizing elections for the controlled participation of the people in the selection of public officials.

Little more has been done institutionally to replace pre-martial law representative institutions. Early in 1973 local meetings were hastily organized to "ratify" the new constitution. These became the subsequent local advisory assemblies—*barangays*, named for the pre-colonial local political unit. Youth *barangays* were subsequently added and *barangays* in general given some role in helping administer local development projects. At the end of 1975 a new hierarchy of "representative" institutions—advisory councils (*Sanggunian Bayan* or "town" councils)—was created by presidential decree. Membership on the councils is generated by a complex ex officio and indirect election system based on the *barangays* and on corporatist "sectors"—professional, "capital," industrial labor, and agricultural labor—given specific representation on each level. The total pyramid has culminated on occasion in a huge national convention made up, in 1976 for example, of more than 4,000 delegates, and in a "National Legislative Advisory Council."[53] In 1978 an element of

53. With the creation of a new interim National Assembly in 1978, this body will probably cease to exist (*Manila Journal*, Feb. 5–11, 1978). The most com-

direct public participation in the selection of nonsectoral, non-appointed, and non-ex officio members of a new interim National Assembly was provided when some 160 of the approximately 200 members were elected. Marcos has made abundantly clear, however, that martial law will continue, that he will determine what is the proper scope for the advisory assembly, and that he will remain the ultimate legislator.[54]

This failure to develop institutions through which controlled political participation might be incorporated into the new order has several possible explanations. The first is fear of the strength of the old political culture, fear that the new regime would not be able to control a government-sponsored political party, elections tied in with the selection of local officials, or a national legislature—even if the latter is a normal accoutrement in authoritarian polities to provide a facade of legitimacy for the international community. Marcos' reluctance to proceed on the political sector gives considerable indirect testimony to the power of the pre-martial law competitive political system.

A second explanation, of course, is Marcos himself and his highly personalistic style of rule. He launches every new program as part of his unfolding plan for development; he personally wages war on the "oligarchs"; he releases individuals (some) from detention when they swear loyalty to him and the New Society; he proudly asserts that the military will not deprive individuals of their rights because "I issued a system of rules and orders which determines exactly under what circumstances arrests may be made";[55] he writes long dissertations for publication in the mass media on the

---

plete study of the *barangay* and *sanggunian* systems is Belinda A. Aquino's "Politics in the New Society: *Barangay* 'Democracy'" (paper presented at the 1977 Association of Asian Studies Meeting). She concludes that both systems "are being integrated more tightly as administrative components of a techno-bureaucratic regime rather than as semi-autonomous political units" (p. 29).

54. In view of the near political disaster resulting from the experiment with elections for the interim National Assembly, it seems highly unlikely that they will be risked again in the near future. Within hours of the closing of the polls on April 7th, many of the handfull of opposition candidates (nearly all centered in Metro Manila) who had dared to stand against the government slate were rounded up and dispatched to detention centers. More than 500 people were arrested and detained for protesting the blatant rigging of the elections. See George McT. Kahin, "Testimony on the Philippines" (presented before the Subcommittee on International Organizations of the Committee on International Relations, United States House of Representatives, April 27, 1978), for details on the scope and methods employed by the government to assure victory for its candidates.

55. *Bulletin Today,* May 14, 1973.

New Society;[56] and he keeps himself—and his wife, Imelda—constantly before the masses, through his weekly radio and TV programs and his near-monopoly of the photographs printed on the front pages of the controlled press. Sycophants support this authoritarian personalism; writers talk about the pride the Philippines should have in the fact that "President Marcos has managed thus far to keep martial law a noble approach to Constitutional authoriarianism,"[57] and repeatedly eulogize the accomplishments of the New Society under Marcos' leadership.

There have been a few tentative indicators that the New Society will move to create corporativist institutions typically associated with authoritarian systems. The tripartite congress of labor, management, and government called to ratify the new labor code could be interpreted as one such indicator, although subsequent developments give little support to this analysis. Similarly—and with equal equivocation—moves to restructure the educational system and to assign it a greater role in guiding the resocialization of society have occurred, but with little structural change; this is not to minimize the significant shifts taking place in curriculum, and the commitment to produce more skilled workers and technicians and to gear the total educational system to the needs of economic development, especially of industrialization in association with foreign corporations. Other indicators exist, such as the move to take over all sports groups in the Philippines and to have them placed under a "National Sports Development Commission." The organization of the youth into advisory assemblies—*Kabataang Barangays*— is another, as is the representative formula built into the upper levels of the more general advisory councils. At the provincial, city, municipal, and national levels of the *barangay* structure, provision has been made for a degree of "functional" representation. These bodies are rather large, but will include only one representative from each of four sectors: the professions, capital, industrial labor, and agricultural labor. Selection of these representatives is left to each sector.[58] These isolated hints at a possible institutionalization of corporativism, even augmented by increased control of the professions, however, remain just that. To date, the Marcos martial law regime has

56. F. E. Marcos, *Notes on the New Society of the Philippines* (Manila: 1973).
57. *Daily Express*, Dec. 28, 1972.
58. See *Manila Journal*, Mar. 14–20, 1976, pp. 1, 5, and Presidential Decrees 824 and 826.

effectively destroyed old institutions, and has expanded the roles played by the civil and military supports typically associated with authoritarianism, but has not moved to create new supporting institutions. It seems unlikely that full institutionalization of a dependent-authoritarian system can take place until this is done.[59]

In contrast with the pattern just described, those charged with implementing martial law moved with extreme rapidity against the leaders of the nationalist movement, arresting hundreds even before the news that martial law had been put into effect was made public. Thousands were jailed, among them leaders and activists from all parts of society joined in the nationalist movement.[60] The drive to suppress the nationalist movement was expanded to include orders to the police to purge the schools of student radicals,[61] for the military to arrest as subversives any person "spreading unfounded rumors and causing anxiety, fear and confusion to undermine the 'New Society',"[62] and for the continued use of "saturation drives" (also called *"Zonas"*) against the people living in areas such as the Tondo, within which nationalist organizations had roots.[63] Near the end of the first year of the new regime, the president announced the institution of a national reference card system for every person living in the Philippines, and on several occasions he has threatened to turn to "revolutionary government" as "an ultimate weapon to clobber the enemies of the state."[64]

59. Others have noted this lack of institutionalization. Jeffrey Race has argued from this that the likelihood of a military coup in the relatively near future in the Philippines is extremely high. "Wither the Philippines?" *Institute of Current World Affairs*, Nov. 30, 1975, especially pp. 15–16.

60. That the military and police were not totally successful in the roundup is suggested by the continuing urban nationalist opposition to the regime as well as the armed resistance in the rural areas. The question of the number jailed by the military remains unclear, especially since the government continually claims that most jailed are "criminal elements." Since this term is frequently used to describe opposition political activity, any breakdown of figures that includes this category becomes meaningless. Further, the continuing arrests and the distinct possibility that provincial arrests are inadequately reflected in government figures leaves the issue clouded. One fact is clear: large numbers have been jailed since martial law was imposed in the Philippines. President Marcos admitted to Amnesty International in November 1975 that some 50,000 had been arrested and detained since September 1972. The government admitted that some 6,000 people remained in detention in May 1975. *Report of an Amnesty International Mission to The Republic of the Philippines* (London: Amnesty International, 1976), p. 6.

61. *Evening Express*, Mar. 3, 1973.

62. *Bulletin Today*, Jan. 9, 1973.

63. Many descriptions of these raids appear in the controlled press. One mentioned that urban guerrilla units, labeled "armed city partisans" by the military, had become active. See *Daily Express*, June 27, 1973.

64. *Daily Express*, Jan. 15, 1973.

Despite the massive pressure, nationalistic resistance to the new order continues and has gained new support from groups previously on the fringes of the movement. Individuals and groups associated with the Catholic Church have become increasingly critical of martial law; the regime has responded by raiding a long list of Catholic institutions scattered throughout the nation. Every year one or more foreign priests have been hurriedly deported for supporting those opposing the regime.[65] The many more Filipino priests, even more deeply involved, cannot be deported. Many have been arrested, some imprisoned, some reportedly tortured, many more harassed.

The attack against the nationalists never ends. It is carried on against any who challenge the claims of the government about the supposed benefits flowing from the Philippines' new dependency. Those raising doubts are frequently students and faculty, and their challenges surface periodically despite the elaborate controls. The government consistently responds with open repression directed at the leaders.[66] The government's attack is also directed at any who would attempt to organize the powerless, urban or rural. The new dependency demands a nondemanding mass base, a depoliticized population.

While the attack against nationalists can never end in a dependent-authoritarian system, the fact remains that the massive measures taken by Marcos have decimated the movement of many of its leaders and activists, destroyed most of the associational forms through which the movement operated, and denied it mass communication channels for reaching the public. Increasingly, the nationalist opposition will have to adopt organizational strategies and tactical policies similar to those of underground movements in authoritarian polities. The long-term consequences—win or lose—of the escalation in the domestic uses of violence in politics instituted by Marcos will be costly to Filipinos and to the political system.[67]

65. Two Italian priests were deported in January 1976 for helping to organize squatters to defend themselves against demolition ordered by Imelda Marcos in her new capacity as Mayor of Metro Manila.
66. See *Pahayag*, December 1973, and "Military Attempts to Muffle the U.P. Collegian," *Pahayag*, January 1976, for accounts of two such cycles.
67. Once martial law was imposed, the military felt free to escalate its campaign against the NPA into one utilizing typical patterns employed by the Americans in Vietnam. The same tactics were shortly applied against the Muslims in the south, with a continuing, grim repetition of Vietnam-like consequences to the civilian population. These costs continue to be imposed, according to current reports from Mindanao.

One immediate consequence of martial law was "the end of the freest press in the world," to use the title of the definitive study of the early phases of authoritarian takeover of the press and of the other sectors of the media.[68] The coup regime moved with remarkable efficiency: in addition to the arrests of leading journalists associated with the nationalist movement, publishers and editors of major metropolitan papers and opinion magazines were also incarcerated, printing plants occupied, radio and TV stations closed down, and a beginning made in guiding the public through strict censorship of the news and the production of a total communications "package" supportive of the policies adopted by the government. The change was dramatic, and even a year later, two middle-aged social scientists from the University of the Philippines attending a conference in the United States agreed that while they totally approved of the changes brought about by martial law, and especially enjoyed the "respect, order in the classrooms, and dedication to study" now typical in students, they both missed the "free press" that had once been the hallmark of the Philippines.

Martial law controls over the communications system remain as effective as in the early days after the takeover. Changes have been made in the methods employed (see Chapter 4 for a full discussion of the mass media in the New Society), but the results are the same: The press continues to publish only upbeat stories about the constant flood of new development projects being carried out by the new government and to push the various themes underlying the changes in Filipinos the New Society hopes to bring about. These include discipline, law and order, greater respect for authority and the rules and regulations of government, greater willingness to work hard, and so on. Nothing negative is allowed to appear, except when criticism is officially sanctioned as against "backsliders"; crime appears to have ceased to exist for the most part, except for an occasional story about the remarkable success the authorities have had in reducing crime rates.

The press devotes considerable space to special development projects of the government, although those that have gained the largest coverage on a regular basis have been the projects directly associated with Mrs. Imelda Marcos. Since martial law, these have

68. D. A. Rosenberg, "The End of the Freest Press in the World," *Bulletin of Concerned Asian Scholars* 5 (July 1973), 53–57.

included her "Green Revolution," which was given a front-page spot for nearly a year; her many cultural activities (her Young Artists' Foundation of the Philippines and the many foreign musicians she brings to the Philippines, such as Van Cliburn and Renata Tebaldi), including the Folk Arts Center; her extravagant gift to the upper classes—the Heart Center—and, most recently, her "beautification" program for Greater Manila.[69] As illustrated in the daily "Green Revolution" column, the average Filipino is admonished to live frugally, to grow more of the food needed for his family, to become less dependent on rice, and to learn to eat other cereals as well as more vegetables. While peasants are pushed to work harder, Imelda Marcos' other projects foster a closer integration of the Philippine elite into an American-centered culture, and further differentiate elite and mass in the Philippines. Development and discipline clearly are to have different meanings to those in different classes, and, judging from reports of the remarkable exploits in extravagance by members of the presidential family, different rewards as well.

The impact of martial law on individuals has varied widely: some have been destroyed, while no one has escaped its impact to some degree or other. Similarly with Filipino organizations: Martial law authorities have outlawed all associations connected with the student nationalist movement, and related intellectual organizations and supporting groups. Professional associations have been more directly co-opted into the authoritarian system than they had been in the more openly competitive pre-coup system; an example of this is the government's move to sponsor a controlled "integrated bar" for the Philippines, thereby forcing a merger of previously competing lawyers' associations and tying them directly to the government.

Attempts by the Marcos regime to reduce the autonomy of agrarian groups have varied between the aggressive use of coercion

69. The enormous outlays for the Heart Center—for intensive care units, equipment and personnel for heart repair and even transplants—will tend to benefit a very small segment of the population. The major killer diseases in the Philippines, as is typical in underdeveloped countries, are tuberculosis, pneumonia, enteritis, diarrhea, infections of the newborn, and other diseases of early infancy, not the diseases and malfunctions associated with the heart and circulatory system, for example, which tend to affect the elites in Third World nations who have adopted Western life-styles. See R. B. Stauffer, "Biopolitics of Underdevelopment," *Comparative Political Studies* 2:3 (October 1969), 361–87. For an analysis of the "beautification" campaign, see R. B. Stauffer, "The Costs of 'Beautification,'" *Pahayag* (February 1976), 5–6.

by the military and the blandishments of various administrative agencies seeking to co-opt selected groups (see Chapter 3 for a broader analysis of changes in rural areas under martial law). Success, while largely achieved by this time, is still more subject to challenge in the rural areas and appears more problematic than similar changes in the condition of urban labor. One of the first moves made by Marcos under martial law was to outlaw strikes. Almost immediately, industrialists began to demand longer work days for the same pay and even to effect reduction in wages.[70] The starting pay for apprentice workers was reduced by a third,[71] and limitations applying to the employment of women and children were either reduced or eliminated; furthermore, most overtime pay was eliminated by making Sundays and holidays regular working days.[72]

President Marcos chose a Labor Day to announce details of the New Society's labor program, which included, in addition to a general commitment to increase employment possibilities, the demand for restructuring trade unions to eliminate "wasteful competition and internecine disorders bordering on anarchy."[73] Very little has since appeared in the Philippine press to indicate what this restructuring will involve; the overall picture, however, is of a greatly weakened labor movement increasingly subject to government domination.

These have been illustrative examples of how martial law has destroyed the autonomy of organized groups in the Philippines that before the coup competed for and enjoyed varying degrees of power. Some associations have been eliminated in the process, others co-opted by the regime, and all traumatically affected by the conditions laid down by the New Society.

In the years since the coup, Marcos has consolidated a dependent-authoritarian system, many of whose component parts he constructed in cooperation with American agencies during the early

70. *Liberation*, Oct. 27, 1972.
71. *Daily Express*, Apr. 15, 1973.
72. *Sugar News*, February/March 1973. Evidence to date demonstrates that the standard of living of the urban workers, as well as of tenant farmers and rural workers, has either gone down or remained at the same pre-1972 low level since the imposition of martial law. For a fuller discussion of the "costs" to the majority of Filipinos of martial law see Robert B. Stauffer, "Philippine Authoritarianism: Framework for Peripheral 'Development'" (*Pacific Affairs*, 50:3 (Fall 1977), pp. 380–384.
73. *Daily Express*, Dec. 10, 1973.

years of his term as president. The system now has more firmly established centralized controls over urban Filipinos and over most in rural areas than was true in the years when the Philippines enjoyed a more competitive, democratic political system. In the language of political developmentalists, the Philippine system now enjoys increased "capabilities" to "cope" with the unstabilizing consequences of rapid development. I prefer to conceptualize the changes less as a "*system* acquiring new capabilities" than as a process in which a small group of Filipinos, representing groups closely allied with Americans and other foreign interests, overthrew the existing political system and imposed authoritarian controls over the rest of Philippine society. These Philippine groups (and the Americans) had been seriously threatened by the nationalist movement in the years before the coup. They had already strengthened their ties before martial law and have rapidly expanded them since. It is through these transnational networks that direction is given to the dependent-authoritarian system, meaning given to refeudalization.

In the first year of his first term as president, Marcos made an aggressive appeal to financial groups in the United States and in Japan to greatly step up the flow of private investments in the Philippines and to expand their support of private enterprise in the Philippines.[74] With the support of the American Chamber of Commerce in the Philippines and the Philippine Association—and presumably the more official Americans—he had his technocrats hammer out legislation that would make investment in the Philippines more attractive. Although the key bill—the Investment Incentives Act of 1967—as modified by Congress, fell far short of giving foreign investors as much as they were offered by neighboring authoritarian regimes in Southeast Asia, it marked a major victory for the emerging alliance opposed to Philippine economic nationalism. It also provided the structural framework (the Board of Investments or BOI) for rationalizing development through close cooperation with the foreign community. The nationalist movement's meteoric rise in the next few years encouraged administrators to hobble the program and legislators to move to challenge the for-

74. F. E. Marcos, *The Philippines and Foreign Investments* (Manila: NMPC, 1966); F. E. Marcos, *Democracy and the Challenge of Economic Development* (Manila: NMPC, 1966); and F. E. Marcos, *Japan and the Option for Progress in Asia* (Manila: NMPC, 1966).

eign-investment model of development. Moreover, the nationalist attacks on the special privileges accorded the foreign business community worked to negate any lures offered by the Marcos administration for new investment, to prevent "normalization" of relations with Japan, and to make rational negotiation of a new treaty with the United States, to replace agreements due to expire in 1974, difficult.

All this was changed by the coup. Marcos immediately proceeded to assure the foreign business community that the New Society would do everything possible to encourage foreign private investment and provide infrastructure supports to facilitate the rapid development of the Philippines. His technocrats moved swiftly. Within months, a number of "service contracts" had been signed with foreign oil companies for the exploration and development of oil fields in the Philippines, including offshore areas, an arrangement that had long been resisted by Congress. Long-standing laws against foreign participation in the rice and corn industries were voided by executive decree and provision made for opening these areas to foreign agribusiness. The BOI began periodically publishing lists of economic areas newly opened to foreign investment; new special tax incentives were opened to foreign businesses who were planning to export their products; any remaining restrictions on capital and profit flows out of the Philippines were removed; and the total tax structure was modified so that the government could claim a year later that the Philippines' "tax incentives are among Asia's best."[75] Major changes were made in the laws regulating the banking and insurance systems to open them up to foreign investment. And at less dramatic levels, the Export Processing Zone in Bataan was pushed ahead, new roads and wharves built, administrative bottlenecks (such as Customs) streamlined, and new facilitative agencies established to provide services for foreign investors. Frequently, the multiple approaches were focused on single themes, as in the drive to provide special physical facilities and government supports for a foreign investment-based electronics industry, or the concentrated drive to make Manila attractive as a base for multinational corporations, a drive that had by the end of 1975 attracted some forty multinational corporations to select the city as their regional headquarters.[76]

75. *Philippine Prospect,* November 1973.
76. *Manila Journal,* Dec. 21–27, 1975, p. 12.

In addition to these many forthright moves to align the Philippine government behind foreign private investment—and reliance on foreign loans—Marcos moved rapidly to undercut the Supreme Court's revolutionary decision on American-held Philippine property. Even before the coup he assured the Americans that he would not honor the decision.[77] Following the coup, he secured provisions in the new constitution that permit continued ownership and, following the expiration of the Laurel-Langley agreement in 1974, issued an executive decree granting nearly a year's grace period during which minor remaining issues relating to land could be negotiated between the Americans and the government, on the basis of an agreement that had been reached prior to September 1972. The negotiations for a replacement of Laurel-Langley and for the military bases agreements focused on rental fees and sovereignty rights. Broad areas of agreement on each have already surfaced in the press: The "special" trade relationship is dead (with the end of the U.S. sugar quota system and with Japan's emergence as the Philippines' first trading partner), and will be replaced with an agreement recognizing that fact. The Philippines' increasing reliance on U.S. military support—for military expansion and for the Mindanao and anti-NPA wars—as well as the greater U.S. need for the Philippine bases, assures an early resolution of the issues being negotiated on new military base agreements.[78]

Direct support for the new regime by the United States has been generous, although probably less generous than hoped by Marcos. For example, the United States has refused directly to finance land reform—although even in that area, more aid than assumed may be flowing to the Philippines through channels such as commodity loans.[79] In general, American government agencies have increased their flow of financial supports for the Philippines since martial law.

77. *Graphic*, Sept. 6, 1972, p. 2.

78. It seems certain that the United States will agree to pay a sizable annual rent for use of the bases. This will provide a method for continuing to support the Marcos regime, should U.S. congressional prohibitions against aid to dictatorships be applied to the Philippines.

79. New loans typically are reported in the controlled press. Earnings from the sale of Public Law 480 commodities are not, probably because of the sensitive issues involved. Claims were made early in the martial law period that the United States was propping up the regime by rapidly expanding this type of support. Later, *Daily Express* included in an overview of foreign financial support a figure for 1973 from Public Law 480 commodities of $200 million, far out of line with any other report but one that alerts us to the possibility of sizable inputs from this source. *Daily Express*, May 13, 1973.

Illustrative are the figures on military assistance. An examination of six main categories of military assistance during the three years prior to and the three years following martial law shows that the U.S. nearly doubled its support, from $60.2 to $118.7 million.[80] This expansion took place at a time when military assistance on the whole was declining in favor of direct sales.

Other U.S. government sources such as the Export-Import Bank have been especially active in the Philippines as the pace of dependent-development has picked up speed. And, quite importantly, multilateral loan agencies within which the United States has a dominant voice have enthusiastically accelerated their approval of Philippine requests for money. A variety of World Bank project loans have been signed since September 1972, new drawing rights provided by the International Monetary Fund, and investment loans provided by the International Finance Corporation. The Consultative Group (the consortium for managing new loans to the Philippines) keeps a firm hand on the direction development will take in the Philippines through its life-and-death power over Philippine indebtedness and new money,[81] and is assisted in this function by the ADB.[82] Private banking consortiums in the United States and elsewhere have responded to the new opportunities and have made sizable loans to investment companies and to various joint ventures in the Philippines. Public and private Japanese money has poured in so fast that Japan has rapidly moved to second place in private foreign investments, from an extremely minor position prior to martial law.

There now exists a formidable network of relationships between representatives of the foreign national and multilateral agencies and governmental units and key financial institutions of the Philippines. Many of these relationships were institutionalized by being built

80. "The Logistics of Repression," *Philippines Information Bulletin* III: 2,3 (July 1975), 5.

81. By the end of 1975 the Philippines had increased foreign indebtedness by more than 400 percent to a figure of $3,842 million, with an increase of 32 percent in 1975 alone (*Business Day International*, Mar. 22, 1976, p. 1). Debt payments in 1975 totalled $459 million against borrowings of $879 million that year. These levels are sufficiently high to indicate that the Philippines is well integrated into the "debt trap." See C. Payer, *The Debt Trap: The International Monetary Fund and the Third World* (New York: Monthly Review Press, 1974).

82. Many of these ADB loans have gone to fund new roads, irrigation schemes, and harbor facilities on Mindanao, and seem tied with the expansion of plantations on that island to supply food for Japan, as well as to facilitate the opening up of new mineral deposits for exploitation. Also see R. B. Stauffer, "The 'Development' of Mindanao," *Pahayag*, June 1975, pp. 32–38.

into the Philippine bureaucracy. This meshing of representatives of the external funding agencies into the Philippine administration has proceeded apace in parallel with the rapid expansion of the role of these agencies in the development of the Philippines.

The game plan behind all these activities has been to encourage private enterprise in the Philippines and especially to create a climate within which the flow of private foreign investment will rapidly expand. Both are obviously taking place, although signs already have appeared to indicate that many Filipino entrepreneurs are not happy with the roles in which they find themselves cast. The president of the Chamber of Commerce of the Philippines wrote, for example: "While the entry of foreign investors with greater capital resources than we can match appears to be prejudicial to our own interests since it will mean more competition in areas where Filipino entrepreneurs with modest resources are already operating, we have taken a position in favor of encouraging the participation of foreign investors . . . because we believe that this is necessary to step up growth."[83]

Foreign private investment has responded to the new conditions. Although firm commitments by new investors were rather slow in the first months after the coup, investigatory visits by business representatives of all important free-enterprise nations began almost immediately, and by 1973 new ventures began to be announced with increasing frequency in the press. By the end of 1975 approximately $500 million in new private foreign investment had been made in the Philippines since September 1972. This investment was concentrated in manufacturing (45 percent, with nearly all going to food, textiles, and petroleum), banks and other financial institutions (30 percent), mining (6 percent), commerce (5 percent), and smaller amounts in public utilities, and the like.[84] The total figure underestimates the magnitude of foreign economic power, since it

83. W. P. Clavecillia, "Trade and Professional Relations in the Philippines," *Commerce* 70 (May 1973), 28–32. Examples of independent Filipino firms that have joined in foreign ventures include Republic Flour Mills (with Swift and Company), Precision Electronics (with Matsushita), and Radiola (with Toshiba). See *Liberation*, Aug. 28, 1973. An indicator of how this can work to invade a field previously reserved for Filipinos is the takeover of Philippine Telegraph and Telephone Corporation by a joint venture made up of the Philippines Overseas Telecommunications Corporation and TRT Communications of Boston. *Bulletin Today*, May 15, 1973.

84. Data from *Manila Journal*, Mar. 7–13, 1976, p. 13. The total for the period 1970–1975 was $566 million. Very little new investment took place immediately prior to martial law. Figures from a year-end report by the Philippine Central Bank, based on Board of Investment data.

does not touch on the amount of local capital raised by foreign corporations on the local capital markets and especially through the greatly expanded network of U.S. private financial institutions created since 1972. Indicative of this is that the huge Ford stamping plant in the Mariveles Export-Processing Zone (publicized as a $100 million investment) reportedly was financed locally. Whether for that reason or for others, its huge input into the manufacturing sector does *not* appear in the government's account of new private foreign investment. And, finally, these figures do not include the cumulative quantity of foreign investments in the Philippines, which had reached $2 billion (largely U.S. in ownership) by the time of the coup, with most of the dynamic sectors safely in the hands of foreign corporations.[85]

Clearly the psychological climate is optimal for foreign private investment in the Philippines today. All the infrastructural agencies to facilitate the process have been built—the foreign banks, export zones, the local development banks, the support structures in the government—and the "climate" made most attractive. The latter includes, of course, the law-and-order, "stability" stance of the New Society, as well as its total package of policies designed to entice new flows of private foreign investment.

A final point remains to be made. In all probability, the hallmark institutional change that will in later years be associated with the new levels of foreign penetration into and control over the Philippine economy will be the new position permitted the foreign banking industry. Before the coup, only a very limited number of foreign banks were permitted to operate in the Philippines and these were prohibited from establishing a network of branches. Furthermore, foreign banks were prohibited from penetrating local Filipino banks. All these restrictions have been brushed aside under martial law. Government pressure has been directed against Philippine banks to force them to merge, and in the process, to admit foreign banking participation. By 1976, the list of Philippine banks involved had lengthened to include more than a score of banks previously free from this type of involvement; on the other side, all the major

85. By 1975, for example, 58 percent of all investments registered with the Board of Investments were foreign, as compared with 28 percent in 1968. See "The State of the Nation after Three Years of Martial Law," Civil Liberties Union of the Philippines (Makati, Rizal: 1975), p. 31. The concluding sentence reads: "Filipino capital, in brief, has been dispossessed of its economic birthright."

American banks interested in foreign investment were represented, as were banks from Japan, the United Kingdom, Germany, and Hong Kong. Similarly, foreign banks have been given the go-ahead to expand their activities in the securities field and to increase their role in the various institutions designed to provide development funds to Filipinos. Since banks play such a crucial role in the developmental processes of free market systems, it would appear that changes already accomplished under martial law have effectively brought the Philippine economy under a type of control infinitely more suited to the needs of multinational corporations than any previous control mechanism since Philippine independence.[86]

The Marcos regime has not only implemented policies highly favorable to foreign interests in the Philippines, but has gone further in institutionalizing new control mechanisms supporting dependent-authoritarianism in this area than it has in the domestic. The New Society has facilitated a rapid refeudalization of Philippine relationships with the dominant nations of the world market economy. The old mechanisms of colonial control have long since been formally eliminated (although in fact many persist in the multitude of foreign and international public advisory agents and agencies participating in decisionmaking in the Philippines). The more subtle and complex instruments of enfeoffment today include as diverse entities as Ford Motor Corporation, First National City Bank, Kawasaki Heavy Industries, the Japan International Cooperation Agency, the Bank of America, Mitsubishi Heavy Industries, Jardine Matheson, Asian Development Bank—and a hundred others. All the pre-martial law constraints (weak as they were) against total foreign domination of the economy, and all those developments in the late 1960s and early 1970s aimed at increasing the autonomy of the Philippines, have been swept aside by the New Society. The Philippines has been fully "opened," incorporated in the more complex network of relationships with the industrial nations of the market-economy world that provide guidelines—and "guides" in the form of resident advisors—for the "development" of the Philippines,

---

86. The potential for control inherent in this flow of foreign investment into the Philippine banking system is suggested in an observation by an official of the Federal Reserve System that 10 percent ownership is all that is "required of the U.S. bank to have a significant say in the management policy of the foreign institution." R. Wolff, "Foreign Expansion of U.S. Banks," *Monthly Review* 23 (May 1971), 25.

a development that will accord the Philippines a place well down on the international division of labor ladder.

Consequences of Refeudalization

This case study documents the input, over time, of authoritarian supports—ideological and material—from a metropolitan nation (in this instance the United States) into a Third World nation (the Philippines), and the cumulative consequences of these supports. Filipino groups (both within the government and outside) that had encouraged and facilitated the infusion of authoritarian supports from outside thereby undermined the existing democratic political institutions and weakened the limited degree of defeudalization that had been accomplished by preceding Filipino nationalists. When a new wave of Philippine nationalism erupted in the late 1960s and early 1970s, the externally strengthened instruments of authoritarian control were used by these Filipino groups to overthrow the existing political system and to institute a dependent-authoritarian system in its place. Changes accomplished after martial law assured that previous gains in defeudalizing the Philippine economy—to a degree at least—would be reversed and that the Philippines would be more closely integrated into the world's market economy on terms laid down by metropolitan centers than had been true in the preceding decades. Put more exactly, martial law institutions have been established to provide a much more rigorous monitoring and control of Philippine development decisions than existed previously.

While this study deals with a rapidly decreasing universe of cases—practically none remain in the category—it does suggest a framework for retrospectively reviewing the circumstances under which other competitive, relatively democratic political systems have been transformed into authoritarian ones, and for examining the consequences of continued inputs from metropolitan nations of supports for authoritarian sectors of these systems.

The findings from this study undermine conventional theory about the roles that the middle classes putatively play in the development process. The "middle sectors" in the Philippines do few of the nation-building things they are supposed to do. Except for isolated individuals, they accept development on terms defined by outsiders. Many actively accept dependency roles in the large number of multi-lateral, multinational, and national (foreign) institutions and corporations integrated into the Philippine system. To the extent that many of the most dynamic individuals accept such roles, leadership in building autonomous political and economic Filipino institutions is lost.

The findings of this case study also underline the vital importance of building intersystem variables into any model of political change, whether it be for charting the forces producing dramatic system change, as in a coup, or the cumulative, incremental modifications taking place within a stable system. Both types were involved in the Philippines, with one making possible the other. The United States provided supports incrementally for strengthening the military, the paramilitary forces, the administrative structures, and the planning agencies, and for shifting the legitimizing ideology from an emphasis on democratic elections and "politics" to one stressing development and reliance on apolitical technocrats. The cumulative consequences of these incremental inputs were to undermine the existing political structures, to greatly expand the power of the authoritative agencies, and to make the coup simple to execute and sustain—and also more probable.

The changes imposed on the Philippine political economy in the years since the coup justify use of the concept of refeudalization. Earlier gains in achieving some degree of autonomy for the Philippine economy and for reserving certain sectors of it for Filipinos have been turned back, and preparations are well advanced for a massive takeover of command positions in the banking system, in the expanding export industries, and in new additions to the typical colonial sectors of the economy: mining and agribusiness.[87] The nationalist drive to achieve meaning for Philippine independence has been silenced, at least temporarily, as the new regime pushes the nation to accept the increasing degree of direction imposed from the agencies of the metropolitan nation and the multilateral institutions over which it has controlling influence.

87. The most important study available on the subject is the National Council of Churches monograph on the role of American business in the Philippine coup and in support of martial law: "The Philippines: American Corporations, Martial Law, and Underdevelopment," *IDOC-International North American Edition*, No. 57 (November 1973). See also F. B. Weinstein, "Multi-National Corporations and the Third World: The Case of Japan and Southeast Asia," paper presented at the 1975 Annual Meeting of the American Political Science Association, September 2–5, 1975; M. Selden, "American Global Enterprise and Asia," *Bulletin of Concerned Asian Scholars* (April-June, 1975); and J. R. Salonga, "Multinational Corporations and Their Participation in Philippine Development," *Unitas* 48 (June 1975).

The Philippine case supports the proposition that powerful metropolitan nations such as the United States find open competitive political systems undesirable in poor Third World nations in which they have important interests. While authoritarian systems may on occasion be used to support nationalist claims for greater autonomy and independence, regimes based on competitive elections backed up by an aggressive free press can be assumed to be more responsive to nationalist demands. And since these demands can be expected to increase as "differentiation" produces wider gaps internally between classes, rural and urban sectors, and regions, and between poor and rich nations, pressures mount for a change to dependent-authoritarianism as a system promising some probability of being able to protect the interests of the dominant center in contrast with a near certainty that democratic systems will increasingly respond to nationalist demands.

The Philippine case study illustrates some of the channels through which Third World nations are manipulated, and especially shows the importance of the newer forms of control—multilateral financial institutions, multinational corporations, the private banking community—as well as of the more traditional mechanisms for maintaining influence over a dependent nation. Some of the costs to Filipinos of changing to a dependent-authoritarian system have been noted. If the Philippine development pattern under the new system follows that of other Third World nations which have been supported in going that route, these costs can be expected to escalate in years to come. And the costs must be added to the bill the metropolitan nations must ultimately pay for having contributed centrally to the building of a total system that distributes costs and benefits disproportionately among the "national" units.

Appendix 1. Statement of President Ferdinand E. Marcos on the Declaration of Martial Law

My Countrymen:

As of the 21st of September, I signed Proclamation No. 1081 placing the entire Philippines under martial law. This proclamation was to be implemented upon my clearance, and clearance was granted at 9:00 in the evening of the 22nd of September. I have proclaimed martial law in accordance with powers vested in the President by the Constitution of the Philippines.

The proclamation of martial law is not a military takeover. I, as your duly elected President of the Republic, use this power implemented by the military authorities to protect the Republic of the Philippines and our democracy. A republican and democratic form of government is not a helpless government. When it is imperilled by the danger of a violent overthrow, insurrection, and rebellion, it has inherent and built-in powers wisely provided for under the Constitution. Such a danger confronts the Republic.

Thus, Article VII, Section 10, Paragraph (2) of the Constitution, provides:

The President shall be Commander-in-Chief of all the Armed Forces of the Philippines and, whenever it becomes necessary he may call out such Armed Forces to prevent or suppress lawless violence, invasion, insurrection, or rebellion. In case of invasion, insurrection, or rebellion or imminent danger thereof, when the public safety requires it, he may suspend the privilege of the writ of habeas corpus, or place the Philippines or any part thereof under martial law.

I repeat, this is not a military takeover of civil government functions. The Government of the Republic of the Philippines which was established by our people in 1946 continues. The officials and employees of our national and local governments continue in office and must discharge their duties as before within the limits of the

Source: *Vital Legal Documents in the New Society* (Manila: Central Book Supply, n.d.), I, 1–7.

situation. This will be clarified by my subsequent orders which shall be given wide publicity. (Refer to General Order No. 3)

We will explain the requirements and standards or details as soon as possible. But any form of corruption, culpable negligence or arrogance will be dealt with immediately.

The Armed Forces is already cleaning up its own ranks. I am directing the organization of a military commission to investigate, try and punish all military offenders immediately. For more than any other man, the soldier must set the standard of nobility. We must be courageous but we must be humble and above all we must be fair. As this is true of the soldier, it must be true of the civilian public officer.

Let no man who claims to be a friend, relative or ally presume to seek license because of this relationship. If he offends the New Society, he shall be punished like the rest.

Persons who have nothing whatsoever to do with such conspiracy and operations to overthrow the Republic of the Philippines by violence have nothing to fear. They can move about and perform their daily activities without any fear from the government after the period of counter-action is over.

The persons who will be adversely affected are those who have actively participated in the conspiracy and operations to overthrow the duly constituted government of the Republic of the Philippines by violence.

But all public officials and employees whether of the national or local governments must conduct themselves in the manner of a new and reformed society.

In addition to this, I issued general orders for the government in the meantime to control media and other means of dissemination of information as well as all public utilities. All schools will be closed for one week beginning this coming Monday. The carrying of firearms outside residences without the permission of the Armed Forces of the Philippines is punishable with death; curfew is established from twelve o'clock midnight to four o'clock in the morning, the departure of Filipinos abroad is temporarily suspended; exceptions are those of official missions that are necessary. Clearances will be given by the Secretary of National Defense. In the meantime, rallies [and] demonstrations are prohibited. So too are strikes in critical public utilities.

I have ordered the arrest of those directly involved in the conspiracy to overthrow our duly constituted government by violence and subversion.

It is my intention beginning tomorrow to issue all the orders which would attain reforms in our society.

This would include the proclamation of land reform all over the Philippines, the reorganization of the government, new rules and conduct for the civil service, the removal of corrupt and inefficient public officials and their replacement and the breaking up of criminal syndicates.

Again I repeat—this is the same government that you—the people—established in 1946 under the Constitution of the Philippines.

There is no doubt in everybody's mind that a state of rebellion exists in the Philippines.

The ordinary man in the streets, in our cities, the peasants and the laborers know it. Industrialists know it. So do the government functionary. They have all been affected by it. This danger to the Republic of the Philippines and the existence of a rebellion has been recognized even by our Supreme Court in its decision in the case of *Lansang* vs. *Garcia,* dated December 11, 1971.

Since the Supreme Court promulgated this decision, the danger has become graver and rebellion has worsened or escalated. It has paralyzed the functions of the national and local governments. The productive sectors of the economy have ground to a halt. Many schools have closed down. The judiciary is unable to administer justice. Many of our businessmen, traders, industrialists, producers and manufacturers stopped their operations. In the Greater Manila area alone, tension and anxiety have reached a point where the citizens are compelled to stay home. Lawlessness and criminality like kidnapping, smuggling, extortion, blackmail, armed robbery, illegal traffic in drugs, gunrunning, hoarding and manipulation of prices, corruption in government, tax evasion perpetuated by syndicated criminals, have increasingly escalated beyond the capability of the local police and civilian authorities.

The usually busy centers of the area such as cinema houses, supermarkets, restaurants, transportation terminals and even public markets are practically deserted. Battles are going on between the elements of the armed forces of the Philippines and the subversives in the island of Luzon at Isabela, Zambales, Tarlac, Camarines Sur,

Quezon; and in the island of Mindanao at Lanao del Sur, Lanao del Norte, Zamboanga del Sur, and Cotabato.

If this continues even at the present rate, the economy of the country will collapse in a short time.

In one province alone—Isabela—where the Communist Party and the New People's Army have sought to establish a rural sanctuary, they are now in control of 33 municipalities out of 37. Other towns are infiltrated severely by these armed elements. In this province alone, the supposed invisible government of the Communist Party has been organized through the Barrio Organizing Committee (BOCs), totalling 207 in twenty-five (25) towns, compared to 161 in 12 towns in early 1971.

In addition to the Barrio Organizing Committees, they have also organized the Barrio Revolutionary Committees (BRCs).

In Angadanan and Cauayan, Isabela, the New People's Army have established communal farms and production bases.

The New People's Army has started to expand its operation to Cagayan, Nueva Vizcaya and Quirino as well as the mountain provinces of Ifugao, Kalinga-Apayao, Bontoc and Benguet. Even the two Ilocos provinces and La Union have been infiltrated.

The New People's Army and the Communist Party have also sought to establish in a similar pattern, a rural sanctuary in the province of Camarines Sur and are attempting to expand into Albay, Sorsogon and Camarines Norte as well as Quezon Province.

The armed elements of the New People's Army under the Communist Party of the Philippines (Maoist faction) have increased to about 10,000, which includes regulars as well as farmers in the daytime and soldiers at night. This is an increase of 100% in a short period of six (6) months. It has increased its mass base to 100,000. Their front organizations' operations have increased tremendously. Example of such a front organization is the Kabataang Makabayan (KM), the most militant organization of the Communist Party which has increased its chapters from 200 in 1970 to 317 up to the end of July 1972, and its memberships from 10,000 in 1970 to 15,000 up to the end of July this year. The Samahang Demokratiko ng Kabataan (SDK), an outspoken front organization, had also increased its chapters from almost none in 1970 to 159 at the end of July this year and has now 1,495 highly indoctrinated and fanatical members.

The crucial point which indicates an increase in the capability, the area of operations as well as the manpower and fire power of the New People's Army is the M/V Karagatan or Palanan incident in Palanan, Isabela last July 4 and 5, 1972. This was a landing by an ocean-going ship of a reported 3,500 M-14 rifles of which only about 900 were recovered by the Armed Forces of the Philippines; about 30 rocket launchers of the M-40 variety of which only six (6) were recovered from the area. Also recovered by our forces were 160,000 rounds of ammunition, two (2) Browning automatic rifles which were originally looted by defector Victor Corpus from the arsenal of the Philippine Military Academy, five (5) Garand M-1 rifles, and one (1) telephone switch board, seven (7) telephone sets, numerous M-14 magazines and many revealing subversive documents.

The landing of military armaments and equipment in the Palanan incident, indicated:

1) that the claim of the New People's Army that they are well-funded has a basis in fact;
2) that they now have sources of funds and equipment not only inside the Philippines but also outside the country;
3) that the Communist Party and the New People's Army are capable of landing armaments, military equipment and even personnel in many points of the long sea coast of the Philippines which is twice the sea coast of the United States.

The Defense establishment has admitted that there have been attempts to infiltrate the military organizations as well as the office of the Secretary of National Defense. There have been various incidents of attempts to sabotage not only operations of the Armed Forces of the Philippines but the operations of the National Government.

It has been reported that the communications system[s] of the Philippine Constabulary are being utilized by the subversives.

The subversives have organized urban partisans in the Greater Manila area. They have been and still are active. They have succeeded in some of their objectives.

The violent disorder in Mindanao and Sulu has to date resulted in the killing of over 1,000 civilians and about 2,000 armed Muslims and Christians, not to mention the more than five hundred thousands of injured, displaced and homeless persons as well as the great number of casualties among our government troops, and the paralyzation of the economy of Mindanao and Sulu.

I assure you that I am utilizing this power vested in me by the Constitution to save the Republic and reform our society. I wish to emphasize these two objectives. We will eliminate the threat of a violent overthrow of our Republic. But at the same time we must now reform the social, economic and political institutions in our country. The plans and orders for reform to remove the inequities of that society, the clean-up of government of its corrupt and sterile elements, the liquidation of the criminal syndicates, the systematic development of our economy—the general program for a new and better Philippines—will be explained to you. But we must start out with the removal of anarchy and the maintenance of peace and order.

I have had to use this constitutional power in order that we may not completely lose the civil rights and freedom which we cherish. I assure you that this is not a precipitate decision—that I have weighed all the factors. If there were any other solution at our disposal and within our capability which we could utilize to solve the present problem, I would choose it. But there is none.

I have used the other two alternatives of calling out the troops to quell the rebellion and suspending the privilege of the writ of *habeas corpus*. But the rebellion has not been stopped. I repeat it has worsened. Thus it was discovered that when the suspension of the privilege of the writ of *habeas corpus* was lifted on January 11, 1972, the organization of the Communist Party had expanded their area of operation as well as increased their memberships.

All other recourses have been unavailing. You are all witnesses to these. So we have fallen on our last line of defense.

You are witnesses to the patience that we have shown in the face of provocation. In the face of abuse and license we have used persuasion. Now the limit has been reached. We are against the wall. We must now defend the Republic with the stronger powers of the Constitution.

To those guilty of treason, insurrection, rebellion, it may pose a grave danger. But to the citizenry whose primary concern is to be left alone to pursue their lawful activities, this is the guaranty of that freedom.

All that we do is for the Republic and for you. Rest assured we will continue to do so.

I have prayed to God for guidance. Let us all continue to do so. I am confident that with God's help we will attain our dream of a reformed society, a new and brighter world.

Appendix 2. Proclamation No. 1081, Proclaiming a State of Martial Law in the Philippines

Whereas, on the basis of carefully evaluated and verified informaiton, it is definitely established that lawless elements who are moved by a common or similar ideological conviction, design, strategy and goal and enjoying the active moral and material support of a foreign power and being guided and directed by intensely devoted, well trained, determined and ruthless groups of men and seeking refuge under the protection of our constitutional liberties to promote and attain their ends, have entered into a conspiracy and have in fact joined and banded their resources and forces together for the prime purpose of, and in fact they have been and are actually staging, undertaking and waging an armed insurrection and rebellion against the Government of the Republic of the Philippines in order to forcibly seize political and state power in this country, overthrow the duly constituted government, and supplant our existing political, social, economic and legal order with an entirely new one whose form of government, whose system of laws, whose conception of God and religion, whose notion of individual rights and family relations, and whose political, social, economic, legal and moral precepts are based on the Marxist-Leninist-Maoist teachings and beliefs;

Whereas, these lawless elements, acting in concert through seemingly innocent and harmless, although actually destructive, front organizations which have been infiltrated or deliberately formed by them, have continuously and systematically strengthened and broadened their memberships through sustained and careful recruiting and enlistment of new adherents from among our peas-

Source: *Vital Legal Documents in the New Society* (Manila: Central Book Supply, n.d.), I, 7–22.

antry, laborers, professionals, intellectuals, students, and mass media personnel, and through such sustained and careful recruitment and enlistment have succeeded in spreading and expanding their control and influence over almost every segment and level of our society throughout the land in their ceaseless effort to erode and weaken the political, social, economic, legal and moral foundations of our existing government, and to influence, manipulate and move peasant, labor, student and terroristic organizations under their influence or control to commit, as in fact they have committed and still are committing, acts of violence, depredations, sabotage and injuries against our duly constituted authorities, against the members of our law enforcement agencies, and worst of all, against the peaceful members of our society;

Whereas, in the fanatical pursuit of their conspiracy and widespread acts of violence, depredations, sabotage and injuries against our people, and in order to provide the essential instrument to direct and carry out their criminal design and unlawful activities, and to achieve their ultimate sinister objectives, these lawless elements have in fact organized, established and are now maintaining a Central Committee, composed of young and dedicated radical students and intellectuals, which is charged with guiding and directing the armed struggle and propaganda assaults against our duly constituted government, and this Central Committee is now imposing its will and asserting its sham authority on certain segments of our population, especially in the rural areas, through varied means of subterfuge, deceit, coercion, threats, intimidations, machinations, treachery, violence and other modes of terror, and has been and is illegally exacting financial and other forms of tributes from our people to raise funds and material resources to support its insurrectionary and propaganda activities against our duly constituted government and against our peace-loving people;

Whereas, in order to carry out, as in fact they have carried out, their premeditated plan to stage, undertake and wage a full scale armed insurrection and rebellion in this country, these lawless elements have organized, established and are now maintaining a well trained, well armed and highly indoctrinated and greatly expanded insurrectionary force, popularly known as the "New People's Army," which has since vigorously pursued and still is vigorously pursuing a relentless and ruthless armed struggle against our duly constituted government and whose unmitigated forays, raids, ambuscades, assaults and reign of terror and acts of lawlessness in the rural areas and in our urban centers brought about the treacherous and cold-blooded assassination of innocent civilians, military personnel of the government and local public officials in many parts of the country, notably in the Cagayan Valley, in Central Luzon, in the Southern Tagalog Region, in the Bicol Area, in the Visayas and in Mindanao, and whose daring and wanton guerrilla activities have generated and sown fear and panic among our people, have created a climate of chaos and disorder, produced a state of political, social, psychological and economic instability in our land, and have inflicted great suffering and irreparable injury to persons and property in our society;

Whereas, these lawless elements, their cadres, fellow-travellers, friends, sympathizers and supporters have for many years up to the present time been mounting sustained, massive and destructive propaganda assaults against our duly constituted government, its instrumentalities, agencies and officials, and also against our social, political, economic and religious institutions, through the publications, broadcasts and disseminations of deliberately slanted and overly exaggerated news stories and news commentaries as well as false, vile, foul and scurrilous statements, utterances, writings and pictures through the press-radio-television media and through leaflets, college campus newspapers and some newspapers published and still being published by these lawless elements, notably the "Ang Bayan," "Pulang Bandila" and the "Ang Komunista," all of which are clearly well-conceived, intended and calculated to malign and discredit our duly constituted government, its instrumentalities, agencies and officials before our people, making it appear to the people that our government has become so weak and so impotent to perform and discharge its functions and responsibilities in our society and to our people, and thus undermine and destroy the faith and loyalty and allegiance of our people in and alienate their support for their duly constituted government, its instrumentalities, agencies and officials, and thereby gradually erode and weaken as in fact they have so eroded and weakened the will of our people to sustain and defend our government and our democratic way of life;

Whereas, these lawless elements having taken up arms against our duly constituted government and against our people, and having committed and are still committing acts of armed insurrection and rebellion consisting of armed raids, forays, sorties, ambushes, wanton acts of murders, spoilage, plunder, looting, arsons, destruction of public and private buildings, and attacks against innocent and defenseless civilian lives and property, all of which activities have seriously endangered and continue to endanger public order and safety and the security of the nation, and acting with cunning and manifest precision and deliberation and without regard to the health, safety and well-being of the people, are now implementing their plan to cause widespread, massive and systematic destruction and paralization of vital public utilities and services, particularly water systems, sources of electrical power, communication and transportation facilities, to the great detriment, suffering, injury and prejudice of our people and the nation and to generate a deep psychological fear and panic among our people;

Whereas, the Supreme Court in the cases brought before it, docketed as G.R. Nos. L-33964, L-33963, L-33973, L-33982, L-34004, L-34013, L-34039, L-34265, L-34339, as a consequence of the suspension of the privilege of the writ of *habeas corpus* by me as President of the Philippines in my Proclamation No. 889, dated August 21, 1971, as amended, has found that in truth and in fact there exists an actual insurrection and rebellion in the country by a sizeable group of men who have publicly risen in arms to overthrow the government. Here is what the Supreme Court said in its decision promulgated on December 11, 1971:

". . . our jurisprudence attests abundantly to the Communist activities in the Philippines, especially in Manila, from the late twenties to the early thirties, then aimed principally at incitement to sedition or rebellion, as the immediate objective. Upon the establishment of the Commonwealth of the Philippines, the movement seemed to have waned notably; but, the outbreak of World War II in the Pacific and the miseries, the devastation and havoc, and the proliferation of unlicensed firearms concomitant with the military occupation of the Philippines and its subsequent liberation, brought about, in the late forties, a resurgence of the Communist threat, with such vigor as to be able to organize and operate in Central Luzon an army—called HUKBALAHAP, during the occupation, and re-

named Hukbong Mapagpalaya ng Bayan (HMB) after liberation—
which clashed several times with the armed forces of the Republic.
This prompted then President Quirino to issue Proclamation No.
210, dated October 22, 1950, suspending the privilege of the writ of
habeas corpus, the validity of which was upheld in Montenegro v.
Castañeda. Days before the promulgation of said Proclamation, or
on October 18, 1950, members of the Communist Politburo in the
Philippines were apprehended in Manila. Subsequently accused and
convicted of the crime of rebellion, they served their respective
sentences.

"The fifties saw a comparative lull in Communist activities, insofar as peace and order were concerned. Still, on June 20, 1957,
Republic Act No. 1700, otherwise known as the Anti-Subversion
Act, was approved, upon the grounds stated in the very preamble
of said statute—that

". . . the Communist Party of the Philippines, although purportedly a political party, is in fact an organized conspiracy to overthrow the Government of the Republic of the Philippines, not only
by force and violence but also by deceit, subversion and other illegal means, for the purpose of establishing in the Philippines a
totalitarian regime subject to alien domination and control;

". . . the continued existence and activities of the Communist
Party of the Philippines constitutes a *clear, present* and *grave* danger
to the security of the Philippines; and

". . . in the fact of the organized, systematic and persistent subversion, national in scope but international in direction, posed by
the Communist Party of the Philippines and its activities, there is
urgent need for special legislation to cope with this continuing
menace to the freedom and security of the country. . . ."

In the language of the Report on Central Luzon, submitted, on
September 4, 1971, by the Senate Ad Hoc Committee of Seven—
copy of which Report was filed in these cases by the petitioners
herein—

The years following 1963 saw the successive emergence in the country
of several mass organizations, notably the Lapiang Manggagawa (now
the Socialist Party of the Philippines) among the workers; the Malayang
Samahan ng Mga Magsasaka (MASAKA) among the peasantry; the
Kabataang Makabayan (KM) among the youth/students; and the Movement for the Advancement of Nationalism (MAN) among the intel-

lectuals/professionals, the PKP has exerted all-out effort to infiltrate, influence and utilize these organizations in promoting its radical brand of nationalism.

Meanwhile, the Communist leaders in the Philippines had been split into two (2) groups, one of which—composed mainly of young radicals, constituting the Maoist faction—reorganized the Communist Party of the Philippines early in 1969 and established a New People's Army. This faction adheres to the Maoist concept of the "Protracted People's War" or "War of National Liberation." Its "Programme for a People's Democratic Revolution" states, *inter alia:*

The Communist Party of the Philippines is determined to implement its general programme for a people's democratic revolution. All Filipino communists are ready to sacrifice their lives for the worthy cause of achieving the new type of democracy, of building a new Philippines that is genuinely and completely independent, democratic, united, just and prosperous. . . .

The Central task of any revolutionary movement is to seize political power. The *Communist Party of the Philippines assumes this task* at a time that both the international and national situations are favorable to taking the road of armed revolution. . . .

In the year 1969, the NPA had—according to the records of the Department of National Defense—conducted raids, resorted to kidnappings and taken part in other violent incidents numbering over 230, in which it inflicted 404 casualties, and, in turn, suffered 243 losses. In 1970, its record of violent incidents was about the same, but the NPA casualties more than doubled.

At any rate, two (2) facts are undeniable: (a) all Communists, whether they belong to the traditional group or the Maoist faction, believe that force and violence are indispensable to the attainment of their main and ultimate objective, and act in accordance with such belief, although they disagree on the means to be used at a given time and in a particular place; and (b) there is a New People's Army, *other,* of course, than the armed forces of the Republic and antagonistic thereto. Such New People's Army is *per se* proof of the existence of a rebellion, especially considering that its establishment was *announced publicly* by the reorganized CPP. Such announcement is in the nature of a public challenge to the duly constituted authorities and may be likened to a declaration of war, sufficient to establish a war status or a condition of belligerency, even before the actual commencement of hostilities.

We entertain, therefore, no doubts about the existence of a sizeable group of men who have publicly risen in arms to overthrow the government and have thus been and still are engaged in rebellion against the Government of the Philippines.

Whereas, these lawless elements have to a considerable extent succeeded in impeding our duly constituted authorities from performing their functions and discharging their duties and responsibilities in accordance with our laws and our Constitution to the great damage, prejudice and detriment of the people and the nation;

Whereas, it is evident that there is throughout the land a state of anarchy and lawlessness, chaos and disorder, turmoil and destruction of a magnitude equivalent to an actual war between the forces of our duly constituted government and the New People's Army and their satellite organizations because of the unmitigated forays, raids, ambuscades, violence, murders, assassinations, acts of terror, deceits, coercions, threats, intimidations, treachery, machinations, arsons, plunders and depredations committed and being committed by the aforesaid lawless elements who have pledged to the whole nation that they will not stop their dastardly effort and scheme until and unless they have fully attained their primary and ultimate purpose of forcibly seizing political and state power in this country by overthrowing our present duly constituted government, by destroying our democratic way of life and our established secular and religious institutions and beliefs, and by supplanting our existing political, social, economic, legal and moral order with an entirely new one whose form of government, whose notion of individual rights and family relations, and whose political, social, economic and moral precepts are based on the Marxist-Leninist-Maoist teachings and beliefs;

Whereas, the Supreme Court in its said decision concluded that the unlawful activities of the aforesaid lawless elements actually pose a clear, present and grave danger to public safety and the security of the nation and in support of that conclusion found that:

. . . the Executive had information and reports—subsequently confirmed, in many respects, by the above-mentioned Report of the Senate Ad Hoc Committee of Seven—to the effect that the Communist Party of the Philippines does not merely adhere to Lenin's idea of a swift armed uprising; that it has, also, adopted Ho Chi Minh's terrorist tactics and resorted to the assassination of uncooperative local officials; that, in line with this policy, the insurgents have killed 5 mayors, 20 barrio captains and 3 chiefs of police; that there were fourteen (14) meaningful bombing incidents in the Greater Manila area in 1970; that the Constitutional Convention Hall was bombed on June 12, 1971; that, soon after the Plaza Miranda incident, the NAWASA main pipe at the Quezon City–San Juan boundary, was bombed; that this was followed closely by the bombing of the Manila City Hall, the COMELEC Building, the Congress Building and the MERALCO sub-station at Cubao, Quezon City; and that the respective residences of Senator Jose J. Roy and Congressman Eduardo Cojuangco were, likewise, bombed, as were the MERALCO main office premises, along Ortigas Avenue, and the Doctor's Pharmaceuticals, Inc. Building, in Caloocan City.

. . . the reorganized Communist Party of the Philippines has, moreover, adopted Mao's concept of protracted people's war, aimed at the paralyzation of the will to resist of the government, of the political, economic and intellectual leadership, and of the people themselves; that conformably to such concept, the Party has placed special emphasis upon a most extensive and intensive program of subversion by the establishment of front organizations in urban centers, the organization of armed city partisans and the infiltration in student groups, labor unions, and farmer and professional groups; that the CPP has managed to infiltrate or establish and control nine (9) major labor organizations; that it has exploited the youth movement and succeeded in making Communist fronts of eleven (11) major student or youth organizations; that there are, accordingly, about thirty (30) mass organizations actively advancing the CPP interests, among which are the Malayang Samahan ng Magsasaka (MASAKA), the Kabataang Makabayan (KM), the Movement for the Advancement of Nationalism (MAN), the Samahang Demokratiko ng Kabataan (SDK), the Samahang Molave (SM), and the Malayang Pagkakaisa ng Kabataang Pilipino (MPKP); that, as of August, 1971, the KM had two hundred forty-five (245) operational chapters throughout the Philippines, of which seventy-three (73) were in the Greater Manila Area, sixty (60) in Northern Luzon, forty-nine (49) in Central Luzon, forty-two (42) in the Visayas and twenty-one (21) in Mindanao and Sulu; that in 1970, the Party had recorded two hundred fifty-eight (258) major demonstrations, of which about thirty-three (33) ended in violence, resulting in fifteen (15) killed and over five hundred (500) injured; that most of these actions were organized, coordinated or led by the aforementioned front organizations; that the violent demonstrations were generally instigated by a small, but well-trained group of armed agitators; that the number of demonstrations heretofore staged in 1971 has already exceeded those of 1970; and that twenty-four (24) of these demonstrations were violent, and resulted in the death of fifteen (15) persons and the injury of many more.

Subsequent events . . . have also proven . . . the threat to public safety posed by the New People's Army. Indeed, it appears that, since August 21, 1971, it had in Northern Luzon six (6) encounters and staged one (1) raid, in consequences of which seven (7) soldiers lost their lives and two (2) others were wounded, whereas the insurgents suffered five (5) casualties; that on August 26, 1971, a well-armed group of NPA, trained by defector Lt. Victor Corpus, attacked the very command post of TF LAWIN in Isabela, destroying two (2) helicopters and one (1) plane, and wounding one (1) soldier; that the NPA had in Central Luzon a total of four (4) encounters, with two (2) killed and three (3) wounded on the side of the Government, one (1) BSDU killed and three (3) KM-SDK leaders, an unidentified dissident, and Commander Panchito, leader of the dissident group, were killed; that on August 26, 1971, there was an encounter in the barrio of San Pedro, Iriga City, Camarines Sur, between the PC and the NPA, in which a PC and two (2) KM members were killed, that the current disturbances in Cotabato and the Lanao provinces have been rendered more complex by the involvement of the CPP/NPA, for, in mid-1971, a KM group, headed by Jovencio Esparagoza, contacted the Higa-onan tribes, in their settlement in Magsaysay, Misamis Oriental, and offered them books, pamphlets and brochures of Mao Tse-tung, as well as conducted teach-ins in the reservation; that Esparagoza was reportedly killed on September 22, 1971, in an operation of the PC in said reservation; and that there are now two (2) NPA cadres in Mindanao.

It should, also, be noted that adherents of the CPP and its front organizations are, according to intelligence findings, definitely capable of preparing powerful explosives out of locally available materials; that the bomb used in the Constitutional Convention Hall was a "Claymore" mine, a powerful explosive device used by the U.S. Army, believed to have been one of many pilfered from the Subic Naval Base a few days before; that the President had received intelligence information to the effect that there was a July–August Plan involving a wave of assassinations, kidnappings, terrorism and mass destruction of property and that an extraordinary occurrence would signal the beginning of said event; that the rather serious condition of peace and order in Mindanao, particularly in Cotabato and Lanao, demanded the presence therein of forces sufficient to cope with the situation; that a sizeable part of our armed forces discharges other functions; and that the expansion of the CPP activities from Central Luzon to other parts of the country, particularly Manila and its suburbs, the Cagayan Valley, Ifugao, Zambales, Laguna, Quezon and the Bicol Region, required that the rest of our armed forces be spread thin over a wide area.

Whereas, in the unwavering prosecution of their revolutionary war against the Filipino people and their duly constituted government, the aforesaid lawless elements have, in the months of May, June and July, 1972, succeeded in bringing and introducing into the country at Digoyo Point, Palanan, Isabela and other undetermined points along the Pacific coastline of Luzon, a substantial quantity of war materiel consisting of M-14 rifles estimated to be some 3,500 pieces, several dozens of 40mm rocket launchers which are said to be Chicom copies of a Russian prototype rocket launcher, large quantities of 80mm rockets and ammunitions, and other combat paraphernalia, of which war materiel some had been discovered and captured by government military forces, and the bringing and introduction of such quantity and type of war materiel into the country is a mute but eloquent proof of the sinister plan of the aforesaid lawless elements to hasten the escalation of their present revolutionary war against the Filipino people and their legitimate government;

Whereas, in the execution of their overall revolutionary plan, the aforesaid lawless elements have prepared and released to their various field commanders and Party workers a document captioned "Regional Program of Action 1972," a copy of which was captured by elements of the 116th and 119th Philippine Constabulary Companies on June 18, 1972, at Barrio Taringsing, Cordon, Isabela, the text of which reads as follows:

Regional Program of Action 1972

The following Regional Program of Action for 1972 is prepared to be carried out as part of the overall plan of the party to foment discontent and precipitate the tide of nationwide mass revolution. The fascist Marcos and his reactionary members of Congress is expected to prepare themselves for the 1973 hence:

January–June:

1. Intensify recruitment of new party members especially from the workers-farmers class. Cadres are being trained in order to organize the different regional bureaus. These bureaus must concentrate on mass action and organization to promote advancement of the mass revolutionary movement. Reference is made to the "Borador ng Programa sa

Pagkilos at Ulat ng Panlipunang Pagsisiyasat" as approved by the Central Committee.

2. Recruit and train armed city partisans and urban guerrillas and organize them into units under Party cadres and activists of mass organizations. These units must undergo specialized training on explosives and demolition and other forms of sabotage.

3. Intensify recruitment and training of new members for the New People's Army in preparation for limited offensive in selected areas in the regions.

4. Support a more aggressive program of agitation and propaganda against the reactionary armed forces and against the Con Con.

July–August:

During this period the party expects the puppet Marcos government to allow increase in bus rates thus aggravating further the plight of students, workers and the farmers.

1. All Regional Party Committees must plan for a general strike movement. The Regional Operational Commands must plan for armed support if the fascist armed forces of Marcos will try to intimidate the oppressed Filipino masses.

2. Conduct sabotage against schools, colleges and universities hiking tuition fees.

3. Conduct sabotage and agitation against puppet judges and courts hearing cases against top party leaders.

4. Create regional chaos and disorder to dramatize the inability of the fascist Marcos government to keep and maintain peace and order through:

    a) Robbery and hold-up of banks controlled by American imperialists and those belonging to the enemies of the people.

    b) Attack military camps, US bases and towns.

    c) More violent strikes and demonstrations.

September–October:

Increase intensity of violence, disorder and confusion:

1. Intensify sabotage and bombing of government buildings and embassies and other utilities:

    a) Congress

    b) Supreme Court

    c) Con Con

    d) City Hall

    e) US Embassy

    f) Facilities of US Bases

    g) Provincial Capitols

    h) Power Plants

    i) PLDT

    j) Radio Stations

2. Sporadic attacks on camps, towns and cities.

3. Assassinate high government officials of Congress, Judiciary, Con Con and private individuals sympathetic to puppet Marcos.

4. Establish provisional revolutionary government in towns and cities with the support of the masses.

5. With the sympathetic support of our allies, establish provisional provincial revolutionary governments.

CENTRAL COMMITTEE
COMMUNIST PARTY OF THE PHILIPPINES

Whereas, in line with their "Regional Program of Action 1972," the aforesaid lawless elements have of late been conducting intensified acts of violence and terrorisms during the current year in the greater Manila area such as the bombing of the Arca building at Taft Avenue, Pasay City, on March 15; of the Filipinas Orient Airways board room at Domestic Road, Pasay City on April 23; of the Vietnamese Embassy on May 30; of the Court of Industrial Relations on June 23; of the Philippine Trust Company branch office in Cubao, Quezon City on June 24; of the Philamlife building at United Nations Avenue, Manila, on July 3; of the Tabacalera Cigar & Cigarette Factory Compound at Marquez de Comillas, Manila on July 27; of the PLDT exchange office at East Avenue, Quezon City, and of the Philippine Sugar Institute building at North Avenue, Diliman, Quezon City, both on August 15; of the Department of Social Welfare building at San Rafael Street, Sampaloc, Manila, on August 17; of a water main on Aurora Boulevard and Madison Aveune, Quezon City on August 19; of the Philamlife building again on August 30; this time causing severe destruction on the Far East Bank and Trust Company building nearby; of the armored car and building of the Philippine Banking Corporation as well as the buildings of the Investment Development Inc. and the Daily Star Publications when another explosion took place on Railroad Street, Port Area, Manila also on August 30; of Joe's Department Store on Carriedo Street, Quiapo, Manila, on September 5, causing death to one woman and injuries to some 38 individuals; and of the City Hall of Manila on September 8; of the water mains in San Juan, Rizal on Sept. 12, of the San Miguel building in Makati, Rizal on Sept. 14; and of the Quezon City Hall on September 18, 1972, as well as the attempted bombing of the Congress Building on July 18, when an unexploded bomb was found in the Senate Publication Division and the attempted bombing of the Department of Foreign Affairs on August 30.

Whereas, in line with the same "Regional Program of Action 1972," the aforesaid lawless elements have also fielded in the Greater Manila area several of their "Sparrow Units" or "Simbad Units" to undertake liquidation missions against ranking government officials, military personnel and prominent citizens and to further heighten the destructions and depredations already inflicted by them upon our innocent people, all of which are being deliberately done to sow terror, fear and chaos amongst our population and to make the government look so helpless and incapable of protecting the lives and property of our people;

Whereas, in addition to the above-described social disorder, there is also the equally serious disorder in Mindanao and Sulu resulting from the unsettled conflict between certain elements of the Christian and Muslim population of Mindanao and Sulu, between the Christian "Ilagas" and the Muslim "Barracudas," and between our government troops, and certain lawless organizations such as the Mindanao Independence Movement;

Whereas, the Mindanao Independence Movement with the active material and financial assistance of foreign political and economic interests, is engaged in an open and unconcealed attempt to establish by violence and force a separate and independent political state out of the islands of Mindanao and Sulu which are historically, politically and by law parts of the territories and within the jurisdiction and sovereignty of the Republic of the Philippines;

Whereas, because of the aforesaid disorder resulting from armed clashes, killings, massacres, arsons, rapes, pillages, destruction of whole villages and towns and the inevitable cessation of agricultural and industrial operations, all of which have been brought about by the violence inflicted by the Christians, the Muslims, the "Ilagas," the "Barracudas," and the Mindanao Independence Movement against each other and against our government troops, a great many parts of the islands of Mindanao and Sulu are virtually now in state of actual war;

Whereas, the violent disorder in Mindanao and Sulu has to date resulted in the killing of over 1,000 civilians and about 2,000 armed Muslims and Christians, not to mention the more than five hundred thousand of injured, displaced and homeless persons as well as the great number of casualties among our government troops, and the paralyzation of the economy of Mindanao and Sulu;

Whereas, because of the foregoing acts of armed insurrection, wanton destruction of human lives and property, unabated and unrestrained propaganda attacks against the government and its institutions, instrumentalities, agencies and officials, and the rapidly expanding ranks of the aforesaid lawless elements, and because of the spreading lawlessness and anarchy throughout the land, all of which have prevented the government to exercise its authority, extend to its citizenry the protection of its laws and in general exercise its sovereignty over all of its territories, caused serious demoralization among our people and have made the public apprehensive and fearful, and finally because public order and safety and the security of this nation demand that immediate, swift, decisive and effective action be taken to protect and insure the peace, order and security of the country and its population and to maintain the authority of the government;

Whereas, in cases of invasion, insurrection or rebellion or imminent danger thereof, I, as President of the Philippines, have, under the Constitution, three courses of action open to me, namely: (a) call out the armed forces to suppress the present lawless violence; (b) suspend the privilege of the writ of *habeas corpus* to make the arrest and apprehension of these lawless elements easier and more effective; or (c) place the Philippines or any part thereof under martial law;

Whereas, I have already utilized the first two courses of action, first, by calling upon the armed forces to suppress the aforesaid lawless violence, committing to that specific job almost 50 percent of the entire armed forces of the country and creating several task forces for that purpose such as Task Force Saranay, Task Force Palanan, Task Force Isarog, Task Force Pagkakaisa and Task Force Lancaf, and, second, by suspending the privilege of the writ of *habeas corpus* on August 21, 1971 up to January 11, 1972, but in spite of all that, both courses of action were found inadequate and ineffective to contain, much less solve, the present rebellion and lawlessness in the country as shown by the fact that:

1. The radical left has increased the number and area of operation of its front organizations and has intensified the recruitment and

training of new adherents in the urban and rural areas especially from among the youth;

2. The Kabataang Makabayan (KM), the most militant and outspoken front organization of the radical left, has increased the number of its chapters from 200 as of the end of 1970 to 317 as of July 31, 1972 and its membership from 10,000 as of the end of 1970 to 15,000 as of the end of July, 1972, showing very clearly the rapid growth of the communist movement in this country;

3. The Samahang Demokratiko ng Kabataan (SDK), another militant and outspoken front organization of the radical left, has also increased the number of its chapters from an insignificant number at the end of 1970 to 159 as of the end of July, 1972 and has now a membership of some 1,495 highly indoctrinated, intensely committed and almost fanatically devoted individuals;

4. The New People's Army, the most active and the most violent and ruthless military arm of the radical left, has increased its total strength from an estimated 6,500 (composed of 560 regulars, 1,500 combat support and 4,400 service support) as of January 1, 1972 to about 7,900 (composed of 1,028 regulars, 1,800 combat support and 5,025 service support) as of July 31, 1972, showing a marked increase in its regular troops of over 100 percent in such a short period of six months;

5. The establishment of sanctuaries for the insurgents in Isabela, in Zambales, in Camarines Sur, and in some parts of Mindanao, a development heretofore unknown in our campaign against subversion and insurgency in this country;

6. The disappearance and dropping out of school of some 3,000 high school and college students and who are reported to have joined with the insurgents for training in the handling of firearms and explosives;

7. The bringing and introduction into the country of substantial war materiel consisting of military hardware and supplies through the MV Karagatan at Digoyo Point, Palanan, Isabela, and the fact that many of these military hardware and supplies are now in the hands of the insurgents and are being used against our government troops;

8. The infiltration and control of the media by persons who are sympathetic to the insurgents and the consequent intensification

of their propaganda assault against the government and the military establishment of the government;

9. The formation at the grass-root level of "political power organs," heretofore unknown in the history of the Communist movement in this country, composed of Barrio Organizing Committees (BOCs) to mobilize the barrio people for active involvement in the revolution; the Barrio Revolutionary Committee (BRCs) to act as "local government" in barrios considered as CPP/NPA bailiwicks; the Workers Organizing Committees (WOCs) to organize workers from all sectors; the School Organizing Committees (SOCs) to conduct agitation and propaganda activities and help in the expansion of front groups among the studentry; and the Community Organizing Committees (COCs) which operate in the urban areas in the same manner as the BOCs.

Whereas, the rebellion and armed action undertaken by these lawless elements of the communist and other armed aggrupations organized to overthrow the Republic of the Philippines by armed violence and force have assumed the magnitude of an actual state of war against our people and the Republic of the Philippines.

Now, Therefore, I, Ferdinand E. Marcos, President of the Philippines, by virtue of the powers vested upon me by Article VII, Section 10, Paragraph (2) of the Constitution, do hereby place the entire Philippines as defined in Article I, Section 1 of the Constitution under martial law and, in my capacity as their commander-in-chief, do hereby command the armed forces of the Philippines, to maintain law and order throughout the Philippines, prevent or suppress all forms of lawless violence as well as any act of insurrection or rebellion and to enforce obedience to all the laws and decrees, orders and regulations promulgated by me personally or upon my direction.

In addition, I do hereby order that all persons presently detained, as well as all others who may hereafter be similarly detained for the crimes of insurrection or rebellion, and all other crimes and offenses committed in furtherance or on the occasion thereof, or incident thereto, or in connection therewith, for crimes against national security and the law of nations, crimes against public order, crimes involving usurpation of authority, rank, title and improper use of names, uniforms and insignia, crimes committed by public officers, and for such other crimes as will be enumerated in Orders that I shall subsequently promulgate, as well as crimes as a consequence of any violation of any decree, order or regulation promulgated by me personally or promulgated upon my direction shall be kept under detention until otherwise ordered released by me or by my duly designated representative.

In witness whereof, I have hereunto set my hand and caused the seal of the Republic of the Philippines to be affixed.

Done in the City of Manila, this 21st day of September, in the year of Our Lord, nineteen hundred and seventy-two.

FERDINAND E. MARCOS
President
Republic of the Philippines

By the President:
ROBERTO V. REYES
Acting Executive Secretary

Appendix 3. General Order No. 1, That President Ferdinand E. Marcos Will Govern the Nation and Direct the Operation of the Entire Government

Whereas, martial law has been declared under Proclamation No. 1081 dated Sept. 21, 1972 and is now in effect throughout the land;

Whereas, martial law has been declared because of wanton destruction of lives and property, widespread lawlessness and anarchy, chaos and disorder now prevailing throughout the country, which condition has been brought about by groups of men who are actively engaged in a conspiracy to seize political and state power in the Philippines in order to take over the Government by force and violence the extent of which has now assumed the proportion of an actual war against our people their legitimate Government; and

Whereas, it is imperative for the undersigned President of the Philippines to assume greater and more effective control over the entire Government, to have the broadest latitude and discretion in dealing with the affairs of the nation, and to exercise extraordinary powers in my capacity as commander-in-chief of all the armed

Source: *Vital Legal Documents in the New Society* (Manila: Central Book Supply, n.d.), I, 23.

forces of the Philippines in order to enable me to restore within the shortest possible time and thereafter to maintain the stability of the nation and to safeguard the integrity and security of the Philippines and to insure the tranquility of its inhabitants, by suppressing lawlessness and all subversive, seditious, rebellious and insurrectionary activities throughout the land, with all the resources and means at my command, and by adopting such other measures as I may deem necessary and expedient to take to contain and resolve the existing national emergency and for the interest of the public;

Now, Therefore, I, Ferdinand E. Marcos, President of the Philippines, by virtue of the powers vested in me by the Constitution as Commander-in-Chief of the Armed Forces of the Philippines, do hereby proclaim that I shall govern the nation and direct the operation of the entire Government, including all its agencies and instrumentalities, in my capacity and shall exercise all the powers and prerogatives appurtenant and incident to my position as such Commander-in-Chief of all the armed forces of the Philippines.

Done in the City of Manila, this 22nd day of September, in the year of Our Lord, nineteen hundred and seventy-two.

Appendix 4. General Order No. 3, On the Continuous Operation of All Government Instrumentalities under Their Present Officers and Employees; On Limitations on the Jurisdiction of the Judiciary

Whereas, martial law having been declared under Proclamation No. 1081 dated Sept. 21, 1972 and is now in effect throughout the land;

Whereas, martial law having been declared because of wanton destruction of lives and property, widespread lawlessness and anarchy, chaos and disorder now prevailing throughout the country, which condition has been brought about by groups of men who are actively engaged in a criminal conspiracy to seize political and state power in the Philippines in order to take over the Government by

Source: *Vital Legal Documents in the New Society* (Manila: Central Book Supply, n.d.), I, 26–27.

force and violence, the extent of which has now assumed the proportion of an actual war against our people and their legitimate Government, and;

Whereas, in order to make more effective the implementation of the aforesaid Proclamation No. 1081 without unduly effecting the operations of the Government, and in order to end the present national emergency within the shortest possible time:

Now, Therefore, I, Ferdinand E. Marcos, Commander-in-Chief of all the Armed Forces of the Philippines, and pursuant to Proclamation No. 1081, dated Sept. 21, 1972, do hereby order that henceforth all executive departments, bureaus, offices, agencies and instrumentalities of the National Government, government-owned or controlled corporations, as well as all governments of all the provinces, cities, municipalities, and barrios throughout the land shall continue to function under their present officers and employees and in accordance with existing laws, until otherwise ordered by me or by my duly designated representative.

I do hereby further order that the Judiciary shall continue to function in accordance with its present organization and personnel, and shall try and decide in accordance with existing laws all criminal and civil cases, except the following cases:

1. Those involving the validity, legality or constitutionality of any decree, order or acts issued, promulgated or performed by me or by my duly designated representative pursuant to Proclamation No. 1081, dated Sept. 21, 1972.

2. Those involving the validity, legality or constitutionality of any rules, orders or acts issued, promulgated or performed by public servants pursuant to decrees, orders, rules and regulations issued and promulgated by me or by my duly designated representative pursuant to Proclamation No. 1081, dated Sept. 21, 1972.

3. Those involving crimes against national security and the law of nations.

4. Those involving crimes against the fundamental laws of the State.

5. Those involving crimes against public order.

6. Those crimes involving usurpation of authority, rank, title, and improper use of names, uniforms, and insignia.

7. Those involving crimes committed by public officers.

Done in the City of Manila, this 22nd day of September in the year of Our Lord, nineteen hundred and seventy-two.

Appendix 5. General Order No. 8, On the Creation of Military Tribunals

Whereas, martial law has been declared under Proclamation No. 1081 dated September 21, 1972 and is now in effect throughout the land;

Whereas, martial law having been declared because of wanton destruction of lives and property, widespread lawlessness and anarchy, and chaos and disorder now prevailing throughout the country, which condition has been brought about by groups of men who are actively engaged in a criminal conspiracy to seize political and state power in the Philippines in order to take over the Government by force and violence, the extent of which has now assumed the proportion of an actual war against our people and their legitimate Government, and;

Whereas, pursuant to General Order No. 3, dated September 22, 1972 issued under Proclamation No. 1081 dated September 21, 1972, I have ordered that certain criminal cases be tried by special military tribunals which may be created by me or upon my orders;

Now, therefore, I, Ferdinand E. Marcos, Commander-in-Chief of all the Armed Forces of the Philippines, and pursuant to Proclamation No. 1081 dated September 21, 1972, do hereby order that henceforth the Chief of Staff, Armed Forces of the Philippines is empowered to create military tribunals to try and decide cases of military personnel and such other cases as may be referred to them.

Done in the City of Manila, this 27th day of Our Lord, nineteen hundred and seventy-two.

Source: *Vital Legal Documents in the New Society* (Manila: Central Book Supply, n.d.), I, 33–34.

Appendix 6. General Order No. 12, On the Jurisdictions of Civil Courts and Military Tribunals

Whereas, martial law has been declared under Proclamation No. 1081 dated September 21, 1972 and is now in effect throughout the land;

Source: *Vital Legal Documents of the New Society* (Manila: Central Book Supply, n.d.), I, 37–40.

Whereas, martial law having been declared because of wanton destruction of lives and property, widespread lawlessness and anarchy, and chaos and disorder now prevailing throughout the country, which condition has been brought about by groups of men who are actively engaged in a criminal conspiracy to seize political and state power in the Philippines in order to take over the Government by force and violence, the extent of which has now assumed the proportion of an actual war against our people and their legitimate Government, and;

Whereas, pursuant to General Order No. 3, dated September 22, 1972 issued under Proclamation No. 1081 dated September 21, 1972, I have ordered that certain criminal cases shall not be heard and decided by civil courts;

Now, therefore, I, Ferdinand E. Marcos, Commander-in-Chief of all the Armed Forces of the Philippines, and pursuant to Proclamation No. 1081 dated September 21, 1972, do hereby order that the military tribunals authorized to be constituted under General Order No. 8 dated September 27, 1972 shall try and decide the following cases exclusive of the civil courts, unless otherwise provided hereunder:

1. Those involving crimes against national security and the laws of nations as defined and penalized in the Revised Penal Code.

2. Those constituting violations of the Anti-Subversion Law as defined and penalized in Republic Act No. 1700.

3. Those constituting violations of the Law on Espionage as defined and penalized in Commonwealth Act No. 616.

4. Those constituting violations of the Hijacking Law as defined and penalized in Republic Act No. 6235.

5. Those involving crimes against the fundamental laws of the State as defined and penalized in the Revised Penal Code, if committed by members of the Armed Forces of the Philippines.

6. Those involving certain crimes against public order as defined and penalized under the Revised Penal Code, namely:

    a. Rebellion or insurrection (Art. 134)

    b. Conspiracy and proposal to commit rebellion or insurrection (Art. 136)

    c. Disloyalty of public officers or employees (Art. 137)

    d. Inciting rebellion or insurrection (Art. 138)

    e. Sedition (Art. 139)

f. Conspiracy to commit sedition (Art. 141)

g. Inciting sedition (Art. 142)

h. Illegal assemblies (Art. 146)

i. Illegal associations (Art. 147)

7. Those involving other crimes committed in furtherance or on the occasion of or incident to or in connection with the crimes of insurrection or rebellion.

8. Those involving crimes constituting violations of the Law on Firearms and Explosives found in the Revised Administrative Code and other existing laws.

9. Those involving crimes on usurpation of authority, rank, title, and improper use of names, uniforms and insignia as defined and penalized in the Revised Penal Code, including those penalized under Republic Act No. 493.

10. Those involving certain crimes committed by public officers as defined and penalized under the Revised Penal Code, provided that civil courts and military tribunals shall have concurrent jurisdiction thereon if the accused is a civilian, namely:

a. Knowingly rendering unjust judgment (Art. 204)

b. Judgment rendered through negligence (Art. 205)

c. Unjust interlocutory order (Art. 206)

d. Malicious delay in the administration of justice (Art. 207)

e. Prosecution of offenses, negligence and tolerance (Art. 208)

f. Direct bribery (Art. 210)

g. Indirect bribery (Art. 211)

h. Corruption of public officials (Art. 212)

i. Frauds against the public treasury and similar offenses (Art. 213)

j. Prohibited transactions (Art. 215)

k. Possession of prohibited interest by a public officer (Art. 216)

l. Malversation of public funds or property (Art. 217)

m. Failure of accountable officer to render accounts (Art. 218)

n. Illegal use of public funds or property (Art. 220)

o. Failure to make delivery of public funds or property (Art. 221)

p. Conniving with or consenting to evasion (Art. 223)

q. Removal, concealment or destruction of documents (Art. 226)

r. Officer breaking seal (Art. 227)

s. Opening of closed documents (Art. 228)

t. Revelation of secrets by an officer (Art. 229)

11. Those constituting violations of the Anti-Graft and Corrupt Practices Law as defined and penalized in Republic Act No. 3019: Provided, that the civil courts shall exercise concurrent jurisdiction with the military tribunals if the accused is a civilian.

12. Those constituting violations of Republic Act No. 6425, otherwise known as "The Dangerous Drugs Act of 1972," provided that civil courts and military tribunals shall have concurrent jurisdiction thereon if the accused is a civilian.

13. Violations of all decrees, orders and regulations promulgated by me personally or upon my direction pursuant to Proclamation No. 1081 dated September 21, 1972.

14. Those involving crimes committed by officers and enlisted personnel of the Armed Forces of the Philippines on the occasion of, in relation to or as a consequence of the enforcement or execution of Proclamation No. 1081 dated September 21, 1972, or of any decree, order and regulation issued or promulgated by me personally or by my duly designated representative, pursuant thereto.

In cases under Nos. 10, 11 and 12 above where jurisdiction is concurrent between civil courts and military tribunals, the court or tribunal that first assumes jurisdiction shall exercise it to the exclusion of all others.

Transitory Provisions

1. Cases now pending in civil courts, whether or not there has been arraignment, shall be tried and decided by said civil courts except criminal cases involving subversion, sedition, insurrection or rebellion and those committed in furtherance of, on the occasion of, incident to or in connection with the commission of said crimes which shall be transferred to military tribunals.

2. Cases filed on or before September 22, 1972 (when General Order No. 3 was promulgated) with the offices of City or Provincial Fiscals or the courts for preliminary investigation except cases involving subversion, sedition, insurrection or rebellion, shall be investigated by the City or Provincial Fiscals or the Judges concerned, and the corresponding information shall be filed in the proper civil courts. Cases involving subversion, sedition, insurrection or rebellion shall immediately be forwarded to the military tribunals through the Office of the Judge Advocate General, Armed Forces of the Philippines.

3. Cases involving crimes within the exclusive jurisdiction of military courts, which are filed after September 22, 1972 with the offices of City or Provincial Fiscals or the courts for preliminary investigation, shall be investigated by the City or Provincial Fiscals or the Judges concerned, but the corresponding information will be filed with military tribunals.

This General Order accordingly modifies General Order No. 3 dated September 22, 1972 issued pursuant to Proclamation No. 1081 dated September 21, 1972. General Order No. 2-A dated September 26, 1972 shall remain in force.

Done in the City of Manila, this 30th day of September, in the year of Our Lord, nineteen hundred and seventy-two.

Appendix 7. Proclamation No. 1102, Announcing the Ratification by the Filipino People of the Constitution Proposed by the 1971 Constitutional Convention

Whereas, the Constitution proposed by the nineteen hundred seventy-one Constitutional Convention is subject to ratification by the Filipino people;

Whereas, Citizens Assemblies were created in barrios in municipalities and in districts/wards in chartered cities pursuant to Presidential Decree No. 86, dated December 31, 1972, composed of all persons who are residents of the barrio, district or ward for at least six months, fifteen years of age or over, citizens of the Philippines and who are registered in the list of Citizen Assembly members kept by the barrio, district or ward secretary;

Whereas, the said Citizens Assemblies were established precisely to broaden the base of citizen participation in the democratic process and to afford ample opportunity for the citizenry to express their views on important national issues;

Whereas, responding to the clamor of the people and pursuant to Presidential Decree No. 86-A, dated January 5, 1973, the following questions were posed before the Citizens Assemblies or Baran-

Source: The New Constitution of the Philippines, comp. F. D. Pinpin (Mandaluyong: Cacho Hermanos, 1973), pp. 1–2.

gays: Do you approve of the New Constitution? Do you still want
a plebiscite to be called to ratify the new Constitution?

Whereas, fourteen million nine hundred seventy-six thousand five
hundred sixty-one (14,976,561) members of all the Barangays
(Citizens Assemblies) voted for the adoption of the proposed Constitution, as against seven hundred forty-three thousand eight hundred sixty-nine (743,869) who voted for its rejection; while on the
question as to whether or not the people would still like a plebiscite to be called to ratify the new Constitution, fourteen million
two hundred ninety-eight thousand eight hundred fourteen
(14,298,814) answered that there was no need for a plebiscite and
that the vote of the Barangays (Citizens Assemblies) should be considered as a vote in a plebiscite;

Whereas, since the referendum results show that more than
ninety-five (95) per cent of the members of the Barangays (Citizens
Assemblies) are in favor of the new Constitution, the Katipunan ng
Mga Barangay has strongly recommended that the new Constitution
should already be deemed ratified by the Filipino people;

Now, therefore, I Ferdinand E. Marcos, President of the Philippines, by virtue of the powers in me vested by the Constitution, do
hereby certify and proclaim that the Constitution proposed by the
nineteen hundred and seventy-one (1971) Constitutional Convention
has been ratified by an overwhelming majority of all of the votes
cast by the members of all the Barangays (Citizens Assemblies)
throughout the Philippines, and has thereby come into effect.

In witness whereof, I have hereunto set my hand and caused the
seal of the Republic of the Philippines to be affixed.

Done in the City of Manila, this 17th day of January, in the year
of Our Lord, nineteen hundred and seventy-three.

FERDINAND E. MARCOS
President of the Philippines

By the President:
(Sgd.) ALEJANDRO MELCHOR
Executive Secretary

Appendix 8. Proclamation No. 1103, Declaring that the Interim National Assembly Provided for in Article XVII (Transitory Provisions) of the New Constitution Be Not Convened

Whereas, Barangays (Citizens Assemblies) were created in barrios in municipalities and in districts/wards in chartered cities pursuant to Presidential Decree No. 86 dated December 31, 1972, composed of all persons who are residents of the barrio, district or ward for at least six months, fifteen years of age or over, citizens of the Philippines and who are registered in the list of Citizens Assembly members kept by the barrio, district or ward secretary;

Whereas, the said Barangays were established precisely to broaden the base of citizen participation in the democratic process and to afford ample opportunities for the citizenry to express their views on important national issues;

Whereas, pursuant to Presidential Decree No. 86-A dated January 5, 1973 and Presidential Decree No. 86-B dated January 7, 1973, this question was posed before the Barangays: Do you approve the New Constitution?

Whereas, fourteen million nine hundred seventy-six thousand five hundred sixty-one (14,976,561) members of all the Barangays voted for the adoption of the proposed Constitution, as against seven hundred forty-three thousand eight hundred sixty-nine (743,869) who voted for its rejection; but a majority of those who approved the new Constitution conditioned their votes on the demand that the interim National Assembly provided in its Transitory Provisions should not be convened;

Whereas, under Article XVII, Section 3 (1) of the New Constitution, the President is vested with the discretion when to convene the interim National Assembly;

Now, therefore, I, Ferdinand E. Marcos, President of the Philippines, by virtue of the powers in me vested by the Constitution and in deference to the sovereign will of the Filipino people, do hereby declare that the convening of the interim National Assembly pro-

Source: *The New Constitution of the Philippines,* comp. F. D. Pinpin (Mandaluyong: Cacho Hermanos, 1973), pp. 133–34.

vided for in Article XVII (Transitory Provisions) of the new Constitution shall be suspended.

In witness whereof, I have hereunto set my hand and caused the seal of the Republic of the Philippines to be affixed.

Done in the City of Manila, this 17th day of January, in the year of Our Lord, nineteen hundred and seventy-three.

FERDINAND E. MARCOS
President of the Philippines

By the President:
(Sgd.) ALEJANDRO MELCHOR
Executive Secretary

Appendix 9. Transitory Powers and Prerogatives of the President as Provided in Article XVII, Sec. 3, of the New Constitution

Sec. 3. (1) The incumbent President of the Philippines shall initially convene the *interim* National Assembly and shall preside over its sessions until the *interim* Speaker shall have been elected. He shall continue to exercise his powers and prerogatives under the nineteen hundred and thirty-five Constitution and the powers vested in the President and the Prime Minister under this Constitution until he calls upon the *interim* National Assembly to elect the *interim* President and the *interim* Prime Minister, who shall then exercise their respective powers vested by this Constitution.

(2) All proclamations, orders, decrees, instructions, and acts promulgated, issued, or done by the incumbent President shall be part of the law of the land, and shall remain valid, legal, binding, and effective even after lifting of martial law or the ratification of this Constitution, unless modified, revoked, or superseded by subsequent proclamations, orders, decrees, instructions, or other acts of the incumbent President, or unless expressly and explicitly modified or repealed by the regular National Assembly.

Source: The New Constitution of the Philippines, comp. F. D. Pinpin (Mandaluyong: Cacho Hermanos, 1973), pp. 51–52.

Appendix 10. Proclamation No. 1104, Declaring the Continuation of Martial Law

Whereas, Barangays (Citizens Assemblies) were created in barrios in municipalities and in districts/wards in chartered cities pursuant to Presidential Decree No. 86 dated December 31, 1972, composed of all persons who are residents of the barrio, district or ward for at least six months, fifteen years of age or over, citizens of the Philippines and who are registered in the list of Citizen Assembly members kept by the barrio, district or ward secretary;

Whereas, the said Barangays were established precisely to broaden the base of citizen participation in the democratic process and to afford ample opportunities for the citizenry to express their views on important national issues;

Whereas, pursuant to Presidential Decree No. 86-A dated January 5, 1973 and Presidential Decree No. 86-B dated January 7, 1973, the question was posed before the Barangays: Do you want martial law to continue?

Whereas, fifteen million two hundred twenty-four thousand five hundred eighteen (15,224,518) voted for the continuation of martial law as against only eight hundred forty-three thousand fifty-one (843,051) who voted against it;

Now, therefore, I, Ferdinand E. Marcos, President of the Philippines, by virtue of the powers in me vested by the Constitution, do hereby declare that martial law shall continue in accordance with the needs of the time and the desire of the Filipino people.

In witness whereof, I have hereunto set my hand and caused the seal of the Republic of the Philippines to be affixed.

Done in the City of Manila, this 17th day of January, in the year of Our Lord, nineteen hundred and seventy-three.

FERDINAND E. MARCOS
President of the Philippines

By the President:
(Sgd.) ALEJANDRO MELCHOR
Executive Secretary

Source: The New Constitution of the Philippines, comp. F. D. Pinpin (Mandaluyong: Cacho Hermanos, 1973), pp. 135–36.

Appendix 11. Report of the National Committee for the Restoration of Civil Liberties in the Philippines

I. The Martial Law Declaration and the Constitution

On September 23, 1972, President Ferdinand Marcos, citing the existence of "an actual state of war against . . . the Republic of the Philippines" carried out by "lawless elements," declared martial law for the whole country.[1] According to the 1935 Constitution of the Republic of the Philippines, which was in force at the time of the presidential proclamation and in the name of which Mr. Marcos justified his action, martial law can only be invoked under highly specific conditions and is subject to the authorization, strict control and review of the two other co-equal branches of the government, Congress and the Supreme Court. A constitution, like that of the Philippines, was carefully designed to insure a workable system of checks and balances among the three separate but equal branches of government. It would therefore have contradicted its purpose and courted self-destruction had it included a provision that gives unlimited powers to the Executive, as Mr. Marcos claims it does in his doctrine of "unlimited martial law."

Article VI, Section 6 of the Philippine Constitution clearly states that "in times of war or other national emergency, the Congress may by law authorize the President for a limited period and subject to such prescriptions as it may prescribe, to promulgate rules and regulations to carry out a declared national policy." The meaning of

Source: "Report of the National Committee for the Restoration of Civil Liberties in the Philippines (NCRCLP) to the U.S. Senate Foreign Relations Committee on Martial Law in the Philippines and United States Relations with the Marcos Administration" (Washington, D.C.: NCRCLP, n.d.). This version of the report is taken from the mimeographed submission to the committee. It excludes the appendixes referred to in the footnotes. The Report of the NCRCLP was also published, in highly summarized form, in the *U.S. Congressional Record—Senate* (Apr. 12, 1973, pp. 12135–145), as part of a statement by Senator Alan Cranston on "Repression in the Philippines." Much of the data in the report's appendixes first appeared in a bimonthly periodical, *Philippine Information Bulletin,* published by the American Friends of the Filipino People in New York City. These data have been updated and expanded in another publication: Walden Bello and Severina Rivera, eds., *Logistics of Repression and Other Essays* (Washington, D.C., and San Francisco: Friends of the Filipino People, 1977).

1. Proclamation No. 1081, "Proclaiming a State of Martial Law in the Philippines," p. 20.

this provision is explicit: Congressional authorization is required in such acts as the declaration of martial law, and the presidential actions carried out during the period of martial law are circumscribed by congressional prescriptions.

Article VIII, Section 2 likewise clearly states that the Supreme Court of the Philippines has the power to review and issue final judgments on "all cases in which the constitutionality or validity of any treaty, law, ordinance, or executive order or regulation is in question." A martial-law declaration and the presidential actions during the period of martial law are thus explicitly subject to a constitutional double-check.

Martial Law and the Courts

Mr. Marcos has, however, chosen to ignore or ride roughshod over these constitutional provisions. With respect to the Supreme Court, Mr. Marcos issued, on September 22, 1972, General Order No. 4, which declared as outside the power of the judiciary all cases "involving the validity, legality, or constitutionality of any decrees, order or acts issued, promulgated or performed by me or by my duly designated representative pursuant to Proclamation No. 1081 [the martial law declaration]."[2] Not only were presidential actions considered exempt from judicial review, but so were those of subordinates, down to the lowliest private, thus magnifying the area of arbitrariness which inevitably attends such periods of military control. What is more alarming, however, is that by wresting away from the Judiciary the power to rule on "crimes against public order" during the period of martial law, Mr. Marcos, through the same General Order, in effect usurped the greater part of the judicial function, since all crime, from rebellion to petty thievery and being a public nuisance, is by definition a violation of the public order. The chilling consequences of such a blanket extortion of judicial power is perhaps best illustrated by the case of Lim Song, an alleged dope peddler. Sentenced by a military court to life imprisonment, Song found his sentence converted to death by Mr. Marcos, and he was executed by a firing squad.[3] There is a possibility that in that distant date when the country returns to "normalcy," the courts may rule his case did not fall under the jurisdiction of a

2. General Order No. 4, p. 2.
3. "Marcos Orders Return to Stringent Regulations," *New York Times*, January 8, 1973; "Manila Broadcaster Jailed for 12 Years," *Washington Post*, November 24, 1972.

military court, that the facts in his case did not justify a sentence of life imprisonment, that the president acted arbitrarily in resetencing him to death. No future judicial ruling, however, will be able to resurrect the man.

Martial Law and Congress

With respect to Congress, Mr. Marcos never sought legislative authorization for his martial-law declaration, nor does he consider the decrees and executive orders promulgated in the martial-law period subject to congressional restrictions. Indeed, the proclamation came as a surprise to a number of senators and congressmen who not only were not consulted but held on charges of subversion or under "protective custody." As in the case with the Judiciary, non-recognition of congressional authority over a martial-law declaration was but a prelude to further usurpation of the legislative power. The clearest instance of this is seen in connection with the so-called "Integrated Reorganization Plan." The plan, a presidential proposal to "reorganize" the national bureaucracy, was simply declared "part of the law of the land" in spite of the fact that it was a bill pending in Congress before martial law.[4] The immediate impact of this arbitrary presidential act was the dismissal of 400 government employees and the forced resignation of thousands more,[5] contrary to civil service laws.

In declaring martial law Mr. Marcos said that he was "utilizing the power vested in me by the Constitution to save the Republic and reform our society."[6] The facts show, however, that the martial-law declaration and the presidential orders immediately following it were subverting the Republic by eroding its keystone—the constitutionally-prescribed separation and equality of the three branches of government—all in the direction of consolidating all power in the incumbent president. Subsequent events, which involved more and graver constitutional violations, would appear to confirm this trend.

II. The Justification of the Martial-Law Declaration

President Marcos justified the imposition of martial law on the grounds that it was needed to deal with a situation of national emergency brought about by "Communist subversion." The fact

4. Presidential Decree No. 1.
5. "Marcos Fires Entire Corps of Civil Service," *The Evening Bulletin* (Washington), p. 2.
6. Statement of the President on the Proclamation of Martial Law, p. 8.

that the slogan of "Communist subversion" has been used to set up oppressive authoritarian regimes elsewhere, notably in Brazil, Greece, Thailand, Bolivia, and Indonesia, should make one initially skeptical of such a claim on the part of Mr. Marcos, especially in the light of his doctrine of "unlimited martial law."

Contradictions of the Declaration

One must first note the ambivalence of the text of Proclamation 1081. While the dominant aim appears to be the creation of an image of national anarchy brought about by the activities of a growing revolutionary left, there is in some parts a noticeable countertendency to minimize the impact of such activities. What are we to draw from the following passage, which Mr. Marcos borrows from a Philippine Senate Committee Report in 1971?:

> In the year 1969, the NPA [New People's Army—military arm of the Communist Party] had—according to the records of the Department of Defense—conducted raids, resorted to kidnappings and taken part in other isolated incidents numbering over 230, in which it inflicted 404 casualties, and, in turn, suffered 243 losses. In 1970, its record of violent incidents was about the same, but the NPA casualties more than doubled.[7]

This passage is in contradiction with other parts of the text, for the only implication we can draw from it is not increasing Communist effectiveness but growing government ability to deal with the activities of the left. Its inclusion suggests that at the time martial law was declared Mr. Marcos had not made up his mind on the extent of the "Communist threat."

What is more revealing, however, is that the Marcos proclamation, again basing itself on the same Senate report and on a judicial analysis, endorses the idea that the Communist Party of the Philippines adheres to both the "idea of a swift armed uprising" and the "concept of protracted people's war."[8] As not only revolutionaries but students of war and revolution will readily attest, these are essentially two different and contradictory politico-military strategies. The strategy of protracted people's war arose in a bitter debate with the deficiencies and defeats of the swift-armed-uprising strategy in semi-feudal countries. Unless it is extremely confused, in which

7. Proclamation No. 1081, p. 7.
8. Ibid., p. 9.

case it would hardly constitute a threat, the revolutionary left must choose one or the other; and whichever strategy it elects would have radically different implications for any assessment of the gravity of the threat that it poses for the status quo at any given moment. The Philippine left is reputedly a "Maoist" left, to use administration parlance, and we would therefore expect it to regard an urban-centered "swift armed uprising" as the height of adventurism and adhere to the strategy of protracted war in the countryside. Is it the left that is caught in self-contradiction, or the presidential analysis?

It is extremely noteworthy that while Mr. Marcos extracts a great number of isolated passages from the 1971 Senate Ad Hoc Committee Report to back up his case for the existence of a "state of actual war," he omits its conclusion, which is that there exists "no clear and present danger of a Communist-inspired insurrection or rebellion."[9]

No assumptions in the field of foreign affairs have been more violently shattered by the events of the past decade, notably by the Vietnam War and the conflict between the People's Republic of China and the Soviet Union, than those of a monolithic Communist bloc and of an "international Communist conspiracy." Yet the martial-law declaration expects us to believe these ideas by endorsing a judicial analysis that the Filipino left seeks to establish a "totalitarian regime subject to alien domination and control" and that its activities are "national in scope but international in direction."[10]

In public and private statements Mr. Marcos and his aides have made vague references to the People's Republic of China as this "foreign conspirator," though we have yet to come across concrete evidence produced by them to prove this "Chinese connection."[11] We can, however, partly judge this claim by taking a brief look at China's record in Asia in the recent past. With regard to aggression, the dominant view in Far Eastern scholarship and, especially after Vietnam, in critical sectors of the foreign policy establishment, is that in those instances when China went to war, it did so largely

9. "No Clear and Imminent Danger," *Philippine Free Press,* September 11, 1971, p. 9.
10. Proclamation No. 1081, pp. 5–6.
11. See for instance working paper for an "Ideology of the New Society" by Fred Elizalde, aide of Mr. Marcos, in *Philippine Information Bulletin,* Vol. 1, No. 1, pp. 28–29.

for reasons of self-defense, as in the case of Korea, or to assert traditionally acknowledged sovereign rights, as in Tibet.[12]

As for "subversion," we must point out that Dean Rusk, one of the implementors of the 'contain-China-in-Vietnam strategy' in the nineteen-sixties, himself admitted that the Chinese were "more cautious in action than in word" in his testimony before this very committee.[13] Current foreign-affairs scholarship on this problem is reflected in the following evaluation by Edwin Reischauer, former ambassador to Japan and professor at Harvard:

> Actually the Chinese have not shown eagerness to spread their faith by conquest beyond their traditional borders. They loudly proclaim the necessity of sweeping the world with "wars of national liberation," but they expect this to be done by the local people in each country. . . . In a sense, they are offering a do-it-yourself kit for revolution.[14]

Mr. Reischauer likewise notes that while "Many Americans . . . think of Southeast Asia as somehow rightfully or inevitably a Chinese zone of influence," this "is a serious error and a grave injustice to the people of that part of the world."[15]

Revolutionary self-reliance appears to have been a key and consistent principle in Chinese foreign policy, and nothing in the record of China's relations with Vietnam, Thailand, Burma, the Philippines, and other Southeast Asian countries indicates that it has ever violated this principle by assuming the leadership and combat role of local revolutionary movements.[16] Furthermore, the

12. "Chinese rhetoric is extremely bellicose, but their actions have tended to be cautious. We have seen how their participation in the Korean War seemed to them to be purely defensive and how even the border war with India was not aggression from their point of view. Even with a large-scale war raging on their southern borders in Vietnam, they have, as of the present writing, injected only some 40,000 engineer troops, in contrast to more than ten times that number of actual combatants whom we have dispatched all the way across the Pacific. Their . . . conquest of Tibet was to them merely rounding out what they considered to be the traditional territories of China. For more than a thousand years the Chinese have considered Tibet to be part of their domains, and during recent centuries they actually have dispatched officials and troops to control it." Edwin O. Reischauer, *Beyond Vietnam*, New York, Alfred Knopf, 1967, pp. 155–156.

13. Dean Rusk, *Statement before the House Committee on Far Eastern Affairs on U.S. Policy toward Communist China*, April 16, 1966, p. 511.

14. Reischauer, ibid., p. 159.

15. Ibid., p. 156.

16. If China has been guilty of anything, it is perhaps of the "sin" of serving as a symbol and model of how to effect rapid and positive structural change, for the left in a society where 90 percent of all families must share only 22 percent of the national income while 2.5 percent and a few corporations monopolize 65 percent

claim of China being the head of a violent-prone international conspiracy must be viewed in the light of the objective reality that the
thaw in U.S.-Chinese relations has become a welcome fact and that,
consequently, the prospects of big-power stabilization in Southeast
Asia have greatly improved.

Communist-Inspired Violent Incidents?

Let us at this point take up the case of the violent incidents which
the administration claims were the triggering circumstances that led
Mr. Marcos to declare martial law and which it attributed to the
revolutionary left.[17] These incidents were a series of bomb explosions in the Manila area in the six-and-a-half months preceding
martial law, and though not explicitly mentioned, an attack on a
police car and the ambush of the convoy of Defense Secretary Juan
Ponce Enrile.[18] On closer examination, however, the methods employed by the responsible elements, as well as the results obtained,
do not lend themselves to facile interpretations as to their motives
and political color. An international weekly presents us with the
following account:

> They came on like a Filipino version of the gang that couldn't shoot
> straight. First, terrorists blew up a police car—while the policemen were
> conveniently off having lunch. Then a series of bombs was set off in
> department stores, city halls, and schools—at night when the buildings
> were unoccupied. Finally, heavily armed guerrillas swooped down on
> the two-car convoy of Philippine Defense Secretary Juan Ponce Enrile,
> riddled an automobile with about 30 bullets and sped away. But Enrile
> was riding in the second, unattacked car and escaped without a scratch—
> as did everyone in his party. A harrowing brush with death. Or was it?[19]

Noting that some observers in Manila believe that the Marcos
administration "even stages incidents which it then blames on the
Communist terrorists,"[20] a Southeast Asian correspondent of a

---

of the national income. This sort of influence, like that of the American Declaration
of Independence, is, however, neither imperialism nor subversion, and Mr. Marcos'
attempt to revive the now-discredited "international Communist conspiracy" theory
should not fool anybody, certainly not the members of this committee.

17. Proclamation No. 1081, pp. 15–16.
18. According to the administration, Proclamation 1081 was signed on September
21 but announced on September 23. The attack on Enrile occurred on Sept. 22.
To any observer the timing would appear uncanny and could not but give rise
to grave suspicions.
19. "Marcos Cracks Down," *Newsweek*, October 2, 1972.
20. "Martial Law a Big Gamble for Marcos," *Washington Post*, Sept. 24, 1972.

Washington newspaper likewise notes the unusualness of the circumstances surrounding the incidents leading up to martial law:

Although the 16 bomb explosions have killed two persons and injured 100 innocent people, they have struck some observers as a strangely-planned terrorist campaign.

For example, the first incident in August, an ambush of a police car, took place while the policemen had parked the car and gone for a walk. The car was riddled by bullets, but the officers were unhurt.

Most of the bombs have gone off at municipal buildings during the night when government officials have been at home.[21]

Focusing on the sixteen bombing incidents, the facts available reveal that the imputation of responsibility to the Communists seemed to be done more by presidential fiat than by the presence of conclusive evidence. As far as we can gather, the military and the police have done very little in the way of solving these cases, having apprehended and questioned only two suspects. And in the case of these suspects, the initial findings were such as to cast grave doubt on the administration's Red Conspiracy Theory. Two men were apprehended in connection with the bombing of Joe's Department Store in Manila on September 5th. Reporting on the investigation, the *Philippine Free Press,* one of the leading weeklies before its forced closure, wrote in its last issue:

After several days of sleuthing, Major Felicisimo Lazaro, Homicide Division Chief of the Manila Metropolitan Police, solved the bombing case by placing under arrest a PC [Philippine Constabulary] sergeant and an ex-convict. Nabbed as suspects in the bombing were PC Sgt. Mario Gabuten, 34, *who was on detail with the PC's Firearms and Explosives Unit in Camp Crame,* and Luisito Lo, 24, alias Ko Lu Si, a canteen operator and an ex-convict.

Manila police sources said that Ko had confessed to his participation in the Carriedo bombing as well as in the repeated threats to bomb a large department store in Rizal Avenue in an attempt to extort about P100,000 from the operator of the establishment. Gabuten denied involvement in the case but Major Lazaro insisted that he had an airtight case against the two suspects[22] [emphasis added].

The initial findings thus indicate that this was no Communist plot, nor was it a simple extortion case, involving as it did an active-

21. Ibid.
22. "More Bombings," *Philippine Free Press,* Sept. 23, 1972, p. 4.

duty Constabulary explosives expert. What is more disconcerting is that in this one case out of 20 where the police had come out with positive results, Manila police sources revealed that, "Before any charges could be filed against the suspects, PC authorities 'borrowed' Sergeant Gabuten for the Manila Police for the usual 'tactical interrogation' at Camp Crame [Philippine Constabulary headquarters in Quezon City]."[23]

One of the reasons observers should critically examine the facile imputation of responsibility for the bombings to the Communists is the obvious parallel between the administration's actions in this situation and its actions during the Plaza Miranda bombing on August 21, 1971. As a result of that incident, which nearly wiped out the whole opposition senatorial slate and which Mr. Marcos immediately branded a Communist terrorist act, the president suspended the writ of habeas corpus to facilitate the detention of "subversives." Subsequent investigation led up, however, to the filing of charges not against Communists but against "living-out" prisoners who had allegedly been "hired to kill,"[24] at which point the case conveniently faded away.

Summarizing, therefore, we find the martial law justification—the existence of a state of insurrection—quite dubious in light of the following:

1. Contradictory assessments of the threat posed by the New People's Army contained in Proclamation 1081.

2. Contradictory interpretations of the strategy of the revolutionary left in the same document, which reveal that Mr. Marcos had a very flimsy basis on which to make his judgment that the left was a decisive threat.

3. The appeal to the now-discredited "international Communist direction" theory in the same document.

4. The selective and biased use of evidence by the president, as shown in his citing isolated passages from a 1971 Senate Report to back up his case of a state of insurrection, without indicating that this same report concluded that such a condition was non-existent.

5. The strange circumstances surrounding the "triggering" cir-

23. Ibid.
24. Editorial, *Philippine Free Press*, Sept. 23, 1972, p. 46; *Pace Magazine*, January 28, 1972, pp. 16–17.

cumstances—the attacks on the Defense Secretary's convoy and the sixteen bombing incidents—and the absolute lack of evidence to support the administration's Red-Conspiracy Theory.

6. The all-too-obvious parallel between the Plaza Miranda bombing case in 1971, when Mr. Marcos suspended the writ of habeas corpus, and the case of the bombings and attacks leading up to martial law.

About a week after the declaration of martial law, when objective assessment of the circumstances leading up to martial law was presumably more possible, the *New York Times* reported that "It is now evident the President exaggerated the extent of the Communist military menace, although it was indeed a growing threat."[25] Likewise, the Philippine correspondent of the *Honolulu Star Bulletin* reported:

There is considerable sentiment here that Marcos exaggerated the danger in order to justify martial law. The government was functioning, although poorly, and total collapse or paralysis did not seem imminent. The nation was in deep trouble, but apparently not on the brink of social revolution.

Independent observers regard the Maoist rebels of the New People's Army and their radical student allies as a serious and growing threat, but believe that it will be several years before they can make a real attempt to seize power.

It was nothing like the early 1950's, when the Huks [members of Hukbalahap, military arm of the Communist Party in the 1950's] were operating right outside Manila, said one source.[26]

III. Violation of Filipino Civil Rights

The presidential actions following the declaration of martial law reveal to even the most disinterested observer a rapid drive to concentrate power in the hands of the current executive through assaults not only on the principle of governmental separation of powers but also on the constitutionally guaranteed rights of the Filipino people. Immediately after the proclamation, the arbitrary arrests of hundreds of individuals were carried out. The arrests were done by the military and in total disregard of all accepted judicial procedure,[27] thus violating Article III, Section 1 of the 1935 Constitution, which states that:

25. "Results by Marcos, but at What Cost?" *New York Times*, Oct. 1, 1972.
26. "Marcos Smashed Democracy," *Honolulu Star Bulletin*, Oct. 5, 1972.
27. Not only was the privilege to the writ of habeas corpus discarded, but all

No person shall be deprived of life, liberty, or property without due process of law, nor shall any person be denied the equal protection of the law. . . .

The nature of the action is quickly revealed by a list of 53 detainees made public by the government on September 25.[28] Among those listed were three senators and three congressmen, including Senator Benigno Aquino, Jose Diokno, and Ramon Mitra, three of Mr. Marcos' best-known liberal critics; two governors; four delegates to the Constitutional Convention, who were conspicuous in their opposition to the maneuvers of the presidential faction in the convention; three newspaper publishers, including those of the *Manila Times* and the *Philippine Free Press,* which have been consistent liberal critics of the Marcos administration; and several well-known newspapermen, notable likewise for their consistent criticism, among whom was Max Soliven, *Manila Times* columnist and former Manila correspondent of *Time Magazine.* The list would be enlarged in the days to come with the inclusion of more established political, journalistic, and even religious figures, but never would it include a top-level or even a middle-level figure of the Communist Party or its supposed "front" organizations. Nevertheless, the presidential press secretary classified all those under detention as "subversives or heads of criminal syndicates."[29] Noting this, an American weekly commented: "Each day the categories under which one can be considered a subversive seem to be broadened. To judge from the names of prisoners thus far available, some of whom are militant anti-communists, the Marcos administration seems intent on silencing any criticism, no matter what its source."[30]

The mass arrests were accompanied by an executive prohibition of all forms of public protest and the shutting down of all but one of Manila's 15 daily newspapers, six of the city's seven television stations, and nine of the major radio stations.[31] "In ordering seizure of the press," the *New York Times* reported, "Mr. Marcos declared

required judicial procedure. Francisco Rodrigo, an ex-senator who was one of those arrested, revealed that in place of the warrant of arrest signed by a judge, those who arrested him simply showed him a xerox copy of an order signed by the Defense Secretary and would not even provide him a copy of this. See Francisco Rodrigo, "Rebuttal Plea before the Supreme Court," p. 5 (mimeo).

28. *Daily Express* (Manila), Sept. 26, 1972, pp. 1 and 5.
29. *Daily Express,* ibid., p. 5.
30. "U.S. Role in the Philippines," *America,* October 14, 1972.
31. *Washington Post,* September 24, 1972.

without further specification that newspapers, magazines, and broadcasting stations had participated in the alleged conspiracy to take over the government by force."[32] These drastic executive measures violated Article III, Section 7 of the 1935 Constitution, which provides that:

No law shall be passed abridging the freedom of speech, or of the press, or the right of the people peaceably to assemble and petition the Government for redress of grievances.

In addition to these violations of Filipinos' basic rights, Mr. Marcos has placed himself above civil-service laws by his arbitrary dismissal of 400 government employees and his demanding the resignation of thousands more; further usurped the legislative power by declaring killings done with unlicensed firearms automatically punishable by death,[33] and "rumor-mongering" as punishable as "subversive propaganda";[34] and further destroyed the judicial function by ordering the start of *military trials* for about 100 of those arrested.[35] For advocating "bloody revolution," a popular television commentator, Roger Arrienda, has already been sentenced to a twelve-year prison term.[36] The government appears to be rather selective as to who shall continue to be detained and tried among those arrested. A *Newsweek* correspondent wrote:

When Marcos first arrested hundreds of politicians, journalists and gangsters, it was said that some of the worst men in the country had been locked up with some of the best. The trouble is that by now many of the worst crooks and cutthroats have been released. The people still in jail are the President's political foes. . . .[37]

IV. Consolidation of One-Man Rule through Manipulation of the Constitutional Convention

Right after the declaration of martial law, Alejandro Melchor, presidential executive secretary, revealed that the period of martial

32. *New York Times*, September 27, 1972, p. 1.
33. "Philippines Decrees Death Penalty . . . ," *New York Times*, January 9, 1973.
34. "Discussions Stops on Philippine Charter," *New York Times*, January 9, 1973.
35. "Manila Broadcaster Jailed for 12 Years," *Washington Post*, November 24, 1972.
36. Ibid.
37. "Marcos' First 100 Days," *Newsweek*, January 22, 1973, p. 49.

law could last as long as two years and result in the cancellation of the 1973 presidential elections.[38] This move gave rise to strong suspicions that President Marcos had plans to disregard another provision—the limitation of the executive's term to four years plus one reelection. Mr. Marcos' final term will end on midnight of December 31, 1973, about one year and three months from the date of imposition of martial law.

It now seems clear that Mr. Marcos utilized the Constitutional Convention to give his plan some semblance of legitimacy. At the time of the declaration of martial law the Convention had been meeting for nearly two years to draft a new charter for the Philippines. On October 20, 1972, the Convention, which, according to the *New York Times,* had come "under the control of forces loyal to Mr. Marcos,"[39] adopted the provisions on the period of transition from one constitution to another. This session took place under martial-law conditions, such that arrested delegates could not participate and strict press censorship kept news of the event from the public. One source claims that in order to be allowed into the convention hall, delegates had to secure "safe-conduct passes" from the Defense Secretary.[40]

Among the provisions approved was Article VIII, Section 3, the first paragraph of which states that:

The incumbent President of the Philippines shall initially convene the *interim* National Assembly and shall preside over the sessions until the *interim* Speaker shall have been elected. He shall continue to exercise his powers and prerogatives under the nineteen hundred and thirty-five Constitution and the powers vested in the President and Prime Minister under this Constitution until he calls upon the *interim* National Assembly, to elect the President and the *interim* Prime Minister who shall then exercise their respective powers vested by this Constitution.[41]

It must first be pointed out that for the executive to exercise the powers provided by both the 1935 Constitution and the new consti-

38. "A High Marcos Aide Says in Washington . . . ," *New York Times,* September 26, 1972.

39. *New York Times,* October 30, 1972, p. 12. A constitutional convention delegate, Eddie Quintero, 72 and a civic leader not engaged in politics, revealed attempts to bribe him and other convention delegates on the part of Malacañang; See "Why Quintero Did It," *Philippine Free Press,* July 1, 1972.

40. *The People* (Philippines), Special Release, December 5, 1972 (mimeo).

41. Proposed Constitution of the Republic of the Philippines, Manila, Bureau of Printing, 1972, p. 47.

tution violates all notion of legality since the 1935 Constitution, including the provisions on the executive power, automatically ceases to be valid once the new constitution comes into existence. With respect to this, too, there exists the very real possibility of a conflict between the powers vested in the president under the 1935 Constitution and those vested in the president and prime minister by the new constitution. We can be assured that where a conflict situation exists, chances are the problem will be resolved by relying on the constitution most favorable to the growth and maintenance of the executive power.

What is more alarming, though, is that this state of affairs, whereby one man exercises the enormous power vested in three different functions, can be maintained *indefinitely,* until the incumbent president chooses to convene the *ad interim* Assembly, the legislative body under the new constitution. If not convened, the *interim* Assembly, even if in existence, cannot function, and no guidelines are at all provided for the presidential discretion to convene the Assembly.

The second paragraph of this section reads:

All proclamations, orders, decrees, instructions, and acts promulgated, issued, or done by the incumbent president shall be part of the law of the land, and shall remain valid, legal, binding, and effective even after lifting of martial law or the ratification of this Constitution, unless modified, resolved, or superseded by subsequent proclamations, orders, decrees, instructions, or other acts of the incumbent president, or unless expressly and explicitly modified or repealed by the regular National Assembly.[42]

This provision seems unusual coming from a Constitutional Convention which was intended simply to frame the fundamental law and not engage in ordinary legislation, a function which falls under the domain of whatever legislative authority the Constitution sets up. Yet it has its logic, not in law but in the context of the presidential actions prior to its approval. We have already shown how the concept of "unlimited martial law" resulted in the usurpation of legislative and judicial authority. This paragraph is obviously intended to make permanent all such violations of the 1935 Constitution and all future arbitrary executive acts in that conveniently

42. Ibid., pp. 47–48.

indefinite period between the promulgation of the new constitution
and the time the executive chooses to convene the *ad interim* National Assembly.

How could such an apparently authoritarian provision be so easily
smuggled into the proposed fundamental law of a democracy? The
264 to 13 vote in favor of the transitory provisions is apparently
explained by Sections 1 and 2 of the same Article. The first section
states:

*There shall be an interim National Assembly which shall exist
immediately upon the ratification of this Constitution and shall continue
until the Members of the regular National Assembly shall have been
elected and shall have assumed office following an election called for
the purpose by the interim National Assembly.* Except as otherwise
provided in this Constitution, the *interim* National Assembly shall have
the same powers, and its Members shall have the same functions, responsibilities, rights, privileges, and disqualifications as the regular National
Assembly and the Members thereof [emphasis added].

The second paragraph reads:

The Members of the *interim* National Assembly shall be the incumbent
President and Vice-President of the Philippines, those who served as
President of the 1971 Constitutional Convention, those Members of
the Senate and House of Representatives who shall express in writing
to the Commission on Elections within thirty days after the ratification
of this Constitution their option to serve therein, *and those Delegates
to the nineteen hundred and seventy-one Constitutional Convention
who have opted to serve therein by voting affirmatively for this Article*
[emphasis added].[43]

To vote for the article on transitory provisions was thus extremely
self-serving for the delegates since they would be automatically
assured a seat in an *interim* National Assembly. What is more, since
the *interim* National Assembly would have the privilege of deciding
when to call elections for the regular National Assembly, it could
be in existence indefinitely—for "20 days or 20 years," as admitted
by the chairman of the Transitory Provisions Committee of the
Convention.[44] While there is a strong possibility that the incumbent

43. Ibid., pp. 46–47.
44. Quoted by Jesus Barrera in "Speech against New Constitution" (mimeo).

president would indefinitely postpone convening the *interim* Assembly, since Article III allows him this privilege, a delegate would not be totally deprived of the benefits of office, receiving as they would more than $36,000 (P216,000) annually in salary and allowances.

Against this apparently clever manipulation of the delegates' self-interest by the dominant Marcos forces, the principled stand of the few opposing delegates, like that of former Supreme Court Justice Jesus Barrera, one of the most respected men in the Judiciary, went unheeded. It is worth quoting from Justice Barrera's rejection speech:

> Mr. President, I am sorry I am constrained to observe that this draft article on Transitory Provisions has been prepared in a hurry without any in-depth consideration of the important issues it has raised. I even dare to state that, as conceived and drafted, it runs counter to what President Marcos himself proclaims to be the answer to Revolution, and that is, Democracy. The draft article is just the opposite. It unwittingly establishes dictatorship that is more or less permanent and, what is worse, institutionalized in the fundamental law of the land.[45]

The warning of Justice Barrera has been brought home by the developments following the approval of the Transitory Provisions article. After an initial period of "free discussion" on the charter, Mr. Marcos reinstituted strict martial law, making "rumor-mongering" punishable as "subversive propaganda."[46] According to the *New York Times,* "It seemed clear the one reason for the presidential order was that free debate had been making obvious and encouraging opposition to the new charter. . . ." It continues, "Speakers against the new constitution have drawn warm responses from audiences, and on a number of occasions, opponents have had platforms all to themselves because advocates have failed to come forward."[47]

On January 19, 1973, Mr. Marcos suspended the required plebiscite on the new charter indefinitely and his administration started organizing "citizens' assemblies" ostensibly for the mere purpose of sampling public opinion on martial law and the new constitution.[48] Guidelines announced for the conduct of these assemblies stated

45. Ibid.
46. "Marcos Orders Return to Stringent Regulations," *New York Times,* January 8, 1973.
47. "Discussion Stops . . . ," *New York Times,* January 9, 1973.
48. "Sponsored Citizens . . . ," *New York Times,* January 11, 1973, p. 5.

that "those in charge . . . have simply to record whether there is a majority for each question and to report this to higher authorities" and that it required "only 5 percent of the registered members of an assembly to constitute a quorum."[49] These assemblies struck uninvolved observers as "totally organized and dominated by supporters of Marcos,"[50] and as "pressured and manipulated expression of opinion."[51] On January 12, 1973, government sources announced that the citizens' assemblies which had met or were about to meet "all showed approval of the new Constitution" and ominously added that "some assemblies had specified seven years when asked how long it should be before general elections were held."[52] Finally, on January 17, what had been strong fears and suspicions appeared to be confirmed. At the meeting of the congress of citizens' assemblies in Malacañang Palace, the body, aside from proposing the continuation of martial law and presidential continuity in office for seven years without general elections, "opposed the holding of a plebiscite on the new Constitution and said the assemblies considered their approval sufficient to constitute national ratification without a plebiscite."[53] Mr. Marcos thereupon "announced ratification of the new constitution, signed a proclamation putting it into effect and similarly adopted with appropriate proclamations, the views of the assemblies on continuation of martial law and on dispensing with the *interim* Assembly."[54]

In his acceptance speech, Mr. Marcos declared "the times are too grave and the stakes too high for us to permit the customary concessions to traditional democratic processes."[55] With this phrase of extraordinary candor, the events which have shaken the Philippines since September 21, 1972, finally and clearly fell into place. Mr. Marcos practically admitted to subverting the constitutional democracy that he had initially declared he was out to save with his imposition of martial law—in his words then, "that we may not . . . lose the civil rights and freedom which we cherish."[56] The pattern should now be clear to even the most uninvolved observer:

49. Ibid.
50. "Marcos' First 100 Days, "*Newsweek,* Jan. 22, 1973, p. 49.
51. "Marcos Gets His Kind of Democracy," *New York Times,* January 21, 1973.
52. "Manila Says . . . ," *New York Times,* January 12, 1973.
53. "Marcos Tightens Control . . . ," *New York Times,* January 18, 1973, p. 9.
54. Ibid.
55. "Marcos Gets . . . ," *New York Times,* January 21, 1973.
56. Statement of the President on the Proclamation of Martial Law, September 21, 1972, p. 9.

The declaration of martial law was the prelude to the progressive concentration of all state powers in one man.

This steady clarification of the meaning of events has elicited worldwide disapproval, especially on the part of the international press which has been the only reliable reporter of events in the country after the suppression of the Philippine press. While at first maintaining a cautious attitude, many publications have finally issued strong condemnations. The case of the *New York Times* is instructive. After suggesting editorially, on September 27, 1972, that the imposition of martial law was "dubious medicine for the fundamental ills that have been sapping the strength and unity of this island republic in the Pacific,"[57] the paper finally and firmly confronted the obvious implications of events in its January 20, 1973 editorial:

Yesterday was another dark day for freedom in Asia as President Ferdinand E. Marcos extended martial rule indefinitely while proclaiming a new Constitution—one which, even if it is eventually revoked, would give him sweeping new powers. Mr. Marcos' resort to obviously rigged citizens' assemblies to gain a figleaf of public approval for his draconian measures, instead of the plebiscite he originally promised, is a clear indication that his descent into tyranny does not enjoy the near-universal acceptance that he has claimed.[58]

Another authoritarian and repressive regime has apparently come into existence in Asia, and for both the American and Filipino people one of the crucial questions at this point is: Will the U.S. Government allow itself to be dragged into supporting another clearly undemocratic government, as has happened in the case of South Vietnam, Pakistan, Greece, South Korea, and Brazil?

V. The U.S. and the Philippines

The Marcos Administration and the U.S.

The United States claims that it had no advance warning of the declaration of martial law.[59] This appears a little unusual. As the correspondent of a West Coast newspaper puts it, ". . . it was obvious to the most casual observer that the American Embassy would have been falling down on its job if it had failed to inform

57. "Marcos Medicine," *New York Times*, September 27, 1972.
58. "Dark Days in Manila," *New York Times*, January 18, 1973.
59. "Martial Law Reports . . . ," *Washington Post*, September 23, 1972.

Washington that martial law was coming, especially when the possibility of it had been openly discussed for more than a year."[60] At any rate, on the very day martial law was declared, Ambassador Henry Byroade and Mr. Marcos conferred for two hours at Malacañang Palace,[61] and according to one press report, Mr. Marcos promised to protect American investments in the Philippines in return for U.S. support.[62]

Mr. Marcos' subsequent actions did nothing to dispel the implications of news reports that in some manner, the United States Government had something to do with developments in the Philippines. Soon after the imposition of martial law, Mr. Marcos hinted at the indefinite maintenance of American bases in the Philippines to offset the Chinese "nuclear threat."[63] He announced that Americans would be allowed to dispose of the $75 million worth of property acquired by them since 1946 at leisure and with no threat of government confiscation, thus going explicitly against a recent Supreme Court ruling that such lands had been acquired illegally and thus were subject to forced sale or confiscation before or after 1974, when parity rights come to an end.[64] Contrary to the same Supreme Court ruling, Mr. Marcos unilaterally declared that American companies would be allowed to retain titles to land provided they met the requirement of 60 per cent Filipino ownership.[65] Marcos likewise indicated that "he would reverse or modify another court decision that would have barred Americans from holding executive jobs in American oil, labor and mining companies after the parity agreement ends."[66] Whereas previous to martial law, foreign companies, mainly American, exploring for oil, needed to acquire formal leases, they will now simply need a government service contract, thanks to another executive order.[67] A similar arrangement is being contemplated for the foreign sector—again mainly American—of the mining industry.[68] Mr. Marcos also

60. Keyes Beech, *San Francisco Examiner*, September 28, 1972.
61. Ibid.
62. Ibid.
63. "Interview with the President of the Philippines," *U.S. News and World Report*, October 16, 1972.
64. *San Francisco Examiner*, September 28, 1972.
65. Ibid., also, "Interview with the President . . .," *U.S. News and World Report*, October 16, 1972.
66. *San Francisco Examiner*, September 28, 1972.
67. "Marcos Seeking Oil Exploration," *New York Times*, October 4, 1972.
68. Ibid.

declared that bulk sales by foreign-owned oil companies to local industries could continue, again in defiance of a recent Supreme Court decision which ruled such sales illegal.[69]

Some commentaries on these developments appear to project the view that Mr. Marcos' moves were unilateral, that they were made with the intention of courting U.S. support which was not there from the start, and that both the U.S. Government and business interests simply stood on the sidelines with a "wait-and-see" attitude. Such an interpretation has no doubt been strengthened by some statements made either by Mr. Marcos or his aides. Defense Secretary Juan Ponce Enrile, for instance, declared, ". . . the US whether it likes it or not, will have to spend money here. . . . If they don't now, it will be more expensive later. They (the U.S.) have as much a stake in our survival . . . as we have. Things could turn out as badly here as they did in Cuba."[70]

If there is anything that the experience of foreign relations in the past decade, especially the experience of the Executive branch's dealings with South Vietnam, Brazil, Greece and Santo Domingo, should have taught us, it is to be critical of such "one-way-flow-of-influence" interpretations. While there is some truth to the explanation that Diem maneuvered the United States into Vietnam and that Ky and later Thieu kept it bogged down there, this is but part of the truth. As records, especially the *Pentagon Papers*, have revealed, due to global misconceptions and the erroneous policies resulting from these, the United States likewise maneuvered to get Diem and Thieu into their positions of power and to keep them there so long as they did not threaten what were perceived by critical sectors of the Executive as genuine U.S. interests. It would thus be more accurate to say that Diem and the United States maneuvered one another to achieve mutually desirable goals.

There is no assurance that the misconceptions of U.S. interests that got the United States little by little into Vietnam have been completely eliminated from the foreign-policy thinking of the United States Government. Together with the still unclarified interaction between the U.S. Embassy and Malacañang Palace at the time of martial-law declaration and the blatant pro-U.S. moves of Mr. Marcos soon afterwards, the promise of a U.S. senator to Marcos

69. Ibid.
70. Lee Lescaze, "Marcos Martial Law . . . ," *Washington Post*, October 7, 1972.

that Congress will soon consider the subject of increased aid to the Philippines should be a cause for unease,[71] as should be those reports of American military support-actions against Filipino guerrillas.[72] What is more disquieting is to realize that these developments have taken place in relation to a country in which due to the same misconceptions in foreign policy that took the United States into Vietnam and to peculiar historical reasons, the United States is in fact substantially involved at this time. Indeed, the United States appears far more deeply embedded economically, politically, and militarily in the Philippines today than it was in Vietnam at the time of the rise of the Viet Cong in the middle fifties.[73]

U.S. Interests and the Philippine Economy

American multinational corporations control assets in the Philippines amounting to over $2 billion at book value. Twenty-four of the fifty largest enterprises in the Philippines are American-owned. A great part of American investments is in oil; the assets of oil companies, most of whom are American, exceed $400 million. Other large investments are found in mining, banking, heavy machineries, chemical-processing, and metal fabrication.[74] American investments alone comprise 80 per cent of the total foreign investment in the Philippines.

How is it that American companies can control such large assets? The Bell Trade Act of 1946, later re-named the Laurel-Langley Agreement in 1954, granted Americans the same rights as Filipino nationals to exploit natural resources and engage in any profitable economic activity in the Philippines. This agreement was originally designed to help develop the Philippines by pumping dollars into its economy. However, between 1956 and 1965 alone, American corporations invested $412 million, 84 per cent of which came from Philippine financial sources,[75] not from American sources, thus

71. "U.S. Senator Hints New Aid for Manila," *Washington Post*, December 11, 1972.
72. Security Agreements and Commitments Abroad, Republic of the Philippines (The Symington Report), U.S. Government Printing Office, Washington, 1967, p. 7.
73. All existing economic and military treaties and agreements between the Philippines and the U.S. are documented in Appendix C.
74. For more detailed statistics on U.S. investments in the Philippines, see Appendix E.
75. This is one of the findings of a study done by the Office of Statistical Coordination and Standards of the National Economic Council of the Philippines. For a breakdown, see Appendix D.

defeating the intent of the Laurel-Langley Agreement. In fact, the same study shows that for every dollar from the United States invested in the Philippines, $5 were taken back to the United States during this same ten-year period. American business operations resulted in an outflow from the Philippines of $386.2 million against a total inflow from the United States of $79.4 million.

Moreover, through the Economic and Technical Agreement of 1951, American advisers have been placed at high levels of the Philippine government to help formulate economic and technical plans for the country. We will not at this point hazard a guess as to the extent these American advisers have interceded on behalf of American business interests.

What has been the relation of U.S. government policy to American economic interests in the Philippines? The following historical account may serve to clarify this.

American bombing in the effort to retake the Philippines left Manila the third most ravaged city in the world after Hiroshima and Warsaw. The U.S. deigned to assist its badly battered colony in the form of the Philippine Rehabilitation Act of April 30, 1946, which offered dollar aid to people whose properties and businesses had been damaged. However, the enjoyment of this act's full benefits was made contingent on the passage of the Bell Trade Act referred to above.[76] The Bell Trade Act stipulated that American citizens and corporations be given equal rights as Filipino nationals to exploit the natural resources of the country and operate public utilities after Independence (the Trade Act was later updated and renamed the Laurel-Langley Agreement of 1954 to expand American rights to include all economic activities).[77] This stipulation clearly violated the Philippine Constitution (Article XIII, Section 1; Article XIV, Section 8), whereupon an *amendment* was made to the Philippine Constitution for the sole purpose of accommodating it. Seen in retrospect, the Philippine government, faced with the economic havoc wreaked by a war not of its own making, had no choice but to accept the American terms.

The granting of parity rights to American nationals in the Philippines was not to be the last time the U.S. Executive branch would exploit its position of superiority vis-à-vis the Philippine govern-

76. Cf. Philippine Rehabilitation Act, April 30, 1946, Chapter 243, Section 601.
77. Cf. Philippine Trade Act of April 30, 1946, Chapter 244, Section 341.

ment on behalf of American business interests. In 1954, the Philippine Congress passed the Philippine Retail Trade Nationalization Law, which would take effect in 1964 to give aliens sufficient time to adjust. This law provides that only corporations or business firms wholly owned by Filipino nationals can engage in retail trade. When the law took effect on June 19, 1964, American businessmen branded it anti-American[78] and proceeded to frustrate its implementation, going to the extent of demanding that President Johnson pressure the Philippine government. In a Joint Communiqué of Presidents Johnson and Macapagal,[79] President Johnson pointed out "that United States economic relations with the Philippines would be seriously impaired if an enforcement of the Philippine Retail Trade Nationalization Law were to prejudice the position of long-established American firms."[80] This undoubtedly contributed a great deal to the notoriously slow and extremely selective implementation of the law.

The wave of nationalism now sweeping the Philippines should be understood in the light of such obvious encroachments on the nation's sovereignty as the parity Amendment. One need but visualize a situation in which the British or the French have equal economic rights to exploit the resources of this country as Americans to see that the Filipino response is predictable and justified. This leads to the realization that friction will not be eliminated but exacerbated by the continuation of this preferential treatment through authoritarian means, as President Marcos appears to be doing.

Military Presence of the U.S. in the Philippines

Militarily, the U.S. operates 23 military bases on 180,000 acres of land leased for 99 years but pays no rent. (Some rough estimates place the probable annual rent at several million dollars.) There are about 20,000 U.S. servicemen now on these bases. Clark Air Base, north of Manila, is one of the largest air bases in the world servicing F-4 Phantom bombers and B-57 squadrons. Subic Bay Naval Base, farther north of Manila, is the largest naval base in

---

78. Todoro Agoncillo and D. Alfonso, *History of the Filipino People*, Malaya Books, Manila, 1967, p. 609.

79. White House press release dated October 6, 1964, printed in the Department of State Bulletin, Vol. 51, No. 1323, 2 November, 1964, pp. 632–634.

80. Ibid.

Asia with nuclear submarine facilities. It is the headquarters and supply base of the Pacific 7th Fleet and aircraft carriers Kitty Hawk, Saratoga, and Coral Sea.[81]

With these military bases in mind, the U.S. commitment in the Mutual Defense Treaty of 1951 is stated best in the words of President Johnson in a 1964 communiqué: ". . . any armed attack against the Philippines would be regarded as an attack against the U.S. forces stationed there and against the U.S. and would instantly be repelled."[82]

During the Senate Foreign Relations Subcommittee hearings of September 30–October 3, 1969, "the (Mutual Defense) Board considers the principal threat to the Philippines to be Communist China with possible assistance from internal dissident groups."[83]

With further questioning by Senator Symington, Admiral Kauffman agreed that "today there is no threat to the Philippines except an internal threat."[84] There is thus a possibility, remote though it may be, that the U.S. commitment to this Mutual Defense Treaty may be interpreted to include armed attacks by Filipino nationals and "would instantly be repelled."

In fact, the Joint U.S. Military Advisory Group (JUSMAG) which was formed under the terms of the Military Assistance Agreement of 1947 placed U.S. military advisers at high levels of the Philippine Military hierarchy to aid the Philippine Command in the planning and implementing of military operations. One of the main tasks of JUSMAG is "to assist in creating a Philippine internal security capability."[85] One of the many military exercises conducted by JUSMAG was specifically designed to train both American and Filipino troops participating in the exercise in the conduct of counter-insurgency activities. This exercise, "Operation Eagle's Nest" and later re-named "Operation Carabao's Trail," was an unconventional warfare exercise series with a guerrilla counter-insurgency setting.

Through joint exercises like this, through provision of American arms, ammunitions and other military supplies to the Philippine

81. See Appendix C, Military and Economic Treaties and Agreements.
82. Security Agreements and Commitments Abroad, Republic of the Philippines, U.S. Government Printing Office, Washington, 1969, p. 7.
83. Ibid., p. 60.
84. Ibid., p. 61.
85. Ibid., p. 13.

Military, and even through some direct participation by American Military personnel in counter-insurgency activities,[86] "U.S. military assistance contributed significantly to the success of the Philippine Armed Forces in suppressing the HUK [Filipino guerilla] rebellion in the 1950's."[87]

Another U.S.-run program which has bearings on counter-insurgency is the "Public Safety Program," a U.S. aid program whose aim is "to strengthen and increase the efficiency and effectiveness of civil police and other Philippine governmental organizations, both national and local, so that the safety of the public can be improved and maintained."[88] Total U.S. expenditures on this program for fiscal years 1969–1973 are estimated at $3.9 million. The Public Safety Program focuses on upgrading capabilities in key operational areas— training, communications, intelligence, mobility, riot-control—so as to improve the capacity of the local police apparatus to deal with guerrilla activities, provide urban policing including the control of the civil disturbances and riots, etc.[89] This program, as well as other U.S. activities in the current counter-insurgency effort, will be further discussed below.

Through the Mutual Defense Board organized in 1958 most of the military planning in the Philippines is done jointly by the U.S. and Philippine Commands. For instance, the Board authorized the establishment of the U.S. Air Force–Philippine Air Force defense system. In the joint planning, the U.S. 13th Air Force is assigned to co-handle the air defense of the Philippines.

All in all, American military aid to the Philippines has totalled $631.7 million since the end of World War II.[90] What we must realize is that together with economic aid, which since World War II has totalled $1.26 billion,[91] this aid must now be reviewed in the light of the qualitatively new character of the Philippine government: from a formal democratic government it has become an authoritarian regime. And as the experience with Pakistan, Greece,

86. Ibid., pp. 161–162; further discussed in next section of this report, below.
87. Ibid., p. 300.
88. "Development Assistance to the Republic of the Philippines, Fiscal Year 1971," Washington, USAID.
89. "Fiscal 1972 Congressional Presentation," Washington, USAID; this report is further analyzed in Appendix F.
90. "Manila Trend . . . ," New York Times, January 18, 1972.
91. Ibid.

and Brazil has shown, the bulk of such aid is used in establishing a military and police apparatus to quell popular discontent.

VI. America's Vietnam Experience and the Philippines: Some Parallels

This report has attempted to show that Mr. Marcos made use of an alleged Communist threat as a pretext in order to establish an authoritarian regime in the Philippines. We have not meant to imply that the Communists do not exist as a social force in the country. They do, but they do not constitute the immediate threat Mr. Marcos would want us to believe and there are, in fact, other nationalistic grass-roots movements which are not necessarily of the same ideological persuasion. Furthermore, what should now be obvious, especially in the light of the Vietnam experience, is that Communism in such countries as the Philippines is an indigenous force for internal structural change that has caught the support of those who, rightly or wrongly, see all other paths to change as blocked.[92] This is not to paint the motives of the Communists in terms too positive. It is to place their movement in the context of the Filipino masses' long and *diverse* struggles to achieve a better life in a society where the upper classes remained appallingly insensitive to their demands,[93] and to search for a path of national development that would be free of foreign interference. It is also to propose that whatever response other nations might have toward the internal demands of the Filipino masses be one that would not violate the universally accepted principles of self-determination and non-interference by other nations in the internal affairs of another. Finally, it is to warn that the United States might be on the brink of again being manipulated to violate these universally accepted principles for the purpose of battling the diverse internal and indigenous forces for change in another Asian country.

The danger of a future large-scale military involvement in another Asian country can be seen in the striking parallels in the conditions imposed in South Vietnam by the unpopular Ngo Dinh Diem and

92. "Social and Political Troubles Deepen . . . ," *New York Times,* September 23, 1972.

93. According to one estimate, 90 percent of all families must share only 22 percent of the wealth, while 2.5 percent and a few corporations monopolize 65 percent of the national income. See, ". . . and an Example," *Washington Post,* April 30, 1972, p. 4.

those created in the Philippines by the Marcos authoritarian regime, and the similarities in the initial U.S. response to such conditions.

As in the case of the Philippines, the United States had had a measure of involvement in Vietnam prior to Diem's rise to power. The French received both military and economic aid in their unsuccessful efforts to defeat the Viet Minh, and, as we all know, the United States refused to be a signatory to the Geneva Agreements after the French defeat. Most observers would readily agree, however, that it was mainly during the Diem years that the United States became bogged down in a situation from which it could have had easily extricated itself previously.[94] American military and technical aid started flowing into South Vietnam to prop up a regime that was not immediately perceived by Washington as highly unpopular. The anti-Communist blinders did not allow to filter through the fact that Diem was so unpopular that armed sects like the Cao Dai and the Hoa Hoa had been driven to the extent of forming a united front against him with a gangster group, the Binh Xuyen. To some experienced observers like Jean Lacouture, the Diem dictatorship was the principal factor behind the insurrection in the South. After 1956 and especially with the repressive legislation of 1959, the Diem "witch hunt" left no other alternatives to those in opposition, whatever their political coloration, except prison, exile, or joining the guerrillas.[95] Faced with vanishing internal support, Diem provoked the United States to stepping in little by little by constantly strumming the U.S. Executive's blind anti-Communist fears.[96]

Like the Diem dictatorship's "witch hunt," Mr. Marcos's "martial law" and mass arrests have left no other choice to the opponents of an unpopular regime, *whatever their political coloration,* except to go into exile or pass into armed, clandestine struggle. As shown earlier in this report, most of those arrested by Marcos are established political-party figures, newspapermen and publishers, non-Communist nationalists, students, trade unionists, and peasant-union leaders. The deportation of two American Franciscan priests and the arrest of other religious figures recall Diem's persecution of some Buddhist sects and other progressive religious groups.[97] Diem's

94. Neil Sheehan, Hedrick Smith, et al., *The Pentagon Papers,* New York, Bantam Books, 1971, pp. 1–25.
95. Jean Lacouture, *Vietnam: Between Two Truces,* New York, Random House, 1966, pp. 54–55.
96. Symington Report, "What worries me . . . ," p. 228.
97. *Los Angeles Times,* October 10, 1972.

1959 legislation created military tribunals which would try "traitors," a move which has now been duplicated in Mr. Marcos' act removing from the civil courts' sphere all jurisdiction over "crimes against public order"—which, as we noted earlier, refer to virtually all types of crime—and transferring it to military courts. One man has already been sentenced to death by the military and executed by firing squad, and another has been handed a twelve-year prison term for "advocating bloody revolution" as a television commentator.[98] Following its historical logic, repression has intensified and will continue to intensify political discontent, "alienating," as the *New York Times* has predicted, "the more moderate elements in Filipino society and driving them into the arms of the . . . groups that Mr. Marcos has vowed to stamp out."[99]

As in the case of Diem when he came to the realization that he had lost his popular base and could only depend on an overarmed military and police for survival, Mr. Marcos has at this point called for increased American aid. Mr. Marcos is obviously aware of the Vietnam parallel, though he is not willing to draw its most profound lessons. How else are we to interpret the statement he made at a televised press conference, in which he coupled a plea for aid with a disguised threat to the American public by invoking a political scenario largely of his own making:

> The American government is the leading power in the world. Of necessity, it has very strong influence on all sources of help and is itself a source of aid. Again I say it is our hope, it is our belief that the [U.S.] government will understand that there is no other way out of the mess in which the Philippines has fallen. There is no other way—unless they [the U.S.] accept a Vietnam-type solution.[100]

Defense Secretary Enrile's remark, which we cited above, betrays even more cynicism and self-complacency than Mr. Marcos': "If they [the U.S.] don't help now, it will be more expensive later."[101]

Is the United States thus at that critical first phase of a Vietnam-type involvement with respect to the Philippines, as historian Gabriel Kolko, among other noted Americans, has warned?[102] This possibil-

98. "Manila Broadcaster Jailed . . . ," *Washington Post*, November 24, 1972.
99. "Dark Days in Manila," *New York Times*, January 18, 1973.
100. Cited in Gabriel Kolko, "The Philippine—Another Vietnam?" *Commonweal*, January 12, 1973.
101. Lee Lescaze, "Marcos Martial Law . . . ," *Washington Post*, October 6, 1972.
102. Kolko, ibid., p. 325.

ity is not at all remote, not only because we have no assurance that the misconceptions which led to Vietnam have been totally eliminated from U.S. foreign-policy thinking, but also because *a measure of U.S. involvement is already present.*

We have mentioned above the various military treaties and agreements which already bind the United States and the Philippines. Let us now take them up in more detail, especially as they bear on the problem of insurgency.

At the hearings conducted by Senator Stuart Symington in 1969 in connection with United States commitments and agreements abroad, James Wilson, Jr., the then Deputy Chief of Mission in Manila, admitted that the United States, through a 1953 agreement with the Philippine Government, is committed "to assist in creating a Philippine internal security capability."[103] Mr. Wilson further confirmed that there are two programs related to counter-insurgency efforts in the Philippines: the A.I.D. Public Safety Program and the Military Assistance Program (MAP).[104]

In 1969, following a period of increased civil strife and incipient guerrilla activity, the United States upgraded the public safety program and renamed it the U.S.A.I.D.–Philippine Internal Security Program. A total of $3.9 million was devoted to this program by the U.S. in the period 1969–73, a substantial increase over the figure of $1.9 million for the period 1961–68.[105] This jump appears to mark a perturbed U.S. reaction to a sudden change in Philippine internal conditions, and much of the program's efforts have been devoted to training local police forces in the latest riot-control, intelligence, and communications techniques.

The Military Assistance Program, coordinated by the Joint U.S. Military Assistance Group, is intended to contribute logistical and training support to the Armed Forces of the Philippines (AFP). The AFP has allocated some of the MAP equipment to units involved in counter-dissident activities, no restrictions being placed on its use for such type of efforts. JUSMAG personnel have a liaison role with the AFP and some of them work *full-time* with it in staff advisory roles, thus opening up the possibility that they have

103. Security Agreements and Commitments Abroad, Republic of the Philippines (the Symington Report), U.S. Government Printing Office, 1967, p. 13.
104. Ibid., p. 229.
105. Mike Klare, "The Police Apparatus of U.S.A.I.D," *Philippine Information Bulletin,* Vol. 1, No. 1; included as Appendix F.

participated in drawing up counter-insurgency plans, especially given the fact that the principal, if not sole, preoccupation of the Philippine Armed Forces over the past few years has been counter-insurgency.

JUSMAG personnel have cooperated with U.S. base personnel in promoting "civic action" projects outside the bases.[106] While sounding harmless, "civic action" is in fact an integral part of modern counter-insurgency methods. First developed during President Ramon Magsaysay's drive against the Huks in the Philippines during the 1950's, it was subsequently employed in Vietnam by the United States.[107] Civic action is not devoid of military purposes and therefore contains concomitant risks. One need only remember that it was sufficient for the Philippines to contribute a civic-action team to the "allied" war effort in Vietnam for it to be considered an enemy by the Provisional Revolutionary Government of South Vietnam, thus exposing its troop-engineers to attack. It is highly probable that the Filipino revolutionary left feels the same way about U.S. civic action teams in the Philippines, thus increasing the chances for an encounter.

One notes that many of the tasks now undertaken by JUSMAG in the Philippines have striking similarities to those carried out by the Military Assistance Advisory Group (MAAG) in Vietnam in the early years of involvement.[108] Similarly, one cannot help but feel that JUSMAG might be the embryo out of which would arise a bigger, more powerful, and more complex military command, as was the case with MAAG, unless the United States radically revises at this point its military policy toward the Philippines.

What is most disturbing, however, are verified reports of the involvement of Clark Air Base personnel in Philippine counter-insurgency efforts that went beyond the usual indirect and diffuse logistical support to direct and specific support-action in concrete anti-guerrilla campaigns.[109] Such type of action is what is meant by the "logistic-type support on an ad-hoc basis" which Mr. Wilson admitted the U.S. military was furnishing the Philippine Government at the Senate hearing mentioned above.[110]

106. Security Agreements . . . , p. 355.
107. Neil Sheehan et al., *The Pentagon Papers,* New York, Bantam, p. 121.
108. Ibid., p. 120.
109. See Appendix C for an enumeration of such incidents, p. II–A–1.
110. Security Agreements . . . , p. 234.

On January 16, 1969, for instance, the Philippine Constabulary requested helicopter support for a raid on an insurgent hideout in Bataan Province. Clark Air Base provided one H-19 *and crew* to furnish transportation and air-to-ground communication for the Constabulary units. This helicopter participated in the encounter for two hours, at the end of which it returned to Clark.[111] It is interesting to point out with respect to this incident that Senator Symington considered Mr. Wilson's claim that no U.S. personnel had been involved in personal combat against the Huks very questionable, especially given the possibility that the helicopter could have been shot down by the insurgents.[112]

It is likewise very disturbing to note unconfirmed reports of increased American direct involvement in the periods prior to and immediately after the declaration of martial law. These reports remain largely unverified because of the general inefficiency of the Philippine media's military correspondents and also because the media came under official government control after the martial law declaration. In 1971, for example, the New People's Army (NPA) claimed in its battle report for that year that it had killed 600 AFP troops, shot down six planes and helicopters, and killed "18 U.S. military advisers over the last three years."[113] The same source claimed that in a post-martial law anti-dissident operation in northern Luzon, "at least 50 U.S. military advisers" were flown in from Clark Air Base to Cordon, Isabela to participate in combat operations.[114] It has constantly been reporting that Filipino-piloted jet aircraft from Clark Air Base conduct bombing raids against them in Northern Luzon.

It would be easy to dismiss these reports as worthless Communist propaganda. However, the Vietnam experience should teach us not to entirely dismiss such reports and instead launch an immediate investigation into them, especially since the U.S. military has been shown to be a not-too-reliable reporter of its activities.[115] Moreover, the Communists have not been the only source of reports of increasing U.S. involvement. In the middle of 1972, for instance, Philippine Senator Leonardo Perez, chairman of the Senate Committee on

111. See Appendix C, p. II–A–1 and Security Agreements . . . , p. 234.
112. Security Agreements . . . , p. 234.
113. *The Guardian,* October 22, 1972.
114. *The People,* Special Release, 1972.
115. *The Pentagon Papers* should have dispelled all doubts with regard to this.

National Defense, claimed that the United States was building another air-sea base in northern Luzon, the base area of the Filipino guerrillas.[116] So far as we know, no official U.S. denial has yet been issued. Another item bearing on American participation in counter-insurgency appeared in the January 7, 1973 issue of the Japanese newspaper *Mainichi Shimbun* which claimed that some U.S. Airborne Brigade men from Okinawa had participated in military activity called "civic action" in war-torn Mindanao. The response to such reports ought not to be blanket dismissal or blanket credulity, but immediate congressional investigation, which, so far, has been one of the effective weapons against the executive and military credibility gap.

To pursue the Vietnam parallel, the present American involvement in the Philippines appears to be similar to that phase of loosely coordinated and diffuse counter-insurgency efforts in Vietnam before Col. Edward Lansdale arrived on the scene to put the U.S. counter-insurgency program on a firmer basis in 1954 and aid began to arrive in large quantities.[117] The point is that as in Vietnam during that period, the United States can still extricate itself safely and honorably. The next step is entirely avoidable and would be to the great benefit of both the American and Filipino people. All of those who have shared the American tragedy in Vietnam would disagree with Secretary of Defense Juan Ponce Enrile's statement to the effect that more aid to the Marcos regime now will make it less expensive for the U.S. later on. It is precisely increased U.S. participation now, in support of an unpopular authoritarian regime, that will make it more expensive, both for the Filipino and American people, later on.

Proposals of the
National Committee for the Restoration of Civil Liberties in the
Philippines to the
Foreign Relations Committee of the U.S. Senate

The United States and the Philippines are entering an entirely new phase in their historic relationship. At the very moment that broad sectors of the American nation have come to realize the folly and injustice of the American involvement in Vietnam and have

---

116. *Ningas Cogon* (New York), May 1972, Vol. 1, No. 8, p. 4.
117. Neil Sheehan et al., *The Pentagon Papers*, pp. 7–25.

succeeded in pressuring their government to secure peace in that war-weary land, another authoritarian regime has arisen in Asia under social conditions very similar to those of South Vietnam during the Diem government and it threatens to drag the United States into another Vietnam-type intervention.

It would be a great tragedy for both the Filipino and American people if the United States government were to refuse to learn at this point one of the most important lessons of the Vietnam War: That there is no firmer basis for friendship between nations than mutual non-interference in each other's internal affairs. It is on this basis that the new relationship between the United States and the Philippines must be securely founded.

With this end in view, the *National Committee for the Restoration of Civil Liberties in the Philippines* advances this basic demand:

The United States must immediately and unconditionally cease all military, economic, and technical aid to the Marcos dictatorship.

It strongly urges the United States Congress to take the initiative in this action by exercising its power of the purse.

We propose two means by which the Senate Foreign Relations Committee can immediately contribute toward making strict U.S. noninterference a reality:

1. It can summon Ambassador Henry Byroade to appear before this committee to enlighten it, and through it, the American people, on the question of whether or not the United States government had a role in the recent political developments in the Philippines.
2. It can likewise initiate a thorough investigation of unconfirmed covert U.S. military support-action against Filipino guerrillas. As a first step in this investigation it can summon those American servicemen who have served in the Philippines and who have indicated their willingness to give testimony.

As the *Pentagon Papers* have so clearly shown, one of the fundamental reasons for the Vietnam involvement was the lack of honest communication between critical sectors of the Executive branch and the people of the United States. Summoning Ambassador Byroade and willing American servicemen and demanding honest testimony from them would be a first and invaluable step in ensuring that the next uncertain step into a new quagmire will not be taken.

Appendix 12. A Statement of the Civil Liberties Union of the Philippines on the State of the Nation after Three Years of Martial Law

The Myth

Three years of martial law have raised many vital questions, questions that the people dare talk about only in the safety of their homes or in the security of small groups of friends. Unfortunately, not all these questions can be ventilated in this paper: there is neither space enough nor time.

But one question demands discussion because around it a myth has risen a myth that seduced by its deceptive simplicity. It is the myth that an underdeveloped nation, like ours, must sacrifice civil liberties and political rights for rapid economic growth.

The Myth's Many Variants

The myth has many variants.

One variant is that developing nations have four objectives—political democracy, full employment, price stability, and economic growth—but can choose only three, not all four, simultaneously. And, of course, the easiest objective to give up is political democracy.

Another variant is that political democracy is a Western imposition not suited to the Asian milieu; that it is too slow, its institutions too unwieldy, its oligarchs too well entrenched, to be capable of pursuing development with the speed, vigor and will that the urgency of the situation demands. "The West could develop leisurely," we are told, "but we do not have time; and so reluctantly, we must give up democracy."

Source: Civil Liberties Union of the Philippines, *The State of the Nation after Three Years of Martial Law,* September 21, 1975. Editors of the statement are Jose W. Diokno, Chairman; J. Antonio Araneto, Commissioner; Jose B. L. Reyes, Commissioner; Lorenzo M. Tañado, Member; and Calixto O. Zaldivar, Member. In published form, this "Statement" appears as Chapter 1, "An Overview" of the full report of the C.L.U.P. Four other chapters discuss "The Economy," "Labor Policy and Agrarian Reform," "Mass Media," and "The Administration of Justice." The C.L.U.P. has also published *A Statement on Foreign Policy and Military Bases under Martial Law* (Makati, Philippines: C.L.U.P., 1977), and a manifesto, "Return to Freedom," issued June, 1977, calling for the end of martial law and the holding of competitive elections.

The Philippine Variant

The Philippine variant is that our society can be restructured only by martial rule. Although President Marcos admits that "martial law was never conceived nor has it ever been utilized to attain revolutionary or radical reforms,"[1] he nevertheless would continue to impose it "beyond the simple need of restoring order, to meet the other and even more important imperative of reforming society."[2]

His implication is clear: only government by martial law can solve the nation's abiding and persistent political, economic and social problems.

Is this true?

Martial Rule Is Dictatorship

To answer this question, one must examine the nature of martial law. Is government by martial law a democracy, an oligarchy or a dictatorship? Is it government by the many, by the few, or by one?

Whatever martial law may mean in other countries, in ours its nature is beyond doubt. Martial law is dictatorship, the rule of one man: The President.

General Order No. 1, dated September 22, 1972, makes no bones about it. There, the President said: "I, Ferdinand E. Marcos, President of the Philippines . . . do hereby proclaim that I shall govern the nation and direct the operation of the entire government, including all its agencies and instrumentalities."[3]

For three years, he has exercised all executive and all legislative powers.

For three years, he has exercised judicial powers; both directly and indirectly. Directly, through military commissions whom he created to try civilians, and whose sentences he must first approve before they can be carried out.[4] Indirectly, through his influence over the Supreme Court and through his power, under the martial law constitution, to remove every member of the judiciary from lowest to highest, at will and even without cause.[5]

---

1. Marcos, "The Democratic Revolution in the Philippines," p. 217.
2. Ibid., p. 128.
3. Emphasis added.
4. Presidential Decree No. 39, November 7, 1972, amended by Presidential Decree No. 566, October 18, 1974.
5. [1973] Constitution, Art. XVI, Secs. 9 and 10.

For three years, he has denied the people any meaningful participation in making public decisions that shape their life and their
livelihood.[6]

For three years, he has kept the constitution, as one member of
the Supreme Court describes it, in a "state of anaesthesia."[7]

In short, martial law "Philippine style" is dictatorship, pure and
simple. It respects no constitutional rights, no civil liberties. It is
subject to no effective checks or balances. It is limited to no fixed
period of time.

Martial Law Cannot Reform Society

Once this is grasped, it becomes absurd to suppose that—in theory
or in practice—martial law is or can be the rational means to
"revolutionize or reform" society.

It is absurd, because our social, political and economic problems
are so grave and so deeply rooted, that no one man is wise enough
to solve them or good enough to be entrusted with unlimited
power to do so. Yet that is what martial law does: it creates a dictatorship and entrusts unlimited power to one man—the President.

It is absurd, because to revolutionize society is to eliminate the
privileges of the few so that the rights of the many may be respected;
but martial law eliminates both the privileges of the few and the
rights of the many, in order to concentrate absolute power in one
man, and privileges only on those he chooses to reward. It is absurd,
because to reform society is to eliminate corruption, but "power corrupts, and absolute power corrupts absolutely," and martial law
creates a dictatorship of absolute power.

It is absurd, because if the dictatorship that martial law creates
acts for its own benefit, it becomes tyranny; and if it acts for the
benefit of the people, it becomes paternalism. In either case, it
affronts the dignity of the people, it belittles their capacity, it de-
grades their humanity—and that is the ultimate corruption.

It is absurd, further, because as its name implies and as the Constitution provides, martial law is military power applied to solve
military problems occasioned by insurrection, rebellion or invasion.[8]

6. Referendums have been held; but no one takes their results seriously.
7. Aquino v. Enrile (1974), 59 SCRA 183 at pp. 420, 432.
8. 1935 Constitution, Art. VII, Sec. 11 (2); 1973 Constitution, Art. IX, Sec. 12.

It was neither designed nor intended to be a military solution for social, economic and political problems, and for two very good reasons:

First, because martial law is to be imposed only in cases of extreme danger, so that its full power must be concentrated in meeting and overcoming that danger. To try to solve military problems at the same time as deep-rooted social and economic problems is to dissipate its strength and to blunt its force, with the result that neither the military problems, nor the social and economic problems, will be solved, as the experience of the present martial law government proves.

Second, because martial law, as the President himself said, "connotes the power of the gun, means coercion by the military, and compulsion and intimidation"[9] but guns cannot kill, nor coercion by the military liquidate, the poverty, the inequality and the injustice that are the most serious of our economic and social problems.

It is absurd, further, because what underlies these problems of poverty, inequality and injustice is the exploitative relation of colonial dependence that we have inherited from our past, so that we cannot eradicate poverty, remove inequality or restore justice unless we simultaneously assert our political independence, strive for economic sovereignty and labor towards cultural liberation. Yet martial law, by entrusting all political power to one man, makes it easier for the colonial power to bribe, to coerce or to deceive him; and in these ways to perpetuate our dependence.

It is absurd, finally, because by the very fact that it is accountable to no one but itself, the dictatorship that martial law creates is destined to excesses, to become bloated as it ages, to seek desperately for—and to create when it cannot find—excuses to justify its perpetuation. Unlike a government that pays at least token homage to the discipline and values built into the institutions of democracy, government by martial law can recognize no limits; and when it cannot feed on anything else, it will feed on itself. Sooner or later, it is bound to devour the very people who created it, as a revolution devours its children.

So martial law that is an indefinite, unlimited dictatorship cannot be the rational means to solve our national problem.

9. *Daily Express,* November 29, 1972.

Martial Law Has Not Reformed Society

In fact, these three years of government by martial law have not only failed to solve our problems, they have aggravated them.

Martial law has neither changed the colonial nature of our economy nor brought us closer to economic independence. On the contrary, as the paper on the economy shows, we are more dependent now than ever before on foreign investments and foreign loans.

The Betrayal of Economic Nationalism

Before martial law, Congress had explicitly adopted "the principles and objectives of economic nationalism."[10] Martial law has betrayed this ideal.

Shortly after martial law was imposed, the martial law constitution
—reversed the Supreme Court decisions in the Quasha case[11] (nullifying all sales of private lands to U.S. citizens after 1945) and the Luzon Stevedoring case[12] (banning foreign directors in corporations engaged in Filipinized industries); and
—gave the President power to disregard all restrictive laws on foreign investments in concluding treaties and executive agreements.[13]
Soon thereafter the President himself:
—extended parity rights unilaterally for one year;
—approved schemes by which U.S. firms divested themselves of title, but otherwise retained the beneficial use and control, of land acquired during parity;
—ratified the Philippine-Japan treaty;
—relaxed Filipinization laws on the retail trade, the rice and corn industry, the interisland shipping industry, and the banking system; and
—opened the door wide to foreign capital and multinational corporations by offering attractive tax and foreign exchange incentives, and an even more attractive labor situation: a large pool of unemployed and under-employed labor, which, though unskilled, is quick to learn and easy to train; which in practice,

10. Investment Incentives Act, R.A. 5786, Sec. 2.
11. Republic v. Quasha (1972), 46 SCRA 160; Constitution, Art. XVII, Sec. 11 and 12.
12. Luzon Stevedoring v. Anti-Dummy Board (1972), 46 SCRA 479; 1973 Constitution, Art. XIV, Sec. 5.
13. 1973 Constitution, Art. XIV, Sec. 15.

if not in law, is denied the right to free self-organization and to job security; and, in both law and practice, is denied the right to strike; while wages and salaries are kept low and made even cheaper with each successive devaluation of the peso, a devaluation that the inflationary policies of the martial law regime make inevitable.

Resurgence Of Crime And Corruption

Martial law has not solved the problem of law and order. Although the crime rate improved markedly at the start of martial law, it is now back to near pre-martial law levels. Crimes against property have increased and will continue to increase as the economic situation worsens. Violence against persons by civilians, is less; but its decline had been made up for by abuses committed by the military, through unreasonable searches and seizures; indiscriminate arrests, indefinite detentions, and frequent torture of political prisoners; repression of some minorities like the Kalingas and Bontocs; and reprisals against unarmed Muslims.

Martial law has not eliminated corruption in government. In fact, it has not even meaningfully reduced it. Abuses of power and privilege by old politicos are gone; but their place has been taken over by new mandarins who, unlike the former, are not accountable to the people.

No Changes in Social Structures

Martial law has not re-structured our society. If at all, the gap between poor and rich has widened because, as the paper on the economy shows, martial law has not solved the problem of unemployment; and the runaway inflation that afflicts us, brought about more by the inflationary policies of the martial law regime than by world economic conditions,[14] has battered the poor much more than it has hurt the rich.

And, as the paper on labor policy and agrarian reform shows, the impairment of the right to free self-organization, the elimination of the right to strike, and the policy of keeping wages low, have

14. Central Bank Twenty-Sixth Annual Report, 1974, p. 40. The 1974 inflation rate was 40% according to the Central Bank (ibid., p. 36); 44.5% according to the NEDA (Report on the Economy for CY 1974, p. 9). Of the 40%, according to the Central Bank, only 16.8% was "due to external price developments," 23.2% was caused by domestic factors.

stripped labor of any defense against both inflation and management abuses; while the slow pace of land reform, the weaknesses of supporting services for tenants, the increase in costs, and the absence of any program for tenants on coconut and sugar lands—and more important—for landless peasants, who far outnumber tenants—all these factors have negated any meaningful gains for our rural population.

In fact, the productivity of agricultural labor, in real terms, dropped from P1,205 per man in 1972, to only P1,167 per man in 1974—a clear indication that our rural population was worse off in 1974 than in 1972.[15]

The government's own statistics show that, despite its claim to greater efficiency and swifter action because of martial law, it is no more capable of pushing land reform now than it was before martial law. Its latest published data show that, by December 31, 1974, of the 1,087,817 tenants of rice and corn lands, only 189,183—or 17%—had received land transfer certificates.[16] Of the 755,649 tenants who work on landholdings smaller than 24 hectares, only 70,679—or 9%—had received their certificates by June 30, 1974. And 395,034 tenants—or 37% of all rice and corn tenants—have no chance to own the land they till, because they work in landholdings of less than 7 hectares, and these lands are not to be sold to them.[17]

So, martial law has not made the poor richer.

Neither has it rid our society of the oligarchy.

As the paper on mass media shows, today the ownership of press, radio and television is concentrated on different, but fewer hands than before martial law, despite the pledge of the martial law regime to "democratize" the ownership of media.

In the world of business and finance, new tycoons have flourished to replace or even surpass the two or three whom the martial law regime has branded as malefactors of great wealth; and other captains of industry remain as firmly at the helm today, as they were before martial law.

The only difference seems to be this: that before, all could—and

15. Obtained by dividing the value of the contribution of agriculture, fishing and forestry to GNP, at 1967 prices, according to NEDA National Income Series No. 3, Table 2, p. 25, by the number of persons employed in that sector, according to the CB Twenty-Sixth Annual Report, 1974, Table 17, p. 32.

16. NEDA Report on the Economy for CY 1974, p. 64; Department of Agrarian Reform Report, June 30, 1974.

17. DAR Report, June 30, 1974; Presidential Decree No. 27, October 21, 1972.

some dared—criticize the economic policies of the government and expose the chicaneries of power; but now, all are as meek towards the martial law regime as labor is docile towards them. Exactions could be resisted and exposed before; now, they must be accepted with a smile; and if the smile be forced, the resentment can find release only in whispers. But this is not too important—because, after all, although real wages have come down, profits are still up.

Why Martial Law Cannot Abolish Oligarchy

The truth is that the one pledge a martial law regime in a mixed economy, like ours, can never keep is the pledge to abolish oligarchy. No matter how dedicated to the ideal of equality it may pretend to be, the best it can ever do is to remove cne set of oligarchs and replace it with another.

The reason for this is fairly obvious. Every martial law regime must have a financial and economic base to maintain its power and keep itself alive. In a mixed economy, such as ours, that base cannot exist without the existing oligarchic structures, because it is these very structures that amass and consolidate the wealth of the nation; it is from the profits they produce that the means come to pay taxes, and from the savings they generate that the funds come for reinvestment to fuel growth. When the mixed economy, moreover, is as biased towards free enterprise as ours has been compelled to be by the imperatives of its export oriented development policy and its dependence on foreign capital and foreign loans, the rise and growth of an oligarchy is unavoidable. In the kind of dictatorship that martial law creates in a mixed economy, an oligarchy is not only necessary, but also inevitable.

So, the "new society" is new only in name. Some faces have disappeared from the scene; others have appeared to take their place. Cadenzas change; the melody lingers on.

Only Political System Has Been Changed

The truth is that martial law has brought about changes only in the political system. Democracy "Philippine style" was far from perfect. But martial law "Philippine style" is not any better.

We had a free but often irresponsible press. Today, as the paper on mass media shows, our press remains irresponsible but it is not free.

We had demonstrations and rallies and marches, marked by inflammatory rhetoric and sometimes marred by violence; but the violence, as Senate investigations concluded, began from the police or military. And some of the counter-violence by demonstrators was instigated by agents of the government who had infiltrated into the student movement. Be that as it may, today we cannot march peacefully to Malacañang or gather elsewhere peacefully to seek redress for grievances.

We had a small standing army of some 60,000 men, on whom we spent some P880 million of our national budget, and who, in the main, knew and kept to their place, accepting the supremacy of civilian rule. Today, our army is programmed to become 275,000 strong by 1976; we are spending some P3.0 billion on it (plus undisclosed millions on intelligence alone); and the military has invaded all spheres of civilian life, including local business, our courts, purely civil quarrels, and labor disputes.

We had courts that were slow, too technical and sometimes corrupt—but we did have an independent judiciary. Today, our courts remain slow, too technical, and sometimes corrupt—and, as the paper on the administration of justice shows, our judiciary is no longer independent.

We had a Congress that some saw as a do-nothing-but-talk-and-make-money assembly; but we could occasionally appeal to curb flagrant abuses by the executive. And, almost invariably, we could ask for protection from Congressmen and Senators when we were victims of injustice. Today, we have no Congress, Congressmen or Senators we can appeal to at all.

We had a system of separation of powers, of checks and balances that sometimes produced paralysis in government. Today, all power is in the hands of one man; and while he can act more swiftly, he can also act precipitately, and, as a result, be constrained to change his mind and policies more often. So uncertainty and insecurity remain.

We had elections that were often a mockery; today, we have referendums that are a sham, with more voters registered by the COMELEC than there are people of voting age, according to the National Census and Statistics Office.

Then, we could—and often did—throw rascals out, even if only to put new rascals in; and we often managed to elect good and honest men. Now, we cannot throw any rascals out; we cannot elect any good and honest men; in fact, we cannot elect any man at all.

Judgment on Political Changes

If the essence of political development is government by increased consensus on vital public issues, then martial law is not development but retrogression: for without free speech, free press and free assembly, and without freedom from fear, there can be no genuine consensus.

If the essence of responsible government is government accountable to the people, because it can be changed peacefully by the people when it no longer serves their good, then government by martial law is irresponsible, because it does not answer to the people, and the people have no peaceful means to change it.

And if the essence of good government is government for the good of the people, then government by martial law is bad government, because like all dictatorships, its primary objective is power, to which all else is subordinated; and because, as government statistics make abundantly clear, the few benefit disproportionately from it.

Thus, all public works projects are "impact projects," not so much in the sense of having the most impact on economic development, as in the sense of having the most impact on the public image of the martial law regime in the eyes of tourists and foreigners.

Economic policies are geared for short-run advantage, regardless of long-run disadvantages; for example, the regime welcomes projects like the Kawasaki Iron Sintering project in Cagayan de Oro City, although such a project can no longer be established in Japan or in other countries because it pollutes the environment.

Foreign investments of all kinds are welcomed because they bring in dollars and add prestige, although their immediate effects are inflationary; and, in the long run, they will not only take out more dollars than they bring in, but make it harder to achieve economic independence.

And so on.

Failure of Martial Law Not Unique to Philippines

The failure of martial law is not unique to the Philippines. There are numerous other dictatorships, in Latin America and in Asia as well, that have given up political democracy and destroyed civil liberties and yet have not achieved either economic democracy or cultural liberation.

Dictatorship never benefits the people in the long run; and seldom, in the short run—even when the dictator comes as a Messiah, untarnished by the crisis he vows to save the people from. When the dictator himself created or contributed to the mess, when his credibility to begin with is low, the chances of effecting meaningful change are infinitesimal.

Why Martial Law Has Spread to Other Asian Countries

"If this is so," it may be asked, "why have other nations, like Korea and India in Asia, Chile in Latin America, and others in other parts of the world, also declared martial law in the last three years?"

The answer is not only personal ambition. Personal ambition may play a role, but rarely the decisive role. No, the real answer is that martial law is imposed, because it is the last defense of an establishment besieged by the forces of progress and change.

Take the Philippine case as an example.

In the late 1960's and early 70's, for the first time in our history, there emerged an organized, vocal, determined and militant nationalist movement for change.

Intellectuals, professionals, small businessmen, students, peasants, laborers and employees, realizing their common interests, began to unite and so to pose a threat both to established political parties and to foreign capital: in particular, the gigantic foreign-owned-and-controlled oil refining industry.

Persons not heretofore active in politics—seminarians, priests, nuns, Catholic school students—were starting to question the injustices of our social system.

Unlike earlier peasant movements, the movement of the 70's counted with membership from the elite, drew elements from both political parties, and support from influential media; and appeared to have a broad base of urban and rural support.

A politics of issues, rather than a politics of personalities, thus became a real possibility; a new party loomed, led by men and women with some experience in local and national politics, who identified themselves with the interests of the masses of our people; opposed the interests of foreign capital and the Filipino elite; and advocated basic social reforms. So strong was the demand for reform that, in the elections to the Constitutional Convention of 1971, independent candidates won about one-third of the seats. Some of those who won were openly identified with the radical left, and campaigned on a nationalist, socialist platform. That they had dared to run at all was significant. That they won, indicated how much the people wanted nationalist change.

Change threatened others besides the Filipino elite and foreign capital. The government of the United States had interests in the Philippines more vital than sentimental ties. For example, the possibility that it might have to get out of Vietnam, required greater protection for its naval and air bases here, against the foreseeable expansion of Soviet naval power into the China Sea. The approaching end of parity demanded a trade agreement equally favorable to U.S. business interests. The Nixon doctrine, which insisted upon more "self-reliance" by America's client governments in Asia, among them the Philippines, and a larger Japanese role in Asia, required a stronger anti-dissident posture, plus easier entry for Japanese and other foreign investments, so that the latter would also have a stake to protect in the Philippines. All these interests felt themselves threatened by the growing nationalist movement, with its egalitarian tendencies.

To eliminate the threat, before the strength of the movement's organization matched the strength of its rhetoric, martial law was the only effective answer. Neither calling out the armed forces nor suspending the privilege of the writ of *habeas corpus*—as had twice been done before—would suffice. In order to squelch the nationalist movement, it was necessary to silence the press that supported it; and to protect the privileged position of foreign and domestic capital, and the interests of the U.S. government, it was necessary to eliminate all debate and criticism, and transfer all power to one man. Only martial law could do this.

Martial law, then, was the result of a confluence of needs. It answered the need of the President to stay in power. It answered the need of the Filipino elite to continue to enjoy and add to their wealth and privilege. And it answered the needs of the U.S. government and business interests to protect U.S. bases, secure U.S. investments, and allow easier entry and greater scope for foreign capital.

It should come as no surprise, then, that shortly after martial law had been declared, a report attributed to the U.S. Senate Majority Floor Leader should praise the imposition of martial law.[18] Nor should it be unexpected that, in the three years following martial law, U.S. military assistance to the Philippines increased by 64%, from $58,433,000, for the pre-martial law fiscal years 1970–72, to

18. Marcos, "The Democratic Revolution in the Philippines," pp. 139–140.

$95,862,000, for the martial law fiscal years 1973-75; and that economic assistance jumped 89%, from $134,230,000, for fiscal years 1970-72, to $254,031,000, for fiscal years 1973-75.[19]

The Only Real Solution: Lift Martial Law

Since martial law cannot be the rational means of the restructing of our society which is essential to the solution of our enduring and stubborn problems of mass poverty, social inequality, and injustice; since the three years that have passed show clearly that martial law is, in fact, incapable of restructuring our society or even maintaining what gains it originally made in restoring law and order; and since the real roots of martial law lie deeper than the personal ambitions of the head of the martial law government, whoever he may be, it follows that, if the nation is to achieve true development, attain real progress and build a better and more just—and not merely a new—society, martial law must be lifted and democratic processes and civil liberties restored to our people.

Whether the head of government be President Marcos or anyone else, martial law must go. Only in freedom, can we really achieve the unity of mind, the strength of will, and the joy of common effort that can move the nation forward, because only in freedom are we truly men—and truly Filipinos.

Appendix 13. Philippine Church-State Relations since Martial Law

I

The initial reaction of the church to Martial Law was that of cautious moderation. While having strong reservations about suppression of basic civil liberties, church leaders nonetheless recognized the poignant need for a radical reform of Philippine society. Rather

---

19. Tables included in "Status of Human Rights in the Philippines," submitted by U.S. Assistant Secretary of State McCloskey in reply to the letter dated June 10, 1975, of U.S. Congressman Fraser, Chairman of the Sub-Committee on International Organizations of the U.S. House of Representatives.

Source: Alex Pescador, "An Overview of Philippine Church-State Relations since Martial Law," *PAHAYAG*, March 1975, pp. 3–6.

than coming out in active opposition to Martial Law, their strategy was one of accommodation, hoping to use their influence to temper authoritarian excesses, aid in effective implementation of reforms, and assist the restitution of a democratic form of government. (See chronology in Appendix 14, entries of Sept. 26 and 28, Oct. 4, and Nov. 9, 1972.) Certain church leaders were against this early policy but their views had little impact on what a majority consensus was. (See chronology, entries of Nov. 26, 1972, Jan. 8, Feb. 7, June 29, and Sept., 1973.) During this period, the first evidence of some form of organized resistance to the regime by churchmen was an unofficial campaign against voting for the passage of a new constitution that would legitimize Marcos' holding of unlimited power and tenure. (See chronology, entries of Dec. 1, 1972 and July 17, 1973.)

Arrests of church personnel at this stage was primarily confined to individuals who were involved in pre-Martial Law activism and/ or social action programs that concerned themselves with issues relating to the exploited masses. The church superior's continuation of a non-interference, wait-and-see strategy resulted in many foreign missionaries accepting either "voluntary deportation" or severing restrictions of freedom so that they could remain in the country. Meanwhile, Filipino clergy was not so lucky. (See chronology, entries of Sept. and Oct., 1972 and Jan. 21 and 29, July 24, Aug. 11, Sept. 7 and 14, and Oct. 20 and 31, 1973.)

II

Between October 1973 and August 1974, a series of events soon brought submerged tensions and criticisms out into the open, leading to a considerable alteration of the church's stand on the Martial Law issue. On October 31, 1973, Fr. Edward Gerlock, M.M., a priest totally involved with social action programs, was arrested on the charge of subversion. He vehemently denied the charges and demanded a public trial of deportation. He claimed that Martial Law was incompatible with the social justice program outlined by Pope Paul VI and the Asian Bishops Conference of 1970 which cited the duty of Catholics to "speak out for the right of the disadvantaged and powerless against all forms of injustice no matter from what source such abuse may come." Fr. Gerlock was the first clergyman to raise these issues in public with the full support of his order. (See chronology, entries of Oct. 31, 1973 and Jan. 13, 1975.)

This period was also characterized by an increase in the number of priests and ministers who criticized the government's reformatory pretensions and the continued exploitation of the people under Martial Law. In some cases, this expression of dissent led to the detention of clergy brave enough to make a public stand. (See chronology, entries of Nov. and Dec., 1973 and March 14 and July, 1974.) Reports on the tortures of a Catholic priest and a Protestant minister while under military interrogation in early 1974 put church-state relations on new grounds. The introduction of physical abuse in the treatment of the clergy put religious organizations on notice that they were no longer accorded the sanctity traditionally provided churchmen. It was noted that the torture-interrogation of these clergymen by the military paralleled the increased use of torture tactics on the "political prisoners." (See chronology, entries of Feb. 20 and March, 1974.) Confronted with the threat of physical violence, the Philippine clergy closed ranks and issued statements condemning the present state of affairs and upholding their right to dissent. (See chronology, entries of April 4 and August, 1974.)

In November 1973, the National Council of Churches in the Philippines (NCCP) passed a resolution at their annual convention suggesting the abolition of Martial Law and the termination of restraints of freedom of speech and the press. In mid-June 1974, the Council issued a much stronger position paper attacking the presence of extensive U.S. military bases in the country. Days later, prominent officers of the Council and notable leaders and laymen of the Protestant church in the Philippines and Asia were arrested and some were later tortured during their interrogation. The event received the attention of the World Council of Churches in Geneva, which stepped in to issue a strong condemnation of the government's high-handed action. (See chronology, entries of Nov., 1973, June 26, July 29, August and Sept., 1974.)

Two months after the NCCP arrests, the military resorted to the use of coercion on the Catholic church to reduce it to silent condonation of the political situation. On August 23, army troopers raided the San Jose Seminary in Novaliches, Rizal, accusing the church of harboring communist leader Jose Ma. Sison within its sanctuary. Many saw the incident as an open act of aggression by the government threatening the Catholic church with greater military reprisals if it continued to allow its priests to publicly criticize Martial Law rule. The integrity of the Catholic church was upheld when Manila Archbishop Sin publicly confronted the government over the raid and ridiculed Marcos for his use of the captive mass media to cover-up the case before the public. Military harassments of Philippine religious leaders had by this time resulted in uniting Protestant and Catholic churches in open hostility to Martial Law. (See chronology, entries of Aug. 23, Sept. 1 and 4, 1974.)

III

Church-state relations deteriorated rapidly as the Philippine churches undertook militant actions involving themselves in direct opposition to the Martial Law government. In September 1974, the 81 members of the Catholic Bishops Conference and the Davao clergy and laymen separately petitioned Marcos to terminate his dictatorial regime. Later, in December, Protestants voiced public dissent over Martial Law and questioned the contradictions in the President's foreign vs. domestic policy on communism. Protestations from church bodies now took the form of open demands and denunciations rather than suggestions or requests. In all these instances, the President either ignored or rejected the petitions. (See chronology, entries of Sept., Nov., and Dec., 1974.)

Archbishop Sin and the Association of Major Religious Superiors investigated reports of maltreatment, torture and murder of political prisoners by the military, and drew national attention to the specific documented cases of such abuse. The condemnation of the ill-treatment of prisoners was heightened by two imprisoned priests, Fr. Ed de la Torre, S.V.D., and Fr. Manuel Lahoz, who went on a hunger strike to protest their own arrests and the torture of 19 fellow prisoners. The Archbishop's campaign achieved a measure of success when the government dismissed seven military enlisted men and ordered the investigation of five officers accused by Fr. de la Torre and Fr. Lahoz. (See chronology, entries of Nov. 22 and Dec., 1974 and Feb. 4, 1975.)

Of far greater significance is the role of the church in the campaign against the attempt by Pres. Marcos to reaffirm and extend his power in the country. His announcement of a public referendum on this matter on Dec. 11, 1974, was challenged by manifestos signed by prominent citizens and educators as well as Catholic and Protestant religious leaders. This was followed by meetings of Catholic leaders ending on January 12 and resulting in such strong denunciations of the President's proposed referendum as "another mockery of democracy" and "another Marcos gimmick to justify his stay in power." Later that same evening Marcos appeared on nationwide television and radio to announce the postponement of the referendum from January 30 to February 27. (See chronology, entries of Dec. 11 and 17, and the two entries of Jan. 12, 1975.)

The announcement of the referendum's postponement did not reduce opposition to it. Individual Catholic bishops continued to publicize their manifestos and letters-to-the-president which were highly critical of the referendum's validity. In Mindanao, a large group of clergy and laymen denounced the referendum and further brought up issues on the torturing of suspected Muslim separationists. (See chronology, three entries of Jan. 1975.) Later, on January 30, fourteen individual citizens, including an imprisoned ex-Senator and five Catholic bishops, presented a petition to the Supreme Court challenging the constitutional legality of Marcos' continued rule and his right to call a referendum. Even though the court dismissed the petition, 96 Catholic bishops immediately issued an appeal for democratic safeguards to make the referendum meaningful. (See chronology, entries of Jan. 30 and the two entries of Feb. 1, 1975.)

In the two and a half years since the declaration of Martial Law, the Philippine church has undergone a radical transformation in its relations with the government. What specific actions the church will take in the future cannot be predicted. However, it is safe to say that the church's role in opposition to the oppressive Marcos government is unalterably set. The three-stage development of church-state relations outlined in this paper also contains within itself an obvious implication for the future which should not be overlooked. Assuming that the Philippine church reflects the aspirations and thinking of its lay members, then the newly-evolved role of the church as an antagonist of the Marcos dictatorship must also indicate heightened mass disillusionment with the regime. This development should have important implications in future considerations of the stability of the Marcos government. . . .

Appendix 14. Chronology of Church-State Conflicts in the Philippines, from September 21, 1972, to February 4, 1975

1972

Sept. 21   President Ferdinand E. Marcos proclaims the imposition of Martial Law in the Philippines.

Sept.   Arrest of Fr. Daniel McLaughlin, M.M., in Panabo, Davao del Norte. He supposedly made a statement during Mass against the declaration of Martial Law in places outside Manila and other troubled provinces.

Sept.   Arrest of Fr. Vincent Cullen, S.J., in Bukidnon province as a result of personal difficulties with local political officials. Also arrested in September was Fr. Lagerway, M.S.C., head of the Social Communication Center, Manila.

Sept. 26   Letter calling for an end to Martial Law as soon as the political situation allows was sent by the Administrative Council of the Catholic Bishops' Conference to Pres. Marcos. (The letter was interpreted by the government-controlled media as an endorsement of Martial Law.)

Sept. 28   Letter sent by sixteen Bishops to President Marcos strongly voicing clergy uneasiness about Martial Law and fears of possible future oppression under such a government.

Oct. 4   Letter expressing concern over the Martial Law situation to Marcos by Bishop Francisco F. Claver, S.J., Bishop of Malaybalay, Bukidnon.

Oct.   Fr. John Peterson, O.F.M., and Fr. Bruno Hicks, O.F.M., both of Guihulngan, Negros Oriental, were arrested. Both men chose voluntary deportation rather than continued detention and left the country on October 20.

Nov. 9   Letter of protestation over Martial Law excesses sent by the Executive Board of the Association of Major Religious Superiors in the Philippines to President Marcos.

Nov. 26   First issue of *Pilipinas,* an underground newspaper published by Christians who oppose Martial Law.

Source: Alex Pescador, "An Overview of Philippine Chuch-State Relations since Martial Law," *PAHAYAG,* March 1975, pp. 7–10.

Dec. 1   Speech by Fr. Pacifico A. Ortiz, S.J., a delegate to the Con-
              stitutional Convention explaining to that body why he
              would not vote for the President's constitution.

1973
Jan. 8   Circular letter to friends by Bishop Claver detailing in-
              creased suppression of dissent under the excuse of subver-
              sion to the state.

Jan. 21   March by ZOTO squatters organization from the Tondo
              district of Manila to Sta. Cruz Church for a Mass to pro-
              test the new government and the loss of Filipino civil
              liberties.

Jan. 29   Arrest of Fr. Jose R. Nacu, (La Salette) advisor and or-
              ganizer for ZOTO. (Released on Feb. 25 but rearrested on
              March 10 and escaped detention on June 4, 1974. Sought
              asylum in the French embassy but was denied. He then
              joined the underground anti-Martial Law movement.)

Feb. 7   Letter sent by Bishop Claver to Pres. Marcos with a long
              cover letter addressed to the Apostolic Delegate, the Most
              Rev. Teopisto V. Alberto, D.D., exposing Marcos' lack of
              credibility, the excesses of the Martial Law government
              which caused additional hardship on the people, and how
              Presidential subordinates are misleading the President.

June 29   Letter by Bishop Nepomuceno, O.M.I., Bishop of Cotabato
              to Archbishop Alberto expressing strong desire for the
              Catholic Bishop's Conference of the Philippines to deal
              more decisively with gut issues of the church's social and
              theological responsibility under Martial Law.

July 17   An open letter to Pres. Marcos denouncing the up-coming
              referendum on the government's new constitution, signed
              by civic and church leaders. (At this time the church came
              out very strongly for a "No" vote on the new constitution
              and expressed opposition via the pulpit and literature urg-
              ing a brave and responsible Christian vote.)

July 24   Arrest of Fr. Henry van den Eeden, parish priest of San
              Remigio, Antique, and sisters Claire, Violeta, and Chris-
              tine Velez for supposed liaisons with an activist youth
              group responsible for ambushing a government patrol.

Aug. 11   Pastoral letter by Archbishop of Jaro, Bishop of Capiz, Bishop of Bacolod, and Prelate Ordinary of Antique protesting the events of July 24.

Sept.   "Underground Priest Speaks," *Philippine Information Bulletin,* Vol. I, No. 4, pp. 12–13. (Interview of Fr. Dagohoy who was working in the countryside with the Maoist New People's Army.)

Sept. 7   Arrest of Fr. Luis Jalandoni, former director of the Bacolod Social Action Committee and co-founder of the Christians for National Liberation, Western Visayas branch. He had gone "underground" upon the declaration of Martial Law.

Sept. 14   Philippine Constabulary (PC) raided the convent of the Good Shepherd Sisters in Davao City, Davao. The Mother Superior and a nun were called for questioning as suspected coordinators of a subversive underground movement in Davao province.

Oct. 20   Arrest of Dr. Nemesio Prudente, ex-President of the Philippine College of Commerce and prominent lay leader in the United Methodist Church. Also on the same date, the PC raided the St. Joseph's College and arrested Sr. Marianni Dimaranan, the school's registrar. Also raided were Trinity College (Episcopalian) and Our Lady of the Holy Angels Seminary (Franciscan) in Novaliches, Rizal.

Oct. 31   Arrest of Fr. Edward M. Gerlock, M.M., of Tagum, Davao, for subversion. Gerlock violently denied charges and insisted that he was only working in church social action project. He challenged the government to come up with evidence in support of their charges. Fr. Orlando Carvajal of the Mindanao Development Center was also arrested and Fr. Tom Marti, M.M., of the Mindanao Social Action Secretariat was brought before military interrogation.

Nov.   Arrests of Fr. Yusingo of Misamis Oriental, ZOTO head Manolito Agoncillo, and Mrs. Lulu Ledesma of the Family Life Apostolate.

Nov.   The annual convention of the National Council of Churches of the Philippines passed a resolution suggesting abolition of Martial Law and ending of restraints of freedom of speech and the press.

Nov. 26   Major Religious Superiors released a summary of the find-
           ings of a nationally circulated questionnaire on Martial
           Law. The Report represented the most complete and inten-
           sive repudiation of Martial Law in both theory and prac-
           tice that had yet been issued by any "objective" source.

Dec.   Arrests of Fr. Woodrow Gabuan, Rev. Emilio Henares,
           Carlos Aliones (lay leader), 2 secretaries under Bishop
           Antonio Fortich of Bacolod, and sought after was Fr.
           Eduardo Saguinsin, all of Bacolod; Fr. Emeraldo Maningo
           of Tacloban City and Fr. Abao of Cebu City.

1974

Feb. 20   Fr. Primitivo Hagad, O.M.I., of Jolo City, was arrested
           and tortured.

March   Arrest of Rev. Cesar Taguba, who was tortured by electric
           shocks resulting in a case of schizophrenia.

Mar. 14   Rev. Toribio, J.C., Cajiuat Highway Hills United Meth-
           odist Church, was arrested and detained for 135 days
           without charges brought against him.

Apr. 14   Statement by the Second Mindanao-Sulu Pastoral Confer-
           ence, citing repression and misery under Martial Law.

June   The National Council of Churches in the Philippines is-
           sued a strong statement via a formal Position Paper con-
           demning U.S. military presence in the country.

June 26   Arrests of Rev. La Verne Mercado, General Secretary of
           the National Council of Churches in the Philippines; Rev.
           Ramon Tiples (Philippine Independent Church), Assistant
           Director of the Committee on Development and Social
           Concerns, NCCP; Rev. and Mrs. Paul Wilson and their
           10 year old son, James; four members of the Karagdag
           family; Ibarra Malonzo, a young lawyer formerly active
           in Christian youth movements; an NCCP caretaker; and
           Rev. Harry Daniel, Assistant General Secretary of the
           Christian Conference of Asia (CCA); and others in the
           home of Rev. and Mrs. Wilson. They were arrested be-
           cause of their acquaintance with a known communist,
           Dante Simbulan, and for having a mimeograph machine.

July   Arrest of Fr. Luigi Ricciarelli (Selesian Order), a teacher
           at the International School and a principal of the Don
           Bosco school in Makati, Rizal.

July 29   "Statement of Concern and Appeal to Authorities" released by leading Protestant laymen and protesting the June 26 raid.

August   Clergy of Kukidnon province asserted the right to protest socioeconomic conditions as cited in the Statement of the Second Mindanao-Sulu Pastoral Conference.

August   World Council of Churches based in Geneva condemned the anti-church actions of the Philippine government.

Aug. 23   150 troopers filling three helicopters raided the Sacred Heart Novitiate and the San Jose Minor Seminary, on the same campus, in Novaliches, Rizal. Arrested were Fr. Benigno Mayo (Jesuit Superior), Fr. Jose Blanco, S.J., and 20 seminary students. Troopers claimed to be searching for Jose Ma. Sison, the head of the Communist Party of the Philippines.

Sept. 1   Manila Archbishop Jaime Sin took actions to restore the integrity of the Catholic Church. He publicly denied the governmental claims of his approval of the raid, as was reported in the government-controlled press and held a Vigil of Prayer at the Manila Cathedral which was attended to overflow capacity. The text of his speech was then circulated as a Pastoral Letter and read in all the Catholic Churches of the country.

Sept. 4   CMLC (Church-Military Liaison Committee) in Cebu City resisted military pressure to stop local priests from reading Archbishop Sin's Pastoral Letter during Mass.

Sept.   Letter by Carmencita Karagdag describing the effects of torture which had been inflicted on her sister Josefina, by military investigators after the June 26 raid on the Wilson home. The interrogation induced a mental breakdown and Josefina is presently a patient in the National Mental Hospital, Mandaluyong, Rizal.

Sept.   An 81-member meeting of the Catholic Bishops Conference petitioned Pres. Marcos to end Martial Law and thereby lift the "climate of fear" pervading over the country.

Sept. 18   Davao clergy and laymen wrote a letter to Pres. Marcos stating their disbelief in Martial Law and demanding that the proclamation be lifted.

Nov.   Pres. Marcos rejected demands of the Catholic Bishops
              Conference.

Nov. 22   Archbishop Sin exposed facts on the torture-murder of
              Marsman Alvarez, brother of presidential foe, Heherson
              Alvarez, who is currently in exile in the U.S.

Dec.   Archbishop Sin, in a letter to Pres. Marcos, strongly
              denounced the continuation of Martial Law.

Dec.   Letter by Discalced Carmelite Nuns of Cebu expressing
              complete support of Archbishop Sin.

Dec.   The Association of Major Religious Superiors reported the
              killing of Santiago Arce to Archbishop Sin. Sin then sent
              a letter to Marcos strongly condemning the military-insti-
              gated murder.

Dec.   48 Protestant ministers and laymen sent a letter to Pres.
              Marcos questioning the morality of his praises for the
              People's Republic of China and the establishment of diplo-
              matic ties while pursuing a communist extermination pol-
              icy at home. They also demanded an end to Martial Law.

Dec. 11   Marcos announced a referendum on the continuation of
              Martial Law and the extension of his powers. The refer-
              endum was to be held on Jan. 30, 1975.

Dec. 17   The release of a Manifesto by 98 prominent citizens, edu-
              cators, and religious leaders denouncing the new referen-
              dum as a farce and demanding an end to Martial Law.

Dec. 13–27   On Dec. 13, Fr. Ed de la Torre was arrested in downtown
              Manila and then detained at Camp Olivas in San Fer-
              nando, Pampanga. On Dec. 24, he began a hunger strike
              after saying midnight Mass for his fellow prisoners. Three
              days later, he was joined by another prisoner, Fr. Manuel
              Lahoz. They cited their imprisonment and the torture of
              19 other prisoners in their camp as the reason for the
              hunger strike.

1975

Jan. 12   Meetings of Catholic leaders end by denouncing the refer-
              endum as "another mockery of democracy," and as "an-
              other Marcos gimmick to justify his stay in power."

Jan. 12   Pres. Marcos announced a deferment of the referendum
           to Feb. 27 because of "incorrect voter lists that had to be
           righted."

Jan. 13   Fr. Gerlock released on a three year probationary period.
           He cannot leave the country or the Greater Manila area
           without military permission because of his "known activist
           sympathies."

Jan.   Bishop Jesus Varela of Ozamis issued a manifesto con-
           demning the February 27 referendum.

Jan.   Bishop Claver authorized his letter to Pres. Marcos to be
           read from all pulpits in his Bukidnon prelature. The letter
           declared his approval of abstention from the referendum
           should a person be convinced that it would be a fraud.

Jan.   Four Catholic Bishops and the social action directors of
           13 Mindanao dioceses denounced the February 27 refer-
           endum and the widespread torture of suspected Muslim
           autonomists in Mindanao and Sulu.

Jan. 30   Fourteen persons comprising 8 civic leaders, 5 Roman
           Catholic bishops, and imprisoned ex-Senator Benigno
           Aquino presented a petition to the Philippine Supreme
           Court challenging Marcos' legal eligibility to be in office
           and to announce the scheduling of a referendum on
           Feb. 27.

Feb. 1   The Philippine Supreme Court in a 10-to-1 decision dis-
           missed the petition of the 14 prominent civic and religious
           leaders presented on January 30.

Feb. 1   69 Roman Catholic bishops representing all of the coun-
           try's dioceses issued an appeal for safeguards to make the
           February 27 referendum meaningful.

Feb. 4   The government responded to pressure exerted by Manila
           Archbishop Sin to investigate the charges made by Fr. de
           la Torre and Fr. Lahoz.

Index

Abueva, Jose Veloso, 20-21
Agpalo, Remigio E., 40-41, 52
Agrarian Reform, Department of, 115-117
Agribusiness, 22, 131-132
Alliance patterns, 18-20. *See also* Elites
American Chamber of Commerce of the Philippines, 189, 195-196, 209
Amnesty International, 36, 42, 72, 204
Antonio, Justice Felix, 99, 105
Aquino, Benigno S., Jr., 56, 108, 159, 192, 263; vs. Commission on Elections, 42
Arrests, 35-36, 262-263. *See also* Detainees
Authoritarian rule: in developing countries, 180-187, 201; in the Philippines, 24, 71-73, 203, 216; and dependency theory, 182-184. *See also* Constitutional authoritarianism

Balance of payments, 59-60, 78. *See also* Investments; Trade
Banking, 214-215
Barangays, 50, 53, 201-203
Barredo, Justice Antonio, 99, 105
Barrera, Justice Jesus, 268
Batasang Bayan (National Advisory Legislative Council), 50
Batasang Pambansa (National Assembly), 50
Benedicto, Roberto, 167
Bernas, Joaquin G., 50
Board of Investments, 209-210. *See also* Investments; Trade

Bombings, 34, 232-233, 236, 259-262
Business community, 192-194, 209

Cariño, Ledivina, 54
del Carmen, Rolando V., 21
Castro, Justice Fred Ruiz, 93, 96, 99, 105
Censorship, 44, 162-165. *See also* Freedom of the press; Mass media
Church-state relations, 19, 25, 29, 45-46, 205, 298-302, 303-309
Citizens' assemblies, 28, 38, 248-249, 252, 268-269
Civil liberties, 23, 44-45, 176-178, 262-269. *See also* Human rights
Civil Liberties Union of the Philippines (CLUP), 25, 41-42, 46, 67, 286-298
Clark Air Base. *See* United States, military bases
Claver, Bishop Francisco, 46
Colonial rule, 14-16, 37
Communicator, 47
Communist Party of the Philippines (CPP), 26, 29-30, 33, 222-223, 230-236
Communist threat: compared to Vietnam, 278-284; and martial law declaration, 161-165, 256-262
Concepcion, Chief Justice Roberto, 38, 88, 97, 105
Congress, 49, 198-199, 255
Constabulary, 48, 191-192, 200
Constitutional Convention, 36-37, 90-94, 248-249, 263-266; manipulation of, 264-270; origins of, 19, 33
Constitution of 1935, 37, 50

Constitution of 1973 (New Constitution), 91-94; and the judiciary, 100-109; ratification, 38, 98, 248-249, 269; transitory provisions, 37-38, 91-99, 250-251, 267-268. *See also* Martial law, constitutionality

Constitutional authoritarianism, 20-21, 49, 56, 71, 81-82. *See also* New Society

Corpus, Victor, 233

Corpuz, O. D., 15, 16

Corruption, 72, 291

de la Costa, Horacio, 67

Counterinsurgency, 281-282

Courts. *See* Martial law, and the courts; Supreme Court; *entries for individual justices and cases*

Crime, 29, 291

Cristobal, Adrian, 39

Cruz, Andres Cristobal, 171

Cruz, Lorenzo J., 168

Cruz, Roman, 190

Dependent-authoritarianism, 204-205, 208-209, 215-216; consolidation of, 198-216; and industry, 195; theory of, 24

Detainees, 36, 39, 263. *See also* Arrests; Dissent

Development, 194; and basic needs, 77-78; five-year plan, 43; goals, 77-79; rural development, 116-117. *See also* New Society, goals

Diokno, Jose, 159, 263

Discipline ("disiplina"), 35, 39

Dissent, 29, 35, 37, 56, 298, 303. *See also* Detainees; Strikes

Economic growth, 27-28, 31, 59-61; and regional disparities, 79

Economic inequalities, 63-66

Economic nationalism, 290-291

Educational system, 203-204

Elections, 49, 56

Elites, 18-20, 52, 55, 70. *See also* Oligarchy

Employment and unemployment, 59, 78

Energy, 78

Enrile, Juan Ponce, 272

Environmental problems, 79

Esguerra, Justice Salvador, 99, 105

Estrella, Conrado, 117

Export-Import Bank, 212

Federation of Free Farmers, 175

Fernando, Justice, 105

Filipino People's Convention on Human Rights, 51

Food supply, 67

Foreign advisors, 195

Foreign aid, 30, 115-116, 119, 191-192, 196, 212. *See also* United States, military aid

Foreign business, 20, 194, 210

Foreign debt, 212

Foreign investments. *See* Investments

Foreign press, 44-45, 173-174

Freedom of the press, 23, 145-147, 151-153, 174, 178-179. *See also* Censorship; Mass media

Galtung, Johan, 183-184

Gerlock, Father Edward, 121-122

Government reorganization, 27, 42-43, 48, 52, 61

Government revenues and expenditures, 39-40, 43, 58

Government structure, 24, 69

Gowing, Peter G., 26

Granada, Ernesto O., 72

Griffin, Keith, 142-143

Grossholtz, Jean, 86

Guerrero, Leon Ma., 26

de Guzman, Raul P., 48

Hicks, Reverend Bruno, 19

Hipe, Victoriano A., 42, 71

Hollnsteiner, Mary, 84

Human rights, 19, 31, 45, 51, 72, 81. *See also* Civil liberties

Ideology. *See* New Society

Ilchman, Warren, 69

Income distribution, 65, 73, 77-78, 291-292
Inflation, 67-68
Insurgents, 239. *See also* Dissent
Interest groups, 54; autonomy of, 208-209; professional associations, 207
Interim Batasang Pambansa (Interim National Assembly), 38, 50-52, 56-57, 250-251, 266-269
Investment Incentives Act, 209
Investments, 60; foreign, 27, 190, 209-214; joint ventures, 213-214; tax incentives, 210

Jacoby, Erich, 144
Japan, 198
Joint U.S. Military Advisory Group (JUSMAG). *See* United States, military aid
Jones Act, 15
Judicial system, history, 85-87
Judiciary. *See* Martial law, and the courts; Supreme Court

Kabataang Barangays, 203
Kabataang Makabayan (KM), 33, 222, 229, 232, 239
Kerkvliet, Benedict J., 22
Kilusang Bagong Lipunan (New Society Movement), 56
Kilusang Bayan (Rural Cooperatives), 127
Kintanar, Agustin, 52
Kolko, Gabriel, 280-281

Laban (Lakas ng Bayan, People's Power), 56
Labor, 208; agricultural, 130-131; urban, 19; wages, 65
Land concentration, 131-132
Land reform, 22, 28, 52, 66-67, 81; compensation provisions, 139-141; as counterinsurgency, 22, 117; critics, 121-122; and farm expenses, 133-137; and "green revolution," 133-139; implementation, 122-124; and land titles, 132-134; and landowners, 124-129,

Land reform (*cont.*)
139-141; objectives, 114-119; results, 120-124; scope, 129-132
Land-Transfer Certificates, 133-134
Lansang vs. *Garcia,* 88-89
Lapiang Manggagawa, 229
Laurel-Langley Agreement, 188, 192, 211, 273-274
Legitimacy, 28-30, 68-69, 172-173, 202
Lopez, Eugenio, Jr., 44, 167, 175-176
Lopez, Fernando, 44, 167, 176
Lopez, Salvador, 51, 84

Macapagal, Diosdado, 51
Magsino, Florencio, 72
Makalintal, Chief Justice Querube C., 93, 96, 99, 105, 111
Makasiar, Justice Felix, 99, 105
Malayang Samakan ng Magsasaka (MASAKA), 229, 232
Malayang Pagkakaisa ng Kabataang Pilipino (MPKP), 232
Mangahas, Mahar, 52, 64-66, 73
Manglapus, Raul, 33
Marcos, Ferdinand E.: and Ngo Dinh Diem, 278-279; on equality, 70; on land reform, 119-120; landholdings, 121; media critics, 155-161; political opponents, 175-176; as prime minister, 57, 251; style of rule, 29, 202-203; *Today's Revolution: Democracy,* 33-35, 82; and the U.S., 270-273
Marcos, Imelda, 48, 55, 167, 206-207
Mariveles Export-Processing Zone, 214
Martial law, 14-20; achievements, 27, 61-63, 74-75; constitutionality, 21-22, 87-90, 253-254; and the courts, 41-42, 109-112, 242-245, 254-255 (*see also* Supreme Court); declaration, 13, 17, 35, 219-241, 256-262; duration, 29-30, 51; explanations of, 16-20, 180-185, 219-241, 255-256, 286-288; legal challenges, 89, 94-100; opposition to, 51, 56, 173, 253, 263, 284-288 (*see also* Dissent); performance evaluation, 80-84; popular support, 28-30, 47-50, 62-63 (*see also* Legitimacy; Political par-

Martial law (cont.)
  ticipation); precedents, 87-88, 228-
  229; U.S. support, 24, 39, 217
Masagana, 99, 116
Mass media, 22-23, 43, 46, 206-207;
  and colonialism, 148-151; and communist subversion, 161-165; concentration of ownership, 154-155, 169;
  credibility, 172; government relations,
  155-159; and the military, 178; and
  national development, 169-172; and
  oligarchic conspiracy, 165-169; politi-
  cization, 153-154; regulation, 145-147,
  161-173; in Southeast Asia, 148-149
Mass Media Council, 166-167
McKinley, President William, 15
Media Advisory Council, 170
Melchor, Alejandro, 190, 264
Menzi, Hans, 168, 175
"Message of Hope to Filipinos Who
  Care," 46, 67
Mijares, Primitivo, 93, 165-166, 168
Military, 29-30, 35-36, 191-192, 200;
  budget, 39; corruption, 39; and devel-
  opment, 191-192; in government, 40
Military aid, 192, 211-212. See also
  United States, military aid
Military tribunals, 41, 107-108, 244-245,
  264
Mitra, Ramon, 263
Monteclaro, Eddie, 174-175
Movement for the Advancement of Na-
  tionalism (MAN), 33, 193, 229, 232
Movement of Concerned Citizens for
  Civil Liberties, 159
Multinational corporations, 20, 28, 60
Muslim resistance movement, 26, 29-30,
  237-238
Mutual Defense Treaty, 276

National Committee for the Restoration
  of Civil Liberties in the Philippines
  (NCRCLP), 25, 253-285
National Economic Development Authority (NEDA), 52, 77, 200
National Legislative Advisory Council,
  201

Nationalism, 14-15, 19; and martial law,
  190, 204-205
New People's Army (NPA), 18-19, 30,
  222-227, 230-239, 283
New Society: goals, 20, 32, 57, 76;
  ideology, 28, 34-35. See also Martial
  law
News media. See Mass media
Noble, Lela, 26

Oligarchy, 32-34, 55, 71, 202, 293; and
  media ownership, 152-153. See also
  Elites
Ongsiaxko, Edmundo, 168
Osmena, Sergio, 44
Overholt, William, 83-84

Pahayag, 27
Parity rights, 271, 274
Parliamentary government, 37, 50, 57,
  91
Paterno, Vicente, 190
The People's Alternative, 51-52
Perez, Juan A., Jr., 168
Philippine Press Council, 151-152
Philippine Studies Bulletin, 27
Plebiscite, 92-94, 268-269
Police. See Constabulary
Political order, 27, 31, 33, 74
Political participation, 28, 49, 55-56,
  201-202. See also Legitimacy
Political power, centralization of, 27, 48,
  70, 90, 216-218, 270
Politics, premartial law, 13-14, 32-34,
  187-196, 198-200
Population growth, 78
Press. See Mass media
Private Development Corporation of the
  Philippines, 196-197
Private enterprise. See Business com-
  munity
Public health policies, 207
Public Information, Department of, 44,
  169-171
Public opinion, 28-30, 62-63, 47-50

Race, Jeffrey, 55, 71

Ramos, General Fidel, 173
Referenda, 47-48, 50-52, 62, 252
Refeudalization, 24, 184-187, 209, 215-217
Reforms, 17, 288-289; economic, 43, 58, 62; social, 22, 28. *See also* Government reorganization
Retail Trade Nationalization Law, 275
Reyes, J. B. L., 109
Rigos, Cirilo, 51
Roces, Joaquin, 160, 164, 167, 175
Romualdez, Enrico P., 167
Romulo, Carlos, 18
Rosenberg, David A., 23, 70, 206
Rural bankers, 65

Saito, Shiro, 26
Salak, Manuel B., 168
Salonga, Jovita, 51, 67, 93, 108
Samahang Demokratiko ng Kabataan (SDK), 222, 232, 239
Samahang Molave (SM), 232
Samahang Nayon (Barrio Associations), 127
Sandiganbayan, 100
Sangguniang Bayan (Local Legislative Councils), 50, 201-202
Shaplen, Robert, 84
Sharing in Development, 27
Signs of the Times, 47
Simpas, Santiago, 54-55
Sin, Cardinal Jaime, 46, 71
Soliven, Max, 263
Soriano, Andre, 175
Soriano, Jose, 175
Stauffer, Robert, 23-26, 40
Strikes, 29, 156, 208. *See also* Dissent; Martial law, opposition
Subic Bay Naval Base. *See* United States, military bases
Supreme Court, 21, 38, 41-43. *See also* Martial law, and the courts

Takahashi, Akira, 122

Tanada, Lorenzo, 108
Tanco, Arturo, 190
Tanodbayan (Ombudsman), 100, 104
Tatad, Francisco S., 165-166, 172
Tax reforms, 43, 58
Technocrats, 40, 188-190, 194-196, 209-210
Teehankee, Justice, 105
Trade, 28, 59-60, 77, 190, 211, 215-216; with Japan, 198
Transitory Provisions. *See* Constitution of 1973
"Trickle down" development model, 197-198
Tuma, Elias, 141-142

United States, 20, 188-189, 270-284; advance notice of martial law, 270-271; and counterinsurgency, 284; economic interests, 272-275; military aid, 39, 276-277, 281-283; military bases, 24, 211, 271, 275-277, 283; model of government, 17-18; Public Safety Program, 277-281
Uphoff, Norman, 69

Valdepeñas, Vicente, 68
Valencia, Teodoro, 76
Violence, 29, 31, 198, 226

Walsh, Tom, 26
Wealth, concentration of, 27, 67; expansion of, 73
Weintraub, Dov, 69, 79
World market. *See* Trade
World peace through Law Conference, 51
Writ of Habeas Corpus, 34, 228
Wurfel, David, 65-67, 84

Yuyitung, Quintin, 157

Zaldivar, Justice Calixto, 51, 97, 105

Library of Congress Cataloging in Publication Data
(For library cataloging purposes only)

Main entry under title:

Marcos and martial law in the Philippines.

  Includes index.
  1. Martial law—Philippine Islands—Addresses, essays, lectures. 2. Philippine Islands—Constitutional law—Addresses, essays, lectures. 3. Marcos, Ferdinand Edralin, Pres. Philippines.
I. Rosenberg, David A.
Law   342′.599′062   78-15145
ISBN 0-8014-1195-5